The politics of alcohol

There is a lot more than drinking involved in drinking.
(Mass-Observation)

The politics of alcohol
A history of the drink question in England

James Nicholls

Manchester University Press
Manchester and New York
distributed in the United States exclusively
by Palgrave Macmillan

Published by Manchester University Press
Oxford Road, Manchester M13 9NR, UK
and Room 400, 175 Fifth Avenue, New York, NY 10010, USA
www.manchesteruniversitypress.co.uk

Distributed in the United States exclusively by
Palgrave Macmillan, 175 Fifth Avenue,
New York, NY 10010, USA

Distributed in Canada exclusively by
UBC Press, University of British Columbia, 2029 West Mall,
Vancouver, BC, Canada V6T 1Z2

British Library Cataloguing-in-Publication Data is available

Library of Congress Cataloging-in-Publication Data is available

ISBN 978 0 7190 8637 3 paperback

First published by Manchester University Press in hardback 2009

This paperback edition first published 2011

The publisher has no responsibility for the persistence or accuracy of URLs for any external or third-party internet websites referred to in this book, and does not guarantee that any content on such websites is, or will remain, accurate or appropriate.

Printed by Lightning Source

Contents

Introduction

In 1925, the economist John Maynard Keynes wrote that he saw 'only two planks of the historic Liberal platform [as] still seaworthy – the Drink Question and Free Trade'.[1] This observation was partly a comment on the parlous state of the Liberal Party at the time, outflanked by the organised labour movement and left with little to distinguish it as a political force. It was also, however, a measure of the extent to which the 'drink question' had come to occupy the political centre ground in the preceding decades. The half century between 1870 and 1920 had seen elections fought and lost on the issue of alcohol control, the creation and abandonment of asylums for the treatment of drunkards, repeated Parliamentary efforts to introduce prohibition, the establishment of a pub company by an Anglican Bishop, the partial nationalisation of the alcohol industry, and drink described by the serving Prime Minister at the outbreak of the First World War as a greater threat than Austria and Germany combined. It was the high water mark of the drink question as a political concern. However, as this book will argue, drink had been an important political issue for a long time before this. It became an object of State regulation in the mid-sixteenth century, and had become a subject of heated political debate by the early seventeenth. Furthermore, while the drink question receded somewhat after the 1940s, this diminishing of the political importance of drink was only temporary. By the start of the twenty-first century, drink was back on the political agenda with a vengeance. The introduction of 24-hour licensing, the rise of city-centre superpubs, and the widespread expressions of public concern over binge drinking and cheap supermarket sales have turned the consumption of alcohol into an issue as feverishly discussed today as it has been at almost any time in the past. The social, political, economic and ethical questions posed by drink have never been fully resolved, and have never gone away. This book is a history of those questions.

By presenting a history of the drink question, this book does not suggest that the same issues have always been associated with drinking; far from it. Because drinking is such a perennial cultural activity, it provides a kind of 'cultural constant', but this is not to say that drinking practices or attitudes to alcohol remain static over time. Indeed, one of the aims of this book will be to trace the way in which ideas about alcohol change. The phrase 'drink question' is an intentional anachronism in this regard. It was used predominantly during the period when political temperance was at its most influential: roughly speaking, from around 1840 to 1940. By applying the phrase to both earlier and later periods I am not suggesting that the specific features of the discourse on drink that characterised Victorian and Edwardian England simply extended back to the seventeenth century and forward to the twenty-first. This book deals with transformations that have characterised thinking about alcohol; however, it also recognises certain constants: worries over heavy sessional drinking and the rituals that encourage those patterns of consumption, heightened concerns over women's drinking, disputes over the proper role of licensing authorities, conflicts between the rights of moderate drinkers and the responsibility of the State to prevent excess, and – often underlying all of these issues – a failure to resolve the tensions between free trade ideologies and the need to maintain social order where alcohol is concerned. Drink has always existed both as an activity and as a set of questions: questions about the rights and wrongs of intoxication, about the role of government in regulating free trade, about the limits of personal freedom, about gender, class, taste and health. In looking at the range of these issues, this book sets out to show that the drink question has never been singular, even when it appeared to be.

While this is a book about the politics of alcohol, it will not scrutinise ministerial meetings, the briefings of civil servants and the actions of policy-makers at the highest level: a detailed study of the 'high politics' of drink has been carried out previously by John Greenaway.[2] Instead I will be looking at the role of drink as a political issue in the widest sense. One of the key claims of this book is that drink not only stimulates public debate, but that it has always tended to expose underlying cultural and political tensions as well. Because drinking is such a ubiquitous social activity, the way it is framed in public discourse – the kinds of problems it is associated with, and the kinds of solutions which are proposed – acts as a barometer of the cultural anxieties and political attitudes which are at work in any particular period. Drink is interesting for many reasons, but the main interest here is how ideas about drink provide an insight into the wider culture. As one writer has put it, 'we can look through the window not only from society to alcohol, but also from alcohol to society'; hopefully this book will go some way towards achieving this perspective.[3]

This book focuses on England partly for the simple reason that any study of such a large subject requires selection. However, the drink question has never been a uniquely English phenomenon and this book is not an attempt to suggest that it is. Nevertheless, drinking does occupy a particularly ambivalent role in English society. The pub is, with good reason, seen as a social institution of unparalleled importance in English cultural life and beer has few equals in the pantheon of cultural signifiers of Englishness. And yet we have recently seen the phrase 'Binge Britain' become a media cliché; and when Tony Blair complained in 2004 that legislators faced a 'new British disease' of binge drinking he was not only repeating a sentiment commonplace in the contemporary press, but one which stretches back to some of the earliest texts we will look at here.

'Binge Britain' refers to more than England, of course. However, it is a slogan which blurs significant differences in consumption between England, Scotland, Wales and Northern Ireland; more importantly for this book, the cultural and legislative histories between the four home nations are significantly different. A lot of the matter discussed here applies to Britain as a whole, but much is specific to England. This should not be taken as indicating that I accept the commonplace idea that the English have a kind of national drinking problem; such simplifications are neither accurate nor especially helpful when attempting to understand drinking culture. Nor am I implying that the political history of drink in England is uniquely complex or varied: the cultural history of drink in America has provided the material for decades of historical inquiry and critical analysis, and the politics of drink in Scotland, Ireland, Russia and many Scandinavian countries has been as complicated and socially divisive as it has been in England. Nevertheless, taking England as the object of study makes it possible to trace the history of one set of national concerns over drinking – and whether the English have a unique drink problem or not, they certainly have a long history of worrying about the possibility that they might. This book will show the degree to which drinking has provided a way of talking about concerns over national identity, economic prosperity, conceptions of freedom, the relationship between the State and trade, and the social effects of free markets – all of which have been arguments pertinent to the social and political contexts of England at the time in which they were being expressed. However, because the drink question has so often really been a question about the nature of open society more generally, many of the arguments looked at here apply equally to any other 'wet' (as in non-abstaining) liberal culture.

While the aim of this book is to explore some of the issues that lie behind public debates on drink, I don't suggest that debates over drink are always simply a cover for something else; rather, concerns which are specific to alcohol (such as its potential impacts on social order or on health) have always been mediated by social context, have usually reflected cultural beliefs and have often driven political decision-making. Drink is not unique in functioning this way, but its special place in culture means that it can provide a distinctive lens for observing the complex relationship between individual consumption, cultural values and social power. In this sense, the drink question provides just one way of mapping social history. However, because drink continues to be an unresolved, contentious and confused political issue, providing a 'long view' of the development of public discourse on drink over time will, hopefully, provide a contribution that is of some relevance today.

For advice, support, comments and discussion along the way, my thanks go to Peter Kavanagh, James Green, Dan Malleck, Catherine Carstairs, Norman Smith and everyone at the Alcohol and Drugs History Society, Betsy Thom, Kristin Doern, Sue Owen, Lucy Burke, Sue Vice, Andy Ruddock, Tom Moylan, Jim Harbaugh, Una McGovern, Colin Harrison, Angela McShane, Phil Withington and everyone at the ESRC network on Intoxicants in Historical and Cultural Perspective. Roger Morris and Alan Peck both helped keep me sane. My anonymous readers at Manchester University Press provided invaluable advice, and the editorial staff ironed out some ungainly glitches. They all did their best, what remains is down to me. The research for this book could not have taken place without the support of staff at the British Library and Bristol University Library, and it couldn't have been completed without research leave provided by the School of Historical and Cultural Studies at Bath Spa University. The one person I couldn't have done any of it without is Thanh, who put up with this project over the years and gave support when things got tough. I hope you like it. Above all, though, my thanks go to Khai and Lily for bursting in and brightening up my days: I treasured every interruption.

Parts of this book have appeared in the *International Journal of Cultural Studies* and the *Social History of Alcohol and Drugs* and are reproduced with permission.

Notes

1   A. Bullock and M. Schock, *The Liberal Tradition: From Fox to Keynes* (Oxford: Clarendon Press, 1967), p. 283.

2   J. Greenaway, *Drink and British Politics Since 1830: A Study in Policy-Making* (Basingstoke: Palgrave Macmillan, 2003).

3   P. Sulkunen, 'Images and realities of alcohol', *Addiction*, 93: 9 (1998), 1305–12, p. 1308.

1

A monstrous plant: alcohol and the Reformation

Let me set down this for my general proposition, that all drunkards are beasts. (George Gascoigne)

Help to blast the vines that they may bear no more grapes, and sour the wines in the cellars of merchant's storehouses, that our countrymen may not piss out all their wit and thrift against the walls. (Thomas Nashe)

In 1628, a writer called Richard Rawlidge published a pamphlet with the eye-catching title *A Monster Late Found Out and Discovered*. That monster was drunkenness. According to Rawlidge, England was suffering from an explosion of social disorder caused by a dramatic rise in the number of alehouses springing up across the country. This, he insisted, had caused a disastrous breakdown in public morality. 'Whereas,' he observed, 'there are within the City's liberties but an hundred twenty two churches for the service and worship of God: there are I dare say above thirty hundred ale-houses, tippling-houses, tobacco-shops &c. in London and the skirts thereof, wherein the devil is daily served and honoured'.[1]

Rawlidge's monster was, in truth, not so 'late found out'. In the previous twenty-five years no fewer than six Acts of Parliament had been passed, and two Royal Proclamations published, targeting alehouses and drunkenness. The licensing of alcohol retail was less than a century old, however, and much of the legislation which had been passed in Rawlidge's lifetime was designed to shore up the power of local magistrates who had been tasked with using their licensing powers to control excessive drinking. Underpinning all this was a wider religious attack on drunkenness and the places where drinking took place. The legislative control of alehouses – initiated by a Licensing Act of 1552 – had been accompanied by a rise in the condemnation of drunkenness from the pulpit and in print. In rough historical terms the development of a public discourse on drink, in which drink was identified as a specific social 'problem' in both literature and legislation, accompanied the spread of the Reformation. This is not to say that there was a direct causal link between the rise of Protestantism and the earliest appearance of the drink question, but it is to say that the social, economic, political, technological and religious transformations that both drove and were driven by the Reformation also created the conditions in which drink became political.

Drunkenness in early modern England

While it would be an oversimplification to draw a neat dividing line between pre- and post-Reformation drinking culture in England, there is no doubt that the sixteenth century saw dramatic changes in the way alcohol was both produced and consumed. In 1500 there were only the most rudimentary of licensing laws. An Assize of Bread and Ale, enacted in 1266, had pegged the price of ale to the price of bread, but it was a law that was only applied in the most ad hoc way.[2] Since 1393, alehouses had been required to display a stake in front of their doors – a practice which eventually led to the development of the pub signboard. In 1494 legislation targeting the itinerant poor gave local Justices the power to 'reject the common selling of ale' where appropriate, but this wasn't the same as requiring a licence to sell ale in the first place.

In the sixteenth century beer made with hops was still a novelty. Instead people drank unhopped ale, which was thicker, weaker, sweeter and far less stable than hopped beer. The ale people drank was mostly brewed domestically and by women. Brewing ale was a poor person's profession – often the last-ditch resort of the desperately needy. There were no big brewers and alehouses were as rudimentary as the laws which governed them: often simply a part of someone's home temporarily opened up for as long as there was a brew for which people were willing to pay. Brewing was seasonal and unpredictable, though reasonably profitable when drinks were actually being sold, and the market for beer was steadily increasing as water sources became increasingly less and less reliable thanks to population expansion and the rise of polluting industries such as tanning.

In the late middle ages, ale also contributed to a rudimentary welfare system. Communal 'ales' – local fund-raising events based around a specially-brewed consignment of ale – were one of the key sources of revenue for both parish churches and secular good causes.[3] 'Bride-ales' for newly-weds, 'bid-ales' for needy individuals, and the notorious 'scot-ales' (which became a form of semi-official extortion imposed by corrupt feudal lords) involved members of the local community contributing to a fund which would finance the preparation of a special ale brewed for the occasion, the profits would then be passed on to the person for whom the ale was held. Not only were 'ales' of this kind an effective way of raising money, they also provided 'a system of circulating aid in which economic activity, neighbourly assistance and festivity were subtly blended'.[4]

The Catholic Church initially frowned on any such activities, often forbidding priests from any kind of involvement whether official or otherwise. However, by the mid-fifteenth century 'church-ales', set up to raise funds for the local parish, had become a common, albeit irregular, feature of community life in many parts of Britain.[5] Church-ales provided a much-needed means of topping up parish finances, but they also provided a useful source of poor-relief. The seventeenth-century antiquarian John Aubrey recalled being told that 'there were no rates for the poor in my grand-father's day; but for Kington St Michael (no small parish) the church-ale at Whitsuntide did the business'.[6]

From the late 1520s links between the Church and ale production became the object of increasing criticism. In 1529 Henry VIII passed legislation targeting the 'plurality of livings' among the clergy, which specifically barred 'spiritual persons' from keeping 'any Manner of Brew-house' other than to produce ale for their own use, a measure which probably contributed to the rise of alehouses by forcing brewer monks to seek new employment.[7] Church-ales also fell foul of wider reforms of local government which saw fixed taxes, such as 'pew-rents', replace more irregular forms of income generation.[8] More broadly, church-ales became the victim of a concerted effort by the Church of England to distance itself from the traditions of its Catholic predecessor. From 1576 checks on whether church wardens had 'suffered any plays, feasts, banquets, church-ales, drinkings or any other profane usages' of their churches began to appear in the visitation articles drawn up by bishops.[9] Nine episcopates included such clauses in their visitation articles between 1571 and 1600, although their application remained sporadic.[10]

Early Puritan reformers in particular found something distinctly unsavoury in local churches relying heavily on the periodic facilitation of mass drunkenness to fund their expensive infrastructure and the upkeep of their clergy. In his splenetic invective against vice, *The Anatomy of Abuses* (1583), Philip Stubbes castigated church-ales, complaining that:

> when the *Nippitatum*, this Huf-cap (as they call it) and the *Nectar* of life, is set abroad, well is he that can get the soonest to it, and spend most at it, for he that sits closest to it, and spends the most at it, he is counted the godliest man of all the rest … In this kind of practise, they continue six weeks, a quarter of a year, yea half a year together, swilling and gulling, night and day, till they be as drunk as apes, and as blockish as beasts.[11]

However exaggerated Stubbes's account may be (and he certainly did have a penchant for rhetorical excess) his argument that drunkenness in the service of God was both immoral and absurd was one that found increasing resonance in Protestant England. Stubbes objected that church-ales 'build this house of lime and stone with the desolation, and utter overthrow of his spiritual house'.[12] Even writers who attempted to defend church-ales were forced to acknowledge that 'drunkenness, gluttony, swearing, lasciviousness' were not unusual features of such events.[13] By the late sixteenth century, however, church-ales were in a state of terminal decline. Four years after Stubbes's broadside, William Harrison claimed that 'church-ales, help-ales, and soul-ales, called also dirge-ales, with the heathenish rioting at bride-ales, are well diminished and laid aside'.[14]

Drink and popular festivity

At the broadest cultural level, the decline of church-ales was one feature of a much wider attack on the festive and ritual culture of medieval Europe. The riotous pre-Lenten carnivals that culminated in Mardi Gras were more a feature of popular culture in mainland Europe than in Britain. Nevertheless, the fundamental elements of carnival – masquerade, the inversion of conventional authority, satire, sexual freedom and considerable drunkenness – were central to festive culture, including church-ales and religious feasts, in medieval England.[15] William Harrison described 'our maltbugs' at fairs getting drunk on 'huffecap, the mad dog, father whoreson, angels food, dragons milk, go by the wall, stride wide, and lift leg' until they 'lie still again and be not able to wag'.[16] Drunkenness fuelled the spirit of temporary disorder and communal freedom (tinged with the palpable threat of violence) that defined carnival periods.

The toleration of carnival excess was always conditional, however, and the drunkenness of popular festivities was one of the common reasons given for their suppression. In 1448 a law passed by Henry VI banning fairs and markets on traditional feast days and Sundays cited 'drunkenness and strifes' as a cause of 'abominable injuries and offences done to almighty God'. Responding to sustained attacks on this aspect of its culture, in 1563 the Council of Trent issued a formal warning to Catholics against allowing religious festivals to be 'perverted into revelling and drunkenness'. Protestant radicals, however, insisted that the problem was intractable. They maintained that popular fairs and church-ales were nothing more than excuses for 'bullbeating, bowling, drunkenness, dancing and such like'.[17]

There has been much debate over the ambivalent role of festive excess in early modern culture.[18] It has been argued that while festive periods often involved outrageous displays of social inversion (the establishment of 'lords of misrule', parodies of the Catholic mass, etc.), carnival was always 'a *licensed* affair in every sense, a permissible rupture of hegemony'.[19] Others have gone further, insisting that the 'supreme ruse of power is to allow itself to be contested *ritually* in order to consolidate itself more effectively', and that popular festivities simply reaffirmed social power by creating periodic spectacles of illusory freedom.[20] We shall see that among nineteenth-century temperance campaigners drink was commonly depicted as a technique by which oppressed peoples were kept in their place by allowing periodic – or even constant – drunkenness to provide a distraction from their actual conditions. Nevertheless, the traditional notion that periodic excess could provide an acceptable, and ecclesiastically sanctioned, safety-valve for otherwise pent-up emotions ran absolutely counter to that Protestant world-view which saw life as a disciplined project of rational endeavour. The post-Reformation suppression of popular festivities, including church-ales, was part and parcel of this. However, this approach risked politicising carnival excess: as Joseph Gusfield has argued, the repression of carnival 'gave to drunkenness and festival behaviour an added feature of social protest that made the emergence of rowdy behaviour even more fearful to those who sought to control it'.[21] The dialectic between the suppression and celebration of the transgressive behaviours associated with drunkenness would become something which characterised the politics of alcohol throughout the modern period.

The development of the alehouse

The attacks on drunkenness penned by the likes of Philip Stubbes were motivated by a religious desire to redefine Englishness as part of a wider moral reformation. For Stubbes, drunkenness was a feature of an old, corrupt England: an England of not only licentious fairs but also sordid drinking dens. Every city, town and village, Stubbes complained ,'hath abundance of alehouses, taverns and inns, which are so fraughted with malt-worms, night & day that you would wonder to se them ... swilling, gulling, & carousing from one to another, til never a one can speak a ready word'.[22] Indeed, from the earliest period of the Reformation alehouses were identified as a particularly pressing problem, for both moral and political reasons. When Coventry magistrates complained in 1544 that 'a great part of the inhabitants of this city be now become brewers and tipplers', they were voicing a common concern.[23] Drunkenness was targeted partly for wider religious and moral reasons, but also because the number of drinking places had increased substantially over the course of the early sixteenth century.

Economic and demographic factors drove this expansion. Both Keith Wrightson and Peter Clark have argued that economic uncertainty and periodic unemployment contributed significantly to the rise of the alehouse as a social institution for two reasons: firstly, more people took to selling ale as a way of keeping the wolf from the door, and secondly, more people had time on their hands which was as well spent in an alehouse as anywhere else. Furthermore, periods of low employment led to an increase in the number of itinerant workers forced to look for work outside their home town or village. For such people alehouses provided both rudimentary lodgings and a place where they could put their ear to the ground and find out what work might be on offer locally.[24]

The other key factor in the rise of the alehouse was hops. It was the addition of hops that, broadly speaking, distinguished 'beer' from unhopped 'ale'. Hopped beer was more stable than ale, which made it possible for brewers to produce more and for sellers to store it for longer. Hops had been occasionally used in brewing for centuries; however, its popularisation followed the arrival of Flemish weavers (and their radical brewing techniques) in Britain around 1400. Their hopped beer had a swift impact, such that in 1436 Henry VI was forced to issue a Proclamation to protect Flemish beer producers from the attacks they were suffering at the hands of disgruntled ale brewers.[25] In 1441 an Assize of Beer was introduced to standardise beer prices and bring them into line with ale. Hops started to be grown commercially in England from around 1520. The introduction of hops was the pivotal moment in the modernisation of brewing: what had once been seasonal, local and domestic was set to become mass produced and highly profitable. By 1587 William Harrison was describing unhopped ale as 'sometime our only, but now taken with many for old and sickmen's drink'.[26]

The rise in the number of alehouses coupled with an expanded capacity for the production of stronger beer (another effect of hops) led to concerns over increased levels of public drunkenness. However, drinking places were also caught up in a wider cultural quarrel over both the proper uses of leisure and the politics of social space. In many ways, sixteenth-century concerns over drinking were one aspect of a bigger anxiety about idleness. While wage labour expanded, the range of commodities remained low. With few commodities to spend money on, and almost no scope for rising up the social scale, there was little incentive for the poor to accumulate wealth. Therefore, there was a strong incentive to work just long enough to earn sufficient money to spend on beer: a commodity that was both pleasurable and readily available. To the social elites of Tudor England, increased numbers of alehouses meant increased opportunities for the lower classes to congregate, drink and spend their time and money in idleness.[27]

Attacks on drinking and alehouses were driven by both religious convictions and concerns over social breakdown.[28] However, because there was no way of controlling alehouses there was no way that the State could put a limit on their expansion. It was this inability to manage the supply-side of beer that led to the introduction of the first Licensing Act in 1552. This Act established the principle of licensing for the first time: it stated that anyone wanting to maintain an alehouse had to obtain a licence to do so from two local Justices and had to give evidence of their good character. Prior to 1552, anyone could open their house up to sell ale, although since 1494 Justices had been given the power to close such establishments down where necessary. In its preamble, the purpose of the 1552 Act was made clear: to counter the 'intolerable hurts and troubles to the commonwealth of this realm' which 'daily grow and increase through such abuses and disorders as are had and used in common alehouses'.

Two things were happening here: the number of alehouses was indeed increasing, but so too was the political anxiety over the risks to social order posed by public drinking. Vesting power in local magistrates provided a means by which the number of alehouses could be controlled and the activities that took place inside alehouses could be regulated. It also reaffirmed the power of local elites by locking them into a national system of control over an institution which formed the hub of lower-class social activity. It was a way of reinforcing politically unifying 'points of contact' between central and local government while identifying an internal threat to national stability which legitimated the introduction of increased controls on the everyday cultural practices of the poor.[29]

While the term 'alehouse' sounds like a rather misty umbrella term for old-fashioned drinking dens, it referred at the time to a very specific institution. Drinking places were divided by culture and practice into three types: alehouses, which generally just sold ale; inns, which were defined by the fact that they provided lodging, food and drink to travellers; and taverns which, in theory at least, just sold wine. The legal distinction between alehouses and other drinking places was not only established by the 1552 Act, it was reinforced by an Act passed one year later, in 1553, ostensibly designed to 'avoid the excessive Price of Wine'. In reality, this Act took an already fairly exclusive establishment – the wine tavern – and enforced its exclusivity by statute. The Act set strict limits on the number of taverns which were to be allowed in each city: forty in London, four in Norwich, six in Bristol and so forth. It also set up a system of licensing for taverns in which tavern keepers, rather than applying for a licence from two local Justices, needed to be 'nominated, appointed and assigned by the head officers and the most part of the common council, aldermen, burgesses, jurats or commonality'. A much higher hurdle, then – and one designed to ensure that only the much better sort opened and ran wine-drinking establishments.

Clearly the aim of this was to formalise an already existing social hierarchy of both drinks and drinking places, and to prevent taverns being dragged down the social scale by springing up willy-nilly under the charge of dubious landlords. Even so, the fact that there were around fifty alehouses for every tavern in the late 1500s meant that for many, alehouses remained the only accessible place where drinking in company could take place.[30] However, there was clearly a desire among some sections of society to isolate the alehouse and to bring it under social control. The success of such legislative interventions was patchy, to say the least. A 1590 Privy Council report noted that alehouses were becoming 'innumerable' and that 'the law for keeping them in order [was] unexecuted' – a complaint that would become a recurring motif in the public discussion of licensing over the centuries.[31] Nevertheless, the result of these social, cultural and economic shifts was that from the middle of the sixteenth century onwards alehouses became increasingly identified with the idle poor, social disorder, political dissent and outright drunkenness.

A monstrous plant

Fairs and alehouses were recognised as traditional features of English cultural life. The condemnation of them tended to arise either from the perception that their proliferation had grown out of hand, or that the Reformation provided an opportunity for all such sordid conventions to be swept away on a tide of moral regeneration. However, a slightly different strand of thinking began to appear in the same period; one which identified drunkenness as a peculiarly modern, and possibly foreign, blight on English society. It was not a dominant theme in the public literature on drinking, but it did reflect the underlying way in which concerns over drunkenness were tied up with concerns over Englishness itself.

In 1576, the English writer and adventurer George Gascoigne published an essay entitled *A Delicate Diet for Dainty-mouthed Drunkards*. In it, he described drunkenness as a 'monstrous plant, lately crept into the pleasant orchards of England'.[32] Its increase, he claimed, reflected a peculiarly English attitude to foreign fashions; one in which continental vices and foibles were adopted in such an exaggerated way as to render them grotesque and absurd. Of the Spanish codpiece, Gascoigne wrote, 'we make an English football', of German drinking habits 'we do make banquets and merriments' by which 'we surpass them very far'.[33] For Gascoigne, the Germans were 'the continual wardens of the drunkards' fraternity and corporation', but it was a role that the English appeared keen to usurp.[34]

Gascoigne's pamphlet illustrates the extent to which concerns over drinking are often overlaid with concerns over national identity. He was, of course, writing at the height of the Elizabethan era of nation-building in the political, military and cultural spheres, and he was not alone in seeing something worrisome in English attitudes to alcohol. Fifteen years later, the popular writer Thomas Nashe observed that excess in drink seemed to have become embedded in English everyday culture, complaining that 'superfluity in drink [is] a sin, that ever since we have mixed our selves with the low-countries, is counted honourable: but before we knew their lingering wars, was held in that highest degree of hatred that might be'.[35] Whatever their views on the morality of individual drinkers, and whoever they blamed for introducing it to England, what both these writers shared was the sense that a culture of excessive drinking presented a tangible social problem which threatened to undermine the nation-building project itself.

Gascoigne and Nashe were both also interested in the rituals of drinking. For both writers, the fundamental problem was not simple excess but the patterns of drinking that seemed to have become established in popular culture. They would be two of the first writers to suggest that the drinking of healths (the ritual of toasting which led to what, in modern parlance, we might call 'heavy episodic drinking'), was the real question that needed to be addressed. Whoever invented it – Danes, Germans or Lowlanders – the problem for both Nashe and Gascoigne seemed to be that the English had adopted it with gusto. Whereas for Stubbes *place* was the fundamental problem (communal drinking dens, by definition, produce drunkenness and immoral behaviour), for Gascoigne and Nashe *pattern* was the primary concern (rituals of drink which encouraged heavy consumption led to drunkenness and disorder). As we shall see, these two issues – place and pattern – would remain two of the fundamental subjects in the debate on drink over the following four hundred years.

An odious sin

In early Stuart England, place remained the focus of legislative intervention – of which there was an enormous amount. The spark for a renewed assault on alehouses was the accession of James VI of Scotland to the throne of England. Within a year of his coronation, in 1604, James I passed an Act 'to restrain the inordinate haunting and tipling in inns, alehouses and other victualling houses'. This Act asserted that 'the ancient, true and principle use of inns, alehouses and victualling-houses was for the receipt, relief and lodging of wayfaring people travelling from place to place'. This was not strictly true. Certainly inns had always been conceived of as resting places for travellers, and the ancient Roman *tabernae* had fulfilled a similar function. Alehouses, by contrast, had never really served this function in any more than the loosest sense. Under the 1604

Act, however, the dubious claim that alehouses existed for lodging rather than for the 'entertainment and harbouring of lewd and idle people' was used to bring in strict rules prohibiting landlords from allowing customers to 'tipple' on their premises. What this meant in practice was that the responsibility to ensure that no one drank for purposes other than necessary refreshment (labourers, for example, were permitted to drink on their lunch breaks) fell on individual landlords. This is an important development: the idea that the people serving drinks should be legally responsible for not allowing customers to get drunk remains a contentious but central element of licensing law today (it proved unenforceable in the early 1600s, a state of affairs that arguably has changed little since). At the same time, fines for serving short measures were included in the legislation – something which conveyed the impression that landlords were stingy as well as immoral.

In practice, the law was largely ignored. The idea that either central government or the local magistrates could keep tabs on exactly how long any one of the 20,000–30,000 alehouse-keepers in the country permitted their customers to hang around was never realistic. It would not be the last example of drink legislation tripping up on the problem of implementation. Indeed, just two years later a further Act was passed to tackle the 'loathsome and odious sin of drunkenness' which had 'of late grown in common use within this realm'. This time drinkers themselves were made subject to the law. A fine of five shillings for drunkenness was introduced, as were fines for anyone tippling (i.e. drinking for more than an hour or so) in their home town. While serving people to the point of drunkenness was outlawed in 1604, drunkenness itself became subject to statutory legislation in 1606.

The 1606 Act was no more effective than its predecessor. Three years later a new Act for the 'reformation of alehouse-keepers' glumly acknowledged that 'the inordinate and extreme vice of excessive drinking and drunkenness doth more and more abound'. It didn't have anything to add to the previous, and obviously unsuccessful, legislation; it simply replaced fines for landlords who broke the law with the draconian measure of banning them from keeping an alehouse for three years on conviction of any offence set out in the Acts of 1604 and 1606.

In 1618 James I released a Royal Proclamation which set out to remedy a situation in which 'many good and wholesome laws' had 'not been duly executed as they ought to be', and which required local Justices to set up annual licensing sessions.[36] As a condition of licence renewal, landlords had to agree to ban cards and other games from their premises. As far back as 1559 there had been official injunctions against 'innholders and alehouse keepers' selling drink 'in the time of common prayer' and the

1618 Proclamation reiterated the ban on Sunday trading during divine service.[37] In addition, however, and the first time such a limit was imposed by law, drinks were not to be served after nine o'clock at night. In order to qualify for a licence, alehouses had to be capable of lodging at least one traveller overnight, and they had to inform local constables of the name of any such travellers who they put up. The 1618 Proclamation also targeted brewers who supplied beer to unlicensed sellers: a rare example of anti-drink legislation taking on the producers.

Charging for licences to run drinking establishments seems to have been James's big idea in 1618, and it provides an early example of how careful we have to be when making sweeping statements about the imposition of cultural power or disciplinary authority. Jacobean legislators may have been engaged in a cultural battle for power in the arena of everyday life, but the State also needed money – and the competing claims of social control and income generation are never more completely at loggerheads than when it comes to alcohol. Drinking may cause all sorts of problems, but an activity so ubiquitous and so economically dynamic is also an irresistible source of State income. Alongside the provisions of the 1618 Proclamation, in the same year King James gave his friend Sir Giles Mompesson the patent to impose a similar system of licences on inns. Mompesson had already carved himself quite a niche in licensing business activities – and reaping the rewards when the licences were broken, or when licence-holders felt it politic to grease his palm in advance of possible prosecutions. In 1621 he was arraigned before Parliament for outrageously misusing his powers: he had prosecuted over 3,000 inns for breaches of their licences, often through entrapment, and was caught providing licences to sixteen inns in Hampshire which local justices had previously closed down for disorder. He was eventually stripped of his knighthood and sentenced to life imprisonment. Like any good disgraced aristocrat, he went into exile and was back pursuing his career in England just a few years later. Nevertheless, in the fallout of the 1621 scandal James was forced to rescind all the legislation requiring licence payments from both inn and alehouse keepers.

At the same time as attempting to regulate alehouse activity, James I moved to reinstate elements of the traditional festive culture, the suppression of which many saw as having contributed to the proliferation of alehouses. In his so-called 'Book of Sports' (1618), James called for the reinstatement of 'May-Games, Whitson Ales' and other festivities, the prohibition of which had led the 'common and meaner sort of people' to 'filthy tipplings and drunkenness, and … idle and discontented speeches in their alehouses'.[38] It was precisely this analysis that framed Richard Rawlidge's pamphlet ten years later. In the past, Rawlidge insisted, 'people scorned to be seen to go to an Ale-house'; what free time they had was spent 'in the commendable exercise of shooting, and of bear-baiting, stool-ball, foot-ball, wasters, and such like'. Now, however:

> those public exercises are left off, by the reason that the preachers of the land did so envay against them as lords of misrule ... and so the preachers and Justices did put down, and forbid all such public sportings on the Sabbath day, but when that the people generally were forbidden their old and ancient familiar meetings and sportings, what then followed? Why, sure ale-house hunting.[39]

While Rawlidge may have agreed with the King on this, there was no overall consensus on the subject and James's call for the restoration of traditional leisure activities went down badly with many of the more puritanical local authorities, even leading to direct confrontations between local magistrates and the Crown over the issue.[40] When Charles I published a new 'Book of Sports' in 1633, it became a significant source of attrition between the King and Parliament. Part of the reason why Puritans objected to the reinstatement of traditional festivities was precisely because their suppression in the early years of the Reformation had represented an attack on a carnival culture which ran counter to Protestant ideas of self-discipline and piety. Reinstating them, even if the goal was to weaken the attraction of the alehouse, seemed to many to represent a lurch towards precisely the kind of continental Catholicism that English Protestantism had defined itself against.

While there were disagreements over the causes of alehouse-hunting, the legislative effort to control alehouse activities continued apace. In 1623 another Act entered the statute books which did away with the un-workable distinction between travellers and locals, and extended the ban on tippling to everyone. In 1625 this was shored up by an Act making landlords liable if anyone, traveller or not, tippled on their premises. In 1627 the system of fines was again updated, to resolve anomalies in the existing legislation.

Drink as a political threat

What was happening here? Certainly there had been an increase in the number of alehouses. Documentary evidence for an ensuing rise in drunkenness is, however, very limited (although, as Peter Clark points out, this doesn't mean there wasn't any such rise).[41] Certainly the beer that was being sold in alehouses was stronger than had been available before the introduction of hops, but it remained significantly weaker than the wine that was being, and had for centuries been, drained by the gallon in the taverns and private homes of the wealthy. There is no compelling evidence that drunkenness per se was significantly on the increase. The reasons for the concerted offensive against alehouses and drunkenness lay elsewhere – in the rise of Puritanism and in the fear of political instability.

The anti-alehouse legislation of the early 1600s suggests something more than the moral condemnation of drunkenness on the part of individual reformers; instead, it looks more like a desire to go after alehouse culture per se, and the wider economic and social networks it both sustained and represented. In part this was driven by a fear of the conspiracies and plots that could be hatched in the murky corners of the lower-class alehouse, or at least of the political disaffection which drunken talk could engender. When 'the drunkard is seated on the ale bench', John Downame complained, 'he presently becommeth a reprover of magistrates, a controller of the state a murmerer and repiner against the best established government ... he thinketh a whole court of Parliament may more easily err in their long deliberated decrees, then he in his present and rash verdict.[42] However, while alehouses may well have been the scene of potentially seditious chatter, there is very little evidence that they were ever actually the source of organised political dissent; alehouse-keepers were business people with little desire to undermine their own interests by allowing their premises to be used by conspirators under the noses of local magistrates.[43] In fact, where political plots did take place, they tended to take place in taverns – which were never subjected to the same degree of official control.

In truth, the Jacobean suppression of alehouses was less to do with preventing revolution and more to do with the assertion of political and cultural control by both new and existing social elites. The late sixteenth and early seventeenth centuries saw an increasing range of popular activities become defined, categorised and made punishable under a raft of new laws.[44] The law, in other words, was increasingly used as a means of controlling the poor by defining parts of their culture as criminal, and therefore subject to both policing and punishment. Alehouse legislation provides an example of this. Taking widespread everyday activities (such as drinking in alehouses) and making them subject to stringent new laws was a powerful way of asserting cultural authority in the domain of everyday life.

Throughout this period, the economics of the beer trade – especially at a local level – remained key to the implementation of legislation. While the Acts of 1623 and 1625 were designed to make prosecutions easier, their effect remained limited. One problem was that local magistrates were often unenthusiastic about arraigning local alehouse-keepers because to do so would be to strip them of an occupation which was often the only thing keeping them off poor relief, and therefore keeping them from adding to the costs of the local parish. Suppressing alehouses could, especially in tight-knit communities, be a lose-lose situation: the local magistrate would incur the ill-will of the alehouse-keeper, his or her patrons and the local brewer while risking adding another family to the ranks of the unemployed. At the same time, however, it was undeniable that in a period of low wages the existence of alehouses in poor communities could only mean the expenditure of much-needed income on drink: something which tended towards increasing poverty.

The tightrope which local authorities had to walk – between alienating their peers and alienating the poor, between facilitating trade and restricting expenditure – was helped to some extent by moves to ensure that revenue from fines imposed under anti-drink legislation went towards funds for local poor relief. An Act of 1627 further updated the law to redress the fact that fining alehouse keepers, and putting them out of business, would often 'leave a great charge of wife and children upon the parishes wherein they live'. To solve this problem, it made any such fines payable to local poor relief. Although the prosecution of alehouse-keepers remained sporadic and dependent on local circumstances, numbers of prosecutions did steadily increase in the period before the Civil War.[45] Partly this was because the revenue from fines was channelled back into ameliorating the nexus of poverty to which alehouses were inextricably tied. However, it was also because as social elites increasingly tried to distance themselves from the poor both economically and culturally, more and more magistrates were prepared to take on landlords and push for wider suppression. The justification given for all this was the threat of crime, the threat of poverty, the threat of sedition and an increasingly coherent religious attack on drunkenness and alehouse culture.

The earliest period of public concern over drink, then, was centred on the threat of social and political disorder. Forms of periodic or socially transcribed transgression that had been a part of pre-Reformation culture were challenged and presented as a threat to both social stability and religious piety. At the same time, however, alehouse numbers were increasing and the beginnings of an organised brewing industry was starting to emerge. The establishment of magisterial licensing put in place a system whereby the will of the State was mediated through decisions made by autonomous local justices; consequently, the tensions between drinkers, producers, religious groups and political elites were always coloured by local circumstance. The localisation of alcohol regulation, through the activities of independent magistrates, would exacerbate an already conflictual situation in ways that would not be resolved for centuries.

Notes

1 R. Rawlidge, *A Monster Late Found Out and Discovered* (Amsterdam: 1628).
2 F. and J. Gies, *Life in a Medieval Village* (London: The Folio Society, 2002), p. 176.
3 R. Hutton, *The Rise and Fall of Merry England: The Ritual Year 1400–1700* (Oxford: Oxford University Press, 1994), p. 59.
4 K. Wrightson, 'Alehouses, order and Reformation in rural England 1590–1660', in E. and S. Yeo (eds), *Popular Culture and Class Conflict 1590–1914* (Brighton: Harvester, 1981), p. 5.
5 Hutton, *The Rise and Fall of Merry England*, pp. 28–59.
6 P. Stubbes, *The Anatomy of Abuses* (London: New Shakespeare Society, 1879), p. 308.
7 G. Austin, *Alcohol from Antiquity to 1800: A Chronological History* (Santa Barbara, CA: ABC-Clio Information Services, 1985), p. 151.
8 Hutton, *The Rise and Fall of Merry England*, p. 145.
9 Church of England, Province of Canterbury, 'Articles to be inquired of, by the church-wardens and sworn men: in the visitation of the Lord Archbishop of Canterbury: within the Diocese of Norwich' (1605).
10 Hutton, *The Rise and Fall of Merry England*, p. 127; R. Hutton, *Stations of the Sun: A History of the Ritual Year in Britain* (Oxford: Oxford University Press, 1996), p. 252.
11 Stubbes, *The Anatomy of Abuses*, p. 150.
12 *Ibid.*
13 T. Coryate, *Coryate's Crambe* (London: William Stansby, 1611).
14 W. Harrison, 'Of faires and markets', in Raphael Holinshed, *The First and Second Volumes of Chronicles* (London: Henry Denham, 1577), p. 138.
15 C. Humphrey, *The Politics of Carnival* (Manchester: Manchester University Press, 2001).
16 Harrison, 'Of faires and markets', p. 202; P. Burke, *Popular Culture in Early Modern Europe* (Aldershot: Wildwood Press, 1988), p. 203.
17 W. Kethe, *A Sermon Made at Blanford Forum* (London: John Daye, 1571), p. 15.
18 M. Bakhtin, *Rabelais and His World*, trans. Hélène Iswolsky (Bloomington, IN: Indiana University Press, 1984); see M. Roth, 'Carnival, creativity and the sublimation of drunkenness', *Mosaic*, 30:2 (1997), 1–18 for a discussion of Bakhtin's failure to discuss the questions of alcohol and intoxication in his discussion of carnival.
19 T. Eagleton, *Walter Benjamin or Towards a Revolutionary Criticism* (London: Verso, 1981), p. 148.
20 G. Balandier, cited in P. Stallybrass and A. White, *The Politics and Poetics of Transgression* (London: Methuen, 1986), p. 14.
21 J. Gusfield, 'Benevolent repression: popular culture, social structure, and the control of drinking', in S. Barrows and R. Room (eds), *Drinking: Behaviour and Belief in Modern History* (Berkeley, CA: University of California Press, 1992), p. 404.
22 Stubbes, *The Anatomy of Abuses*, p. 107.
23 P. Clark, 'Alehouses and alternative society', in D. Pennington and K. Thomas (eds.), *Puritans and Revolutionaries: Essays in Seventeenth-Century History* (Oxford: Clarendon, 1978), p. 50.
24 *Ibid.*, p. 52; Wrightson, 'Alehouses, order and Reformation in rural England', p. 4.
25 P. Haydon, *Beer and Britannia: An Inebriated History of Britain* (Stroud: Sutton, 2003), p. 33.
26 Harrison, 'Of faires and markets', p. 170.

27 J. Warner, 'Good help is hard to find: A few comments about alcohol and work in preindustrial England', *Addiction Research*, 2:3 (1995), 259–69, pp. 262–3.

28 H. L. Sharpe, *Early Modern England: A Social History, 1550–1760* (London: Arnold, 1996), p. 106.

29 *Ibid.*, pp. 118–20.

30 Clark, 'Alehouses and alternative society', p. 50.

31 R. F. Bretherton, 'Country inns and alehouses', in R. Lennard (ed.), *Englishmen at Rest and Play: Some Phases of English Leisure 1588–1714* (Oxford: Clarendon, 1931), p. 154.

32 G. Gascoigne, *A Delicate Diet for Dainty-mouthed Drunkards*(London: Richard Jones, 1576), n.p.

33 *Ibid.*

34 *Ibid.*

35 T. Nashe, *Pierce Penilesse, His Supplication to the Divell* (Edinburgh: Edinburgh University Press, 1966), p. 75.

36 James I, *A Proclamation concerning ale-houses* (London: Bonham Norton, 1618), p. 1.

37 England and Wales, Sovereign, *Injunctions given by the Queen's Majesty* (1559).

38 James I, *The King's Majesties declaration to his subjects, concerning lawful sports to be used* (London: Bonham Norton and John Bill, 1618), pp. 4–5.

39 Rawlidge, *A Monster Late Found Out*, pp. 12–13.

40 P. Heylyn, *Cyprianus Anglicus* (London: A. Seile, 1688), p. 257.

41 Clark, 'Alehouses and alternative society', p. 58.

42 J. Downame, *Four Treatises, Tending to Dissuade all Christians from four no less heinous than common sins namely the abuses of Swearing, Drunkenness, Whoredom, and Bribery* (London: Michael Baker, 1613), p. 87.

43 Clark, 'Alehouses and alternative society', p. 68.

44 Sharpe, *Early Modern England*, p. 113.

45 Wrightson, 'Alehouses, order and Reformation in rural England', p. 21.

2

Healths, toasts and pledges: political drinking in the seventeenth century

He is reputed a peasant, a slave and a bore, that will not take his liquor pro-foundly. (Thomas Young (after Thomas Nashe))

He is foxt, he is flaw'd, he is flustered, he is subtle, cupshot, cut in the leg or back, he hath seen the French King, he hath swallowed an hair or a tavern-token, he hath whiptd the cat, he hath been at the scriveners and learn'd to make indentures, he hath bit his grannam, or is bit by a barn-weasel. (Thomas Heywood)

In the seventeenth century, the stream of alehouse legislation was ac-companied by a rising tide of religious anti-drink literature. That ale-houses posed a secular threat to the ideological power of religion had long been recognised. Following the publication of the Bible in English, Thomas Cranmer had sent a declaration to be read to congregations, forbidding any 'open reasoning' on scripture 'in your open taverns or alehouses … and other places, unmet for such conference'.[1] 'Open reasoning' was a threat to ecclesiastical power, and alehouses – demo-cratic by nature – were no place to fathom the mysteries of organised religion.

However, the application of reason was the least of the worries ex-pressed by most seventeenth-century religious writers on drink. Their concern was the 'voluntary madness' of drunkenness: something they saw as both a species of gluttony and the wilful destruction of the ra-tionality which God had uniquely bestowed upon Man.[2] Drunkenness was, in St Augustine's words, a 'bewitching sin' and some religious writers were already starting to describe its attractions in terms com-parable to what we would now recognise as addiction. However, most of the energy expended by preachers and moralists alike was directed towards the cultures and rituals of drinking which encouraged exces-sive consumption. Most prominent among these targets was the drink-ing of healths.

A bawd and pander unto drunkenness

The drinking of healths, toasts and pledges caused particular anxiety among seventeenth-century religious writers. Indeed, it was nothing less than 'an engine invented by the devil, to carry on the sin of drunkenness'.[3] Alehouses, and the less salubrious taverns, may have been violent, criminal and possibly seditious places, but, so numerous writers claimed, the drunkenness which occurred in them was the result of drinking rituals.

In *Pierce Penilesse*, Thomas Nashe had complained that 'now he is a no body that cannot drink *supernagulum*, carouse the hunter's hoop, quaff *upsey freze crosse*, with healths, gloves, mumps, frolics, and a thousand such domineering inventions'.[4] He went on to complain that the rituals of drinking were 'as good as printed precepts, or statutes set down by Act of Parliament'.[5] Nashe's description of drinking rituals would provide the model for numerous later diatribes against drink (many of which simply plagiarised whole chunks of Nashe's Elizabethan text while claiming to present eyewitness accounts of drinking in Jacobean England). One work which leaned heavily on Nashe's blueprint was a pamphlet entitled *Philocothonista, or the Drunkard, Opened, Dissected and Anatomized* by the celebrated playwright Thomas Heywood (1635). Heywood's study dwelt extensively on the drinking of toasts – an activity for which he blamed the Danes, insisting that they were 'the first upon record, that brought their wassail-bowls and elbow-deep healths into this land'.[6] Heywood went on, however, to note that 'the cooler the climates are, the more the inhabitants are addicted to strong and toxing drinks'. Of those more bibulous north European nations, the English, Heywood regretfully concluded, were 'the most forward to commit this grievous and abominable sin of drunkenness'.[7]

However, for both Heywood and most of his contemporaries it was cultural, rather than climatic, influences which were the cause of excessive drunkenness. In 1612, the Anglican preacher Thomas Thompson complained that in England anyone refusing to drink healths 'is accounted no good fellow, but a meacock, or a puritan'.[8] Shortly afterwards Thomas Young, who had just become tutor to a young John Milton, published a pamphlet entitled *England's Bane*, in which he repeated whole sections of Nashe's work, including the condemnation of anyone who 'forceth and goads his fellows forward to be drunk with his persuasive terms, as I drank to you, I pray pledge me.'[9] Young also echoed Nashe in blaming the wars of the Low Countries for introducing drunkenness to England. The persistent borrowing of Nashe's colourful writing by pamphleteers such as Young tells us as much about the extent to which drink had started to produce its own discourse as it does about the realities of drinking practices at the time. As we shall see throughout this book, the rhetoric of drunkenness – both visual and linguistic – has often played as much a part in shaping public debates on alcohol consumption as have the actual realities of drinking behaviour.

The grounds for condemning health-drinking were religious as well as cultural. 'Woe to him that giveth his neighbour to drink', said the Bible, 'and makest him drunken also'.[10] In his *Delicate Diet* George Gascoigne had cited St Augustine's warning that pledging 'doth yet smell of the smoke of paganism'.[11] 'There is no true fellowship in [pledging],' wrote the influential religious writer Arthur Dent, 'it is mere impiety'.[12] The condemnation of health-drinking by religious writers became increasingly widespread in the first half of the seventeenth century, and, as the work of ministers such as Dent, Young and Thompson shows, attacks on drunkenness were not limited to Puritans. Nevertheless, preachers with puritan leanings were often responsible for the more explosive diatribes against alcohol. Perhaps the most sustained and voluminous broadside of the time was penned by the maverick lawyer and religious pamphleteer William Prynne. Published in 1628, *Healthes: Sicknesse* contained a relentless condemnation of the 'odious, swinish, unthrifty and state-disturbing sin' of health-drinking, and especially its normalisation within courtly circles.[13]

In *Healthes: Sicknesse* Prynne set out to explain why drunkenness 'doth so much increase and superabound among us'. He blamed the cultural tolerance of drunkenness: the 'many specious, beautiful, popular, amiable, and bewitching' terms whereby 'this ugly, odious and filthy sin' was 'beautified, gilded and adorned'. He blamed 'the negligence and coldness of justices, [and] magistrates' in applying the existing licensing laws to control excess. But more than anything, he blamed those rituals of health-drinking which were a 'bawd and pander unto drunkenness'. While often a frenetic and rambling attack on all aspects of drinking culture, at other times Prynne's essay carried a precise political weight. Specifically, Prynne walked a dangerous line between the generalised condemnation of public drinking and the suggestion that the corruption of drunkenness was in some way analogous to corruption in the royal court of Charles I. Warning the King against the increasingly commonplace courtly ritual of drinking to his health, Prynne acerbically pointed out that healths 'ordinarily and usually tend to the honour, praise, applause, and commemoration, of vain, of evil, wicked, and sinful men, especially, among the baser and looser sort'. Prynne left it to the reader to decide what this told us about a King who routinely accepted healths from his courtiers. This elliptical technique of leaving readers to make connections between the objects of his censure and real, often courtly, individuals would eventually cost Prynne dear: five years later his ears were removed for sedition after he publicly condemned theatrical performances just as the King's wife was taking part in a play.[14]

Prynne's attack on courtly health-drinking reveals the extent to which, by the middle of the seventeenth century, anti-drink literature was targeted not just at plebeian alehouses but also at the aristocratic culture of the court. The drinking of toasts and healths was by no means a uniquely lower-class activity, and it was by no means limited to the drinking of ale or beer. Indeed, as England lurched towards civil war in the 1640s, the wine-drinking rituals of the Royalist court would become charged with religious, political and cultural significance. So much so, that for the second half of the 1600s, choice of drink, and ritual of consumption, would become some of the leading signifiers of the cataclysmic political division opened up by the Cromwellian Revolution.

Wine, beer and ale, together by the ears

The Interregnum, perhaps surprisingly, brought no new legislation regarding alehouses. It might have been expected that the Puritans, in their moment of victory, would have pressed home their advantage and moved to finish off the alehouse. That they did not lends some credence to the idea that the suppression of alehouses in the three decades prior to the Civil War, while fuelled by religious indignation, had more to do with shoring up new class alignments through aggressive cultural politics than ushering in God's Kingdom.

Things changed temporarily when Cromwell set up a system of direct military rule under the so-called Major-Generals in October 1655. Three months prior to this, Cromwell had issued a Proclamation stating that no new licensing legislation was necessary, but that local magistrates needed to get on with implementing the law as it stood: closing down unlicensed premises, prosecuting drunkards and stripping irresponsible landlords of their right to sell beer.[15] When the Major-Generals were appointed, Cromwell's call for the stern application of the law was carried out with zeal. Having been charged with reinforcing strict standards of moral rectitude, the Major-Generals spent two years closing thousands of disorderly and unlicensed alehouses. In Warwickshire, for example, one-third of all existing alehouses were shut down.[16]

Unfortunately for the moral guardians of the Protectorate, such rigidly coercive enforcement of virtuous behaviour was destined to burn itself out in a relatively short time. By 1657 both Parliament and the population had tired of the Major-Generals' strong-arm tactics. Cromwell saw the obvious dangers in sustaining such an unpopular system and agreed to have it dismantled. With the collapse of the Major-Generals, the suppression of alehouses returned to the status quo: a cat-and-mouse game between local justices and alehouse-keepers in which, where justices had the will and the means to do so, they gained the upper hand, but where otherwise alehouses continued to function as before.

Perhaps one reason why the suppression of alehouses under the Protectorate was relatively half-hearted is that brewers were precisely the kind of people who made up much of Parliament's core support. Cromwell himself was rumoured to have had a family connection to brewers in Huntingdon – and although this was never proved, it provided Royalists with some minor propaganda material.[17] In this context, Cromwell's purported ties with brewing were not politically significant because they implied that he had a role in promoting drunkenness. Simply being associated with brewing was not something that, as yet, could be construed as morally dubious. Royalists never tried to portray Cromwell as corrupting public virtue by hawking ale; instead, the satirical potential of Cromwell's brewing ties lay in the fact it allowed Royalists to depict Cromwell as dull and provincial: just like ale.

The Civil War led to a new intensification of the political symbolism of alcohol – both in terms of drinks and drinking rituals. For defeated Royalists in particular, the consumption of wine and the rituals of toasting the exiled King became ways of sustaining their cultural and political values. The already elitist status of wine became explicitly political when the traditional wine-drinking elite were forced from power by the Cromwellian insurgency. Once that happened, wine ceased to be simply part of a cultural milieu and came instead to stand for a specific set of political beliefs.

There is a whole sub-genre of Royalist literature from the Interregnum which codifies the struggle between the two sides of the conflict as a battle between wine and ale.[18] Wine consumption was, by dint of the fact that it was an imported product, mostly confined to the wealthy (a cultural feature which is by no means universal – in France wine has always fulfilled a much more democratic role). However, the political potential of this was never truly realised until new economic and cultural divisions began to be thought about in terms of consumption and the places where consumption occurred. Alehouses had been condemned in the early seventeenth century as sites of drunkenness and criminality, but behind this was an attempt to isolate and manage a new plebeian culture. For Royalists, defeat in the Civil War seemed to have handed victory to that mob-like, plebeian world which the alehouse in many ways represented. Exiled Royalist poets and letter-writers repeatedly analogised the political situation at home in terms of wine and ale: complaining that 'Beer and Ale makes you prate / of the Kirk and State' while 'sack does divinely inspire us ... to do what our Ruler require us'.[19] With the world having been turned upside down by the victory of Parliament, what was once merely dull and bucolic was now revolutionary and destructive; hence one Royalist poet could write: 'From hops and grains let us purge our brains; / They do smell of anarchy'.[20] As the traditional drink of the court, wine represented both stability and sophistication; ale and beer, by contrast, seemed to stand for a provincial dullness which had erupted into a horrifying Puritan enthusiasm.

The cultural and political distinctions embodied in wine, combined with a more mundane desire to find some kind of pleasure in defeat, meant that the practice of drinking healths to the King became an important feature of Royalist culture. Drinking healths provided a clandestine, but easily recognisable, way of reinforcing the bonds within a social class that was otherwise in danger of fragmentation.[21] The fact that this was the case says much about not only about the social significance of drinking rituals, but the distinctive place of wine in British drinking culture.

Historically, wine was subject to far more legislative control than ale or beer. As early as 1330 legislation was enacted to control the selling of 'corrupt wines' and to ensure that 'none be so hardy as to sell wine but at a reasonable price'. In 1536 the pricing of wines was handed over, by law, to the 'Lord Chancellor, Lord Treasurer, Lord President of the King's most honourable Council, Lord Privy Seal and the two Chief Justices of either Bench'. Clearly, wine prices were too important to be left to any less august a body. Considered alongside the 1553 Act, it is clear that the regulation of wine was seen as a business to be entrusted to only the highest State officials. Furthermore, just as the cultural status of beer drinking was as much about the cultural status of the alehouse, so wine drinking was inextricably linked to the culture of the tavern. In 1628, John Earle wrote that a tavern is 'a degree or (if you will) a pair of stairs above an Alehouse, were men are drunk with more credit and apology'.[22] While the same author was far less generous in a Restoration redraft, adding that a 'tavern is an academy of debauchery, where the devil teaches the seven deadly sins instead of sciences',[23] even the most disorderly elements of tavern life carried with them the sheen of social and intellectual sophistication – as the celebratory tavern poetry of Ben Jonson and his associates showed.

'Our age,' wrote the so-called 'Water Poet' John Taylor, 'approves that Sack is the best lining or living for a good poet; and that it enables our modern writers, to versify most ingeniously'.[24] While Taylor himself preferred to drink old-fashioned ale (his name was a reference to his early career as a waterman, not his drinking habits), the upper-class, tavern-haunting literati of sixteenth- and seventeenth-century England certainly saw wine as the key to their own inner brilliance. Robert Herrick, one of the more enthusiastic of the tavern poets, eulogised wine thus:

> 'Tis thou, alone, who with thy mystic fan,
> Work'st more then wisdom, art, or nature can,
> To rouse the sacred madness.[25]

Herrick was playing here on the ancient idea of Dionysian inspiration, something that we will look at more closely in later chapters. Celebratory drinking literature, in particular the anacreontic poetry which had been fashionable since the late sixteenth century, was understandably popular among young upper-class men with literary pretensions.[26] It provided an excellent excuse to drink wine and it imbued their social activities with the aura of classical learning and poetic inspiration. The Royalist paeans to wine discussed above owed as much to this tradition – which depicted wine as dashing, daring, sophisticated and inspiring – as they did to the specific rituals of drinking healths.

Traditional religious connotations were undoubtedly one aspect of the Royalist uses of wine. However, it was connotations of tradition, wealth, social status and cosmopolitanism which mattered most. Where 'base … muddy ale' was provincial, wine was urbane; where beer provided refreshment, wine bestowed taste.[27] In the comic play *Wine, Beer and Ale Together by the Ears* (1629), a bar-room dispute between the three drinks over social status is only resolved when water allocates them three domains: ale to the country, beer to the city and wine to the court. John Taylor's *Drink and Welcome*, published eight years later, set out an inventory of British drinks which gave as much attention to the cultural significance of drinks as it did to either taste or geography. Generally speaking, ale was seen as the traditional drink of the peasantry, beer as the drink of urban artisans and commercial types, while wine was, stereotypically, the courtly drink.[28] The Civil War transformed this politics of taste into the concrete politics of ritual expression. As the sociologist Pierre Bourdieu once famously observed, 'taste classifies, and it classifies the classifier';[29] this was never truer than among Royalist drinkers under the Protectorate.

By drinking healths to the exiled King, Royalists not only kept his cause alive, but constantly reminded themselves what the Royalist cause stood for: the restitution of that aristocratic hegemony so rudely and violently interrupted by Cromwell and his henchmen. It must, then, have come as something of a blow when – within days of his Restoration – Charles II issued a Royal Proclamation against those 'vicious, debauch'd, and profane persons' who:

> spend their time in taverns, tipling-houses, and debauches, giving no other evidence of their affection to us, but in drinking our health, and inveighing against

all others, who are not of their dissolute temper; and who, in truth, have more discredited our cause, by the licence of their manners and lives, then they could ever advance it by their affection or courage.[30]

Charles later ordered that his Proclamation be read by every minister in the land to their congregations once a month for six months. Even at the risk of alienating some of his most loyal supporters, Charles II was keen to avoid the impression that a restored British monarchy meant a celebration of those licentious aspects of English courtly life which the likes of Prynne had castigated prior to the Civil War.

One important feature of the 1660 Proclamation is that it does not attack alehouses or taverns, and it does not make general statements about public drunkenness; instead, it specifically condemns the drinking of healths. It illustrates the extent to which concerns over drunkenness among the English in particular were tied to concerns over patterns and rituals of drinking. It also illustrates how these patterns of drinking – the drinking of healths and toasts, and later the convention of buying rounds – transcended the kind of class distinctions which overlaid concerns about place. While *what* and *where* people drank was commonly seen as a marker of social class, those rituals which tended towards excessive drinking in groups were more often perceived, for better or worse, as a feature of national culture.

For its part, Charles II's Proclamation was unlikely to have a significant effect on aristocratic drinking rituals: the availability of drink was not reduced, nor was the desire to engage in convivial drinking. Neither, crucially, were the cultural and political divisions between gentry and bourgeoisie, between court and country, or between conformist and nonconformist made any less complex by his return to power. As long as people drank, and as long as what they drank said something about who they were, then the rituals which accompanied social drinking would take on political significance. If anything, this became even more pronounced after the Restoration of the monarchy than it had ever been previously.

Political drinking in the Restoration

Charles II may have publicly condemned drunkenness, but it was the wine-drinking Royalists who won the war between Parliament and the Crown and they were not about to celebrate victory by taking on the puritanical habits of their enemies. The cultural turmoil which led up to the Civil War had seen the beginnings of the politicisation of sobriety – a process that would become much more pronounced over the course of the eighteenth century – and it was Cromwell's men who had most explicitly allied their political and religious world-view to the state of being not-drunk.

Royalists saw the Restoration as supplanting the sober seriousness of the Interregnum with, if not some kind of anarchic licence, then certainly a celebration of pleasurable liberty. Indeed, refusing to engage in convivial drinking quickly became a questionable trait: to remain po-faced and sober was to draw suspicion that you perhaps hankered after a return to the Protectorate. Why remain conspicuously sober by choice when you no longer had to – unless you were with those who had turned sobriety into a religious and political virtue? Following the Restoration, for many the 'connection between sobriety and sedition was clear'.[31]

Even allowing for his personal proclivities, Samuel Pepys's diary provides perhaps the clearest evidence that in Restoration England even relative sobriety (by twenty-first century standards) was unusual. Conspicuous sobriety would have aroused suspicion for its plain oddness alone, never mind the worrying religious passions it might signify. Drinking and drunkenness remained common, and attacks on the latter continued to be penned by writers who clung to the Puritan vision of the virtuous society.[32] Whichever way the political wind blew, drinking retained its central role in public life – even after the appearance of coffee-houses from 1650 onwards. Among the political elite in particular, the connotations which had attached themselves to wine in the previous few decades meant that it became inextricably associated with a courtly culture that had close ties with continental Europe and which tended towards a greater tolerance of Catholicism. Wine and beer remained at each other's throats, and even more so after the establishment of Whig and Tory parties following the Exclusion Crisis of 1679.

In practice, the kind of people who made up the political elite in the late seventeenth century all drank wine – at least, in the privacy of their own houses.[33] Nevertheless, in the political discourse of the Restoration drink became a symbolic marker of cultural difference in which Tories stood for claret, and Whigs stood for beer. Certainly, this was the principle on which the two sides pursued their public drinking, and on which they hurled insults at each other in print. The political symbolism of Tory wine and Whig beer was relatively straightforward. For the Tories, wine stood for sophistication, conviviality, wit and good taste. It also stood for loyalty to the crown – a residual effect of the Royalist pledging during the Interregnum. For Whigs, wine stood for snobbishness, continental effeteness and, most damningly, a suspiciously Catholic-looking Francophilia. On the other side, Whigs depicted beer as honest, hearty, unpretentious and, crucially, English; the Tories depicted Whig beer drinkers as tedious, miserable and even violent when in their cups.[34] The poet John Dryden, in his prologue to Nathaniel Lee's *Caesar Borgia*, complained that London was swarming with unsophisticated and Whiggish arrivistes, neurotic about trumped-up foreign Catholic plots: 'So big you look, tho' claret you retrench / That arm'd with bottled ale; you huff the *French*'.[35] Commenting on this passage, Susan Owen has wondered 'which is the worst offence to the Tory Dryden: criticizing the French or drinking bottled ale'. The two, it seemed, were inseparable.[36]

Late seventeenth-century satire often relied on caricaturing Tories as ridiculously pretentious faux-connoisseurs or Whigs as backwater bumpkins parading as the nouveau-riche. One Whig victory which was especially irksome to the Tories was the ban on French imports which they imposed in 1679. This aggressive measure obviously hit imports of French wines hard, so it doubled as an attack both on French trade and on Tory values. An interesting effect of this policy was that the old problem of wine adulteration was swiftly corralled into the burgeoning metaphorical armoury of political satirists. Tories complained that the embargo forced vintners and wine-retailers to adulterate their products, an act they saw as analogous to the adulterated loyalty of the Whigs – a loyalty which didn't extend to allowing for the natural rules of succession to be followed, for example.[37] Whigs were ready with a response: that adulteration was endemic in the wine trade anyway, just as the royal absolutism – itself an adulteration of proper government – was endemic among Tory ranks. That the leading Whig politician was Anthony Ashley Cooper provided Tory pamphleteers with plentiful ammunition for puns on the name – a cooper being a barrel-maker. Fuel for more vicious satire, however, was provided by the fact that since 1668 Cooper had had a tap fixed to his side which drained an abscess on his liver. Images of 'Tapski' dispensing adulterated bodily fluids to a populace deprived of proper French wine abounded.[38]

One further effect of the 1679 embargo on French goods was the rapid development of the wine trade with Portugal. The vineyards of the rocky Douro valley in northern Portugal did not produce wines capable of matching those produced in the main wine-growing regions of Europe, but the discovery of a technique by which the fermentation process was halted early through the addition of brandy allowed the Douro producers to make a wine that was both unique tasting, strong and reasonably reliable. It did as well as any in lieu of claret, and promoting trade with Portugal meant discouraging trade with France. While Tory traditionalists paid higher prices for French wines that evaded the embargo, forward-looking Whigs took to drinking the new 'port wine' with gusto: here was a way to huff the French and drink something more sophisticated than muddy ale. Port sales went up by over 30 per cent in the last quarter of the seventeenth century.[39] The establishment of port as *the* gentleman's drink in the eighteenth century was helped significantly by the Treaty of Methuen in 1703. This agreement, drawn up by the diplomat John Methuen as part of an attempt to bring Portugal onside during the War of Spanish Succession, allowed for lower duties to be imposed on Portuguese wines in exchange for similar duty reductions on woollen goods being imported into Portugal from Britain. Port, in fact, is a wine born of political necessity – something that the sight of such un-Portuguese names as Cockburns, Sandemans and Croft lining the banks of the Douro to this day confirms.

By the 1680s, then, historical and cultural distinctions between wine and beer-drinking had become embroiled in the new party politics which followed the Exclusion Crisis. Wine, always the drink of the privileged classes, had come to signify the loyalism of those who supported the monarchy through the Interregnum and the urbane anti-Puritanism of Cavalier culture and its legacy. Beer, the grass-roots national drink, had survived persistent attacks on alehouses in the early years of the century and re-emerged as the symbol of honesty and a down-to-earth Protestantism – with all the political potential that associating such values with 'Englishness' could afford. With the Restoration of the monarchy, popular anxieties over political instability became focused on the threat of a resurgent Catholicism, an anxiety which reached a head over the trumped-up 'popish plots' in 1678. France was seen as the major source of Catholic threat, and French wines became targeted as both culturally popish (doubtless an idea bolstered by the role of wine in Catholic sacramental ritual) and as an economic drain which directed money straight to the coffers of the French treasury. Largely in response to this, new alcohol markets emerged, dealing in new drinks. In particular, port wine became available and swiftly popular: a drink that was new not only in its taste, strength and method of production, but in demonstrating how the perennially money-spinning trade in alcohol could act as a weapon of economic warfare. Drink had moved from creating a focus for the establishment of power along broad cultural lines, to acting as a symbol of political allegiance, to providing a weapon in the armoury of political and economic strategists. A few years later, the introduction of gin to this mix would show just how dramatic a social impact the strategic use of alcohol could have.

Notes

1   J. Strype, *Memorial of the Most Reverend Father in God, Thomas Cranmer* (London: Richard Chiswell, 1694), pp. 42–3.
2   T. Thompson, *A Diet for A Drunkard* (London: Richard Bankworth, 1612), p. 20; A. Dent, *The Plain Man's Path-way to Heaven* (London: 1607), p. 162; Downame, *Four Treatises*, p. 83.

3   S. Ward, *A Warning Piece to all Drunkards and Health-Givers* (London, 1682).
4   Nashe, *Pierce Penilesse*, p. 76.
5   *Ibid.*, p. 79.
6   T. Heywood, *Philocothonista, or the Drunkard, Opened, Dissected, and Anatomized* (London: Robert Raworth, 1635), p. 28.
7   *Ibid.*, p. 91.
8   Thompson, *A Diet for A Drunkard*, p. 63.
9   T. Young, *England's Bane, or the Description of Drunkenness* (London: William Jones, 1617).
10   Habakkuk 2:15.
11   Gascoigne, *Delicate Diet*, n.p.
12   Dent, *The Plain Man's Path-way to Heaven*, p. 165.
13   W. Prynne, *Healthes: Sicknesse* (London, 1628).
14   *Ibid.*
15   'Protector', *A Proclamation Commanding a Speedy and Due Execution of the Laws Made against the Abominable Sins of Drunkenness, Profane Swearing and Cursing, Adultery, Fornication, and Other Acts of Uncleanness* (London: Henry Hills and John Field, 1655), p. 1.
16   Bretherton, 'Country inns and alehouses', p. 160.
17   S. Earnshaw, *The Pub in Literature: England's Altered State* (Manchester: Manchester University Press, 2000), p. 91; A. McShane-Jones, A. 'Roaring Royalists and ranting brewers: the politicisation of drink and drunkenness in political broadside ballads from 1640 to 1689', in A. Smythe (ed.), *A Pleasing Sinne: Drink and Conviviality in Seventeenth-Century England* (Cambridge: D. S. Brewer, 2004), pp. 73–4.
18   M. Kebluseck, 'Drinking and the Royalist experience, 1642–1660', and A. McShane-Jones, 'Roaring Royalists and ranting brewers', both in Smythe (ed.), *A Pleasing Sinne*; Earnshaw, *The Pub in Literature*, pp. 90–3.
19   Kebluseck, 'Drinking and the Royalist experience', p. 56.
20   J. Phillips, 'In Praise of Canary', in *Wit and Drollery Jovial Poems* (London, 1661).
21   Kebluseck, 'Drinking and the Royalist experience', p. 58.
22   J. Earle, *Micro-cosmographie, or A Piece of the World Discovered* (London: William Stansby, 1628), Chapter 13.
23   J. Earle, *The Character of a Tavern* (London: D. A., 1675), p. 1.
24   J. Taylor, *Drink and Welcome* (London: Anne Griffin, 1637).
25   R. Herrick, 'His farewell to Sack', in *Hesperides* (London: John Williams and Francis Eglesfield, 1648).
26   S. Achilleos, 'The *Anacreonta* and a tradition of refined male sociability', in Smythe (ed.), *A Pleasing Sinne*, p. 24.
27   'Gallobeligicus', *Wine, Beer and Ale, Together by the Ears* (London: John Grove, 1629), p. 8.
28   A. Findlay, 'Theatres of truth: drinking and drama in early modern England', in J. Nicholls and S. Owen (eds), *A Babel of Bottles: Drink, Drinkers and Drinking Places in Literature* (Sheffield: Sheffield Academic Press, 2000).
29   P. Bourdieu, *Distinction: A Social Critique of the Judgement of Taste* (London: Harvard University Press, 1987), p. 6.
30   Charles II, *A Proclamation against vicious, debauch'd and profane persons*, London: Christopher Barker and John Bill, 1660), p. 1.
31   McShane-Jones, 'Roaring Royalists and ranting brewers', p. 78.
32   See, for example, A. Jones, *The Dreadful Character of a Drunkard* (London: Elizabeth Andrews, 1663); Ward, *A Warning Piece to all Drunkards*.

33 C. Ludington, '"Be sometimes to your country true": The politics of wine in England, 1660–1714', in Smythe (ed.), *A Pleasing Sinne*.
34 McShane-Jones, 'Roaring Royalists and ranting brewers', p. 77; S. Owen, 'The politics of drink in Restoration drama', in Nicholls and Owen (eds), *A Babel of Bottles*.
35 N. Lee, *Caesar Borgia, Son of Pope Alexander the Sixth* (London: R. E., 1680).
36 Owen, 'The politics of drink in Restoration drama', p. 46.
37 Ludington, '"Be sometimes to your country true"', pp. 92–5.
38 Earnshaw, *The Pub in Literature*, p. 92.
39 Ludington, '"Be sometimes to your country true", p. 91.

3

A new kind of drunkenness: the gin craze

If therefore it be thought proper to suppress this vice, the legislature must once more take the matter into their hands; and to this, perhaps, they will be the more inclined, when it comes to their knowledge, that a new kind of drunkenness, unknown to our ancestors, is lately sprung up amongst us, and which, if not put a stop to, will infallibly destroy a great part of the inferior people. (Henry Fielding)

The use of other liquors is not as bad; because the drinking of spirituous liquors is a kind of instantaneous drunkenness, where a man hath no time to recollect or think, whether he has had enough or not. (Josiah Tucker)

So far, we have seen that the changing dynamics of public debates over alcohol have been driven by social, political and economic factors. While hopped beer and port both represented technological developments, their impact was mediated by the wider social contexts which gave those material changes political significance. So far culture, not drink per se, has moulded the drink question. The 'gin craze' represents a change of emphasis in this regard. As we shall see, the feverish public debate on gin was shot through with anxieties over class, the economy, national identity and the protection of moral norms; similarly, the popularisation of gin was the result of political decisions which were framed by cultural and economic concerns. Nevertheless, gin was also a qualitatively new kind of intoxicant: it was not the first distilled spirit to be drunk in England, but it was the first to gain widespread popularity. In most cases, the social history of alcohol is a story of how culturally constant materials (e.g. wine or beer) change their meaning according to social context; the story of the gin craze, however, shows that sometimes new technologies and new commodities reverse that relationship so that culture *reacts* to new materials, rather than only acting upon them.

At the start of the eighteenth century gin stood for modernity, free trade and economic security. By 1750 gin stood for urban decay, social disintegration and economic collapse. At the start of the century its production and retail was actively encouraged by the state. Forty years later

Parliament would be searching for something – anything – that could quell consumption, everything else having failed spectacularly. Writers who once championed the distillers' cause would have long since thrown their weight behind legislative suppression. In fifty years, enthusiasm descended into panic and prohibition. In the process, gin exposed fundamental contradictions at the heart of the new market economy of which London was the crucible.

The spirit of the times

Gin was the result of a technological revolution. The production of alcoholic drinks has always required technology, but that technology has conventionally been geared towards harnessing more or less effectively the natural process of fermentation. Distillation was a technological paradigm shift because instead of simply manipulating a natural occurrence it involves a process that otherwise would simply not occur. Left alone, alcoholic liquids will not distil themselves.

The history of distillation is obscure. It was probably introduced to Europe by Islamic chemists; the word 'alcohol' is itself Arabic. It goes without saying, then, that distillation was not first used for the mass production of intoxicating drinks; it took a European sensibility to exploit that particular potential. Once introduced to the West, the change of use came fairly quickly. References to *uisge beatha* (the Gaelic for *aqua vitae*, from which we get the word 'whisky') start to appear in British historical records from the fifteenth century. As early as 1584, the Lord Deputy of Ireland passed a decree restricting access to whisky among the Irish peasantry, claiming that it 'sets the Irish mad and breeds many mischiefs'.[1] However, whisky consumption remained localised in parts of Scotland and Ireland. In England, spirit-drinking only began to take hold in the seventeenth century when brandy began to enter the market. Because brandy was primarily imported from France, it soon became embroiled in the same system of trading sanctions which had reduced the levels of wine importation at the end of the seventeenth century. Like wine, brandy was an alchemical luxury that turned English pounds into French francs.

It was the 'Glorious Revolution' – the accession of William of Orange to the throne of England in 1688 – that triggered the development of an indigenous distilling industry. Within a few years of taking the throne, William III set about popularising Dutch 'geneva' – a name soon shortened, 'by frequent use and the laconic spirit of the nation', to *gin*.[2] There were a number of reasons for this. For a start, gin had none of the popish connotations that adhered to brandy and the social symbolism of drinks, as we have seen, mattered enormously in early modern England. The production of a native distilled spirit was a gesture of cultural status. However, there were good economic reasons for developing the trade in gin as well. Being made from corn rather than grapes, it could be produced using British raw materials to supply a British market. Even more than port, gin represented a cultural and an economic bulwark against Catholic France. Within a year of William's coronation, Parliament banned the import of all foreign brandy, aqua vitae, and other spirits. This ban was only lifted five years later – and even then the ban on French imports was retained. In 1690 the monopoly of the London Guild of Distillers was rescinded. This meant that whereas the trade had previously been tightly restricted by the guild system, now anybody who wished to do so could set up shop as a producer or retailer of gin. Most importantly – and in complete contrast to the wine and beer trades – there was no requirement for a licence of any kind. While the internal market was protected against French imports, free trade was encouraged to stimulate competition and consumption. Here was a new economic dispensation: no guilds, no protected interests, no licensing. Gin was a commodity nurtured in that ideal modern marketplace in which supply is left to find a natural level with demand.

That competition stimulates, rather than simply meeting, demand became apparent soon enough. In 1700 consumption of gin stood at less than half a gallon per person annually – although this may have been affected by a temporary ban put on domestic distillation in 1699 following concerns over corn prices. By 1720 it was nearer to 1.3 gallons.[3] The increased consumption that followed liberalisation benefited the powerful landowning interests because they got to sell off the surplus grain that was the result of newly improved farming techniques; distillers and retailers were happy at the development of an obviously popular new market; and Parliament was happy because, thanks to incremental increases in duties, gin helped to fill coffers which were depleted by the ongoing wars with France.[4]

Nevertheless, not everyone saw the trade in gin as an unalloyed good. By the 1720s magistrates and preachers were starting to call for controls to be placed on the trade, to such an extent that in 1726 Daniel Defoe thought it necessary to defend distillers against such demands. In his *Brief Case of the Distillers*, Defoe established a free-trade defence of the distilling industry. Legal and moral responsibility, he claimed, had nothing to do with the working of the market. 'As for the excesses and intemperance of the people,' Defoe wrote, 'the distillers are not concern'd in it at all, their business is to prepare a spirit wholesome and good.' He concluded that if 'the people will destroy themselves by their own excess … 'tis the magistrates' business to help that, not the distillers'.[5] For Defoe, the poor had become tired of 'tedious and dull' ale and distillers were simply providing a commodity which the State had no right to suppress.[6] Any responsibility for drunkenness lay with the consumer, not the producer.

Defoe's complacency would be short-lived. Over the course of the 1720s the ever more visible social effects of gin consumption on the streets of London led to increasing levels of alarm among even the distillers' closest allies. Indeed, just three years after penning his defence of the distillers Defoe complained that 'now so far are the common people infatuated with *Geneva*, that half the work is not done as formerly' and threw his weight behind direct government intervention.[7] The change in tone was quite a turnaround, even by Defoe's standards.

By 1729 just under five million gallons of spirits were being drunk in England per year.[8] While accurate per capita figures are almost impossible to extrapolate from existing statistics, levels of consumption were high by any measure. Patrick Dillon has estimated gin consumption in London in the early 1720s as being around a pint a week for every man, woman and child in the city, Roy Porter worked it out as twice that amount at the peak of the gin craze in the early 1740s.[9] Such figures are thumbnail sketches at best. Nevertheless, it is clear that by the late 1720s this new and potent type of drink, virtually unknown just thirty years earlier, was being drunk in considerable quantity by large numbers of people. Parliament's response was to introduce licensing. In 1729 legislation was introduced imposing a £20 licence on all gin retailers. In addition a two-shilling excise duty was placed on every gallon of compound spirits.

The 1729 Act produced a small drop in consumption the year it was passed, but twelve months later consumption was back at pre-1729 levels.[10] To get around the law on compound spirits, distillers produced raw spirits which became known, sardonically, as 'Parliamentary Brandy'. Parliamentary Brandy did nothing to reduce drunkenness, but much to reduce tax revenues. In 1733, in recognition that the measures introduced in 1729 had 'not answered the good purposes thereby intended', the Act was repealed. This volte-face angered many who saw it as a dereliction of parliamentary duty. As levels of drunkenness continued to rise a small but well-organised group of campaigners led by Thomas Wilson, the Bishop of Sodor and Man, the physician Stephen Hales and Sir Joseph Jekyll, MP for Reigate, began to lobby for a radical and previously untried strategy: gin legislation which was 'in its nature a prohibition'.[11]

The path to prohibition

The year 1736 saw an explosion (in one case, literally) of printed material on the subject of gin as medical tracts, sermons, political broadsides, satirical plays and popular poems flew off the presses. Heated debates took place in Parliament and demonstrations took place in the streets. The occasion for all this activity was an Act, which was passed successfully, placing such high duties on the production and sale of gin as to effectively ban its consumption by law. The 1736 Gin Act imposed a £50 annual licence on anyone wanting sell gin in quantities of less than two gallons. In addition it imposed a duty of 20 shillings per gallon on spirits – ten times the amount put on the same quantity in 1729. The aim was de facto prohibition on the grounds, in the words of the Act itself, that gin-drinking had become:

> very common especially amongst the people of lower and inferior rank, the constant and excessive use whereof tends greatly to the destruction of the healths, rendering them unfit for useful labour and business, debauching their morals, and inciting them to all manner of vices.

What is more, the consequences of this were 'not confined to the present generation but extend to future ages, and tend to the devastation and ruin of this kingdom'.

This charge sheet expresses precisely the concerns of the time: that gin led to vice among the lower classes, that it made them unfit workers, and that it threatened future prosperity through its impact on unborn children. In order to understand how the 1736 Gin Act came about we need to understand how this message of economic collapse gained currency, and how the destruction of a successful indigenous industry was made palatable in an age when the self-definition of England so often hinged on its role as a trading nation.

To successfully achieve legislative intervention of this kind, the prohibitionists had to win an argument about the social effects of vice and the role of the State in managing those effects. It wasn't as simple as arguing that because gin had negative social effects it should be outlawed. Vice, as Bernard Mandeville had argued some years earlier, was not necessarily a bad thing for mercantile economies because the consumption that vice stimulated created jobs and developed the economy. Mandeville's notorious poem 'The Fable of the Bees' had made a persuasive case for the social value of vice as a source of wealth creation and distribution. 'The worst of all the multitude', Mandeville wrote, 'did something for the common good.'[12]

The 1724 edition of the 'Fable of the Bees' included a lengthy explanation of this seemingly perverse statement, and Mandeville used gin to illustrate his point. Gin, he stated, was a drink 'that charms the unactive, the desperate and crazy [and] makes the starving sot behold his rags and nakedness with stupid indolence'.[13] However, Mandeville's purpose was not to condemn gin but to show that even this most diabolical commodity had a role to play in promoting the common good. Gin may turn people into 'brutes and savages', Mandeville claimed, but it also created jobs: toolmakers, corn-reapers, maltsters, carriage-drivers and so forth. The money spent on gin fed the exchequer 'prodigiously'. For every hopeless sot, there were countless moderate drinkers for whom gin provided relief from grinding poverty or physical pain; for every bar-room brawler fired up on gin there was a soldier on whose Dutch courage the security of England depended. Most importantly, even if the majority of gin-sellers were rank topers only a small number had to become rich through the trade to have a disproportionately beneficial social impact. A man made rich through gin, Mandeville concluded, could well 'be as industrious in spreading loyalty, and the reformation of manners throughout every cranny of the wide populous town, as once he was in filling it with spirits'. Thus a gin-seller could become a model of 'shining and illustrious ... virtue!'[14]

Mandeville's irony aside, his remarks provide an example of the extent to which, by the 1720s, gin had become the focus of reflections on the moral economy of the market. Mandeville's proposition was that the social benefits of accumulated wealth had the potential to override the social evils necessary to that accumulation in the first place. It was a proposition which went to the heart of the capitalist project and which raised fundamental questions about the role of the modern state.

Because gin was both new and more or less unregulated, it exposed these kinds of issues in stark terms. It also presented a kind of legislative tabula rasa, being unencumbered by either centuries of tradition or the muddle of laws which covered the licensing of both wine and beer. Basic principles could be addressed, and the exponential increase in consumption drove calls for drastic action. Both Thomas Wilson and Stephen Hales produced lengthy tracts in support of prohibition.[15] Wilson warned that England faced the threat of a *drunken ungovernable* set of people' both 'intoxicated and enervated by the fatal love of a *slow* but *sure poison*'.[16] The ineffectuality of the 1729 Act in reducing the levels of consumption was, for Wilson, proof of the necessity 'to make a law, that shall amount to a PROHIBITION'.[17] Because gin was new, because it wasn't anchored in centuries of tradition, prohibition was a conceivable course of action.

The disease of drunkenness

Both Wilson and Hales built many of their arguments around the language of disease. As we shall see in Chapter 4, this had been quite common among anti-drink writers since the late seventeenth century. Hales's insistence that there 'is no one so far gone in the disease of *drunkenness* ... but there is room for a cure' based on 'diligent and fervent prayer' is indistinguishable from many earlier writings on the same subject.[18] However, this convention was given an explicitly political slant in Hales's *Friendly Admonition* through the argument that because it was 'extremely difficult, for the unhappy habitual *dram-drinkers* to extricate themselves from this prevailing vice; so much more it becomes the duty of the governors of the nations, to withhold from them so irresistible a temptation'.[19] Earlier anti-drink writers had called for the suppression of drinking places on the grounds that they posed a risk to social order, and they had also called for drinkers themselves to guard against falling into destructive habits. Hales, however, was the first to explicitly argue that the 'disease of drunkenness' legitimised State intervention in the otherwise free agency of the individual. This argument – that the slavery of compulsive habit justified coercive restrictions on individual freedom by the State – would become the cornerstone of prohibitionist thinking in the nineteenth century. Hales's use of this argument gives an early illustration of how the concept of compulsion undermined ideas of individual sovereignty precisely as they were becoming the philosophical engine of modernity itself.

Another of Hales and Wilson's innovations was to apply the language of disease to society. In their work drunkenness was not simply a disease that afflicted individuals, instead it was a condition afflicting the whole of society – an 'infection [that] 'daily spreads' throughout the entire nation.[20] Nowhere is this more evident than in their repeated descriptions of the effects of spirituous liquors on the unborn child. Hales and Wilson filled their pages with dire images of diseased offspring 'scorched up by [these] *fiery* and pernicious *liquors*'.[21] In later editions of his study, Hales introduced statistics from the bills of mortality which appeared to show a dramatic fall in christenings after 1724 coupled with an increase in burials. Clear evidence, so he claimed, that gin was decimating the population.

The image of the diseased child became a staple of eighteenth-century anti-gin literature. Writers complained of a '*pigmy* generation', a 'parcel of poor diminutive creatures' born to gin-soaked parents.[22] Wilson, anticipating later claims about inherited alcoholism, warned that countless children were being born with a 'love of strong liquors'.[23] Daniel Defoe warned that 'in less than an age, we may expect a fine spindle-shank'd generation';[24] Henry Fielding asked how those 'wretched' children 'conceived in *gin*' could become 'our future sailors, and our future grenadiers'.[25] This vision of economic and military decline was conjured up in typically dramatic terms by Hales in his *Friendly Admonition*. 'What must be the end thereof,' he asked 'but the *final ruin* of this *great and trading nation*.'[26]

As Jessica Warner has pointed out, here was the 'political arithmetic' that powered the drive for prohibition.[27] Gin could be condemned on all sorts of moral grounds, but the argument could not be clinched so long as a pragmatic case for the economic value of the gin trade could be put forward effectively. The prospect of streets crowded with half-mad starvelings, and of a nation defended by enfeebled armed forces, trumped even the most optimistic visions of distillers boosting the money supply by turning the annual corn harvest into a sea of lucrative spirits. What is more, the focus on damage to children concentrated otherwise less concerned minds on what was often presented as the truly diabolical aspect of gin: the fact that it was popular with women.

The gin craze gendered the alcohol debate in entirely new ways. Gin was popular with women for numerous reasons: not only were there large numbers of unattached women with disposable income in the capital (an effect of the expanding market in domestic service), but gin bypassed the rigorous gender exclusions of the alehouse and the tavern. The popular soubriquets 'Mother Gin' and 'Madam Geneva' reflected the novel gender balance among gin drinkers. To the likes of Hales and Wilson, this was the worst of all worlds. It was awful enough that the '*softer* and more *delicate* part of the creation', as Wilson coyly put it, drank.[28] That they should abandon their sacred, not to mention economically crucial, role as the mothers of the nation's labourers was simply horrifying. Indeed, whereas Hales identified compulsive drinking as the ethical justification for legislation, Wilson made the case based on the threat to future generations. '*Distilled spirituous liquors* are the greatest enemies to *fertility*,' he insisted, adding that 'for this reason, if there were no other, the *legislature* will think it worth their most serious consideration, how to put a stop to an *evil* that directly tends to the *decreasing* as well as *weakening* of the *breed* of the nation.'[29]

While it is a term that needs to be used with caution, the gin craze can be described as exhibiting aspects of moral panic. This is especially so in that the activities of a specific social group (in this case the urban poor, and especially poor urban women) were identified in the mass media, such as it was, as the source of a moral threat.[30] It is certainly the case that tales of infanticide, neglect, abuse and abandonment on the part of drunken mothers and nurses, fed a media market hungry for spectacle and scandal.[31] The truth or otherwise of such stories mattered little; what mattered was that they bolstered the drive for prohibition by using the image of the drunken mother to depict gin as both morally and economically ruinous.

The trial of the spirits

The anti-gin campaigners did not have a monopoly on the debate, however, and there were plenty of people willing to attack the social snobbery that they saw as driving anti-gin agitation. When one anonymous author,

who foresaw a nation 'destitute of both labourers and soldiers' and ter-
rorised by 'desperadoes', insisted that 'the *gin-trade* must be destroy'd',
an irate respondent demanded to know why gin was singled out when
'the public peace is as often broke by alehouse-sots and wine-drinkers
as any other'.[32] Anti-gin campaigning was unmistakeably class-specific
and popular satirists pointedly exposed the hypocrisy which underpinned
much of its literature. As the character in one satirical play observed, the
disastrous effect of gin drinking on mothers was the shared opinion 'of
some eminent doctors'. But, he asked:

> I wonder how the d- - -l they should understand the constitutions of poor men
> and their wives, and how they beget and breed up children; it cannot be by their
> practice … for they'll be hanged before they attend to a poor woman, in the
> utmost extremity, to see what she brings forth.[33]

Popular authors depicted the 1736 Act as an elitist attack on lower-class
culture. Drunkenness was endemic in Georgian England and it was pat-
ently absurd to try and suggest it was only the poor who had an aversion to sobriety. Daniel Defoe claimed drunkenness was a 'national vice'
among the English of all classes (one which he claimed dated back to 'the
Restoration … or within a very few years after').[34] The punch-drunk an-
tics of the upper classes were hardly a well-kept secret; indeed, William
Hogarth's most popular print in his own lifetime was 'A Midnight Modern
Conversation' (1733): a scene of alcohol-fuelled pandemonium among a
group of wealthy young bucks which Jenny Uglow has convincingly argued was perceived at the time as a scene of 'lusty English freedom'.[35]
Few people in Georgian England were sober in the sense that we would
understand the term today and the kind of freedom implicit in the act of
getting drunk chimed with a certain model of individualistic liberty which
underpinned that notion of Englishness illustrated in many of Hogarth's
works. Anyone arguing for the effective prohibition of gin had to answer the charge that unless they called for the prohibition of all alcoholic
drinks (an idea which would have been simply unthinkable), then they
were engaged in a form of hypocrisy.[36]

Anti-gin campaigners responded by arguing that spirits produced a new,
'instantaneous' kind of drunkenness'.[37] But why this craze for gin-soaked
excess had caught on was a question that was shot through with class
anxieties. In the 1750s, it became commonplace to claim that the fashionable excesses of social elites trickled down to the poor.[38] In 1736, Thomas
Wilson saw things the other way around. He feared that 'the vice is grown
epidemical, since it has got not only amongst *mechanics,* and the *lowest
kind of people*, but amongst persons of the highest *genius*'.[39] For Wilson,
drunkenness was a kind of hideous miasma arising from the swamp of
urban poverty, not Defoe's more universal and oddly democratic 'national

vice'. Consequently, it was to the enlightened self-interest of the elite legislature that Wilson appealed, claiming that because direct appeals to the poor 'will not have the desired effect' it was on 'behalf of *these persons* ... and of their unhappy *offspring*, we presume to address our selves to the legislature, and to implore the powerful assistance of that, against the spreading infection'.[40]

Wilson's appeal to government was not mere elitism, however. By speaking to the legislature as the guardian of public morals he tapped into a key political question of the time: at what point is sumptuary legislation justified? When does government have both the right and responsibility to intervene in the consumption of otherwise freely available commodities by its subjects?

Protecting the public good

In effect, the campaign for prohibition forced the question of where the proper limits of government lay in relation to consumption. Debating the 1736 Act, Lord Hervey noted that 'every legislature has claimed and practised the right of withholding those pleasures which the people have appeared to use to excess'.[41] This was a thorny problem given that, even as a leading anti-gin campaigner acknowledged, 'mankind, in a *trading nation* especially, live upon the *vices* and *extravagancies* of one another'. However, the same writer continued by insisting that if a trade 'directly strikes at the well-being of the *community*, so as in a very short time either greatly to wound it, or to bring it nothing, that *art, trade* or *manufacture* ... ought to be prohibited'.[42]

This worked as an abstract principle, but it left the legislature in the position of having to decide how to define the extent to which the harms caused by a particular trade outweighed the benefits. If it was indeed a '*universal concession*, that a *public good* ought *always* to be preferred to a *private one*',[43] then lawmakers were left with what would become the classic liberal problem of identifying who, exactly, occupied the social position from which benefit and harm could be accurately judged. Furthermore, the problem for any legislature addressing this question was not simply deciding whether an activity produces more harm than good, but whether the measures required to curtail a particular activity would themselves produce harms that outweigh any intended benefits.

The 1736 Act was, in many ways, a test case for these kinds of political questions. The Middlesex Justices, whose doom-laden reports on levels of gin consumption in London had played a pivotal role in creating the impression of an epidemic of drunkenness, argued that prohibition would restore '*religion, sobriety* and *industry*' to the people.[44] The social harms identified by anti-gin campaigners were the same as had been identified by Puritan preachers a century earlier, and as would be outlined by teetotallers and prohibitionists a century later: that intoxication undermined religious piety, reason and the desire to work. Put differently, it set up a series of alternative goods to those on which the social order relied: it replaced the desire to seek out religious consolation with the desire for the consolations of the bottle; it replaced the cultivation of reason with willing cultivation of the irrational; and it provided a pleasure for which the pleasure of labour was no match. One of the fundamental political problems posed by intoxication is that it has always had the capacity to undercut ideological efforts to make things which are socially necessary (such as work and self-discipline) appear inherently pleasurable: which is why, as many frustrated temperance zealots of nineteenth-century England would later discover, attempts to curb drinking by positing the sober life as fundamentally more enjoyable are often doomed to failure.

The effects of the 1736 Gin Act were a salutary lesson for those who felt that the practical difficulties of prohibition were surmountable. They were not. Only a tiny handful of £50 licences were taken out while the vast majority of gin-sellers simply continued to ply their trade regardless. Most sellers weren't conventional licensed retailers anyway. Gin had always been sold by chandlers, grocers and street-hawkers and they were in no position to either buy licences or give up their most lucrative trade. Reflecting on the effects of the 1736 Act, one commentator observed that:

> Even from the beginning, this law was so far from effecting a prohibition, that it really heightened, and spread the evil; for one distiller's-shop was shut up, ten places were open for the sale of drams, they were cried about the streets, publicly vended in markets, people sat with them by the road-side; and tho' they might not be so frequent as they were in chandlers-shops, yet they were as common at the green-stalls as potatoes.[45]

The disastrous impacts of the 1736 Act were compounded when in 1737, in an attempt to help enforce the regulations, the government hit upon the idea of providing a £5 reward for information leading to the conviction of illegal gin-sellers. Soon an army of the zealous, the acquisitive and the vindictive were providing information to the authorities, often on the most questionable grounds.[46] To make things worse, attacks on informers became a serious social problem, as did attacks on constables arresting popular retailers. In response an Act was passed allowing for anyone gathering in numbers of five or more for the purpose of rescuing offenders to be transported to America for up to seven years. The consumption of gin continued to increase, while the quality of the product declined as unscrupulous merchants adulterated their product safe in the knowledge that no one was in a position to complain when they did. Far from restoring religion, sobriety and industry, the 1736 Gin Act bred violence, corruption and a widespread contempt for the law. In the end, the *soberizing Act* ... furnish'd more tempters to the excessive use of spirituous liquors, than ever were to be met with in [the] streets before'.[47]

Prohibition also provided the opportunity for Robert Walpole's political opponents to exploit legislation widely perceived as an attack on individual liberty. Jessica Warner has argued that because the 1736 Act 'pursued an agenda of blatant social control, it had the unintended consequence of transforming an unthinking indulgence into a conscious act of political protest against an already unpopular government'.[48] Soon after the Act was passed in 1736, Jacobites exploded a bomb in Westminster Hall containing the text of five Acts of Parliament, one of which was the Gin Act. Such gestures were a testament to how easily a perceived attack on the rights of the poor could be turned to political advantage by oppositional groups keen to 'embrace the opportunities of heightening the murmurs that ... necessarily arise, from depriving the commonalty of a darling attachment'.[49] Prohibition was a disaster. It did nothing to reduce levels of gin drinking, and when the 1736 Gin Act was repealed in 1743 it had been effectively a dead letter for quite some time.

After prohibition

The 1743 Gin Act reduced the annual licence fee from a prohibitive £50 a year to an eminently affordable 20 shillings a year, but with the proviso that only people already keeping 'taverns, victualling-houses, inns, coffee-houses, or ale-houses' could take out a spirit licence. The aim was to encourage legitimate retailers to become licensed and to ensure that those with licences were already experienced traders.[50] By making gin a legitimate commodity once again, the 1743 Act 'stripped gin of its symbolic value among London's proletariat'.[51] The amount of gin being drunk did fall significantly in the following years, and it has been argued that 1743 marked the beginning of end of the gin craze as far as consumption is concerned.[52]

However, the gin craze was always as much about discourse as consumption and 1743 certainly did not mark the end of the public debates. Indeed the perception remained that gin-drinking was as bad as ever. In 1750, Thomas Wilson revived his campaign for anti-gin legislation and encouraged a number of prominent public figures to lend their support. Henry Fielding, for example, was persuaded by Wilson to join the campaign for gin legislation after they met in December 1750.[53] In 1751, Fielding published a study of street crime in London which blamed gin-drinking for much of the problem. In its description of diseased offspring and the imminent demise of the labouring (and soldiering) classes, Fielding's essay echoed the anti-gin propaganda that had preceded it. However, it differed in its claim that lower-class crime was largely caused by a desire to emulate the lifestyles of the wealthy. 'Bad habits,' Fielding wrote, 'are as infectious by example, as the plague itself by contact.'[54] He argued that luxury among the wealthy led to crime among the poor for two reasons: firstly by creating a desire for commodities which only crime would finance, and secondly by promoting the idea that wastefulness and indulgence were social virtues. So long as the aristocracy indulged themselves in expensive drinks, Fielding wrote, the poor would imitate them by indulging in cheaper alternatives. Habits which were regrettably effete among the rich became positively dangerous when taken up by an imitative lower class. Vice was never a good thing, Fielding insisted, but when it 'descends downward to the tradesman, the mechanic, and the labourer, it is certain to engender many political mischiefs'.[55] For Fielding the failure of the civil authorities to 'stem the tide of luxury would destroy the free state, and thus individual liberty, and reduce the nation to slavery'.[56]

The campaign of 1750–51 drew interventions from an array of public figures, such as the economist Josiah Tucker and the physician David Hartley.[57] However, by far the most significant event was the publication of William Hogarth's twin engravings 'Gin Lane' and 'Beer Street' in 1751. In Hogarth's own words, 'Gin Lane' and 'Beer Street' were designed to juxtapose the 'dreadful consequences of gin drinking' with the 'thriving industry and jollity' of beer.[58] 'Gin Lane' rendered into startling visual form all the anxieties thrown up by lower-class gin consumption: child neglect, sexual licence, religious impiety, urban decay, poverty, idleness, sloth and brutality. In doing so, it neatly illustrated the extent to which anxieties over gin consumption were at the same time anxieties over urbanisation and the rise of a potentially lawless mass society. Indeed, while 'Gin Lane' is ostensibly about the effects of mass drunkenness on urban society it is also perhaps the first piece of art which uses intoxication as a way of describing the urban experience itself: a technique which would become commonplace among modernist painters and writers a century later.

In 'Gin Lane', Hogarth also implied a connection between alcohol and poverty which his peers rarely expressed: the idea that – in the words of one of Hogarth's few contemporaries to make the same point – 'Poverty may not only be the effect, but the cause of dram-drinking'.[59] How much we can read this into 'Gin Lane' is a matter for some debate. Charles Dickens certainly thought this was Hogarth's intention, observing in 1848 that 'Gin Lane' 'powerfully indicate[s] some of the more prominent causes of intoxication among the neglected orders of society, as any of its effects'.[60] Some recent scholars have gone further, arguing that to Hogarth's intended audience 'it would have been most evident that not gin drinking per se but the oppression of the governing class as a *cause* of gin drinking was the real subject of the prints'.[61] One reason that Hogarth's prints remain so ambiguous today, however, is precisely because it was by no means clear who Hogarth would have defined as the 'governing class' of his time – or whether his definition would have chimed with that of the people to whom 'Gin Lane' was addressed.

The end of the craze

The public pressure exerted over the issue of gin in 1750–51 led to the passing of the last great Gin Act of the period. The 1751 Act was designed not to reinforce gin's outlaw status, but instead to drag it into the orbit of respectability.[62] It achieved this by adding a further 20 shillings to the annual licence, and only allowing licences to be granted to publicans who worked out of establishments rented for at least £10 a year and who donated to the church and the poor. It made small debts for spirits non-recoverable in law, thus undermining the credit economy of many back-street sellers, and it banned spirits sales from prisons and workhouses (a measure which, by the fact it was needed at all, says much about the ubiquity of alcohol in eighteenth-century England). It broke the potentially corrupt relationship between licensing magistrates and the alcohol trade by barring brewers, inn-keepers or distillers from acting as justices in matters relative to the sale of gin. It also increased duties on spirits, though not by a spectacular amount.

The 1751 Act was seen by many subsequent historians as finally bringing the gin craze to an end. In the years following, commentators observed that the common people had become 'more sober, decent, healthy, and industrious',[63] and that they did not see 'the hundredth part of the poor wretches drunk in the streets' as used to be commonplace.[64] However, this was due in large part to a run of poor harvests and a subsequent ban being placed on domestic distillation in 1757. Jessica Warner has shown that while gin consumption diminished between 1743 and 1750, it rose to significantly high levels by 1759.[65] Indeed, while concerns over gin-drinking receded after 1751, neither the legislation on drink nor public debates on licensing went away.

By gentrifying gin the 1751 Act sought to defuse the political threat which had become attached to its consumption, but its historical impact is almost certainly more to do with the nature of the campaign that led to its implementation than the effects of the Act itself. After 1751 the urban poor did not disappear and neither did gin consumption enter a period of terminal decline; the latter, however, ceased to signify the former in the way it had previously. Understood as a combination of extraordinarily high levels of consumption, repeated attempts at legislation, bouts of widespread public disorder and a fevered public debate carried out in newspapers, pamphlets, plays, sermons and political broadsides, the gin craze certainly petered out after 1751. To this extent, the historical importance of the 1751 Act lies in the way it helped to redefine the cultural significance of gin. In the long run, however, the most significant legacy of the 1751 Act was not its impact on gin consumption; it was the fact that the campaign leading up to the Act produced the single most memorable image not only of the gin craze, but perhaps of eighteenth-century London itself. 'Gin Lane' would go on to become a touchstone image of early modern England, and it would give a depiction of drunkenness an extraordinary prominence in the shared cultural imaginary. When people claim that the English have always liked to get drunk, it is often this image which hovers in the background, providing such assertions with a commonsense historical legitimacy. It should be remembered, however, that 'Gin Lane' is not a documentary image: it was a political statement which reflected not only Hogarth's innovative desire to draw classical imagery into the ambit of popular art, but also the accumulated rhetoric of anti-gin campaigning that had been developed in the preceding decades. This is not to say the gin craze as represented by Hogarth was a mere fiction, but rather to say that the gin craze tells us as much about attitudes to, and the politics of, drink as it does about what people at the time actually did.

Notes

1   E. Malcolm, *Irel and Sober, Ireland Free* (Dublin: Gill and Macmillan, 1986), p. 2.
2   B. Mandeville, *The Fable of the Bees: Or Private Vices, Publick Benefits* (London: J. Tonson, 1724), p. 86.
3   J. Warner, *Craze: Gin and Debauchery in the Age of Reason* (London: Profile, 2003), p. 3.
4   *Ibid.*, p. 30.
5   D. Defoe, *A Brief Case of the Distillers and of the Distilling Trade in England* (London: T. Warner, 1726), p. 11.
6   *Ibid.*, p. 24.
7   D. Defoe, *Augusta Triumphans* (London: J. Roberts, 1728), p. 45.
8   P. Dillon, *The Much-Lamented Death of Madam Geneva: The Eighteenth-Century Gin Craze* (London: Review, 2002), p. 74.
9   *Ibid.*, p. 28; R. Porter, *London: A Social History* (Harmondsworth: Penguin, 2000), p. 219.
10 Warner, *Craze*, p. 100.
11 Anon., *A Letter to a Friend in the Country In Relation to the New Law Concerning*

Spirituous Liquors (London: M. Cooper, 1743), pp. 14–15; T. Wilson, *Distilled Spirituous Liquors the Bane of the Nation* (London: J. Roberts, 1736), p. 5.

12 Mandeville, *The Fable of the Bees*, p. 85.

13 *Ibid.*, p. 86.

14 *Ibid.*, p. 92.

15 Wilson, *Distilled Spirituous Liquors* and S. Hales, *A Friendly Admonition to the Drinkers of Gin, Brandy and other Distilled Spirituous Liquors* (London: SPCK, 1751 [originally published in 1734]).

16 Wilson, *Distilled Spirituous Liquors*, pp. 8 and ix.

17 *Ibid.*, p. 5.

18 Hales, *A Friendly Admonition*, p. 28.

19 *Ibid.*, p. 31.

20 *Ibid.*, p. vi.

21 Hales, *A Friendly Admonition*, p. 20.

22 Anon., *The Trial of the Spirits, or Some Considerations Upon the Pernicious Consequences of the Gin-trade to Great-Britain* (London: T. Cooper, 1736), p. 9; Anon., *A Dissertation on Mr Hogarth's Six Prints Lately Publish'd* (London: B. Dickinson, 1751), p. 14.

23 Wilson, *Distilled Spirituous Liquors*, p. 39.

24 Defoe, *Augusta Triumphans*, p. 45.

25 H. Fielding, *An Enquiry into the Causes of the Late Increase of Robbers and Related Writings* (Oxford: Clarendon Press, 1988), p. 90.

26 Hales, *Friendly Admonition*, p. 20.

27 Warner, *Craze*, p. 90.

28 Wilson, *Distilled Spirituous Liquors*, p. xi.

29 *Ibid.*, p. 43.

30 P. Borsay, 'Binge drinking and moral panics: Historical parallels?' *History and Policy Papers* (2007) www.historyandpolicy.org/papers/policy-paper-62.html#top, accessed June 2007.

31 P. Dillon, *The Much-Lamented Death of Madam Geneva: The Eighteenth-Century Gin Craze* (London: Review, 2002), pp. 96–7.

32 Anon., *The Trial of the Spirits*, pp. 9, 16, 28; 'T. S.', *A Proper Reply to a Scandalous Libel Intituled The Trial of the Spirits In a Letter to the Author* (London: J. Roberts, 1736), p. 12.

33 Anon., *A Short History of the Gin Act* (London: H. Goreham, 1738), p. 10.

34 Defoe, *Brief Case of the Distillers*, p. 17.

35 J. Uglow, *Hogarth* (London: Faber & Faber, 1997), p. 230; D. Bindman, *Hogarth and his Times* (London: British Museum Press, 1997), p. 71.

36 Anon., *Occasional Remarks upon the Act for laying a Duty upon the Retalers of Spirituous Liquors &c. and for Licensing the Retailers Thereof* (London: A. Dodd, 1736), p. 17.

37 Fielding, *An Enquiry into the Causes of the Late Increase of Robbers*, p. 88; J. Tucker, *An Impartial Inquiry into the Benefits and Damages Arising to the Nation from the Present Very Great Use of Low-priced Spirituous Liquors* (London: T. Trye, 1751), p. 21.

38 Fielding, *An Enquiry into the Causes of the Late Increase of Robbers*; Anon., *A Dissertation on Mr Hogarth's Six Prints*; Anon., *The Consequences Of Laying an Additional Duty on Spirituous Liquors, Candidly Considered* (London: H. Whitridge, 1751).

39 Wilson, *Distilled Spirituous Liquors*, p. 47.

40   *Ibid.*, p. xv.
41   B. Montagu, *Some Enquiries into the Effects of Fermented Liquors* (London: J. Johnson, 1814), p. 199.
42   Anon, *The Trial of the Spirits*, p. 14.
43   *Ibid.*, p. 15.
44   Wilson, *Distilled Spirituous Liquors*, appendix II, p. xx.
45   Anon., *A Letter to a Friend in the Country*, p. 15.
46   P. Clark, 'The "mother gin" controversy in the early eighteenth century', *Transactions of the Royal Historical Society*, 5th ser:5 (1987), 63–84, p. 80.
47   Anon, *A Short History of the Gin Act*, p. 6.
48   Warner, *Craze*, p. 132.
49   Dillon, *The Much-Lamented Death of Madam Geneva*, p. 141; Anon., *The Consequences Of Laying an Additional Duty on Spirituous Liquors*, p. 17.
50   Warner, *Craze*, p. 191.
51   *Ibid.*, p. 218.
52   *Ibid.*, p. 192.
53   Dillon, *The Much-Lamented Death of Madam Geneva*, p. 244.
54   Fielding, *An Enquiry into the Causes of the Late Increase of Robbers*, p. 77.
55   *Ibid.*, p. 78.
56   F. Dodsworth, '"Civic" police and the conditions of liberty: the rationality of governance in eighteenth century England', *Social History*, 29:2 (2004), 199–216, p. 205.
57   I. Maddox, *An Epistle to the Right Honourable the Lord-Mayor, Aldermen and the Common-Council of the City of London, and Governors of the Several Hospitals* (London: H. Woodfall, 1751), pp. 44–9.
58   W. Hogarth, *The Analysis of Beauty*, ed. Joseph Burke (Oxford: Clarendon, 1955), p. 226.
59   Anon., *The Consequences Of Laying an Additional Duty on Spirituous Liquors*, p. 6.
60   C. Dickens, 'Cruikshank's "The Drunkard's Children"', in *Miscellaneous Papers* (London: Chapman Hall, 1908), p. 106.
61   R. Paulson, *Hogarth Volume III: Art and Politics, 1750–1764* (Cambridge: Lutterworth, 1993), p. 26.
62   Dillon, *The Much-Lamented Death of Madam Geneva*, p. 261.
63   T. Smollett, *The History of England from the Revolution to the Death of George the Second, Vol. IV* (London: T. Cadell, 1800), p. 433.
64   G. Burrington, *An Answer to Dr William Brakenridge's Letter* (London: J. Scott, 1757), p. 36.
65   Warner, *Craze*, p. 207.

4

The politics of sobriety: coffee and society in Georgian England

It was said of Socrates, that he brought philosophy down from heaven, to inhabit among men; and I shall be ambitious to have it said of me, that I have brought philosophy out of closets and libraries, schools and colleges, to dwell in clubs and assemblies, at tea-tables and in coffee-houses. (Thomas Addison)

This is one of the disadvantages of wine. It makes a man mistake words for thoughts. (Samuel Johnson)

The prohibitory Gin Act of 1736 had a number of political consequences: it revealed the extent to which public concerns over drunkenness provided a way of reinforcing social hierarchies; it exposed the limitations of State control in the area of private consumption; it showed the extent to which the right to get drunk could be hitched to the idea of personal liberty; and it showed, for the first time, that the prohibition of intoxicants can increase their attraction through imbuing them with an aura of political transgression. It also made explicit some of the inherent contradictions which beset any attempt politically to manage a market economy. Although this was not the first time drunkenness had become politically significant, it was the first time that that significance had so clearly exposed the extent to which alcohol behaves as a kind of archetypal commodity: an object in which consumption, pleasure and waste are inextricably bound together and on which a complex, diverse and politically significant economy rests. With hindsight we could say that in 1736 it became clear that the modern world was going to have to deal with drunkenness, but that to do so effectively might just push the political logic of the market beyond its own limits. As the 1736 Act came up for repeal in 1742 members of the House of Lords complained that facilitating the 'vices, debaucheries, and destruction of millions, is a manifest inversion of the fundamental principles of national polity';[1] but their idea of national polity had turned out to be neither practical nor in the interests of a powerful coalition of traders and landowners. Furthermore, facilitating expenditure was necessary to the economy. As a commodity with the capacity to expand its market share by mere dint of being made available, and which had an extraordinary capacity to dematerialise money, alcohol turned out to have a striking affinity with the ideal logic of capital itself. The gin craze uncovered the fact that the logic of intoxication was not entirely distinct from the logic of the market. However, gin was also caught up in a wider cultural dialectic; one which began to open up meaningful and politically significant distinctions between being drunk and being sober.

In addition to the deep-rooted political impacts of prohibition, something else was happening in Georgian England which would shape the politics of consumption in a profound way, and which would prepare the ground for the Victorian temperance movement. This was the beginnings of a politics of sobriety – a strange concept in what was perhaps the most drunken period of British history, but one whose seeds were sown in the attempt by the emerging middle class to carve out a cultural territory from which its already well-developed assault on established aristocratic power could be consolidated. If wine, beer and port acted as signifiers of party allegiance after the Restoration, then that resonance was echoed by the way in which coffee came to signify a set of cultural, political and philosophical values which transcended the fuzzy party lines of Georgian England.

A wakeful and civil drink

The first coffee houses appeared in England in the 1650s.[2] In 1734 there were 551 registered coffee houses, but the real figure was more likely to have been in the thousands.[3] While this was not a lot in comparison to the number of alehouses and 'brandy shops' (there were reckoned to be almost 9,000 alehouses in London alone in 1739), it was comparable to the number of inns and taverns.[4] Coffee houses mattered primarily because they acted as hubs for the explosion of new intellectual, economic, artistic and political activity which characterised Georgian London. Stock-jobbers bought and sold at Man's and Jonathan's, maritime insurers struck deals at Lloyd's, and traders bought and sold at Garraway's. Leading Whigs gathered at St James's, while the Cocoa Tree was popular with Tories and Jacobites. London's coffee houses were the meeting places par excellence of the new middle class. They acquired the nickname 'penny universities' for their role in disseminating education beyond the closeted and elitist groves of contemporary academe. For David Hume they were 'a sign of the liberty of the constitution' and for the French writer Abbé Prévost they were the 'seats of English liberty'.[5] It was primarily in coffee houses that the new journals and newspapers – the *Evening Post*, the *Daily Courant*, the *Spectator*, *Tatler*, the *London Journal* – were read and discussed. The middle-class challenge to traditional aristocratic political, intellectual and economic authority was mounted largely from the coffee houses – a fact reflected by a Royal Proclamation released by a panicky Charles II in 1675 ordering the complete suppression of coffee houses as 'the great resort of idle and disaffected persons', only to be hastily withdrawn a year later.[6] Coffee houses represented the aggressive carving out of a new cultural middle ground: neither the ivory towers of aristocracy, nor the alehouses of the poor.

In his influential study of democracy and the public sphere, the German social theorist Jürgen Habermas claimed that the coffee houses of Georgian London were fundamental to the rise of modern democratic culture.[7] Philosophically, Habermas argued, they played a crucial role in what he called 'the project of modernity', one of the key features of which Habermas identified as the desire to arrive at meaningful explanations of the world through rational discussion. Modernity (and democracy) were, therefore, founded on a combination of scepticism and what Habermas called 'communicative rationality': that is, a model of reason which assumes rationality is the outcome of public intellectual exchange rather than more or less individualistic endeavour. Modernity, in other words, is characterised by the tendency to subject explanations of the world to *public* debate and *public* scrutiny.

The reason Habermas thought that the Georgian coffee houses were so important to the 'project of modernity' is precisely because they were centres of *rational* debate. They were not, by definition, centres of drunken debate. And this is exactly how the coffee-drinkers of their day liked to present themselves: they drank coffee because, while mildly stimulating, it was not intoxicating; it was what Francis Bacon had once called a '*wakeful and civil drink*'.[8] The reason coffee houses sprang up throughout London was only partly because of the availability of this new commodity, it was also because coffee houses provided a cultural space which contrasted significantly with alehouses, taverns and inns. Rural alehouses had, by the mid-eighteenth century, acquired some of the respectability previously limited to rural inns.[9] However, in the cities alehouses were still often seen as 'receptacles of sots, and the scum of the Earth' and tavern clubs were all too often mere 'suck-bottle Assemblies' bearing a closer resemblance to gatherings of 'swill-belly'd wine-porters, than a formal body of ... reputable members'.[10] By contrast, the coffee houses appeared civilised, urbane and reasonable.[11] It was their very sobriety that made the coffee houses the centre of what Habermas identified as the new 'public sphere'.

The politics of politeness

More than anything else, what coffee houses provided was a social space that reflected 'politeness' and 'manners'. Partly by way of re-evaluating some of Habermas's more sweeping claims, Brian Cowan has argued that what the likes of Addison and Steele were attempting to achieve by cultivating a coffee-house culture of conversation and politeness was not so much to develop a project geared towards the universal adoption of 'communicative rationality', but rather to use politeness as a way of asserting cultural power.[12] The image of Georgian coffee house society which has survived in the popular imagination is in many ways the image conscientiously developed in the pages of the *Spectator*: one in which sophistication and good manners guaranteed a degree of liberty in speech and thought which set the ground for not only modern business practices but the democratic sensibility itself. However, the Georgian coffee house was an exclusive institution, open to women and the poor in principle only. Moreover, the idealisation of politeness which found its concrete expression in the coffee house was one which effectively turned the cultural predilections of a particular social group into a normative model for society as a whole.[13]

The depiction of coffee-house culture as uniquely sober was crucial here, especially in an age beset with anxieties over the anarchic tendencies of gin. Where drunkenness meant violence, criminality and conflict, sobriety meant civility, manners and politeness. Politeness was idealised, especially in the work of the Earl of Shaftesbury, on the grounds that it was the guarantee of liberty. For Shaftesbury, unlike more conventional civic republicans, good manners were not merely an indicator of the successful internalisation of the law; that is to say, people did not only behave well because they had fully absorbed strict social rules which protected other liberties, nor because they had successfully internalised social norms.[14] Instead, Shaftesbury argued that politeness and good manners were the foundation on which liberty rested: people could only be free if they were well-mannered towards one another.[15] In other words, it was only by cultivating social behaviours which celebrated 'amicable collision' that true liberty (which, for Shaftesbury meant a successful modus vivendi) could be sustained.[16] From this perspective, drunkenness is at best an illusion of liberty and at worst an enemy of it. This idea had the advantage of condemning upper- and lower-class drinking alike: while it was agreed by many that gin drinking among the poor tended towards anarchy, the 'lusty English freedom' of the sozzled toff could also be condemned as mere illusion. For the likes of Shaftesbury drunkenness undermined politeness by encouraging boorishness; it encouraged heated exchanges rather than amicable collisions. From this perspective, polite coffee-house culture was the model for the modus vivendi which was only possible when the heat was taken out of interpersonal conflict.

Coffee-house culture, then, was presented as more civil because it was more sober. It was not, however, completely sober and nor did it pretend to be. There were some entirely practical reasons for this, not least that clean, safe water was almost impossible to get hold of – and no amount of tea or coffee would entirely replace the need for other forms of liquid refreshment. However, there were also a number of reasons why total sobriety would have been seen as extremely impolite. One was the deeply-held idea of conviviality: the empirically grounded belief, dating back at least as far as the Greek symposium, that drink facilitates free and easy conversation just as much as it can push such conversation into conflict. Of course, sympotic drinking was as much a form of disciplinary training as it was a means to oiling the wheels of philosophical exchange: in Plato's *Symposium* Socrates was not, strictly speaking, sober; he just knew better than anyone else how to hold his drink. There was also the crucial concept of *in vino veritas*: which implied that to truly get to know, and therefore trust, someone you were as well to see them drunk. Few Georgian champions of good manners demanded absolute sobriety. In his later, teetotal, years, Samuel Johnson insisted that wine provided 'neither … knowledge nor wit', and he chided a tipsy Joshua Reynolds for not realising that wine 'makes a man mistake words for thoughts'.[17] However, Johnson still accepted that wine had both social and psychological benefits. Like many people, the very idea of demanding sobriety from others would have struck Johnson as both unsociable and fanatical, and thereby deeply ill-mannered.

Nevertheless, in polite culture such liberty as drink produced – the liberty of convivial exchange – still had to be disciplined through the adoption of rigorous social codes in order to prevent it descending into the licence of drunkenness which threatened the very foundations of true political freedom. For the disciples of politeness, this was an unarguable form of social progress – for the likes of Ned Ward, by contrast, it meant that coffee houses lacked 'the excitement and conviviality that a good tavern provides'.[18] The rigorous ideal of controlled drinking (something which Samuel Johnson came to see as beyond his own capacities) was a typical example of the civic republican principle that only self-discipline guarantees social freedom.

For mid-eighteenth-century civic republicans, freedom was imagined as a condition requiring the adoption of certain responsibilities, rather than a simple right which the State challenged at its peril.[19] However, it does not fully explain the culture of self-discipline and sobriety that characterised the polite coffee house. By contrast to the explicitly coercive enforcement of social control achieved through legislation and policing, politeness represented an inward discipline, rather than one imposed by the law. Crucially, however, the polite model of discipline was one which was only available to those immersed in the patterns of social exchange and behaviour out of which the rules of politeness emerged. Politeness 'set up reciprocal relations between elite social status and cultural expression' in such a way as to 'fortify the distinctions between patrician and plebeian in culture'.[20] Moreover, its avowedly middle-class rejection of both aristocratic and plebeian cultures of physical excess meant that the Whig culture of politeness could act as 'a form of policing just as stringent, just as socially exclusive, as Tory persecution'.[21]

Sobriety as ideology

Habermas's assertion that coffee houses were the primary site for political debate in Georgian London has been challenged on the grounds that the alehouse remained 'the single most important locale where people engaged in political discussion', if only because there were so many more alehouses than coffee houses.[22] Formal politics certainly centred around drinking establishments with both Whig 'mug houses' and Tory alehouses briefly acting as hubs for organised political activities.[23] The continuing role of alehouses in the management (and corruption) of voting is vividly recorded in Hogarth's famous 'Election' series. All of which certainly contributes to the impression that the Habermasian view of the London coffee house is one so heavily shaped by the literature of its own propagandists as to be deeply problematic. In many ways Habermas buys rather naively into what was an ideological sleight of hand on the part of certain coffee-house habitués. The polite type personified in the fictional 'Mr Spectator' was only ever an idealisation. Coffee-house conversation was distinguishable from alehouse or tavern conversation within limits, but any idea that coffee houses were uniquely sober institutions is misguided. Coffee houses rarely sold non-alcoholic drinks exclusively: cider, brandy, whisky and beer were also widely available.[24] Indeed, one contemporary claimed that 'nothing is more common, even in our public coffee-houses, than to hear brandy, or as the more polite term it, *French* cream, called for to mix in coffee'.[25] Furthermore, there was nothing to stop people from combining all sorts of different drinks in all sorts of different establishments, depending on their mood. On one boozy perambulation, the satirist Ned Ward observed that coffee was 'a liquor that sits most easily on wine', before staggering into a Temple Gate coffee house to 'check the aspiring fumes of the most Christian juice by an antichristian dose of Muhammadan loblolly'.[26]

Nevertheless, the fact that sobriety in Georgian England was only ever relative should not lead us to dismiss the sober coffee-house ideal as mere hypocrisy. Habermas may have been rather too keen to accept the self-mythologisation of the Georgian middle classes, and as a result he may have proposed overly grand claims for the role of strictly rational discourse in early democracy; however, if we accept Mr Spectator as an ideological figure, then Habermas's claims still stand albeit as the description of a concept, not a reality. What matters is the fact that sections of the urban middle class claimed sobriety for themselves, not that they still drank. What this meant was that sobriety became a means by which new social and political attitudes could be articulated in concrete terms. To be even a bit more sober than the aristocracy or the labouring classes was politically significant; to hitch that sobriety to the idea of social progress was a way of imbuing an act of cultural distinction with grand historical importance. It was precisely this fusion of social progress and sobriety which would drive the great temperance campaigns of the nineteenth century. In Georgian London the idea was still in its infancy, but it was clearly identifiable in the politics of politeness and the emergence of a bourgeois political public sphere centred on the coffee house rather than, as might otherwise have been the case, the tavern.

Notes

1   House of Lords, *The Lord's Protest Against an Act for Repealing Certain Duties upon Spirituous Liquors* (London: 1743), p. 10.
2   B. Lillywhite, *London Coffee Houses* (London: Allen and Unwin, 1963), p. 17.
3   B. Cowan, *The Social Life of Coffee* (London: Yale University Press, 2005), p. 154.
4   Lillywhite, *London Coffee Houses*, p. 23.
5   Cowan, *The Social Life of Coffee*, p. 148; Porter, *London: A Social History*, p. 206.
6   Charles II, *A Proclamation for the Suppression of Coffee-houses* (London: John Bill and Christopher Barker, 1675); Charles II *An Additional Proclamation Concerning Coffee-Houses* (London: John Bill and Christopher Barker, 1676).
7   J. Habermas, *The Structural Transformation of the Public Sphere*, trans. Thomas Burger (London: Polity Press, 1989).
8   F. Bacon, *The Virtues of Coffee* (London: W. G, 1663), p. 8.
9   P. Clark, *The English Alehouse: A Social History* (London: Longman, 1983), p. 237.
10 C. Parfect, 'The number of alehouses shown to be extremely pernicious to the public' (London: R. Baldwin, 1758), p. 10; N. Ward, *A Complete and Humorous Account Of all the Remarkable Clubs and Societies in the Cities of London and Westminster* (London: J. Wren, 1756), p. 2.
11 Cowan, *The Social Life of Coffee*, p. 48.
12 B. Cowan, 'The rise of the coffeehouse reconsidered', *Historical Journal*, 47:1 (2004), 21–46.
13 L. Klein, 'Liberty, manners, and politeness in early eighteenth-century England', *Historical Journal*, 32:3 (1989), 583–605, p. 589.
14 *Ibid.*, p. 591.
15 *Ibid.*, p. 603.
16 *Ibid.*, p. 602.

17 J. Boswell, *The Life of Samuel Johnson* (London: J.M. Dent, 1978), pp. 233–5.

18 Earnshaw, *The Pub in Literature*, p. 123.

19 Dodsworth, '"Civic" police and the conditions of liberty', p. 210.

20 Klein, 'Liberty, manners, and politeness in early eighteenth-century England', p. 589.

21 B. Cowan, 'Mr Spectator and the coffeehouse public sphere', *Eighteenth Century Studies*, 37:3 (2004), 345–66, p. 351.

22 A. Houston and C. Pincus, *A Nation Transformed: England After the Restoration* (Cambridge: Cambridge University Press, 2001), p. 141.

23 Haydon, *Beer and Britannia*, p. 101.

24 Cowan, *The Social Life of Coffee*, p. 82.

25 Anon, *The Consequences Of Laying an Additional Duty on Spirituous Liquors*, p. 21.

26 N. Ward, *The London Spy* (London: Colleagues Press, 1993), p. 219.

5

A fascinating poison: early medical writing on drink

Drunkenness is nothing but a state of self-induced insanity. (Seneca)

It is impossible to fix precise limits, and to determine where soundness of mind ends, and madness begins. (David Hartley)

The social, medical and philosophical changes which took place in the eighteenth century are a crucial stage in the history of attitudes to alcohol for a number of reasons. As we have seen, the introduction of gin politicised alcohol use such that debates over how to control consumption became embroiled in fundamental questions about the role of the State in managing both markets and private behaviours. Furthermore, questions about intoxication and sobriety that had previously been couched in purely religious terms started to become enmeshed in secular questions about the relationship between reason, civility and social progress. This second issue was partly an extension of earlier debates about propriety and public morality, however, it also tied in with newer questions about psychology and consciousness. This partly impacted upon the way in which the distinction between sobriety and intoxication was conceived, but it also began to reshape thinking about compulsion.

The eighteenth century witnessed significant developments in the 'medicalisation' of problem drinking. It has often been argued that the modern concept of addiction was developed, or 'discovered', in America in the final third of the eighteenth century.[1] In reality, the key features of the modern 'disease model' of addiction were being developed in Britain throughout the eighteenth century, and had become fairly well established by the 1770s.[2] It was these developments that would lay the ground for some of the most critical aspects of the nineteenth-century drink question: debates over the treatment of habitual drunkards, their moral responsibility, and the role of the State in protecting them from their own destructive desires. Related to the burgeoning medical discourse on drink were long-running philosophical disputes over the nature of consciousness. These fuelled heated speculation over what drunkenness told us about the relationship between mind and body, and what the moral implications of that relationship might be.

Body, mind and spirits

The Enlightenment sparked innumerable controversies as to the nature of reason and its relationship to moral responsibility. In Britain, the neat Cartesian division between body and mind had always been treated with some scepticism.[3] Far from the health of the mind being divorced from the actions of the body, it seemed self-evident to many that physical well-being was inextricably, and causally, tied to mental health. Joseph Addison hitched this idea to a polite defence of physical exercise, describing the body as 'a bundle of pipes and strainers, fitted to one another after so wonderful a manner as to make a proper engine for the soul to work with'.[4] Addison's own fondness for the bottle didn't prevent him from aspiring to his own rather higher ideals. Debates raged in the medical literature over the relative benefits of different diets and regimens. The prolific medical writer Thomas Short noted that few subjects 'have of late afforded greater matter of discourse and writing than water-drinking'.[5] Such debates were part of a far wider discussion about physical and mental health which spoke volumes about the complexity of thinking on the subject in eighteenth-century Britain. And, of course, it was a debate taking place right in the middle of the gin craze.

For doctors such as Stephen Hales, drink was a lifelong political concern. However, Hales was unusual in abstracting his discussion on drink from wider health concerns. More typical were doctors such as George Cheyne who incorporated a discussion of alcohol into broader studies of physical and mental well-being. George Cheyne had especially good reason to worry about the effects on alcohol on health. In *The English Malady* (1733) he included a brief narrative of his own medical history: a torrid tale of weight swings, skin infections, lethargy, fever, constipation, diarrhoea, gout, shaking, vomiting and vertigo, which left the clear impression that when Cheyne dispensed advice to sickly patients – whatever their disease – he spoke of that which he knew. The turning point in Cheyne's narrative was the moment when, after moving to London, he fell in with '*bottle-companions*'. After spending some time acquainting himself with the life of the tavern he found that his 'health was in a few years brought into great distress', he 'grew *fat, short-breath'd, lethargic* and *listless*'.[6] What followed anticipated later temperance novels in its description of excess, despair and recovery.

Having recovered from one of many bouts of sickness, Cheyne spent the next twenty years '*sober, moderate* and *plain* in my diet, and in my greatest health drank not above a quart, or three pints at most, of *wine* any day'.[7] As an illustration of the levels of consumption considered frugal in the mid-eighteenth century, this is certainly revealing. More important, however, is the emphasis Cheyne subsequently put on water-drinking as crucial to healthy living. 'The benefits a person who desires nothing but a *clear head* and *strong intellectual faculties* would reap by religiously drinking nothing but *water*,' he wrote in 1740, 'are innumerable'.[8] Cheyne was perhaps the first secular doctor (in the sense that, despite his open religious convictions, he was not a cleric of any sort) who saw total abstinence as both possible and advisable.

Sobriety and sanity

Abstinence, though unusual, was not completely unknown in Georgian England. Indeed, Thomas Short complained that among a certain class of doctors it had become one of 'those general and groundless invectives, which have been thrown about of late'.[9] Samuel Johnson gave up drinking once it stopped agreeing with him, and he was more than happy to discuss his abstinence in public – although he never tried to convince others that his was a universally applicable course of action. Cheyne's original contribution was to propose a specific physiological reason why intoxicating drinks might be detrimental to mental health. Cheyne worked with a mechanistic and neurological model of consciousness of the sort which would be developed in more depth by David Hartley; one in which thoughts were seen as arising from the activities of the nerves; and because in this model the action of the nerves was dependent on other bodily processes (such as the response of the stomach to foodstuffs), it collapsed the division between body and mind. For Cheyne, intoxicating drinks were 'sensible causes' of '*madness* and *lunacy*' precisely because of their detrimental impact on the nerves.[10] Cheyne challenged readers to find a case of madness in 'any one who soon after twenty, *entered on water-drinking* only ... for it is *fermented* liquors only that inflame the *membranes* and *membranous tubuli* (the *nerves*) which are the bodily organs of *intellectual* operations'.[11] Here was a convincing medical argument for total abstinence, by one of the most famous physicians of his day, and avoiding any explicit appeal to moral or religious reasons for temperance.

Cheyne was part of a generation of doctors who began to look at the workings of the mind in ways which demanded that they account for the impact of intoxication, and who helped turn the subject of drunkenness from one concerning moral rectitude and social responsibility into one that also involved the nature of consciousness itself. Central to their new approach were the ideas of John Locke, who posited the notion that identity did not exist independently of, or prior to, consciousness; instead identity was simply what emerged out of every individual's awareness of their own thought processes. Conventionally it was assumed that one's consciousness was subordinate to one's essential identity: to 'know thyself' was to apprehend *through* one's consciousness a true, higher self which lay beyond the distractions and illusions of daily existence. From this perspective to be, or to get, drunk meant either to intensify the clutter of consciousness such that one's true nature was obscured, or – the flipside – to slice through that curtain of social convention and habitual thinking to reveal one's true nature, for better or for worse. The problem Locke posed for both positions was the idea that there was no super-identity which drunkenness could either reveal or more deeply obscure. Instead, Locke suggested, identity was simply the product of whatever state of mind a person may find themselves in. One of Locke's friends, Anthony Collins, illustrated this philosophical position mischievously by asserting that 'the mad man and the sober man are really two as distinct persons as any two other men in the world'.[12] It was a dangerous proposition, but one which would nag at politicians, philosophers and jurists for a very long time.

The problem all this posed was how to distinguish securely between rationality and irrationality given that, in the case of intoxication, the line was blurred. Madness could not simply be defined as a deficit of rationality because the separation between sanity and insanity was complicated, not simplified, by developments in the philosophy of mind. For Locke, consciousness (and, by extension, identity) rested on the transformation of sense-experience into mental activity. By locating madness in the constantly shifting and contingent domain of the imagination – a domain which could easily and temporarily be disrupted by the simple act of taking a drink – madness was brought *closer*, not further, from everyday life. Thus, understanding the 'voluntary madness' of intoxication became an ever more pressing concern, as did understanding the 'willing slavery' of habitual drunkenness.

One person who developed Locke's 'associationism' in directions which would further blur the distinction between intoxication and madness, was the philosopher and doctor David Hartley, whose influential *Observations on Man* was first published in 1749. Hartley was a friend of Stephen Hales and added his voice to the clamour for anti-gin legislation in 1751. However, his position on alcohol owed more to the physiological speculations of George Cheyne than the moralistic campaigning of Hales. Hartley developed a complex theory of the relationship between body and mind based on the idea that mental activity arose from physical activity (in the form of tiny vibrations) in the nerves. He claimed that ideas were the mental effect of vibrations in the nerves which were carried into the brain where they stimulated both simple sensory responses and highly complex associative reactions. It was the nature of these simultaneous mental reactions to the stimulation of neurological vibrations that produced ideas and, by Lockean extension, identity. This model of the mind, taken together with Hartley's assertion that because of the complexity of mental activity 'it is impossible to ... determine where soundness of mind ends, and madness begins', had profound implications.[13]

What happens to the mind when an intoxicating substance is taken into the body? For Hartley the 'greatest and most immediate effect arises from the impressions made on the stomach, and the disorderly vibrations propagated thence into the brain'.[14] Erasmus Darwin concurred, defining drunkenness as an experience in which the 'irritative motions are much increased in energy by internal stimulation'.[15] This is a deeply materialist model of intoxication – in which it is merely the result of a series of physical impressions; paradoxically, however, when applied to a model of the mind in which consciousness and, by extension, identity proceed from physical impressions it turns the act of getting drunk into an act of literal self-transformation. Anya Taylor has suggested that Hartley was both reflecting and further entrenching the 'spirit of the age' here by drawing his readers' attention to a 'concern with intoxication, personal dislocation and oblivion'.[16] That is, Hartley's interest reflected a more widespread concern with what the fluidity of identity – as posited by Locke and developed to its radical extreme by Hume – meant for human self-realisation and self-creation: a concern in which the drinker, precisely because of the unique questions intoxication posed, acted as a 'test case'.[17]

The associationism of Hartley and Cheyne was an important part of the context in which ideas about drinking began to shift. They represented a move away from simply decrying drunkenness as a temporary madness to identifying drunkenness as one exemplar of the complexity of the mind: both its inextricable ties to the body, but also the impossibility of constructing an impenetrable wall between sanity and insanity. The bodily causes of madness, Hartley wrote, were 'nearly related to drunkenness'.[18] The capacity to *willingly* rearrange the very mental structures which gave rise to individual identity posed the thorniest of philosophical questions, and the job of exploring the implications of this would, as we shall see, be taken up by Romantic writers with some enthusiasm. However, the philosophical implications of willingly intervening in one's own identity construction was only one side of this coin; on the other side was the question of whether one could willingly enslave oneself to the experience of intoxication. If drunkenness was a voluntary reordering of the self, then which part of an individual's humanity was curtailed when a person apparently lost the capacity to choose whether to drink or not? Such questions would come to play a key role in the evolution of modern ideas of addiction, and in wider debates over the idea of human freedom itself.

The idea of addiction

Writing in 1751, Josiah Tucker suggested there were three types of gin-drinkers:

> First, such as are obstinately addicted to it; – secondly, such as have no unconquerable attachment, yet cannot withstand the temptation, when thrown in their way; – thirdly, young children, and the rising generation.[19]

The fact that Tucker uses the word 'addicted' here does not tell us much. The verb 'addict' is an ancient one meaning to attach oneself to someone or something. It could be used to denote devotion to virtue: John Bunyan's exhortation that we 'addict ourselves to the belief of the scriptures of truth' was not untypical.[20] Nevertheless, as Johnson pointed out in his *Dictionary*, while 'to addict' meant to devote or dedicate, it was nevertheless 'commonly taken in a bad sense; as, *he addicted himself to vice*'.[21] Whether positive or negative, however, the crucial point about the use of the phrase 'to addict' was that it functioned as a reflexive verb; as something one did to oneself. Addiction, therefore, implied both choice and freedom. The uniquely paradoxical aspect of the concept, however, was that it also implied a willing renunciation of that very freedom. To addict oneself implied making a conscious choice to give up the capacity to make a similarly free choice in the future. For a believer to addict themselves to God meant that they chose to give themselves up to that higher power; for a drinker to addict themselves to spirituous liquors implied the same thing.

Modern conceptions of addiction are, of course, very different. Now we speak of someone *becoming addicted to* a substance or activity: a crucial inversion of responsibility. We also have, as part of our commonsense understanding of the world, the idea that one can *become an addict*. This shift from reflexive to passive verb, and from verb to noun, is the linguistic trace which marks the transformation of addiction from a premodern to a modern concept. That the idea has metamorphosed over time is beyond question; however, where and when this metamorphosis occurred has been subject to some dispute.

It has long been argued that the modern idea of addiction was first outlined in a coherent and unified form by the American physician Benjamin Rush in his *Inquiry into the Effects of Ardent Sprits on the Human Body and Mind*, first published in Philadelphia in 1784.[22] The reality, however, is that Rush's *Inquiry* contains little that was not already commonplace in England prior to its publication, and rather a lot that was anachronistic. Indeed, it has often been claimed that the spur to Rush's *Inquiry* was the publication of a sermon entitled 'The Mighty Destroyer Displayed' by the Quaker preacher Anthony Benezet.[23] Less commonly noted, however, is the fact that Benezet's sermon is littered with references to the work of both George Cheyne and Stephen Hales. It also cites William Cadogan's *Dissertation on the Gout*, which contains a discussion of abstinence.[24] Rush himself acknowledged his intellectual debt to Cadogan in the preface to a series of sermons on 'temperance and exercise' which Rush published in 1772.[25] Taken together with the fact that Rush lived in London in the early 1770s, and was close friends with the influential London surgeon John Coakley Lettsom – who published an essay on hard drinking shortly after Rush's *Inquiry*, it is difficult to imagine how Rush remained immune to the range of medical and religious literature on habitual drunkenness that was being published in England at the time. However, the important question is not so much whether Rush knew that problematic drinking was a common feature of public debate in Georgian England, but whether what he had to say on it was distinctively original.

The principal features of Rush's analysis of 'addiction' that have been identified as original are that that he described it as a *progressive disease* characterised by a *loss of control* over drinking, the cure for which is *total abstinence*. That Rush was only actually writing about distilled spirits somewhat undermines this claim from the start. The description of gin-drinking as a progressive disease, characterised by a loss of control, for which the only cure was total abstinence from distilled spirits was at the heart of Stephen Hales's *Friendly Admonition*, published half a century before Rush joined the debate. Furthermore, the idea of just abstaining from distilled spirits, rather than all alcohol, would have struck George Cheyne as oddly half-hearted – though Thomas Short may have approved. Rush's essay should, in fact, be seen as a conduit for ideas that had been developing in England for over a century. Furthermore, the roots of some of the principles which characterise modern ideas about addiction, such as the idea that it involves a loss of control so profound as to undermine the capacity to make free, moral choices, stretch back over a century before Rush's intervention.

Directions against drunkenness

One striking example of a pre-eighteenth century work which anticipated features of the disease model are the 'directions against drunkenness' contained in Richard Baxter's compendious work of casuistical reasoning, the

Christian Directory (1673).[26] Baxter was one of the most prolific doctrinal commentators of the late seventeenth century, and so his analysis of the causes and effects of drunkenness is framed in deeply religious terms (though we should remember that Rush's approach was far from secular). However, his desire to reveal the minutiae of drink's effects on behaviour forced Baxter to meticulously divide habitual drinkers into different groups according to what their circumstances, motivations and patterns of consumption were. Loss of control – a specific vitiation of the will as opposed to a more general irrationality – was key to his definition of problem drinking. Among the many types of drinkers he described, there were those who:

> keep the soundness of their *reason*, though they have lost all the *strength* and *power* of it, for want of a *resolved will*: and these confess that they *should abstain* but tell you, *they cannot: they are not so much men.*[27]

Loss of control and abstention both feature here; so too does the typically modern idea of denial. A second class of drinkers, according to Baxter, had 'given up their very *reason* (such as it is) to the service of their *appetites*; and these will not believe … that their measure of drinking is too much, or that it will do them hurt'.[28] Baxter described drinkers suffering from self-delusion ('their appetite so mastereth their very reason, that they can choose to believe that which they would not have to be true'); as enslaved by instant gratification ('they judge all by *present feeling*'); and as driven by guilt (such that they 'fly from themselves' and drink 'as if they were resolved to be damned').[29] Baxter's suggested cures for habitual drinking also anticipated some modern approaches, such as calling for drinkers to renounce alcohol in front of their peers, and to 'give up [themselves] to the government of some other'.[30] He also suggested drinking a cup of wormwood after every 'cup of excess', though how effective this form of aversion therapy was in practice we have no way of knowing.

Baxter's work was certainly not typical of his time, but the extensive and detailed discussion of motivation, psychology, cause and cure contained in his 'directions against drunkenness' illustrates the fact that such approaches were already being worked out in the late sixteenth century. Given this, and the proliferation of public discussions on habitual drinking from the 1720s onwards, it becomes clear that the key question in determining how and when an identifiably modern conception of addiction appeared does not lie in identifying when it was first described in terms of loss of control; Baxter provided a forensic analysis of that phenomenon in 1673. Nor does it lie identifying when drinking was first described by doctors as a disease; the physician Everard Mainwaring wrote that 'drunkenness … hath all the requisites to constitute a disease' as early as 1683.[31] It does not reside in the principle of total abstinence, the idea of which was irritating Thomas Short by 1727, nor in the suggestion that abstinence should be sudden and immediate (William Cadogan rejected that technique in 1771).[32] Neither did it reside in the combination of all these ideas with regards to spirit drinking; Stephen Hales set out that argument in 1734.

In reality, there was no moment when thinking on addiction changed, no paradigm-shifting text. Instead, approaches to habitual drinking were moulded by a collapse in the distinction between identity and action, between *what* you did and *who* you were, which occurred over the course of the eighteenth century. Richard Baxter clearly fell on one side of this divide. He insisted that, ultimately, the drinker was master of his own fate – that a true self existed above and beyond that part which had sunk into excess. 'If thou *wilt* not', Baxter demanded, 'say thou *wilt* not, and say no more thou *canst not*; but say, *I will keep my sin and be damned*: for that's the English of it'.[33] The work of Cheyne and Hartley marks a significant shift, however, because of its concern with the material source for the formation of habits. For the likes of Baxter, habit was like an object that the self picks up and then forgets how to throw away again. Samuel Ward, writing shortly after Baxter, wrote that the 'reason why this sin is so hardly left, and so few recovered from it, may be partly from the strength this sinful habit gets in the soul by the many repeated acts'.[34] However, this retains the idea that the self is autonomous; habit *gets into* the soul, but it does not *transform* it. It was the decentring of the self that followed Locke's insistence on the role of sensory activity in consciousness, and Hume's assertion that our selves are nothing more than a bundle of perceptions, which opened the door to the possibility that habits may be less like things picked up by selves, and more like part of the fabric out of which selves are actually formed. If we become habituated to certain experiences, then those experiences play a role in shaping the mental processes out of which our identity emerges. Habitual drunkenness seemed to provide one especially worrisome illustration of this.

The conventional religious perspective was that some part of the drinker's self, however deeply mired in the habitual use of strong drink, could, albeit through the intercession of a higher power, drag that drinker back into the light of sobriety. But the blurring of the line between body and mind, and between consciousness and identity, made the habitual consumption of intoxicants the material cause of a radical restructuring of the self. Writing in 1740, even the conservative Bishop of London was forced to tackle this unsettling proposition, insisting that:

> We must carefully distinguish between desires of nature *before* a habit of intemperance, and *after* it. Nature, not vitiated with custom or habit, is easy and content with a *reasonable* and *moderate* refreshment; but the cravings of nature

under the dominion of habit (if we may then call it *nature*) are unlimited and endless.[35]

He continued, in language typical of the time, by insisting that the desires of habit 'are as much a disease, as thirst in a fever'; the habit of drunkenness was, he continued, 'the worst kind of slavery'.[36] For the likes of Stephen Hales, this truth had important political implications: it meant that the drunkard must be 'as it were, forced into his liberty … and be bound down to keep him from destroying himself' and everyone around him.[37]

An infernal spark

In conventional religious discourse, habitual drunkenness had been a species of gluttony: a sin – albeit strangely bewitching – for which the drinker was morally responsible. By the second half of the eighteenth century, however, it had become commonplace to describe habitual drunkenness as something more extraordinary again: something which seemed to effect a metamorphosis through which the drinker was transformed into a different kind of person, just as a body was transformed by the actions of a disease. This was both disturbing, but also strangely intriguing. In 1774, the popular moralist Edward Harwood published an essay entitled *Of Temperance and Intemperance: Their Effects on the Body and Mind*. In it he insisted that a 'sober person':

> knows nothing of the perturbation, tumult and darkness of an intemperate man's soul, and is a stranger to those craving, impetuous and ungovernable passions, that tyrannize over him.[38]

Harwood's drinker was an object of horror and pity, but also of fascination: a helpless sinner, but also a figure of extremity, passion and alienation; the victim of 'an infernal spark which is absolutely inextinguishable'.[39]

As the century progressed, increasing numbers of medical professionals began to look towards this extraordinary phenomenon, and the range of explanations, prognoses and cures began to increase noticeably. The published studies of heavy drinking became lengthier, more detailed, and also more reliant on the direct observation of patients by the authors. John Coakley Lettsom's *Hints Respecting the Effects of Hard Drinking*, first published in 1787, presented a detailed study of the physical symptoms which marked the progressive stages of habituation to what Lettsom calls 'this fascinating poison'.[40] Lettsom acknowledged his debt to his close friend Benjamin Rush by appending a version of Rush's 'moral thermometer' to his own essay; however, he sided with Cadogan's earlier position on total abstinence – insisting that 'where the habit of drams has long continued, the total and sudden omission of them, has sunk the person into irretrievable debility'.[41]

The most substantial and detailed medical statement on the issue was undoubtedly Thomas Trotter's book-length study, *An Essay Medical, Philosophical and Chemical on Drunkenness and its Effects on the Human Body* (1804). There, Trotter asserted that 'in medical language, I consider drunkenness, strictly speaking, to be a disease' and that '*the habit of drunkenness is a disease of the mind*'.[42] As should now be clear, this language was not in any way startling or original. However, his rigorously clinical approach, as well as his attempt (not always successful) to push moral judgement to the side of his analysis did mark a significant shift in thinking.[43]

For Trotter, the disease of drunkenness was 'produced by a remote cause'.[44] However, that cause was neither sin nor moral weakness. Trotter, like Cheyne before him, was concerned with the environmental and psychological causes of excessive drinking, and especially the extent to which drinking arose from deeper, psychological and affective problems. Describing drunkenness among old people, Trotter observed that:

> Young persons, distracted by other passions, are not much addicted to drinking; but when love, departing with youth, leaves a vacuum in the mind, if its place be not supplied by ambition or interest, a taste for gaming, or religious fervour, it generally falls prey to intoxication.[45]

Trotter was unusual in the extent to which he sympathised with drinkers – especially what he saw as vulnerable drinkers: women, the poor and the old. He saw habitual drunkenness as a disease, but he saw the source as often being a kind of spiritual malaise. He did not see drinkers as sinners, nor did he see them as victims of a nervous disorder brought on by physical exposure to alcoholic liquids. As a result the cures that he proposed were not as simple as prayer, piety, aversion or abstinence; his preferred approach was a kind of moral counselling: the rousing of 'particular passions, such as the parent's love for their children, desire of fame, the pride of reputation, family pride etc.'[46] For Trotter the drinkers became a 'case' whose treatment required exploration and observation rather than either regimen or religion. Consequently, he saw treating the motivation to drink as more important than treating the act of drinking itself.[47] In a sense, it is Trotter's sympathy with drinkers that sets him apart from earlier religious and medical writers. However, it is a sympathy which, looked at from a critical perspective on medical history, opened the door to a new and arguably more invasive form of control: a control which required drinkers to not just stop what they were doing, but to subject themselves to observation and categorisation by doctors so that, eventually, they could change who they were.

The medicalisation of drunkenness, and its subjection to the 'clinical gaze' was undoubtedly the most critical development in thinking about habitual drinking over this period.[48] The description of habitual drinking as a 'disease' – at first metaphorically, then increasingly literally – represented the birth of a new understanding of addiction which sought to strip it of its moral weight (although, as we shall see, this reconceptualisation would never be fully established). The eighteenth century saw the development of an array of treatment regimes which sidestepped conventional calls to prayer and piety. Debates abounded over the relative merits of partial and total abstention, of sudden and gradual withdrawal. Primitive forms of aversion therapy were proposed and explorations into the psychological roots of addiction began to be developed.[49] Religious conceptions of habitual drinking remained dominant, however, and there were very few writers who did not fall back into conventional condemnations of the vice of drunkenness even when they were attempting to define it in the language of science. Nevertheless, the rise of new ideas about addiction served to isolate and treat a newly defined illness, and to that extent they formed part of a wider process of medical empire-building. However, the other story about addiction is the story of how it became an object of fascination. Both drunkenness and habitual drinking posed problems regarding identity, the will, the nature of disease and the meaning of habitual behaviours at large. Few activities provided a more stark illustration of the complexity of this newly deconstructed relationship between body, mind and selfhood than drinking; hence the opprobrium conventionally targeted towards habitual drinkers became mixed with intrigue. Furthermore, whether couched in secular *or* religious language, the idea that the innermost self could be transformed through drinking – and, by extension, through abstaining – was a revolutionary development which would have an enormous impact on ideas about drink in the nineteenth century. The emergence of drunkenness as the object of fascination, as well as mere control, would become key to the development of the drink question in later years.

Notes

1   H. G. Levine, 'The discovery of addiction: Changing conceptions of habitual drunkenness in America', *Journal of Studies on Alcohol*, 39:1 (1978), 143–74; P. Ferentzy, 'From sin to disease: differences and similarities between past and current conceptions of chronic drunkenness', *Contemporary Drug Problems*, 28 (2001), 362–90.

2   R. Porter, 'The drinking man's disease: The "pre-history" of alcoholism in Georgian Britain', *British Journal of Addiction*, 80 (1985), 385–96; J. Warner, '"Resolved to drink no more": Addiction as a preindustrial construct', *Journal of Studies on Alcohol*, 55:6 (1994), 685–91; J. Nicholls, 'Vinum Britannicum: the "drink question" in early

modern England', *Social History of Alcohol and Drugs*, 22:2 (2008), 6–25.

3 R. Porter, *Flesh in the Age of Reason* (Harmondsworth: Penguin, 2004), pp. 59–60.
4 *Ibid.*, p. 119.
5 T. Short, *A Rational Discourse on the Inward Uses of Water* (London: Samuel Chandler, 1725), p. v; see also J. Smith, *The Curiosities of Common Water* (London: J. Billingsley, 1723); G. John, *Flagellum, or a Dry Answer to Dr. Hancock's wonderfully Comical Liquid Book* (London: Thomas Warner, 1723); Anon., *The Juice of the Grape, or Wine Preferable to Water* (London: W. Lewis, 1724).
6 G. Cheyne, *The English Malady* (London: George Strahan, 1733), p. 326.
7 *Ibid.*, p. 342.
8 G. Cheyne, *An Essay on the Regimen* (London: C. Rivington, 1740), p. 24.
9 T. Short, *Vinum Britannicum* (London: D. Midwinter, 1727), p. 51.
10 G. Cheyne, *The Natural Method of Cureing the Diseases of the Body and the Disorders of the Mind Depending on the Body* (London: George Strahan, 1742), p. 93.
11 Cheyne, *An Essay on the Regimen*, p. xxv.
12 Cited in Porter, *Flesh in the Age of Reason*, p. 78.
13 D. Hartley, *Observations on Man, his Frame, his Duty and his Expectations* (London: J. Johnson, 1791), p. 230.
14 *Ibid.*, p. 232.
15 E. Darwin, *Zoonomia* (London: J. Johnson, 1794), p. 248.
16 A. Taylor, *Bacchus in Romantic England: Writers and Drink, 1780–1830* (London: Macmillan, 1999), p. 65.
17 *Ibid.*, p. 5.
18 Hartley, *Observations on Man*, p. 236.
19 Tucker, *An Impartial Inquiry*, p. 22.
20 J. Bunyan, *The Greatness of the Soul* (London: Joseph Marshall, 1730), p. 79.
21 S. Johnson, *A Dictionary of the English Language* (London: J. Knapton, 1756).
22 Levine 'The discovery of addiction'; Ferentzy, 'From sin to disease'.
23 T. Jason Soderstum, 'Benjamin Rush', in J. S. Blocker, D. M. Fahey and I. R. Tyrell (eds), *Alcohol and Temperance in Modern Society, Vol. 2* (Oxford: ABC-Clio, 2003), pp. 527–8; A. Benezet, *The Mighty Destroyer Displayed, &c.* (Philadelphia, PA: Joseph Cruikshank, 1774).
24 W. Cadogan, *A Dissertation on the Gout* (London: J. Dodsley, 1771), pp. 40–1; 60–1.
25 'A Physician', *Sermons to the Rich and Studious on Temperance and Exercise* (London: Edward and Charles Dilly, 1772).
26 R. Baxter, *A Christian Directory* (London: Robert White, 1673).
27 *Ibid.*, p. 381.
28 *Ibid.*
29 *Ibid.*, pp. 382–3.
30 *Ibid.*, p. 393.
31 E. Mainwaring, *The Method and Means of Enjoying Health, Vigour, and Long Life* (London: Dorman Newman, 1683), p. 125.
32 Cadogan, *Dissertation on the Gout*, p. 41.
33 Baxter, *Christian Directory*, p. 393.
34 Ward, *A Warning Piece to all Drunkards*, p. 59.
35 E. Gibson, (1740) *An Earnest Dissuasive from Intemperance in Meats And Drinks* (London: M. Downing, 1740), p. 16.
36 *Ibid.*, p. 20.

37   Hales, *Friendly Admonition*, p. 12.
38   E. Harwood, *Temperance and Intemperance: Their Effects on the Body and Mind, and Their Influence in Prolonging or Abbreviating Human Life* (London: T. Becket, 1774), pp. 6–7.
39   *Ibid.*, p. 52.
40   J. C. Lettsom, *Hints Respecting the Effects of Hard Drinking* (London: C. Dilly, 1798), p. 14.
41   *Ibid.*, p. 16.
42   T. Trotter, *An Essay Medical Philosophical, and Chemical on Drunkenness and its Effects on the Human Body* (London: Routledge, 1988), pp. 8, 172.
43   R. Porter, 'Introduction', in *Ibid.*, p. xv.
44   *Ibid.*, p. 8.
45   *Ibid.*, pp. 83–4.
46   *Ibid.*, p. 188.
47   *Ibid.*, pp. 190–1.
48   M. Foucault, *The Birth of the Clinic: An Archaeology of Medical Perspectives* (London: Routledge, 1993).
49   Lettsom, *Hints Respecting the Effects of Hard Drinking*, p. 17.

6

Ungovernable passions: intoxication and Romanticism

He will come to know it, whenever he shall arrive in that state in which, paradoxical as it may appear, reason shall only visit him through intoxication. (Charles Lamb)

Hence the drunkard ceases to attend to external stimuli, and as volition is now also suspended, the trains of his ideas become totally inconsistent as in dreams or delirium. (Erasmus Darwin)

The question above all others that nagged at philosophers, political thinkers and doctors throughout the eighteenth century was: 'What is it to be human?' Was humanity by nature solitary and aggressive, as Hobbes had claimed, or was it, as Shaftesbury insisted, communal and reasonable? Were our identities impermeable things with which we were born, or were they, as Locke claimed, merely the outgrowth of our self-consciousness? Was morality based in the contingencies of experience and emotion, as Hume thought, or was it, as Kant was determined to prove, the product of a transcendent rationality? Were our thoughts the domain of a Cartesian *res cogita*, or were they, as Hartley and others contended, intimately connected to our bodies through the action of our nerves? In this new and uncertain world ontological questions were as pressing as moral ones. A drunk, from a conventionally Christian perspective, was a sinner and sin, like virtue, had a status in the universal scheme of things which meant that however culpable a sin may be, it was also meaningful. By contrast, if we are just a bundle of pipes and strainers – or a bundle of nerves – then that which makes us unique, which gives our lives meaning, resides somewhere in this mass of conscious, semi-conscious, subconscious and unconscious activity.

Anthony Cascardi has described the problem of modern subjectivity as being that of 'imagining purposive and coherent possibilities for self-transformation where the ends of action are no longer fixed according to nature and where the terms of transcendence have been rendered suspect'.[1] In other words: how do you give your life purpose when the religious foundations of meaning have been undermined? One answer to that

73

question was to make a mark in the world; to be unique. Politeness set out a model for achieving this through a kind of tip-of-the-iceberg approach to one's own brilliance. To be brilliant was to be singular. However, for those whose social proclivities or position disbarred them from entry into the clubbable world of Georgian wits, asserting one's uniqueness was not so simple. The development of 'sensibility' in the latter half of the eighteenth century provided another route. Politeness located individuality in the performance of wit, but at the same time developments in medical thought had created a smorgasbord of conditions each of which could bespeak a kind of uniqueness. This was the age of politeness, but it was also the age of hypochondria.[2] The expansion of medical literature produced a fashion for self-diagnosis which tapped into the self-scrutiny born out of increasing uncertainty over what the self actually was. When the terms of transcendence are suspect, and the opportunities for the display of brilliance are tightly circumscribed, suffering, as Roy Porter put it, 'might purchase the privilege of being different'.[3]

We have already seen the extent to which habitual drinkers were becoming the subjects of fascinated enquiry. Those 'craving, impetuous and ungovernable passions' certainly smacked of a uniqueness of some kind, and they indicated a propensity for high emotions which might even signify a brilliance of some destructive kind. Furthermore, as Hogarth had inadvertently shown, intoxication was so much more *interesting* than sobriety. The simple jocularity of 'Beer Street' paled next to the dramatic concatenation of distorted religious imagery that turned 'Gin Lane' into one of the most memorable and iconic images of its time. Looking back at 'Gin Lane', William Hazlitt had become enthralled by the gothic projection of drunkenness onto the physical landscape, the way the buildings reeled 'as if drunk and tumbling about the ears of the infatuated victims below'.[4] Charles Lamb called 'Gin Lane' 'sublime', and he described the central figures as 'terrible as anything Michelangelo ever drew'.[5] No-one ever used that kind of language to describe 'Beer Street'.

The drunkard's confession

The 'ungovernable passions' which characterised the habitual drinker took on a new resonance as sensibility mutated into full-blown Romanticism. For a generation obsessed with the limits of experience, the drunkard was far too intriguing a figure to remain confined to the pages of sermons and medical tracts. The drinker's literary confession (a genre so extraordinarily commonplace now it is hard to believe it was once unknown) was about to make its appearance. Whereas habitual drinkers had previously been described, diagnosed, defined and dissected from the outside – by sober preachers, doctors and moralists, they were about to start speaking for themselves.

The first example of this appeared in a book called *Some Enquiries into the Effects of Fermented Liquors*, published in 1814 by 'A Water Drinker'.[6] That 'water drinker' was the lawyer and writer Basil Montagu who was close to a number of leading Romantic writers including William Hazlitt and Charles Lamb. *Some Enquiries* was a strange and idiosyncratic book which fused an early temperance moralism with a deeply Romantic sensibility. It contained an extraordinary collection of disparate bits of writing gleaned by Montagu from an array of sources: excerpts from *The Life of Samuel Johnson*, from Benjamin Franklin's memoirs and from Thomas Clarkson's *Portraiture of Quakerism*; it cited Thomas Trotter, Benjamin Rush and Erasmus Darwin; and it contained lengthy excerpts from parliamentary exchanges which took place in the run-up to the 1736 Gin Act. More chaotic than encyclopaedic, it was unlike anything printed on the subject previously. While most of the material was already in print, two pieces of writing stood out as remarkably novel: one an anonymous piece called 'On the origin and progress of drunkenness in a letter to a young gentleman', and the other Charles Lamb's 'Confessions of a drunkard'.

The first of these prefigured in almost every detail the kind of temperance narratives which would become widespread from around 1830 onwards. Written in the form of a letter from father to son it describes the journey from convivial pleasure to poverty, sickness, tragedy and death; from the student drinker as the 'prince of fine fellows' to his deathbed as 'a martyr of INEBRIETY!'[7] Had it been written twenty years later, it would have been utterly conventional. In 1814, however, it was a literary oddity.

'Confessions of a drunkard' is an even more remarkable example of early temperance literature. We know far more about 'Confessions of a drunkard' than the epistolatory tale discussed above. Though anonymous, it was written by Charles Lamb and had been originally published a year earlier in *The Philanthropist*, a journal edited by Montagu's friend, and leading Quaker, William Allen. We also know that Lamb later published it as an Elia essay in the *London Magazine* in 1822 – and that this time he appended an irate riposte to a suggestion in the *Quarterly Review* that the essay was autobiographical (a contention which failed to convince those who knew Lamb well). The fact that it was first published eight years before Thomas De Quincey's *Confessions of an English Opium-eater* makes it the earliest example we have of the 'confessional' narrative of addiction – a narrative form which would play a central role in shaping wider cultural beliefs about both what addiction was and how it should be treated.

'Confessions of a drunkard' was unique because it was written from the perspective of a habitual drinker and it describes the ungovernable passions of that life from the inside. While it is framed by a somewhat ambivalent discussion of total abstinence, the essay is not really a discussion of cause and cure, but the delineation of a character – the tortured 'drinker' himself. 'Confessions of a drunkard' depicts the drunkard as a person of extremes: alienated, sensitive and conflicted; in other words a profoundly Romantic figure. Anya Taylor points out that Lamb's essay 'illuminates Romanticism for its self-consciousness, its confessional outpourings even when ringed with irony, its turbulence and passion, its recognition of the nearness of despondency and madness.'[8] Lamb's use of Miltonic allusion both aggrandises the experience of addiction, and creates an analogy between intoxication and the Fall of Man. The paradox that in the moment of intoxication 'self-transcendence and self-abasement lie embedded in each other' was an irresistible one to Romantics reacting against the polite idea that Man was capable of always rationally pursuing his own best interests.[9]

The idea of intoxication incorporating gestures of both transcendence and fall lurks behind the bathetic impact of the 'person from Porlock' in Coleridge's 'Kubla Khan'. It is also something that Coleridge commented on in a notebook entry in 1808 in which he imagined a 'delightful Poem' depicting mankind as passing through three stages: the prelapsarian in which Man is 'possessed of the Heavenly Bacchus'; 'Man in a savage state as a water-drinker'; and finally the period in which 'the Bastard Bacchus comes to [Man's] relief'.[10] Here intoxication was imagined as an imperfection but also a gesture of the highest human aspirations. Intoxication, for many Romantics, was all-too-human, but heroically so.

Taken by itself 'Confessions of a drunkard' could be seen as a kind of novelty, possibly influencing aspects of De Quincey, but otherwise coincidentally prefiguring the confessional narrative as found in later temperance literature. However, 'Confessions of a drunkard' directly influenced the development of later temperance literature, specifically through its influence on the writing of one of the first mainstream American temperance novels: Walt Whitman's *Franklin Evans* (1842). *Franklin Evans* quotes Lamb's dramatic description of the prospect of withdrawal verbatim:

> But what if the beginning be dreadful? The first steps, not like climbing a mountain, but going through fire? What if the whole system must undergo a change, violent as that which we conceive of the mutation of form in some insects? What if a process comparable to flaying alive, have to be endured?[11]

Lamb's influence on temperance literature has often been overlooked.[12] However, his originality lay not in what he described, but in the language he used to describe it. 'Confessions of a drunkard' not only depicted the experience of addiction from the perspective of the addict, but it turned that experience into a literary event.

Dionysus reborn

Of course, intoxication has always had a special relationship with art. Classical concepts of Dionysian inspiration fed into early modern poetry: symposiastic poetry, which praised alcohol for both its conviviality and its ability to inspire, was popular from the Renaissance onwards, despite being rejected as boorish by elements of polite society.[13] Indeed, the 'Anacreontic Society', which flourished in the late eighteenth century, left a lasting mark on history in that its signature drinking song – 'Hymn to Anacreon' – provided the tune for the Star-Spangled Banner. Robert Burns revitalised the tradition of symposiastic verse in poems such as 'Scotch drink', as well as incorporating them into 'Tam O'Shanter': a poem which celebrated the pleasures of convivial drinking in the warmest terms, while using drunkenness as the occasion for the wildly hallucinogenic imagery of the denouement. Taylor suggests that both Burns's poetic celebrations of drink and his own notorious proclivities provided an inspiration and blueprint for later Romantic writers searching both for means of inspiration and a way of exploring those questions of consciousness that dogged the age.[14]

However, attitudes to intoxication among the Romantics remained mired in class snobbery and racial elitism. Writing in *The Courier* in 1811, Coleridge railed against the dangers of allowing the Irish access to drink, complaining that the 'quantity of stimulus, which taken by a man of education, surely as it will hasten his decay of powers, would yet, for the time, only call them into full energy ... The same quantity renders an uneducated man, of undisciplined habits, a frantic wild beast.'[15] Thomas De Quincey would make some very similar comments in his writings on opium, overlaying them with an ugly racism.

Burns aside, the Romantics tended to draw an unyielding distinction between the finer aesthetic sensibilities, and grandiose existential torments, of the refined drinker and the poisonous bestiality of the lower-class drunk. Such distinctions were not limited to writers and poets. Thomas Trotter had insisted that while the 'cultivated mind ... commits no outrage' when drunk, drunkenness among the 'ignorant and illiterate' was 'human nature in its vilest garb, and madness in its worst form'.[16] Nevertheless, aesthetic sensibilities put an additional spin on this by fusing it to the notion of the painfully sensitive artiste. Basil Montagu, in warning against the use of drink as a means of overcoming shyness, was careful to distinguish between the 'timidity of merit' – by which he meant the shyness of sensitive poets – and the 'timidity of ignorance'.[17] Poets,

Montagu claimed, should not use drink for this purpose because it risked turning them into victims of addiction; the ignorant, by contrast, should not overcome timidity through drink because, being stupid, they should be timid anyway.

Ambivalence and paradox ran through Romantic writing on drink. Was it a source of pleasure or pain? Did it produce flashes of transcendence, or did it suck the drinker into the mud? Did it inspire art or illusion? Nicholas Warner suggests that Coleridge's 'notion of "two wines"' allows for two different readings of intoxicants; they can be 'denigrated as vulgar counterfeits of the true sublime or celebrated as humble yet nonetheless genuine avatars of intoxication on a higher plane'.[18] It was this degree of heightened intensity that Romanticism added to the existing discourse on drink. Never had the Dionysian muse been taken so seriously: Keats's 'blushful hippocrene' hardly sparkled with gaiety, even if Keats wanted it to. However, in turning away from the convivial and the light-hearted, Romantic writers were able to mine the interiority of the (refined) drinker to an extent not previously attempted. One effect of this was to make it possible to conceive of the addict as a fascinating, and thereby marketable, literary character.[19] A second effect, however, was to romanticise drinking in both its positive *and* negative aspects. Positively, drunkenness could be presented as an indication of the desire for aesthetic and spiritual transcendence; however bathetic such a yearning may prove. But even the most horrendous outcomes of habitual drinking could be framed in these terms. Lamb's narrator describes a tale of woe, but also a journey with plenty of seductive intensity for a generation of readers for whom Thomas Chatterton's suicide provided the model of brilliant, but doomed, sensibility. In the Romantic exploration of intoxication, the idea that you could live fast, die young, and leave a trail of beautiful fragments behind, was born. It remains one of the most important cultural influences shaping attitudes to intoxication today.

Notes

1 A. Cascardi, *The Subject of Modernity* Cambridge: Cambridge University Press, 1992), p. 7.
2 Porter, *Flesh in the Age of Reason*, pp. 401–2.
3 *Ibid.*, p. 402.
4 W. Hazlitt, *The Selected Writings of William Hazlitt*, ed. Duncan Wu (London: Pickering and Chatto, 1998), p. 129.
5 C. Lamb, *The Prose Works Vol. 1* (London: Edward Moxon, 1838), pp. 190–1.
6 Montagu, *Some Enquiries into the Effects of Fermented Liquors.*
7 *Ibid.*, pp. 224, 229.
8 Taylor, *Bacchus in Romantic England*, p. 91.

9   M. Cooke, 'De Quincey, Coleridge, and the formal uses of intoxication', *Yale French Studies*, 50 (1974), 26–40, pp. 27–8.

10 S. T. Coleridge, *The Notebooks of Samuel Taylor Coleridge, Volume 3: 1808–1819*, ed. K. Coburn (London: Routledge and Kegan Paul, 1973), n. 3623.

11 W. Whitman, *Franklin Evans, or The Inebriate: A Tale of the Times*, in T. Bresher (ed.), *Walt Whitman: The Early Poems and Fiction* New York: New York University Press, 1963), p. 179; Montagu, *Some Enquiries into the Effects of Fermented Liquors*, p. 192.

12 M. Warner, 'Whitman Drunk', in B. Erkkila and J. Grossman (eds), *Breaking Bounds: Whitman and American Cultural Studies* (Oxford: Oxford University Press, 1994), p. 33.

13 J. Scodel, *Excess and the Mean in Early Modern English Literature* (Oxford: Princeton University Press, 2002), p. 226.

14 Taylor, *Bacchus in Romantic England.*

15 S. T. Coleridge, *The Collected Works of Samuel Taylor Coleridge: Essays on His Times in* The Morning Post *and* The Courier *II* (London: Routledge and Kegan Paul, 1978), p. 175.

16 Trotter, *An Essay Medical, Philosophical, and Chemical on Drunkenness*, p. 23.

17 Montagu, *Some Enquiries into the Effects of Fermented Liquors*, p. 305.

18 N. Warner, *Spirits of America: Intoxication in Nineteenth-Century American Literature* (London: University of Oklahoma Press, 1997), pp. 18–19.

19 A. Clej, *A Genealogy of the Modern Self: Thomas De Quincey and the Intoxication of Writing* (Stanford, CA: Stanford University Press, 1995), p. 20.

7

Odious monopolies: power, control and the 1830 Beer Act

And it may be observed that the law leaves justices at their absolute discretion, in granting a licence to a new person. (John Disney)

The power of selling beer ought, on the face of things, be no more obstructed or restrained than that of selling potatoes. (*The Times*)

While the second half of the eighteenth century saw the emergence of new philosophical and medical speculations on the nature of intoxication and addiction, it also saw the return of some much older concerns over licensing and the social role of the alehouse. In 1753, just two years after the last of the great Gin Acts, a Licensing Act was passed which required all new licence applications to be accompanied by a certificate, signed by a local clergyman and 'three or four reputable and influential household-ers' verifying that the applicant was 'of good fame and sober life and conversation'. This meant that for the first time anyone intending to open an alehouse had to prove in advance that they were respectable members of the community. In addition alehouse licences, which until now had been granted in perpetuity, were to be renewed annually. Both measures increased the power of local magistrates in the matter of granting licences, and it was a power that many were keen to exploit. Over the next half century there was a trend towards increasing licence restrictions in many areas as magistrates tried to reduce the number of alehouses in their ju-risdictions. However, this trend conflicted with the desire of increasingly powerful drinks manufacturers to expand their markets, and the desire of government to increase its tax revenue by encouraging an industry which provided a lucrative source of excise duties. These tensions would come to a head in 1830 with the passing of a Beer Act which would, in one dramatic move, undo almost three centuries of work towards placing beer retail under magisterial control. The 1830 Beer Act represented a victory of free trade capitalism over the established power of local economic and political elites and was an experiment as radical, in its own way, as the at-tempted gin prohibition of 1736. One impact of the 1830 Beer Act would be to transform an anti-spirits movement which stretched back to the days of the gin craze into a radical and well-organised teetotal temperance campaign. A confluence of anxieties over gin drinking and alehouses, radicalised by the pressures of a drift towards laissez-faire capitalism, kick-started a temperance movement which, while remaining singularly unsuccessful in achieving its specific goals, would become one of the dominant political forces of Victorian England.

The power of the brewers

In London and a few other major cities the gin craze distracted attention away from the traditional stand-off between magistrates and alehouse-keepers, but that convoluted relationship was never resolved at any point in the eighteenth century. Magistrates still negotiated a path between their own cultural values, economic necessity and political expediency as publicans tried to make a living wage while not falling foul of the local authorities. All the while, beer sales were dwindling. Having fallen by around 30 per cent between 1689 and 1750, beer production remained virtually static for the next fifty years at around 16 million barrels per annum while the population increased from six to nine million.[1] This decline in per capita consumption of beer continued to well into the nineteenth century. The key change in the beer market over this period was not an increase in consumption, then, but the increased concentration of production in the hands of common brewers. Although brewers had been major players in the beer trade for a long time, until the latter half of the eighteenth century the majority of retailers still brewed their own beer. The emergence of powerful regional (and later national) brewers such as Whitbread saw huge profits being accumulated by a relatively small number of companies while the number of home-brewing alehouses started a terminal decline. Even though beer consumption was not growing the market remained enormous. As a result, companies who could produce and distribute their product on an industrial scale were able to make vast sums of money.

Most of the eighteenth-century brewing giants made their fortune through porter. Porter, although virtually unknown outside the world of real ale specialists today, revolutionised the brewing industry. The popular story, though disputed by some beer historians,[2] is that one Ralph Harwood invented porter in the Bell Brewery, Shoreditch while searching for a recipe that would replicate a popular drink called 'three-threads'. Though its precise nature remains uncertain, three-threads was a mix of different beers which was strong, dark and affordable. Some time around 1720 it was found that a drink similar to three-threads could be made by brewing from malt that had been over-heated during the drying process.

Conventionally, malting requires drying soaked barley in such a way as to arrest the sprouting process while preventing it from roasting; however, it seems that a batch of 'blown' malt – dried too quickly and at too high a temperature – was delivered to either Harwood or another brewer and added to the mash tun as normal. The result was a dark, strong beer which caught on like wildfire and quickly acquired the name porter, after the London porters among whom it was first popularised.

Porter transformed the beer industry because, unlike all previous beers and ales, it lent itself to economies of scale. It was much less susceptible to spoiling than other beers, and it could be stored in bulk and transported long distances. The most efficient way to produce porter was in large vats, which meant that while it was extremely economical once production was under way it required a sizeable capital outlay in the first place. Brewers with the capacity to create large brewing and storage facilities, and who were able to transport their product long distances, benefited enormously. Porter contributed to a considerable concentration of the brewing industry, and it was, according to Peter Clark, 'one of the first truly mass-produced consumer items ever retailed in England'.[3] It established those brewers who came to monopolise the market as some of the first giants of the new industrial economy.

Porter, like gin and port before it, was a marker of progress. It relied on new brewing technologies and it illustrated the extent to which new commodities could transform even static markets. From one perspective it showed the wealth-creating power of capitalism in its best light as huge profits were derived from the invention and enterprise of such humble self-starters as Samuel Whitbread (who began his life as a brewer's apprentice). From a more conservative perspective, however, it seemed to confirm all that was wrong with the brave new world of capitalist trading: that it was an economic system which too often relied on not only pandering to the worst aspects of human nature, but actively encouraging consumers to, as it were, addict themselves to commodities which were at best useless and at worst downright dangerous. It was bad enough that the porter trade encouraged drunkenness, but worse that its retail outlet was the alehouse – that hoary den of iniquity which generations of magistrates had been trying to suppress.

In fact, alehouses had acquired a measure of respectability in the mid-eighteenth century. The patriotic celebrations of ale that accompanied the condemnation of gin hardly squared with a suppression of public houses. The relationship between magistrates and alehouse-keepers was as complex and tense as ever, but it was not always recriminatory. Where possible, it was in the interests of landlords to cultivate good relationships with local authorities and over time this inevitably encouraged a more professional approach to management.[4] In addition, alehouses became increasingly tied into formal politics over the course of the eighteenth century through their use as both campaign headquarters and polling booths during elections. This was not an especially strange phenomenon since alehouses were often the largest and most well-resourced public buildings in any community. Nevertheless, it opened the door to all sorts of corruption, not least when the local licensing magistrates had a clear preference for one party over the other. Alehouse-keepers, keen to keep on the right side of the authorities, had the wherewithal to be very persuasive come election time – as Hogarth's 'Election Series' shows in typically carnivalesque terms.

Despite this, many local magistrates remained suspicious. The relationship between public houses and social and political elites was always going to be tenuous, and as the spirit of evangelicalism began to spread among the middle classes in the second half of the eighteenth century so old denunciations of godless alehouse culture began to return. In 1773 the Quaker John Scott described the alehouse as an 'infernal mansion, where demons of avarice, extravagance, fury, and prophaneness hold their perpetual residence'. He went on to suggest that the system of certificates introduced in 1753 was being abused because the four reputable householders required to confirm the publican's character could easily be 'brother tipplers, or gamesters, or poachers, or perhaps worse'.[5] Three years later the magistrate John Disney published a plea to fellow Justices in which he insisted it was 'the duty of every good magistrate and citizen' to reduce the ease with which licences were granted, and thereby 'stem that torrent which must finally overwhelm the liberties of this country'.[6] Disney pointed out that it had been established by legal precedent that, however certificates may be obtained, 'the law leaves the Justices at their absolute discretion, in granting a licence to a new person' and he urged that 'every argument against … new licensing ought to be allowed its full force, before they receive our fiat'.[7] The rigorous application of magisterial discretion, as called for by Disney, would remain one of the most contentious and divisive issues in public debates on alcohol for the next two centuries.

The principle of 'need'

The kind of concerns expressed by reforming magistrates were given official sanction in 1787 when George III was cajoled by William Wilberforce into issuing a Royal Proclamation against vice, profaneness and immorality. The Royal Proclamation, and the Proclamation Society that Wilberforce immediately set up to support its implementation, called on magistrates to apply existing laws more rigorously in order to suppress licentious behaviour, gambling, sexual impropriety and drunkenness. In an official statement of aims the Proclamation Society made it clear that it saw the 'regulation of public houses [as] a point of vast importance' which had 'engaged much of the Committee's Attention'.[8] A backlash of sorts was under way against the public house which would lead to what Sidney and Beatrice Webb would later call 'the most remarkable episode in the whole history of public-house licensing in England'.[9]

The impact of the Royal Proclamation was to give magistrates across the country free reign to apply the existing law with the stringency urged by the likes of Disney. One consequence of this was an attack on unlicensed beer-selling which culminated in a 1795 Act imposing draconian punishments on black marketeers. However, the more important long-term effect was the widespread application of a key principle in licensing known as the 'principle of need'. In 1768, Henry Fielding's brother, Sir John Fielding, had outlined this idea in a critical commentary on licensing law. He urged magistrates to 'unanimously agree to reduce the number of alehouses, by suppressing those that appear to be unnecessary, from the number there are in the neighbourhood, who only starve one another'.[10] In other words, he wanted magistrates to use their discretion to determine what number of alehouses was appropriate to the population and issue licences accordingly. Disney concurred, arguing that it 'should be well considered, how far the accommodation of the public in general, or the circumstances of that particular township, require [a new licence], or make it necessary', thereby making the role of the magistrate not simply to ascertain the good character of potential publicans but also to decide in advance whether there was any need for a new alehouse or inn to be opened up at all.[11]

For one writer at least, this meant that 'if his Majesty's most gracious Proclamation … is seriously to take place' magistrates should 'permit no alehouse to exist, within *four* miles of any market town'.[12] Such draconian prohibitions were never going to take place without making magistrates appear to be a law unto themselves. Instead many local magistrates adapted the requirement for a signed certificate of character such that any application had to be agreed by a vestry of respectable local inhabitants which was convened especially for the purpose. This was a remarkable episode in licensing history because, for the first time, local residents in a limited number of areas were given a decisive say in how many licensed premises would be allowed in their area. Other benches formally agreed to grant no new licences 'but where the convenience of the public absolutely required it'.[13] The idea that licence numbers should be set by magistrates according to population, even if that meant actively reducing the number of existing alehouses, became established in this period. It was a concept that would re-emerge as a dominant concern towards the end of the nineteenth century as temperance campaigners actively packed the benches of the licensing authorities, and towards the end of the twentieth century when the principle of 'need' was finally abandoned.

One prominent campaigner on the principle of need was the Tower Hamlets magistrate Patrick Colquhoun. In 1795 Colquhoun published a report on public houses which claimed to show that a large number of the 6,000 licensed public houses in London were 'houses of little trade'.[14] He argued that large numbers of poor tenants were drawn by the promise of high earnings into running public houses even though the trade was already saturated. As a result, they allowed their pubs to 'be prostituted to the purpose of harbouring *thieves, pick-pockets,* or *lewd* and *profligate people of either sex*', since that was the only way they could ensure custom.[15] Colquhoun concluded that it was the duty of magistrates to prevent this from occurring by limiting the number of licensed premises to just one for every fifty families in the neighbourhood and to close premises where the tenancy had changed hands constantly over the previous two years (a sure sign that the business was failing). Colquhoun also argued that, rather than simply attacking all licensees, magistrates should actively encourage men 'of some respectability, and of good moral characters' to become landlords.[16]

An odious monopoly

Colquhoun's main targets were the unrespectable drinking dens that he claimed littered the streets of London. However, his other target was the system of tied houses which he felt distorted competition at the retail end of the beer market and contributed to the problems outlined in his study. A tied house is a pub which is owned by a brewery and leased back to the landlord, or in which the landlord is directly employed by the brewery. By contrast, a 'free house' is owned wholly by the landlord. Colquhoun was writing at a time when breweries were actively engaged in buying up properties which they then rented back out to tenant landlords. The advantage this provided was that the breweries had a secure outlet for their beers and they retained the capital value of the licensed property for themselves. Versions of the tied-house system had been in existence for some time; since the late seventeenth century brewers had been in the habit of allowing landlords to run up credit which they then recovered by taking partial or whole ownership of the landlord's property. Indeed, on these grounds the distinction between a tied and a free house became very blurred: so-called freeholders often entered in to 'loan ties' with brewers, which meant they borrowed from brewers to buy their properties, often at low interest, thereby mortgaging their bricks and mortar to the company that supplied their beer. Outright ownership of pubs by brewers increased in the second half of the eighteenth century. The big porter brewers had capital to invest and by vertically integrating their business so that they controlled both production and supply they were able to further secure their position in a highly competitive market. Ironically, the demands of reforming magistrates often strengthened the hand of the big brewers in this regard by forcing landlords to improve their properties in order to retain licences, and thereby run up bills which could only be met by borrowing from the brewers.

The tied-house system brought together concerns over both the management of alehouses and the corporate power of the brewing giants. To many observers, it seemed that by buying up public houses across the country porter brewers were skewing the property market, turning landlords into vassals, and creating what a *Times* editorial would later call a 'most odious monopoly'.[17] Patrick Colquhoun was circumspect in attacking the big brewers, remarking obsequiously that most were 'men of high character for integrity and humanity', but he was insistent that the creation of tied houses completely undermined the free competition necessary for an equitable and socially responsible drinks market to thrive.[18]

Colquhoun believed that intrusive regulation could exist alongside free competition because he believed that State intervention was necessary to prevent markets from becoming distorted. To this extent he uncomfortably straddled three corners of an increasingly vociferous debate on the role of the State in regulating the consumption of alcohol. On the one hand, reforming magistrates, backed by the Proclamation Society and, from 1802, its successor the Society for the Suppression of Vice, sought to bring the weight of judicial authority to bear on the alcohol trade. However, while widespread fears over the organising role of drinking places in revolutionary France bolstered support for a judicial clampdown,[19] such noisy interference from an elite patrician class raised the hackles of both Whigs and Radicals who objected to what they saw as the arbitrary imposition of power by a self-serving, not to mention corrupt, elite. Finally, the big brewers were starting to throw their political weight around having muscled their way into the higher echelons of political life (the term 'bung aristocracy' was in common use from at least the 1820s)[20] and they were actively working to consolidate their already considerable economic power. Again both Whigs and Radicals objected to what they saw as the continuation of vested interests by a new means: landowners were often close to brewers and it was clear that they had shared interests which worked to benefit traditional elites and undermine the social mobility from which they had previously benefited.

In this context, arguments for a free trade in beer became all the more compelling. To free-traders the beer industry was as an exemplar of all that was wrong with the protectionism of markets still dominated by established interests. It also appeared to illustrate the tendency for excessive government management to allow producers to overcharge for their product. From a free trade perspective, the power of magistrates to limit the number of licences in any one area simply increased the likelihood that existing beer retailers would exploit their customers since they were only exposed to limited competition. The 1820s witnessed a feverish spate of often contradictory and badly framed drink legislation (five significant Acts between 1822 and 1828) passed by governments who struggled to manage the contradictory political, economic and juridical problems posed by the drinks industry. In the face of obvious confusion, free-traders seized their opportunity and pushed through a measure which allowed the entire beer retail trade to be thrown open.

The brewers condemned

The movement towards liberalising the trade in beer was motivated in part by a suspicion that local magistrates were abusing their power in providing licences. While some magistrates appeared to be imposing their moral values on local residents by suppressing licences others seemed to be in the pockets of the drinks trade, using their powers to refuse licences to independent landlords while shoring up the tied-house system by granting licences to anyone in cahoots with brewers. As the *Times* put it:

> Though brewers in person cannot grant licences, there is nothing that we know of to prevent an individual from canvassing his brother justices to join with him in setting up any tenant of his own to vend the beer of a friendly brewer, and thus to serve the interests of a pair of jobbers at once.[21]

In some places licences were being unfairly suppressed, while in others they were being granted 'with great facility, and far beyond what appear[ed] to be necessary for the public accommodation'.[22] Any claims magistrates may have had to be protecting the public good by the management of licences faced the counter-claim that the exercise of such powers was an invitation to corruption. And while magistrates could always respond that they were public servants who, at their best, were above such murky activities, brewers had no credible claim to the moral high ground. The rise of brewing giants only served to increase public suspicion that they were more concerned with securing profits than with providing a wholesome product.

Anxieties over possible corruption among the big brewers came to a head over the problem of adulteration. The malt used in brewing had been taxed since 1644, and between 1760 and 1815, as the government sought tax revenues to fund wars in America and with France, duties went up from 9½d to almost 6½s per bushel. The price of porter, however, had remained virtually static since 1722 and the force of tradition meant it was very difficult for retailers to put the price up.[23] Increased duties, therefore, hit brewers and retailers hardest. In the 1780s the saccharometer, which allowed brewers to measure the amount of fermentable liquor they were extracting from their malt, was introduced. To their surprise, porter brewers found that the dark malts they were using were less efficient than pale malts used in standard brewing.[24] Before long unscrupulous porter brewers were using paler malts and then colouring and flavouring the resulting brew with a cocktail of additives. Observers complained loudly about the 'noxious ingredients', including opium and coculus indicus, added to porter by brewers.[25] An excise officer giving evidence to a Select Committee on the beer trade listed, among other adulterants he had come across, opium, liquorice, orange peel, copperas, gentian, treacle, coriander and ground ginger.[26]

Adulteration made the brewers look guilty of the worst kind of corruption. Not happy with skewing the market through the system of tied houses, they were also both fleecing and poisoning their own customers through the adulteration of their product. In 1814, 14,000 Londoners voiced their anger by signing a petition against both adulteration and high beer prices.[27] The monopoly created by the big brewers exacerbated the problem by encouraging smaller brewers to cut corners in order to maintain a foothold in a market which was squeezing them on every side. Beer sales continued to fall overall, and publicans were forced into unscrupulous practices to sell enough drinks to turn a profit. A Licensing Act passed in 1822 addressed some of these concerns by instituting rules on opening hours and clarifying the law on standard measures. Alehouses were to close for part of Sunday and 'during late hours of the night or early morning', although these regulations were inadvertently rescinded by the 1828 Licensing Act which neglected to reinstitute them, having repealed all previous licensing legislation.

To many the problem seemed to be lack of competition, and much of the legislation passed in the 1820s contained more or less ineffectual schemes to remedy this situation. In 1823 an Act 'to encourage the consumption of beer' encouraged smaller brewers to produce 'intermediate' strength beers which could compete with porter. Unfortunately, the Act was so badly framed that six years later there were only twenty-nine 'intermediate brewers' in the entire country – as compared to 1,477 common brewers.[28] More successful was an Act the following year designed to encourage smaller 'retail brewers' by introducing a new system of licence fees under which licences for common brewers were charged according to rate of production, so that the bigger brewers paid more.

While much of the licensing legislation passed in the 1820s was designed to encourage liberalisation through government intervention, it was a change to the tax on spirits which provided the final catalyst for a radical overhaul of the beer trade. In 1825 an Act was passed aimed at reducing spirits smuggling and strengthening controls on legitimate distilling. The Act banned distillers from acting as retailers, outlawed distillation without a licence, instituted extensive powers of inspection and seizure for officers of the excise, banned distillation on Sundays, introduced annual licences for spirits retailers, and banned the sale and consumption of spirits in prisons and workhouses. The 1825 Act significantly tightened controls over the distillation and spirits retail industries as a whole. However, it also repealed existing taxes on spirit production and replaced them with new, much lower, duties designed to reduce the persistent smuggling which previously high levels of taxation had encouraged.

The impact of the 1825 Act was immediate. The amount of spirits produced for consumption in England more than doubled between 1825 and 1826. The number of spirits retail licences, which had been increasing in only the hundreds annually since 1815, went up by 5,000 between 1824 and 1826 to 42,599.[29] Of course, some of this increase can be accounted for by consumers switching from illicit to licit suppliers. Nevertheless, the perception at the time was that the tax reduction had led to a massive increase in both the consumption of spirits and a rise in the social disorder associated with drunkenness. It looked to some as if the government might have opened the door to a new gin craze by ignoring the key lesson of the past: that so long as spirits were cheap, people would consume them in high quantities. One result of this widespread concern over the impact of the 1825 Act was that just as numerous social commentators had sung the praises of English beer during the gin craze, so an increasing number of people after 1825 began to look for ways to encourage beer-drinking as an alternative to spirits. Combined with concerns over the monopolistic power of big brewers and the widespread corruption of magistrates, fears over a new epidemic of gin-drinking gave impetus to the already noisy campaign to liberalise the trade in beer.

Laissez-faire

Sidney and Beatrice Webb, in their Fabian analysis of liquor licensing, complained that 'it was an obsession of every enlightened legislator' between

1820 and 1830 'that cheapness and good quality could only be secured by an absolutely unrestricted competition'.[30] This was a decade in which laissez-faire economics achieved a level of hegemonic power hitherto unimagined. The beer industry was a case study in the need for reform precisely because it was an example of how monopolies short-changed consumers. What was needed, so free traders argued, was both a stimulation of the beer trade so that it could compete fairly with spirits, and the encouragement of competition within the trade so that disreputable houses could be swept out of business by the invisible hand of the market. This was the application of Smithian economics to the beer trade – and it was something Adam Smith himself had called for. In *The Wealth of Nations* he had argued that a free trade in beer would lead, after 'a pretty general and temporary drunkenness among the middling and inferior ranks of people' to an 'almost universal sobriety'.[31] He had also challenged the idea that competition necessarily encouraged consumption by using the example of alehouse, claiming that:

> It is not the multitude of alehouses ... that occasions a general disposition to drunkenness among the common people: but that disposition arising from other causes necessarily gives employment to a multitude of alehouses.[32]

In other words, opening up the trade in beer would not increase drunkenness (that would only happen if other factors were at work), but it would allow market forces to ensure that both the product and the environments in which it was consumed were improved across the board. The free-trade attitude to beer retail was summed up by *The Times*. The 'power of selling beer,' it argued succinctly, ought 'to be no more obstructed or restrained than that of selling potatoes'.[33]

The 1830 Beer Bill proposed something not far from this ideal. Its key provision was that anyone wanting to sell beer should be allowed to do so as long as they bought an excise licence costing £2 2s. No application to magistrates, no certificate of character, no alehouse licence – just a small tax payment. It was this proposal that drove a coach and horses through the whole principle, in place since 1552, that the sale of beer had to be managed by the local magistrates through a system of licences. The radical nature of this idea, especially in this light of the politically charged and culturally significant struggle that had persisted between magistrates and alehouses for the preceding two centuries, cannot be overstated.

A Select Committee looking into the possible impacts of the Bill took evidence from a range of interested parties: brewers, publicans, excise officers and spirits retailers. Both brewers and publicans argued against the liberalisation of licensing. Brewers had obvious reasons for wanting to maintain the status quo since widening access to beer licences threatened to undermine the system of tied houses which shored up the sale of their product. Many of the publicans who testified argued that increased competition from new beer shops would put them out of business – something they could ill-afford given that most of them were in debt to the brewers and needed to protect their revenues in order to avoid losing their homes. At the same time most also agreed that spirit consumption had increased considerably since 1825. One publican claimed his spirits sales had increased from 100 to 400 gallons a month following the reduction in duties. Another stated that customers were asking for a quartern of gin and a pint of water instead of a pint of beer since the former was now the cheaper option. He went on to complain that a new 'gin-spinner' in his neighbourhood had benefited from the 1825 Act so much that he now drove 'his carriage and four in as great a style as almost his Majesty'.[34]

The imprecations of brewers and retailers fell on deaf ears, however. The 1830 Select Committee was determined to back liberalisation and its final report did so in no uncertain terms. The Act which was finally passed introduced the £2 2s excise licence for beer shops and scrapped the requirement for beer-sellers to acquire a licence from magistrates. It did introduce fines for allowing drunkenness on the premises as well as fixed opening hours, and – perhaps as a sop to irate magistrates – it allowed them to close beer-houses which allowed 'riot or tumult'. However, full alehouse licences, as defined by the 1828 Licensing Act, were now only needed by pubs selling wines and spirits in addition to beer.

Fresh with beer

The 1830 Act was the result of a combination of factors: concerns over corruption in the trade, a widespread mistrust of the power of local magistrates, increased spirit drinking, the increasing dominance of free-trade economics, and (not least) political manoeuvring in advance of a general election. Wellington's Tory administration may not have seemed the natural source for such a radical piece of legislation, but Wellington was about to face the country and, for all the reasons outlined above, liberalisation was a popular measure. It was also one that split the Opposition.[35] Whigs were torn between their free-trade instincts and the prospect of backing an Act which seemed to encourage moral laxity, while recalcitrant Tories were torn between their conservative desire to retain the status quo and the risk of appearing puritanical. As would remain the case throughout the nineteenth century, politicians voting on a licensing issue found that their economic principles often did not square with their moral or cultural values, not to mention their political pragmatism, where the subject of alcohol was concerned.

The immediate effect of the 1830 Act, not surprisingly, was an explosion in the number of premises selling beer. More than 24,000 beer shops opened within a year of the Act becoming law, and the number was nearer 40,000 by 1835.[36] The Act did little to constrain the power of the big brewers. They already had the advantage of economies of scale and so, rather than beer shops turning to smaller suppliers, the big brewers simply undercut the competition and sold both to their own tied houses and the new beer shops. One paradoxical feature of the Beer Act was that it tried to protect the holders of alehouse licences by ensuring that only they could sell wine and spirits, indeed publicans addressing the 1830 Select Committee were constantly reminded that this distinction should act in their favour. The problem was that this encouraged full licence-holders to push spirits sales in order to maintain their market share. Brewers, who had a material interest in maintaining the value of licensed properties that they either fully or partially owned, invested heavily in the physical appearance of their pubs with the aim of enticing customers through their doors by a combination of lavish interiors and the promise of access to an array of spirits. To a large extent the response of property-owning brewers to the 1830 Beer Act was the development of the gin palace, though large-scale gin shops were not unknown before 1830. Trade liberalisation did encourage beer consumption (although levels had in fact begun to increase in the mid-1820s); however, it did little to reduce the demand for spirits, which dipped slightly from 1830–33 but then increased quickly to reach record levels in 1839.[37] The overall rate of increase in the number of public houses with beer, wine and spirits licences was almost completely unaffected by the 1830 Act.

Perhaps predictably, almost as soon as the 1830 Act was passed people began to complain that it had unleashed a torrent of drunkenness. Within weeks of its enactment Sydney Smith complained that 'Everybody is drunk. Those who are not singing are sprawling. The sovereign people are in a beastly state'.[38] Not everyone was so dismayed. *The Times*, sticking doggedly to its free-trade line, mocked 'certain philanthropists' who noted with alarm that 'people have now and then, since the Act was passed, been seen "summot fresh" with beer'.[39] *The Times* was confident that in the long run liberalisation would encourage beer-drinking and, if not produce Smith's universal sobriety, then certainly reduce the number of people getting 'delirious on poison'. However, within a year concerns over the effects of the Act had returned to haunt even those who had pushed it through. Debating beer shops in September 1831, Wellington himself announced that he now 'wished these houses to be placed under the control of the magistrates just as public houses were'.[40]

In 1833 a new Select Committee was convened to consider the impacts of the Beer Act. The tenor of both its questions and conclusions contrasted starkly with the report produced three years previously. The 1833 Committee heard from a procession of witnesses who, often responding to rather leading questions from the members, testified that the Beer Act had led to an increase in drunkenness, poverty and crime. Many witnesses blamed the so-called Swing Riots – a wave of popular unrest that had spread across southern England in the autumn of 1830 – on the new beer shops. One Norfolk magistrate insisted that there 'decidedly was' a connection between the two.[41] Another claimed, ironically for a rural magistrate, that rioters gathered in beer shops rather than alehouses because 'the characters are more respectable' in the latter.[42] The Essex magistrate John Disney, whose father had published his broadside against alehouses fifty years earlier, stopped at blaming beer shops for the riots but insisted they had nonetheless led to an overall increase in crime.[43]

The 1833 Select Committee concluded that 'considerable evils' had arisen from the provisions of the 1830 Beer Act and it recommended a return to magisterial control, including a revival of the requirement for certificates of character to accompany licence applications.[44] The following year an Act was passed implementing most of the Committee's recommendations. Noting in its preamble that 'much evil has arisen from the management and conduct of houses in which beer and cider is sold by retail', the Act re-introduced the certificate of character. It also created a distinction between beer shops that sold beer for consumption on and off the premises (hence introducing the rudiments of the modern off-licence) while giving an added advantage to fully licensed public houses by allowing them to sell for consumption both on and off premises under the same licence. It also introduced new powers allowing constables to enter beer shops at any time of day or night to monitor activities as well as allowing magistrates to set fixed opening hours for their jurisdictions annually.

The Times condemned these last two provisions as 'capricious' and oppressive, seeing in them a return to the arbitrary power of local justices. 'Men of the better sort,' it protested, 'must soon be driven from a trade which lays them open to the tyranny of every petty constable, not to mention the prejudices and caprices of the magistrates'.[45] Such opinions chimed well with those who still saw the beer trade as an honest occupation which had only to be protected from the deleterious influence of vested interests. However, the credibility of the free trade argument had been seriously undermined by the results of the 1830 experiment. Not only were one-time supporters of liberalisation beginning to voice doubts, but the experience had given rise to a newly invigorated campaign to not only return to the pre-1830 status quo, but to tackle the practice of alcohol consumption head-on and in radically new ways. Far from tackling spirit-drinking by reinvigorating the traditional British love of beer, the

1830 Act made it possible for groups which might previously have only condemned gin to throw beer into the mix and condemn alcohol consumption altogether. If the gin palace was the response of property-owning brewers to the Beer Act, then the response of anti-drink campaigners was organised teetotalism: an idea which would transform the discourse on drink permanently.

Notes

1 J. Burnett, *Liquid Pleasures: A Social History of Drinks in Modern Britain* (London: Routledge, 1999), p. 179.
2 See, for example, M. Cornell, *Beer: The Story of the Pint* (London: Headline, 2003).
3 Clark, *The English Alehouse*, p. 293.
4 *Ibid.*, p. 238.
5 J. Scott, *Observations on the Present State of the Parochial and Vagrant Poor* (London: Edward and Charles Dilly, 1771), pp. 58–60.
6 J. Disney, *Thoughts on the Great Circumspection Necessary in Licensing Public Alehouses* (London: J. Johnson, 1776), p. 14.
7 *Ibid.*, pp. 8–10.
8 Proclamation Society, 'Brief statement of the origin and nature of the Society' (London: George Stafford, 1789), p. 19.
9 S. and B. Webb, *The History of Liquor Licensing in England Principally from 1700–1830* (London: Longmans, Green & Co., 1903), p. 49.
10 J. Fielding, *Extracts from Such of the Penal Laws as Particularly Relate to the Peace and Good Order of this Metropolis* (London: H. Woodfall and W. Strahan, 1768) p. 106.
11 Disney, *Thoughts on the Great Circumspection Necessary in Licensing Public Alehouses*, p. 9.
12 Anon., *An Essay on Tea, Sugar, White Bread and Butter, Country Alehouses, Strong Beer and Geneva and other Modern Luxuries* (Salisbury: J. Hodson, 1777), p. 18.
13 Webb and Webb, *The History of Liquor Licensing in England*, p. 57.
14 P. Colquhoun, *Observations and Facts Relative to Public Houses* (London: J. Downes, 1795), p. 19.
15 *Ibid.*, p. 22.
16 *Ibid.*, p. 26.
17 Anon., 'Licensing system' (*Times*, 30 August 1827), p. 2.
18 Colquhoun, *Observations and Facts Relative to Public Houses*, p. 34.
19 Clark, *The English Alehouse*, p. 324.
20 Anon., 'Licensing system'.
21 Anon., 'Editorial' (*Times*, 22 September 1829), p. 2.
22 House of Commons, *First Report from the Committee on the State of the Police of the Metropolis* (1817) 233, p. 9.
23 Haydon, *Beer and Britannia*, p. 111.
24 Cornell, *Beer*, pp. 111–12.
25 R. Macnish, *The Anatomy of Drunkenness* (Glasgow: W. R. McPhun, 1827), p. 19.
26 House of Commons, *Report from the Select Committee on the Sale of Beer* (1830) 253, p. 31.
27 Haydon, *Beer and Britannia*, p. 153.

28 House of Commons, *An account of the number of brewers, retail brewers, licensed victuallers and intermediate brewers, in England, Scotland and Wales* (1830) 208, p. 3.
29 G. Wilson, *Alcohol and the Nation* (London: Nicholson and Watson, 1940), p. 395.
30 Webb and Webb, *The History of Liquor Licensing in England*, p. 87.
31 A. Smith, *The Wealth of Nations Books IV-V* (Harmondsworth: Penguin, 1999), p. 71.
32 A. Smith, *The Wealth of Nations Books I-III* (Harmondsworth: Penguin, 1986), p. 461.
33 Anon, 'Editorial' (*Times*, 22 September 1829), p. 2.
34 House of Commons *Report from the Select Committee on the Sale of Beer* (1830) 253, p. 37.
35 Greenaway, *Drink and British Politics Since 1830*, p. 21; Harrison, *Drink and the Victorians: The Temperance Question in England, 1815–1872* (London: Faber and Faber, 1971), p. 75.
36 Wilson, *Alcohol and the Nation*, p. 394.
37 *Ibid.*, p. 332.
38 Haydon, *Beer and Britannia*, p. 171.
39 Anon., 'Editorial' (*Times*, 21 October 1830), p. 2.
40 Anon., 'Parliamentary Intelligence' (*Times*, 7 September 1831), p. 1.
41 House of Commons, *Report from the Select Committee on the Sale of Beer* (1833) 416, p. 70.
42 *Ibid.*, p. 13.
43 *Ibid.*, p. 28.
44 *Ibid.*, p. 3.
45 Anon., 'Editorial' (*Times*, 31 October 1834), p. 2.

8

The last tyrant:
the rise of temperance

Through the influence of strong drink, we are now living in worse than Egyptian oppression. Banish this pernicious article from common use and we shall at once breath in all the freedom and happiness of Canaan. (*Temperance Magazine and Review*)

If they would rest their cause on the fair ground of temperance for those who can be temperate, and total abstinence for those who cannot be temperate … we should regard them as a good example and a public benefit. But, running a-muck like mad Malays, we look upon them as a bad example, and a public evil, only less intolerable than drunkenness itself. (Charles Dickens)

As Brian Harrison has pointed out, the single factor which distinguished the Victorian temperance movement from the raft of anti-drink activity that preceded it was the emergence of organised temperance societies.[1] That is, local, and later national, associations whose defining feature was their goal of reducing or eradicating alcohol consumption across society. The Society for the Reformation of Manners had been active in the late seventeenth century and a raft of 'loyal associations' emerged towards the end of the eighteenth century.[2] The Proclamation Society existed alongside other groups such as The Society for the Reformation of Principles, not to mention campaigning organisations like the Society for the Abolition of the Slave Trade. The Society for the Suppression of Vice boasted 1,200 members in 1804 and included a number of groups based outside the capital.[3] William Wilberforce's prominent role in the Proclamation Society, the Abolition Society and the Vice Society illustrates the extent to which many of these associations drew their membership from the evangelical wing of upper-class Anglican society. Evangelicalism was spreading the message of organised social and moral reform at the same time as increasing numbers of individuals were publicly mooting the idea of partial or even total abstinence from alcoholic drinks. However, it was the 'fusion of the idea of association with the idea of abstinence' which was needed to kick-start the temperance campaign proper.[4]

Organising temperance

One or two idiosyncratic total abstention societies had sprung up in the early nineteenth century. In June 1817 a nailer from Skibereen, one Jeffrey Sedwards, set up a total abstinence society with twelve friends. Similar groups followed in nearby communities, but the movement was short-lived and soon fell into obscurity.[5] In Manchester a religious sect calling themselves the Cowherdites renounced alcohol in 1809, but this was part of a wider asceticism which also included becoming vegetarian. Large-scale and well-organised temperance associations were, as later temperance campaigners were always quick to recognise, an American idea. Small anti-spirits societies had begun to form sporadically in America as early as 1808, including the sizeable Massachusetts Society for the Suppression of Intemperance (founded in Boston in 1813). However, it was the formation of the American Temperance Society (ATS) in 1826 which marked a turning point. The ATS was a not just a society whose members pledged to abstain from drinking spirits, but one whose ambitions were national, indeed international, reform.

In post-colonial America, as in Hanoverian England, alcohol consumption tapped into deep-set concerns about both freedom and national identity. In England, as we have seen, there was tension between the liberty of the 'free-born Englishman' to drink alcohol and the polite idea of rational social progress. In America high levels of alcohol consumption in the late eighteenth century raised questions that went to the heart of what the newly independent nation's idea of itself was. W. J. Rorabaugh has shown the extent to which the right to get drunk became entrenched in post-colonial popular culture almost as an expression of the freedoms that the War of Independence had secured, while at the same time religious preachers, railing against the sinfulness of drunkenness in terms already familiar, hitched their arguments to both the notion of America's religious destiny and its achievement of historically unprecedented political freedoms.[6] Lyman Beecher, whose 'Six Sermons on Intemperance' (1825) had a direct influence on the founding of the ATS,[7] warned that once the people were 'perverted by intemperance, ambition needs no better implements with which to dig the graves of our liberties, and entomb our glory'.[8]

The sermons of American preachers associated with the ATS, brought over to Britain by American seamen commanding ships which ran on temperance principles, triggered the formation of organised anti-spirits societies in Britain. Remarkably, a number of anti-spirits societies were founded almost simultaneously in the late summer of 1829 by people who were apparently unaware of each others' activities. In August Dr John Edgar, secretary of the Belfast Religious Tract Society, wrote a public temperance appeal, while at the same time in New Ross, Wexford, Revd George Carr established a temperance society at his local Quaker meeting house. Meanwhile one John Dunlop was on the verge of setting up a temperance society in Greenock, just outside of Glasgow. Within a year there would be temperance societies in the major cities throughout Britain, including Glasgow, Manchester, Leeds, Dublin, Birmingham, Bristol, Newcastle, Bradford and, from November 1830, London.

It is important to emphasise that none of the temperance societies which were formed between 1829 and 1831 preached total abstinence. They only required their members to foreswear spirits (except, in most cases, for 'medicinal purposes') and to campaign for the reduction of spirit consumption and drunkenness in their communities. They caught on for a number of reasons. Certainly, the increased levels of spirit consumption after 1825 had prepared the ground for an organised response to what some saw as the beginnings of a new gin craze, but the new temperance societies also tapped into (and were largely driven by) the evangelical spirit of social reform. What is more, they gave that desire for social reform a concrete object: the use of spirituous liquors. Abstaining from spirits was manageable, meaningful, visible and culturally significant. Just as coffee-drinking had allowed sectors of the urban middle class to claim a portion of the moral high ground in the midst of the gin craze, so the conspicuous rejection of spirits signified the moral rectitude of a section of the more evangelically-minded middle class. In the 1820s spirit-drinking remained a predominantly lower-class activity (although more than one witness to the 1830 Select Committee noted that the main increase in spirit consumption after 1825 had been among middle-class householders buying in bulk for home consumption). Abstaining from spirits, even when coupled with the promise to only use other drinks in moderation, was without doubt an act of cultural self-assertion as much as it was an act of moral reform. Indeed, John Dunlop – who had as good an understanding of the cultural politics of drink as anyone at the time – claimed later that he had tried, unsuccessfully, to include a pledge against wine-drinking when forming the Glasgow and Edinburgh Temperance Societies, but had been unable to persuade enough people to sign up to such an intrusive requirement.[9]

The early temperance societies were born out of an evangelical spirit of social reform which had already produced numerous associations for moral improvement such as the Proclamation Society and the Society for the Suppression of Vice. The American Temperance Society presented a model of how the specific practice of spirit-drinking, which had been the source of widespread social anxiety for most of the preceding century, could provide a coherent focus for evangelical reform. Finally, the reorganisation of spirits duties in 1825, and the ensuing increase in consumption, sparked off a wave of social anxiety which provided fertile ground for cultivation of organised temperance. However, had the temperance movement remained the marginal activity of a few relatively affluent evangelicals it is unlikely it would have had much of a social impact; it certainly would not have led to the long-running and politically charged disputes over temperance that will be discussed in the following chapters. In order for that to happen the conservative notion of partial abstinence and moderate drinking which underpinned the first temperance societies had to be supplanted by the radical idea of total abstinence which drove the second wave of the temperance campaign.

The teetotal revolution

As we have seen, the idea of total abstinence was not new in 1830; and while it was extremely unusual to abstain from all alcohol, it was not something limited solely to a handful of cranks and eccentrics. Indeed, a debate had already been taking place as to the relative merits of abstention as against moderation. In 1794, the author of a *Treatise on the True Effects of Drinking Spirituous Liquors, Wine and Beer* argued against moderate drinking on the grounds that 'the words *moderately taken* express nothing at all, for a certain quantity may not affect a strong man and another may be very much hurt by it'.[10] Basil Montagu, writing twenty years later, set out a detailed refutation of the Quaker doctrine of moderation and listed a series of arguments for total abstinence, including the claim that 'abstinence is easier than temperance'.[11] While apparently counter-intuitive, the idea that it is easier to give up a pleasure entirely than to indulge in that activity with complete self-control was one that would later become critical to the teetotal temperance message.

Despite the existence of arguments for total abstention, the idea of not drinking beer remained largely untenable so long as it was popularly agreed that the serious social problems which arose from drunkenness were attributable to spirits. As long as beer and spirits were perceived as qualitatively different, then anti-spirits campaigns had no use for total abstinence. However, once that distinction began to collapse then anti-spirits temperance became open to question. Gin had raised the prospect of an 'instantaneous drunkenness' and had created the novel idea that drunkenness need not necessarily arise from gluttony, nor from extended bouts of drinking. By the later eighteenth century, once technological developments had made it possible to measure levels of alcohol in drinks, there was no question that gin and beer were qualitatively different drinks, they simply contained alcohol in different degrees of concentration. If, as anti-spirits campaigners felt, drinking gin was an unquestionably bad thing then there was no logical reason why all alcoholic drinks should not be condemned as simply lesser versions of the same evil. Total abstinence arose as an idea partly out of the breakdown in the distinction between different types of alcoholic drinks. There was no reason why beer, taken in quantities, could not achieve precisely the same effects as gin.

By expanding access to beer and, apparently, increasing levels of drunkenness, the Beer Act opened the door for total abstentionists to make precisely this argument. The most notable and influential total abstention campaigner to emerge in the wake of the Beer Act was a cheese-maker from Preston called Joseph Livesey. In his testimony to a remarkable Select Committee on Drunkenness, convened in 1834, Livesey made this point clearly by insisting that there had been a significant rise in drunkenness in his home town of Preston since 1830 and that the rise in disorder was attributable solely to beer. When asked if there had not also been a rise in spirit-drinking, Livesey responded 'I do not think there has ... the drunkenness in Preston is principally owing to the consumption of beer'.[12] Livesey's determination to lay the blame for increased drunkenness at the door of beer led one bemused-sounding member to ask whether the Committee were 'to understand that you object, as a general principle, to the consumption of beer?' 'Yes', Livesey responded.[13]

The reason that Livesey, a mere cheese-factor, found himself testifying to a Parliamentary committee was that he was also the most prominent member of the Preston Temperance Society. It was the Preston Temperance Society which had made the crucial leap from moderation to total abstinence in August 1832 when Livesey, along with five fellow members, signed a pledge to abstain from all intoxicating drinks, rather than just spirits. Since then Livesey had been tireless in spreading the total abstinence message throughout the country. Within three years of establishing teetotalism as a viable concept (the word teetotal is widely attributed to one Dicky Turner, a member of the Preston Temperance Society), the anti-spirits movement in Britain was on the verge of collapse. Its self-assured message of middle-class moral ascendancy was steam-rollered by a radical, energetic and visionary movement of largely working-class teetotallers whose fundamentalism allowed for a clarity of message which made the existing temperance movement seem both smug and confused by comparison.

Organised teetotalism was a revolutionary idea, especially among the working class. Whatever the debates taking place among doctors, lawyers, priests and poets as to the benefits of abstinence, drinking remained absolutely central to working-class culture. As Brian Harrison put it, for the working man in the early nineteenth century ,'to abandon drink was to abandon society itself'.[14] Magistrates and politicians had historically been suspicious of the alehouse precisely because it was, as it were, the 'parliament of the people'. The already pivotal role of the alehouse in lower-class society became, if anything, even more vital in the early years of the Industrial Revolution. Public houses provided working communities with their only social space outside of work and home. They were places to drink, but they were also the working people's social clubs, trading and entertainment centres, meeting places for societies and unions, labour exchanges and reading rooms.[15] Before organised sport, public libraries, parks and museums – not to mention cinemas, concert halls and holiday resorts – there was often literally nowhere for working people to socialise other than the pub. To remove the pub was to tear out the heart of the community; to stop drinking was to make oneself an outcast.

The annihilation of alcohol

Far from being diminished by this, the early teetotal movement thrived on it. It gained its intensity, like many religious movements, from the fact that the demands it placed on its adherents left them with no home other than the Society itself. Furthermore, the genuinely revolutionary nature of what teetotalism proposed – the complete abandonment of alcohol and all the cultural rituals, exchanges and economies associated with it – gave it a sense of mission which went far beyond anything dreamt up in the cosy meeting rooms of the anti-spirits campaigners. By necessity, as well as by design, teetotalism saw its ultimate goal as the transformation of society.

The evangelical zeal which fired the temperance movement ensured that, from its earliest days, it was infused with millenarian rhetoric. American temperance preachers, employing a declamatory style that combined religious enthusiasm with a sense of historical destiny, were fond of describing sobriety in the most utopian terms. It 'will be a mater of rejoicing', proclaimed Lyman Gilbert, when '*temperance* shall so entirely prevail, that a generation shall finally arrive, that can say, Behold the last drunkard is gone!'[16] Livesey enthusiastically adopted this tone, but went further than prophesying the day when there were be no more drunkards; for him the teetotal revolution promised more again. In the first edition of his *Preston Temperance Advocate* he implored his readers in fiery terms:

Brethren! Let us arouse ourselves! Let the love of God, of men, and of truth, be our impelling principle … let the martyr's zeal burn quenchless in our breasts; and let our object be nothing less than the ANNIHILATION OF ALCOHOL from Britain and the world, *and the consequent deliverance of all people from his tyrannic yoke!* [17]

This style swiftly became the lingua franca of teetotalism. 'Nerve your arm for the conflict,' wrote one campaigner to the people of Northampton, 'and drive the tyrant from the earth'.[18] In making the dramatic shift to total abstention, teetotallers convinced themselves that they had identified the last tyrant, the last shackle holding mankind back from its progressive destiny. Livesey was no nostalgic pastoralist looking back to some pre-industrial golden age. For him, teetotalism was the gateway to the future, not an escape route to the past, and his movement was an early exponent of that utopian notion of social transformation which would influence European political movements throughout the nineteenth and early twentieth century.

The utopianism of the teetotal movement was quickly identified by its opponents as its greatest absurdity. In a public rebuff to the teetotal New British and Foreign Temperance Society, one writer asserted that:

> The total abandonment of intoxicating liquids is one of the most extravagant projects of this inventive age ... [Let] the impartial observer seriously ask himself, if to overthrow all the drinking customs of society is not almost to re-model the social condition; if it be not a very revolution which would convulse the empire from its pinnacle to its base.[19]

The *Times*, agreeing with the surgeon Astley Cooper's description of teetotalism as 'too utopian' complained that 'drunkenness is a heinous vice and a detestable nuisance, but it is not half so demoralizing or disgusting as the cant of the Pharisaical prigs' in the teetotal movement.[20] In 1849 Charles Dickens accused teetotallers of promoting 'demoralisation' by their fanatical insistence that alcohol was the root of all evil.[21] Two years later Dickens fell out badly with his one-time collaborator George Cruikshank over the latter's conversion to teetotalism and he publicly rebuked the 'whole hoggism' of teetotal fundamentalists, Cruikshank very much included.[22]

Teetotalism was indeed a utopian concept, even if teetotallers denied the term, which tended to be used pejoratively, at the time. Early teetotal literature revelled in the language of total social transformation and, like all utopian movements, it showed complete conviction in the belief that it had identified the means to achieve that transformation. As we shall see in Chapter 9, however, the teetotal movement would soon split over the question of means. Livesey always believed the sober millennium had, by necessity, to be achieved through the free choice of the people; he had an unshakeable belief in both the possibility and the righteousness of grass-roots change based on individual ethical choices. From 1851, however, this entire principle would come under attack from teetotallers who lacked Livesey's belief that, given clear enough moral guidance, everyone would freely choose sobriety over drunkenness.

The belief that everyone, drunkards included, could be made better through what became known as 'moral suasion' meant that teetotalism not only took a new approach to the idea of abstention, but it also took a completely new view of habitual drunkards. Rather than condemn drinkers as immoral, or even as diseased, teetotallers saw them as victims of a destructive habit who could be reclaimed through proper moral guidance and the acceptance of teetotal principles. It was early teetotal organisations that pioneered the technique of bringing drinkers to public meetings to hear the testimony of ex-drinkers who had found sobriety. At teetotal gatherings processions of ex-drinkers would regale the audience with tales of desperation and debauchery – all, inevitably, ending in the discovery of the light of temperance.[23] Respectable moderationists may have hated it, but the movement struck a chord with large numbers of working people, not least because it suggested that both personal salvation and social transformation were in their hands rather than the hands of priests or politicians. Teetotalism spoke directly to that class of people whose exclusion from the mainstream political process had just been confirmed by the 1832 Reform Act and it offered them, among other things, a stake and a role in social change. It held out, especially to those who had previously been reviled as drunks, the promise of more than mere emancipation or even respectability. It told them they could spearhead the dawn of a new age: the sober millennium.

This radical message was both teetotalism's strength and its greatest weakness. While it required an extraordinary commitment from its adherents, teetotalism had the advantage of paying more than lip-service to the real lives of the people it reached out to. Between 1832 and 1836 teetotalism spread throughout both the major cities and the provinces – especially North Wales and Cornwall. The British Teetotal Temperance Society was founded by Joseph Livesey in London in September 1835 while at the same time existing 'moderationist' temperance organisations clashed with the teetotallers. Anti-spirits temperance groups, such as the original British and Foreign Temperance Society, had, by this time, established themselves as the kind of respectable organisation that members of the social elite were happy to be associated with. They were horrified when Livesey's horny-handed teetotallers arrived on the scene and were extremely reluctant to join with them. The New British and Foreign Temperance Society split from its more respectable forebear in 1836 to pursue a line supporting both total abstention and a condemnation of the drinks trade. Meanwhile, numerous other teetotal groups sprang up including the British Teetotal Temperance Society, the British Temperance Association, and a teetotal-friendly society founded in 1835 grandly titled the Independent Order of Rechabites.

To many outsiders, teetotallers were frankly mad. The Chartists held teetotalism at arm's length. While there were some teetotal Chartist groups, many were wary of the teetotal insistence that emancipation should be driven, first and foremost, by abstention.[24] Teetotallers blamed the sufferings of the poor on alcohol rather than systemic inequalities. Livesey's famous Malt Liquor Lecture, which he delivered in towns and cities throughout Britain, hitched teetotalism specifically to successful development of modern capitalism. 'The Temperance Society is an insurance for the safety of every man's property,' Livesey insisted. 'Drunkenness and disorder are sure to drive capital away; but in the midst of a reformed population it will find a secure investment'.[25] The Chartists blamed the suffering of the poor on the exclusion of the labouring classes from the levers of power; Livesey blamed it on drink. However, while Livesey saw sobriety as an end in itself, teetotalism did make it possible for others to see sobriety as a stage in the achievement of wider political freedom. Millenarian teetotallers may have dreamed of the dry utopia, but it appeared to others that more practical emancipatory goals might also be achieved by the adoption of sobriety.

Sobriety and liberation

This was certainly the case in Ireland where teetotalism (promulgated through the spectacular temperance 'crusade' of Father Theobald Mathew between 1838 and 1841) was taken up by a number of nationalist politicians. Since as far back as the sixteenth century, the supposed drunkenness of the Irish had been seen by English colonialists as exacerbating the threat of insurrection.[26] Coleridge voiced a typical complaint in 1811, writing that the Irish, after 'the third of fourth glass of whisky' are likely to 'itch for a riot and … begin to enquire after a rebellion!'[27] The stereotype of the savage, drunken Irishman remained extraordinarily widespread in mainland Britain throughout the nineteenth century, especially as agitation for Home Rule began to bite. Even Friedrich Engels, presumably trying to speak on behalf of poor Irish immigrants, fell into absurd caricature as he explained how the 'crudity' of the Irishman, his 'contempt for all humane enjoyments', coupled with grinding poverty, led to widespread drunkenness. 'How can society blame him when it places him in a position in which he almost of necessity becomes a drunkard,' wrote Engels, 'when it leaves him to himself, to his savagery?'[28]

Understandably, many nationalist politicians angrily rejected such offensive representations, not least because to ascribe a kind of genetic propensity for drunkenness to an entire people was an extremely effective way of justifying the 'civilising mission' of colonial rule. Irish drunkenness was seen as contiguous with Irish savagery and Irish childishness – all of which were central elements in the ideological justification of English power. Falling in with the teetotal temperance movement provided a range of benefits to nationalists in the 1830s and 1840s. It allowed them to conspicuously reject the charge that the Irish were any more drunk than the English, but the sheer scale of the Mathewite Crusade also provided an unprecedented platform and infrastructure through which nationalist ideas could be disseminated. It was estimated that between four and five million people signed up to Father Mathew's teetotal pledge between 1839 and 1841; it was an extraordinary campaign, albeit one which revolved entirely around the personality of Father Mathew himself. Many Protestant teetotallers on the mainland were suspicious of the sacerdotal focus of a movement in which pledges appeared to be dispensed rather than adhered to (the joke was that many signatories were later seen drunk complaining that 'the pledge hadn't worked'). But the impact of the movement, which combined the expression of collective cultural pride with the conspicuous celebration of sobriety, was deep and lasting. Daniel O'Connell took the pledge in October 1840, and in 1846 he presided over a meeting of the National Temperance Society in London.[29] However, it has been argued that O'Connell's enthusiasm was based on the fact that the vast juggernaut of the Mathewites provided an ideal vehicle to which O'Connell could hitch the 'monster meetings' of his campaign for Repeal.[30] Meanwhile other temperance-minded nationalists, such as Thomas Davis of the Young Irelanders, argued that teetotalism provided 'the offering of incipient freedom'.[31] The phrase 'Ireland sober, Ireland free', popularly, though apocryphally, ascribed to Father Mathew himself, became a touchstone over the following decades and drove the often radically anti-drink agenda of later nationalist organisations such as the Gaelic Athletics Association.

In America, the Washingtonian Movement, founded in 1840, echoed the British teetotal campaign in focusing on the reclamation of drunkards and in positing the idea that social change could be driven by a sober working people. Many abolitionists would later draw direct parallels between the tyranny of drink and the tyranny of slavery.[32] The role of alcohol in the subjugation of Native Americans had been highlighted by anti-spirits campaigners as far back as the mid-eighteenth century (one speech by a Creek chief, published in London in 1754, described spirits as 'the tyrant ... which our pretended *white friends* artfully introduced' for the enslavement of the Creek nation).[33] Abolitionists drew parallels between drunkenness and subjugation, but they also pointed to the practical uses of drunkenness by slave-owners as a means of managing their slaves. Frederick Douglass, whose slave narrative became so central to

the abolition movement, dwelt at some length on the custom of allowing slaves periodic 'holidays' in which they could get drunk. Douglass
castigated the 'liberty' given to slaves to go on periodic drinking bouts,
pointing out that such holidays were 'among the most effective means in
the hands of the slaveholders in keeping down the spirit of insurrection'
by serving as 'safety-valves, to carry off the spirit of enslaved humanity'.[34]
Over the course of the nineteenth century, the 'safety-valve' uses of drunkenness would be identified by abolitionists, nationalists and, later, many
socialists as one of the key means by which exploitative social systems
were sustained.

Temperance and the idea of freedom

Throughout this period we see, once again, that debates over drink provided a way of talking about the meaning and nature of freedom. We can
also see some of the areas around which this debate began to crystallise.
One was the extent to which the freedom to engage in certain activities (such as frequenting alehouses, or getting drunk in public) could be
regulated by the state, and on what grounds. The control of alehouses
was always a matter of the control of lower-class social spaces, for all
the political and social reasons described above. The control of drunkenness was also, from the early eighteenth century, partly a health issue.
From this perspective, drunkenness raised the question of how free we
should be to damage our own bodies, and also to what extent physical ill-
health limited our freedom to pursue other activities. Politically, personal
ill-health was increasingly condemned during the gin craze as impacting
disastrously on the common good. This was a gendered discourse: it was
specifically the impact of alcohol on the bodies of mothers that was condemned in terms of its effect on their offspring. But drunkenness also, of
course, raised questions about public order. The freedom to drink clearly
impinged on the freedom of others to go about their daily business when
drunkenness led to either violent crime or public disorder. As we shall see
in Chapter 9, this question of where personal liberty encroached on the
liberties of others would become ever more heated as modern liberalism
took shape across the course of the nineteenth century. Equally concerning to liberals was the question of market freedom. The 1830 Beer Act
was an experiment in market freedom as much as the 1736 Gin Act was
an experiment in market control. Neither achieved their desired goals.
After 1830, it became impossible to ignore the extent to which the abstract notion of market freedom had a direct impact on the other questions regarding the nature of personal freedom which liberalism took as
its fundamental concern. A free trade in beer implied an increased liberty

to consume a commodity which in many cases visibly impacted on the freedom of others when the consumer of that beer became drunk. Finally, we see the question of the extent to which intoxication itself was an act of freedom or, even leaving addiction aside for the moment, either an act of enslavement (because it undermined the rationality on which liberty was taken to be founded) or an action which made the drinker more susceptible to enslavement or subjugation by others. The drink question, in many ways, was a question of liberty itself.

Teetotalism, though limited in terms of its number of adherents, and though ridiculed by its many opponents, forced a debate which required the clarification of these issues. It did so primarily because it expressed the problem in fundamentalist terms, and partly because it had an energy and a single-mindedness which propelled its vision of the sober millennium onto the political agenda. It was the utopian strain in the discourse of total abstention, the idea that society could be transformed fundamentally and permanently by the abolition of alcohol consumption, which would be the principal legacy of teetotalism. Anti-drink writers had linked the idea of individual freedom to the issue of drunkenness for centuries; however, it was after the teetotallers conjured up their vision of a sober millennium that it became possible to think about entirely new levels of social and political freedom as being achieved through sobriety. The early teetotallers never had the practical means to achieve this goal: their reliance on persuasion really did, to use a later utopian slogan, 'demand the impossible'. However, it was not long before a new raft of temperance campaigners, committed not to the regeneration of society through persuasion but to the transformation of society through the force of legislation, took up the baton and drove temperance headlong towards the politically explosive principle of total alcohol prohibition. By hitching the utopian elements of teetotalism to the principle of legitimate State coercion, prohibitionism brought underlying debates over the nature of freedom to the surface of the drink question. By doing so, it further shifted the focus of drink discourse from the practical management of public behaviours to the most basic principles of liberal thought.

Notes

1 Harrison, *Drink and the Victorians*, p. 101.
2 A. Hunt, *Governing Morals: A Social History of Moral Regulation* (Oxford: Oxford University Press, 1999).
3 M. J. D. Roberts, 'The Society for the Suppression of Vice and its early critics', *Historical Journal*, 26: 1 (1983), 159–76, p. 163.
4 Harrison, *Drink and the Victorians*, p. 101.
5 Malcolm, *Ireland Sober, Ireland* Free, p. 77.

6   W. J. Rorabaugh, *The Alcoholic Republic: An American Tradition* (Oxford: Oxford University Press, 1979).
7   Blocker, Fahey and Tyrell (eds), *Alcohol and Temperance in Modern History*, p. 92.
8   L. Beecher, *Six Sermons on Intemperance* (Boston, MA: T. R. Marvin, 1828), p. 57.
9   J. Dunlop, *The Philosophy of Drinking Usage in Great Britain* (London: Houlston and Stoneman, 1839), p. 110.
10 Anon., *A Treatise on the True Effects of Drinking Spirituous Liquors, Wine and Beer on Body and Mind* (London, 1794), p. 10.
11 Montagu, *Some Enquiries into the Effects of Fermented Liquors*, p. 366.
12 House of Commons, *Report from the Select Committee of Inquiry into Drunkenness* (1834) 559, p. 92.
13 *Ibid.*, p. 95.
14 Harrison, *Drink and the Victorians*, p. 50.
15 *Ibid.*, p. 52.
16 L. Gilbert, *Reasons for Temperance: A Discourse* (Boston, MA: Lincoln and Edmonds, 1829), p. 22.
17 J. Livesey, *The Preston Temperance Advocate* (1 January 1837), p. 2.
18 Anon., 'An appeal to the inhabitants of Northampton by the committee of the Temperance Society' (undated), p. 3.
19 Anon. (I. C. Y.), 'Teetotalism: Absurd in its object and censurable in its agency' (London: E. Grattan, 1838), p. 5.
20 Anon., 'A Temperance Society' (*Times*, 6 September 1833), p. 2.
21 C. Dickens, 'Demoralization and total abstinence', in M. Slater (ed.), *Dickens' Journalism, Vol. 2* (London: J. M. Dent, 2003), pp. 159–69.
22 C. Dickens, 'Whole Hogs' (*Household Words*, 23 August 1851).
23 Harrison, *Drink and the Victorians*, p. 130.
24 L. L. Shiman, *Crusade Against Drink in Victorian England* (Basingstoke: Macmillan, 1988), p. 33.
25 J. Livesey, *The Malt Liquor Lecture* (Ipswich: J. M. Burton, 1850), p. 31.
26 Malcolm, *Ireland Sober, Ireland Free*, p. 2.
27 Coleridge, *The Collected Works*, p. 176.
28 F. Engels, *The Condition of the Working Class in England* (Harmondsworth: Penguin, 1987), p. 125.
29 S. Couling, *History of the Temperance Movement in Great Britain and Ireland* (London: William Tweedie, 1862), p. 180.
30 Malcolm, *Ireland Sober, Ireland Free*, pp. 127–9.
31 *Ibid.*, p. 131.
32 D. Herd, 'The paradox of temperance: Blacks and the alcohol question in nineteenth-century America', in Barrows and Room (eds), *Drinking: Behaviour and Belief in Modern History*; J. Crowley, 'Slaves to the bottle: Gough's *Autobiography* and Douglass's *Narrative*', in D. S. Reynolds and D. J. Rosenthal (eds), *The Serpent in the Cup: Temperance in American Literature* Amherst: University of Massachusetts Press, 1997).
33 Anon., 'The speech of a Creek-indian against the immoderate use of spirituous liquors' (London: R. Griffiths, 1754).
34 F. Douglass, *The Narrative of the Life of Frederick Douglass, An American Slave* (Harmondsworth: Penguin, 1986), p. 115.

9

A monstrous theory: the politics of prohibition

The power to apply correction by legislative means, cannot be doubted, without supposing the intelligent, the just and the moral portion of the community unable to control the excesses of the ignorant and disorderly, which would be to declare our incapacity to maintain the first principles of Government by ensuring the public safety. (Select Committee of Inquiry into Drunkenness, 1834)

The Traffic is corrupt at the core ... its 'good' is only the good of limited mischief. (Frederic Lees)

The 1830 Beer Act triggered the most intense period of public debate on alcohol since the 1750s. By radicalising the temperance movement it gave an entirely new complexion to the long-standing campaigns to regulate public drunkenness. At the parliamentary level, the effects of the Beer Act moved one MP, James Silk-Buckingham, to establish a Select Committee of Inquiry into Drunkenness which reported in August 1834. Silk-Buckingham's committee (dubbed the 'Drunken Committee' by sceptical observers) insisted that the State had a central role to play in the control of drinking, and it proposed some novel interventions. These included firmer regulatory powers to limit the number of licences according to population, to reduce Sunday opening and to ban the common practice of distributing wages in public houses. They also included proposals which would have a profound influence on the Victorian 'rational recreation' movement: the establishment of public parks, municipal libraries, museums and reading rooms and the abolition of the stamp duty on newspapers which many campaigners saw as a 'tax on knowledge'.[1]

While Silk-Buckingham's committee did not pull its punches in its condemnation of drunkenness (blaming it for everything from 'debility and decay in the young' to the 'extinction of all moral and religious principle'), its remedies fell short of demanding that the State encourage, far less demand, absolute sobriety.[2] Radical as Silk-Buckingham's position was, it was not utopian. The idea that the State should enforce absolute sobriety on its citizens was more or less unthinkable in 1834, despite Silk-Buckingham's clear admiration for teetotalism. Twenty years later, however, an energetic and tenacious campaign for the State prohibition of all alcohol would have established itself in Britain. The appearance of prohibitionism would split the temperance movement, but it would also bring to a head the questions of liberty and State regulation which had always been part of public debates on drink but which had often been obscured by the messy practicalities of conventional licensing. Prohibition certainly clarified things, and it would make the drink question a pressing concern of some of the leading political thinkers of the time.

An American pledge

The radical spirit of organised teetotalism ensured that its rise to prominence was swift. Within four years of the Preston Temperance Society adopting the new pledge, teetotal societies had not only appeared throughout Britain but the idea had been taken up by the largest temperance organisation in America. In 1835, James Silk-Buckingham sent a series of letters to the American Temperance Society describing the dramatic impact of teetotalism on the British temperance movement.[3] The American Temperance Union adopted a teetotal pledge the following year, an event described by one chronicler as a 'triumphant *cap of the climax* ... which gave zest to every pulsation of the universal system of temperance reform'.[4]

While the movement of temperance ideas went both ways across the Atlantic, temperance campaigners in Britain always saw America as 'the grand source of temperance reform'.[5] This was partly because it was in the interests of temperance campaigners to ally their movement with the transformative political potential symbolised by the New World, and it partly explains why Victorian temperance campaigners in Britain had so little to say about their forebears in Georgian England. However, it was also because the political successes of temperance activity in America provided a model and an aspiration for British campaigners. American temperance always appeared to be more radical, more progressive than the English version (even when it was not) and so the innovations of American campaigners invariably had an impact on their British counterparts.

One example of this was the attempted introduction of the 'American Pledge' by members of the New British and Foreign Temperance Society in 1839. The 'American pledge' – teetotalism returned with interest – required that signatories not just abstain from alcohol, but that they abstain from offering drinks 'as an article of entertainment' to friends or family.[6] This may look like a relatively minor point of principle. However, when the issue came up for debate at the Society's annual meeting in Exeter Hall, what followed was described by one contemporary as 'the most extraordinary and tumultuous meeting ever held within the walls of that building'.[7] Amid a scene of 'perfect anarchy' the chairman of the Society, Lord Stanhope, was forced to abandon his seat as the platform was more or less stormed by supporters of the American pledge who loudly announced to the hall that it would be adopted by the Society from now on.[8] Stanhope stormed off and formed his own 'short pledge' temperance organisation, the British and Foreign Society for the Suppression of Intemperance, hence adding further confusion to what was an already crowded field of 'British and Foreign' temperance groups of one kind or another. It took a further three years for the feud to be resolved and for the two groups to join forces in founding the more succinctly named National Temperance Society (although Stanhope, still not content, refused to join unless Father Mathew was made its president).

This damaging schism over an ostensibly minor question of social niceties was, in fact, the first shot across the bows in a rumbling debate over the future of temperance. American pledgers felt strongly that in addition to private abstention teetotallers had a responsibility to intervene in the habits of those around them. In its own small way, this signalled the arrival of the principle that teetotalism could be forcibly imposed on others, even if only in the private sphere. In doing so it undermined the conviction, deeply held by moral suasionists, that abstention should always be the result of individual moral choice.

Ultimately, the short pledge faction won the skirmish: the National Temperance Society retained the 'short pledge', and an American pledge-based True Teetotal Union, set up after the merger, failed to last. For a decade the question of compulsion receded to the background, but when news reached Britain in 1851 that the State of Maine had successfully prohibited the trade in alcohol, a new lease of life was given to those who felt that sobriety should be imposed rather than volunteered.

The evil of moderation

By the late 1840s every sizeable town had a local temperance society and 'teetotalism' had become a recognised term everywhere. In 1852, the London Temperance League claimed it had financed 500 lectures by its agents throughout the country and had sent 3,000 petitions to Parliament.[9] Bands of Hope, designed to inculcate temperance principles in young people, were springing up in towns and cities across Britain, and in February 1852 a Band of Hope meeting in London was attended by 6,000 children. John B. Gough, the American 'Demosthenes of total abstinence', toured Britain between 1853 and 1855 addressing up to half a million listeners in total and, according to temperance campaigners at least, persuading around 12,000 people to sign the pledge. In 1848, a coalition of temperance sympathisers and sabbatarians successfully saw the Metropolitan Police Act of 1839, which enforced the closure of all public houses before noon on Sundays, extended to the whole country with additional measures closing pubs on Christmas Day and Good Friday. It was a small, but significant, step forward for the proponents of piecemeal temperance reform.

Nevertheless, taken in its entirety British teetotalism produced more heat than light. For all its fiery rhetoric it made precious little impact on actual levels of beer and spirit consumption. Despite dipping slightly during the recession of the early 1840s, by 1851 per capita consumption of alcohol was almost exactly the same as it had been twenty years earlier.[10] Teetotallers were undoubtedly good at publicly reclaiming drunkards: that small but significant proportion of the drinking population for whom alcohol had become a serious problem. What they failed to do, however, was make any measurable headway towards changing the drinking patterns of moderate drinkers. This posed a fundamental problem for teetotallers because, although they expended much of their energy on the reformation of 'habitual drunkards', their utopian project required the eradication of alcohol consumption in all its forms. Standing between radical teetotallers and the sober millennium was an enormous army of moderate drinkers for whom teetotal reclamation meant nothing, and to whom the likes of Joseph Livesey were nothing more than 'pharisaical prigs'.

The arch-enemy of teetotalism was the moderate drinker. Moderate drinking threatened to undermine the whole temperance project by showing that alcohol was not inherently destructive. In order to counter this, teetotallers had to depict moderate drinking as a snare which drew vulnerable drinkers into debauchery and ruin. It was easy for teetotallers to convince drunkards or their families that alcohol was the root of all evil, but it was far harder to convince the thousands of ordinary people for whom alcohol was a source of great pleasure (not to mention the centre of their social lives) that they should embark on the narrow path to sober liberation. Not surprisingly, moderate drinkers found teetotallers deeply irritating. Charles Dickens complained that the temperance movement suffered from an inability 'to distinguish between use and abuse'.[11] His feelings were typical. One London mechanic who was cajoled into attending a temperance meeting by zealous teetotal colleagues recalled sitting through a series of 'enthusiastic' speeches from an array of reclaimed drunkards culminating in an oration – which 'failed to either anger or interest' him – on the 'Evil of Moderation'.[12] It was a title which could have provided a motto for the entire teetotal campaign.

Enter prohibition

Teetotallers saw themselves as the vanguard of a two-pronged mission of salvation: to save individual drunkards through the practice of reclamation, but also to save society itself through the overthrow of King Alcohol. The problem was that while they were rather good at the first of these, they had no means whatsoever by which to achieve the second beyond an optimistic faith in progress. Their reliance on 'moral suasion' meant that they had no means at their disposal for ushering in the sober society beyond lectures and parades – hardly the most compelling alternatives to a warm night in the pub. Without bringing in a sober society, teetotalism would always be nothing more than a novel social safety net. In truth, moral suasionist teetotalism was doomed from the start by the obdurate contradiction between its goals and its methods.

John Dunlop, founder of the Glasgow Temperance Society and one of the leading figures in British temperance, saw the solution as demanding a root-and-branch assault on the cultural roots of drinking practices. In 1839 he published a monumental study of 'drinking usages' which detailed the link between workplace cultures and rituals of drink, exposing the often bizarre ways in which drinking was enforced as a workplace norm throughout Great Britain. Dunlop's novel conclusion was that much socially inscribed drinking was not, in fact, popular; rather, it was the outcome of the social pressure that drinking customs imposed on individuals. What followed was that 'Teetotalism must abolish the usages, or the usages will abolish Teetotalism'.[13] For Dunlop, social pressure created a culture of consumption which could only be destroyed on a social, not an individual, level.

Dunlop's desire to look beyond individual decision-making reflected a shift in the focus of temperance campaigning towards the wider social contexts in which drinking took place. The 'rational recreation' movement formed part of this process, and in the 1840s a number of the ideas contained in Silk-Buckingham's report made it into legislation: the Public Museums Act (1845) and the Public Libraries Act (1850) were significant steps towards the development of precisely those counter-attractions that Silk-Buckingham had called for. However, the business of enacting legislation and building local amenities was slow and arduous, and there was still no guarantee that the reading room would actually prove more of an attraction than the taproom for the majority of working men. The pace of moral suasion and counter-attraction was slow, so when the notion of prohibiting the alcohol trade started to take shape in America, frustrated temperance activists in Britain were quick to adopt the idea.

In 1851, the Quaker Governor of Maine, Neal Dow, introduced a law outlawing the sale and manufacture of alcohol. Dow, like many in the American temperance movement, sympathised with moral suasion but found that its strategies rendered it largely ineffectual. This disillusionment with moral suasion was intensified in America by the collapse of the Washingtonian movement, which had achieved spectacular levels of support in the 1840s (including the backing of a young Abraham Lincoln) but which had died back towards the end of that decade, having failed to achieve anything like the temperance reformation it had promised. Ever since the American Temperance Society had adopted a pledge promising not to supply alcohol, it had been possible to think seriously about imposing temperance on others as part of a programme of social reform. With the passing of the so-called 'Maine Law' in 1851, this idea reached fruition. Within four years similar laws had been adopted by eleven other states including Connecticut, Vermont, New Hampshire and, briefly, New York. It was a testament to the dramatic political impact of radical teetotal movements like the Washingtonians that such a law could even have been contemplated, much less enacted. The turn to legislation rather than persuasion was also, however, a testament to their failure.

In some ways this novel idea of using the law, rather than persuasion, to restrict alcohol consumption simply represented a change of strategy on the part of those who had fallen in with Washingtonians, but been disillusioned by their collapse. In truth, however, it represents far more than that. The shift from persuasion to compulsion represented a complete reconsideration of the role of the State in the management of private morality. The significance of this political shift, hidden behind what at first appeared as a mere change of tactics, only began to reveal itself, in Britain at least, when mainstream political thinkers turned their attention to the drink question after a vociferous lobbying campaign to push similar legislation through the British Parliament.

A political association

The Maine Law reignited the fire of British temperance campaigning. It sidestepped the limitations of moral suasionism by identifying the source of the problem not in drinkers, but in the drinks trade itself. While setting its sights on what looked to be a similar goal, the principle of alcohol prohibition actually inverted the moral universe of suasionism and it was never accepted by many of the leading teetotallers. Joseph Livesey denounced the sacrifice of 'the temperance cause proper' to the 'wild and impracticable scheme' of prohibition.[14] Prohibitionists insisted that sobriety was not an issue of individual moral regeneration, but rather the object of practical politics. With the rise of prohibitionism, alcohol control began to be talked about in terms of legitimate State coercion rather than individual moral choice.

The prohibitionist conception of the relationship between citizen and State may have been offensive to Joseph Livesey but it caught on quickly with many other frustrated British temperance campaigners. In 1853 a prohibitionist organisation was founded in Manchester called the United Kingdom Alliance for the Suppression of the Trade in Alcohol (a name generally shortened to 'the Alliance'). The foundation of the Alliance formalised the division between those who favoured moral suasion and those who favoured legislative action. Perhaps more importantly, however, it marked the moment at which the drink question broke into wider British political discourse. Prohibitionism posed a political question – indeed, Frederic Lees, the most serious-minded theorist of prohibition, insisted that 'the Alliance is not a temperance, but a *political* association' – and the Alliance developed a sophisticated brand of single-issue lobbying techniques.[15] As Harrison puts it,

> The Alliance, though now less well known than its predecessors the Catholic emancipation, parliamentary reform, anti-slavery and anti-corn law movements, represents the culmination – even the *reductio ad absurdum* – of the techniques elaborated by these campaigns.[16]

The Alliance began by campaigning for state-wide prohibition on the model of the Maine Law. By 1857, acknowledging perhaps that even the most wildly optimistic of their number had to take account of political reality, they switched tactics and began to campaign for the introduction of new legislation which would allow local areas to vote on whether to impose a form of prohibition regionally. Under the guidance of their indefatigable Parliamentary champion Sir Wilfrid Lawson, the Alliance drew up a so-called 'Permissive Bill' proposing just such measure, which Lawson introduced to Parliament in 1864. The Permissive Bill was defeated in 1864, and would go on being defeated as Lawson reintroduced it repeatedly over the next two decades. However, the Alliance, aiming its sights on a social revolution, was not put off by such short-term losses. Lawson's Bill put prohibition on the political map and a version of it would, forty years later, be adopted by the governing Liberal Party in an ill-fated move which brought England as close to allowing limited prohibition as it would ever get. It is a measure of the effectiveness of the Alliance that prohibition would, throughout the second half of the nineteenth century, expose deep divisions within political and cultural liberalism; divisions between those who located freedom in individual liberty (including the liberty to drink) and those who saw freedom as the outcome of progressive legislation (including prohibition), however much that progress may involve the restriction of personal liberties.

Two conceptions of liberty

Prohibition, illiberal as it may seem to a twenty-first-century mind, was based on solid liberal foundations. Prohibitionists did not believe in outlawing alcohol for the sake of their own puritanical proclivities (though this, doubtless, played a part). They believed in outlawing alcohol because they believed that, in the long run, what appeared to be an infringement on individual liberty would turn out to add greatly to the store of human freedom by releasing all individuals, even those who did not realise that they needed it, from an activity which diminished their rationality as well as their prosperity. For prohibitionists (as for moral suasionists) drink was a form of bondage disguised as freedom. Prohibition, then, was an expression of the liberal belief in enlightened progress, in this case progress towards the realisation that drink was a form of slavery, even if that progress had short-term costs. However, it also contradicted the equally liberal principles of toleration and individual freedom.

Frederic Lees tackled some of these questions head-on in an essay on prohibition which sold in significant numbers on publication in 1856. The 'best conception of Government,' Lees stated, 'includes the right and the duty of repressing socially injurious trades, whenever such trades materially interfere with the social and moral advancement of the community'.[17] Furthermore, he insisted that 'the only just liberty is "rational liberty" [and] among just examples of rational liberty, actions which are socially evil, whether evil in their issue or their tendencies, cannot be fairly included'.[18] The right of the publican to sell alcohol was, for Lees, not a natural right but merely 'the *privilege*, and the licensed liberty, of contributing to degrade his country'.[19] The correlative of all this was that, because the drinks trade was 'inherently and tremendously evil' – a claim which anti-prohibitionists flatly rejected – the State had the right and duty to repress it on the grounds that it '*must*, not only resist wrong, but do many things necessary to *prevent* wrong'.[20] Throughout his essay Lees appealed above all to Jeremy Bentham as his moral guide; however, prohibition was a concept which some of the heirs of Bentham, not least John Stuart Mill, would contest vigorously.

The battle-lines in this debate can be traced in some of the many letters that appeared in *The Times* between 1850 and 1870 on the subject of Wilfrid Lawson's Permissive Bill. In October 1856, an exchange was published between Samuel Pope, a radical Liberal MP and Secretary of the Alliance, and the liberal-minded Tory, Lord Stanley. This exchange revealed key points on which the interventionist liberalism of the Alliance clashed with the Millian liberalism of anti-prohibitionists. J. S. Mill would later comment on these letters in *On Liberty*, concluding that prohibitionism, as presented by Samuel Pope, represented a 'monstrous' theory of social rights 'far more dangerous than any single interference with liberty [as] there is no violation of liberty it would not justify'.[21]

The exchange of letters was triggered by Lord Stanley turning down an invitation to attend the annual meeting of the Alliance in Manchester. Stanley decided to make his response to the invitation public, and, while claiming to 'entirely approve' of 'the voluntary temperance movement', he outlined a list of objections to the principle of legally enforced prohibition.[22] Firstly, he argued that prohibition was impractical: that it would lead both to widespread evasion and 'contempt for law', and that it would reduce excise revenue considerably. Secondly, he argued that far from making alcohol less attractive, prohibition would turn alcohol into the source of two suspect pleasures: the pleasure of intoxication and the pleasure of resisting an unjust law. Finally, Stanley claimed that any 'moral' behaviour which resulted from legislative compulsion, rather than from autonomous choice, was not in fact moral behaviour in any meaningful way, it was simply obedience to coercion. As a consequence, however much it may ameliorate the short-term effects of drunkenness, prohibition could not contribute to genuine social progress. Warming to his theme, Stanley concluded that:

> The principle ... of personal liberty of action, permitted wherever it does not come into collision with the personal liberty of others is at once the result and guarantee of modern civilization. Encroach upon it, under whatever idea of benefiting mankind, and you will find that compulsion has produced resistance – that the best feelings of men are enlisted in support of their worst vices – that intemperance has gained defenders in those who would otherwise have been foremost to denounce it – and that you will have given to bigotry, political and religious, a precedent of which it will not be slow to avail itself.[23]

Prohibitionism, Stanley insisted, was wrong morally, practically and politically, not least because the 'absence of temptation cannot confer moral strength'.[24]

Stanley's argument rested on the common liberal presupposition that 'moral strength' or virtue consisted of a set of values that everyone would come to agree on once the right social conditions were in place. As a Millian liberal, he felt that the 'right conditions' would apply when individuals were given maximal freedom from State compulsion (allowing for the principle that their actions did not restrict the freedom of others). Samuel Pope disagreed. For him, as for all prohibitionists, the role of the State was to 'be the great educator of the habits of the people'; that is, to actively intervene in improving the moral condition of its citizens.[25] This disagreement over the role of the State in guiding the moral choices of its citizens – the conflict between what Isaiah Berlin would later call 'negative' and 'positive' conceptions of liberty – lay at the heart of liberal debates over alcohol in the second half of the nineteenth century.[26]

The idea of prohibition highlighted a fundamental problem for liberal thinkers regarding the relationship between moral responsibility and reason. Liberal moral objectivism – the belief that there were universal and knowable moral absolutes – was influenced by Immanuel Kant's argument that there were universal moral laws, and that those laws were discoverable through, and only through, the exercise of *reason*. For Kant himself, one implication of this was that one could not be held morally responsible for actions carried out while drunk. The 'actions ... of a madman or a drunkard,' he wrote 'can be attributed, though not imputed to them. In imputation the action must spring from freedom'.[27] In other words, responsibility was based on freedom, and freedom was dependent on the proper functioning of reason. To be irrational – or drunk – was to be no longer a free moral agent. The legal implication, for Kant, was that the 'drunkard cannot ... be held accountable for his actions, but he certainly can, when sober, for the drunkenness itself'.[28]

As we have seen, however, this model of moral responsibility was unsettled by the emergence of addiction discourse. This was because the idea of addiction suggests that, in some instances, individuals are not, in fact, free to decide whether to get drunk or not. In other words, drink did not only undermine moral responsibility after it had been taken, it had the potential – so long as it was held to be addictive – to undermine moral responsibility without even being ingested. This was critical to the prohibitionist argument. For prohibitionists 'the appetite for drink ... unlike every other appetite ... is never satisfied. Indulgence is not followed by satiety, but by increased craving.'[29] Prohibitionism, then, rested on the new idea that alcohol produced not just desire, but addiction.

In *On Liberty*, J. S. Mill followed Kant in arguing that while drunkenness itself was 'not a fit subject for legislative interference' it was:

[P]erfectly legitimate that a person who had once been convicted of an act of violence to others under the influence of drink should be placed under a special legal restriction, personal to himself; that if he were afterward found drunk, he should be liable to penalty.[30]

However, it was a matter of fundamental principle for Mill that drinking could only be legislated against in terms of its public effects. Drinking – in and of itself – could not be subject to legislation because the decision to drink was always taken freely. Prohibitionists disputed this, and they leapt on Mill's own famous insistence that no one should be 'free not to be free' to justify intervention to prevent drinkers from turning themselves into enslaved drunkards.[31]

In November 1868, Mill clashed with Dawson Burns – a founding member of the Alliance – in *The Times* on the subject of the Permissive Bill. Defending the Bill against Mill's public opposition, Burns complained that Mill ignored the 'indisputable peculiarity of the drink traffic, and its acknowledged connection with all the evils that impoverish, criminalise and degrade immense masses'.[32] Mill responded by reasserting his belief that 'the use or non-use of alcoholic liquors is a subject on which every sane and grown-up person ought to judge for themselves under his own responsibility'.[33] For Mill, and like-minded liberals, the job of the State was to allow individuals to make their own choices and their own mistakes so long as those choices and mistakes did not actively restrict the opportunity of others to do the same. For prohibitionists, the role of the State was actively to create the conditions in which individuals would be able to apprehend moral truths – and since that required sobriety, the State had a responsibility to outlaw the drinks trade.

As the prohibitionists pointed out, however, Mill's own arguments could also be applied in support of prohibition. Dawson Burns observed that 'if the question were one of mere personal taste (as of one kind of food in preference to another) ... the Permissive Bill could never have been drafted'.[34] It was only drafted because alcohol was not like most other commodities: it had a unique potential to create negative social impacts, and it had been shown to be, in some cases, addictive. For prohibitionists the principles of free choice did not apply to trade which, by its nature, undermined the capacity to choose freely.

Mill did not dispute either the deleterious effects of the alcohol trade or the 'great moral value of the end [temperance campaigners] pursue'.[35] What he did not accept was that, just because the boundaries of individual liberties were broken by some drinkers, it followed that *all* drinkers should be compelled to abstain. For Millian liberals, prohibition presented an unjustifiable infringement on individual liberty by insisting that moderate drinkers should also be prevented from access to alcohol – even though their drinking caused no apparent harm to anyone.

T. H. Green, perhaps the only other British philosopher who could match Mill's status as a theorist of liberalism, disagreed fundamentally. Green joined the Alliance in 1872 and became a vice-president in 1878 and his advocacy of outright prohibition hardened over time,[36] partly on the grounds that he regarded the drink question as 'that question of all others which is of the most pressing social importance in our towns'.[37] Green, like all prohibitionists, insisted that moderate drinkers would, and should, simply forgo the minor (and, at best, morally suspect) pleasure of drinking in the cause of the greater good. That greater good was, ultimately, a society freed from the primitive urges and instincts which kept the greater part of humanity in bondage.

Green's support for prohibition was in keeping with his wider political conception of the relationship between the State and individual liberty. In a famous defence of State intervention he wrote that

> Our modern legislation ... involving as it does manifold interference with free-dom of contract, is justified on the ground that it is the business of the state, not indeed directly to promote moral goodness, for that, from the very nature of moral goodness, it cannot do, but to maintain the conditions without which a free exercise of human faculties is impossible.[38]

This argument is coherent by its own lights. If one believes, as Green did, that there are objective moral absolutes, and if one believes that the understanding of those absolutes requires certain knowable conditions, then it is reasonable that the role of the State is to create those conditions. Peter Nicholson argues that the apparent contradiction between Green's belief in moral autonomy and his support for prohibition is resolved by his belief that the common good must, by definition, be the same for all.[39] Therefore, creating the conditions in which people will *choose* this good is not the same thing as moral coercion.

Prohibitionism, then, was a concrete expression of 'positive' concep-tions of liberty. It presumed that the simple expansion of individual liber-ties would merely give free reign to the worst aspects of human nature (and prohibitionists assumed, of course, that the desire to drink was never a good thing). Consequently, they saw the role of government as being to actively construct conditions which 'liberated' people from their own worst desires. As Berlin pointed out, utopian forms of positive freedom always require a grand political intervention after which those illusory desires which had previously tied humans to their worst natures would wither away, leaving behind a transformed society. Samuel Pope expressed just this sensibility, writing that the Alliance 'have faith in a millennial fu-ture, when law shall have accomplished its work, and the people trained in virtue shall be a law to themselves'.[40] Looking back from a twenty-first century perspective, we know of course that prohibition has never achieved any such thing.

Sobriety by Act of Parliament

The Alliance saw no reason to entertain concerns over the possibility that prohibition might make things worse rather than better. Their reports were that prohibition was a success in the states of America where it had been implemented. When states (including Maine and New York) repealed prohibitive legislation after 1855 prohibitionists blamed the perfidy of the drinks trade, the corruption of local officials, the lack of will among law enforcers: anything but the idea itself. This certainty as to the rightness of both its principles and its means made the Alliance formidable but also rigid and inflexible. While it threw its resources into the almost annual introduction of the Permissive Bill, and into applying pressure on MPs in marginal seats to support 'local option' (as the key provision of the Bill was known), it refused to dirty its hands engaging with the piecemeal licensing legislation that was actually being put onto the statute books. For many this represented a missed opportunity just as the backlash to the 1830 Beer Act was starting to produce concerted attempts to regain governmental control over the trade.

Perhaps its peripheral role in an embarrassing debacle over Sunday closing put the Alliance off. In 1854, a Select Committee looking at further restrictions on Sunday trading took evidence from 'several zealous promoters of an association established to procure the enactment of [the Maine Law] in England'.[41] These Alliance witnesses (including both Frederic Lees and the Alliance's founder Nathaniel Card), testified that the majority of working people wanted an extension of Sunday closing because they wanted to be spared the temptation presented by pubs for at least one day a week. The idea that working people were desperate to be saved from the temptation of the drinks trade was a key Alliance claim – and one rubbished by Livesey, who doubted that the evidence of pubs on a Saturday night pointed to a population 'in the fangs of the traffic, longing for "protection"'.[42]

The 1854 Committee, however, was persuaded and it recommended that Sunday closing be extended to include most of the afternoon and later evening. These measures were duly incorporated into a Sale of Beer Act the same year which required pubs to close between 2p.m. and 6p.m. on Sundays, and to close for the night at 9p.m. Widespread condemnation in the press, and two days of rioting in Hyde Park the following June – blamed by most observers on anger at the new Sunday closing restrictions – led to a hasty amendment reducing Sunday afternoon closing to two hours in the afternoon and extending evening opening to 11p.m. So much for a population desperate to be spared from temptation.

While the Alliance pursued its purist path of 'local option' or nothing, momentum was building for further government action to curb drunkenness. One idea was to encourage a more sophisticated approach to drinking. In 1860 Palmerstone's Liberal administration introduced an Act, supported by the then Chancellor William Gladstone, which allowed shopkeepers to apply for a special licence to retail wine, and which also allowed restaurants to sell wine to customers. Cynics saw Gladstone cosying up to his friends in the wine trade, and temperance campaigners threw their hands up in horror at the prospect of the 'grocer's licence' spawning a whole new raft of drinks outlets. However, others saw the measure as encouraging more respectable and responsible drinking. By making it possible for the lower classes to purchase wine more easily, and by making restaurants a viable alternative to the pub, the Wine and Refreshment House Act foreshadowed some of the efforts to encourage more 'continental' style of drinking in Britain over a century later. Wine consumption did increase significantly after 1860, but whether this was at the expense of other drinks is a moot point: by 1865 consumption of wine, spirits and beer were all higher than they had been five years earlier.

In 1869 the free-trade experiment of 1830 was finally repealed by the Wine and Beerhouse Act, which required all new licences to be approved by magistrates. After almost forty years it was clear that the increased competition produced by free trade had not, as the Smithian model predicted, flushed out bad traders. Instead it had dramatically increased the number of outlets selling drinks – a 'very large proportion' of which remained tied to brewers – while beer adulteration remained, according to one Select Committee report an 'almost universal' practice.[43] Gladstone, now installed as Prime Minister, did not need a temperance campaign to tell him that the licensing system was desperately in need of reform and he set out a timetable for new licensing legislation to be introduced in 1871, with the 1869 Act providing a stopgap. The hope was that a major new Licensing Act would iron out the anomalies which had crept into existing legislation and provide a robust framework for the management of all areas of alcohol retail. Gladstone may also have wanted to appear to be doing something about levels of alcohol consumption, which – despite forty years of temperance – had reached unprecedented levels, but he did not want to pick a fight with the brewers, many of whom had always seen the Liberal Party as best reflecting their interests. Unfortunately for Gladstone, when the Home Secretary Henry Bruce introduced his Licensing Bill in 1871 it triggered a debate of such intensity that it would badly damage the Liberal Party and define the relationship between temperance and mainstream politics for decades to come.

Charged with drawing up a new Licensing Bill, Bruce produced something as radical in its own way as the Beer Act of 1830. However, where the Beer Act was based on an idea of startling simplicity, Bruce's 1871 Bill proposed an extraordinarily complicated system of licences. To resolve anomalies in the existing licence scheme, Bruce proposed not to simplify things but rather to introduce a system of 'general' and 'limited' licence certificates including inn certificates, eating certificates, railway refreshment room certificates, theatre certificates, 'special refreshment room' certificates, beershop certificates and the inelegantly titled 'closed vessel retail certificates'. The Bill also put in place systems by which the role of licensee and licence manager were to be distinguished, complicated procedures for the renewal of licences at annual sessions, and a system of licence rents designed to return to local coffers some of the excess market value which tended to be added to any property after it was granted a licence. Taken alone, the complexity of the certificate and rent system would probably have been enough to ensure a rough passage for the Bill through Parliament. However, it was a radical proposal for local control of licences which caused uproar and vilification from all sides.

The 1871 Licensing Bill is a testimony to the influence that the temperance movement, and the Alliance in particular, had begun to exert at the highest political level. The key proposal in the Bill was that local ratepayers should be able to vote on the number of licences granted in their area each year. This was not the 'local option' contained in Wilfrid Lawson's Permissive Bill, but it was as close as was realistically possible at the time. Rather than allowing a two-thirds majority of local ratepayers to enforce local prohibition – which was what Lawson wanted – Bruce's Bill proposed that each year licensing authorities would publish the number of licences they intended to grant, and that a petition of one-third of local ratepayers could then trigger a ballot of the entire electorate on whether or not to accept that number of new licences. A three-fifths majority in the subsequent vote could then overturn or alter the proposed number. In addition, the Bill set out a statutory maximum number of licences for any area: one per thousand inhabitants in towns and one per six hundred elsewhere. Any attempt to grant more licences would require approval by vote. Once the number of licences was agreed, the local authorities would then tender them to the highest bidders. Finally, the Bill proposed that licences could be renewed annually for ten years, but be treated as new applications after that. In effect this made it possible for significant reductions in licences to take place every ten years, although the rigorous procedures for licence renewal also meant that zealous authorities would be able to suppress unwanted licences on an annual basis.

Were the Alliance a pragmatic campaign group, they would surely have seen Bruce's Bill as a victory: a significant step towards temperance reform which, for the first time, legally instituted the principle that licences could be subject to systematic suppression where there was clear local support for such a move. They were nothing of the sort, though. The Alliance objected to all licensing on the principle that the drinks trade was a social evil, therefore a Bill which proposed merely to make licence applications difficult, rather than impossible, was of no use to them. They dismissed Bruce's Bill as a feeble sop to the trade, and refused to give it support. The drinks industry, unsurprisingly, attacked the Bill with as much vigour as it could muster. The timing of Bruce's Bill was unfortunate: coinciding with the Paris Commune and a consequent wave of anti-'communist' feeling among British industrialists, it was a measure which the brewers were able to depict as outrageously socialist.[44] Gladstone himself seemed unimpressed by the proposed measures, perhaps all too aware that a Bill of this sort would gain few friends and make countless enemies. In a diary entry from December 1871, Bruce ruefully observed that he had 'a cabinet today, when I hope to have my Licensing Bill in its main principles definitely settled. Unfortunately Gladstone cares for nothing but "free trade" … and I cannot get him really to interest himself in the subject'.[45]

The Parliamentary debates over Bruce's Licensing Bill were tortuous and often chaotic.[46] Most famously, during a debate in the Lords the Bishop of Peterborough William Magee argued that the State had no legitimate right to try and enforce greater sobriety by statute. 'If I must take my choice … whether England should be free or sober,' the Bishop stated,

> I should say it would be better that England should be free than compulsorily sober. I would distinctly prefer freedom to sobriety, because with freedom we might in the end attain sobriety; but in the other alternative we should eventually lose both freedom and sobriety.[47]

It was a memorable expression of the principles set out previously by both Stanley and Mill, and it deeply angered prohibitionists who accused Magee of encouraging drunkenness in the name of an abstract liberal principle.

Magee's intervention was a remarkable inversion of the Alliance position that to be drunk was to be enslaved. It also carried palpable echoes of the Irish nationalist slogan 'Ireland sober is Ireland free' (and Charles Stuart Parnell would echo Magee in parliamentary debates on Irish licensing nineteen years later).[48] William Magee's comment was immediately condemned by the Alliance, but it was far closer to the prevailing opinion than that of the prohibitionists. In the midst of all this, Bruce's Licensing Bill found itself beset on all sides. The drinks trade attacked it, the Alliance attacked it, moderate liberals feared that it misjudged the balance between the rational management of public affairs and oppressive legislation,[49] and Gladstone saw a political millstone being ground out before his eyes. In the end a version of the Bill was passed in 1872, but so effectively neutered that it was hardly recognisable. The 1872 Licensing Act, as finally passed, retained original sections on adulteration, fines for drunkenness and the physical condition of public houses. It also set out new opening hours – though these were much longer than Bruce had intended – and banned the sale of spirits to children under sixteen. All mention of licence limits, variable certificates and local voting, however, were entirely removed.

The extensive revision of Bruce's Bill was not enough to appease the drinks lobby. Many powerful producers switched allegiance to the Tories, who themselves made much political capital out of depicting the Liberal administration as nanny-ish and puritanical. Disraeli enthusiastically presented the Tories as the party best placed to defend those long-cherished English freedoms of which the right to drink beer had always provided such a powerful symbol. By presenting themselves as a party set against the legislative tinkering of the Liberals, the Tories also succeeded in reinforcing the idea that the Liberals were in league with the radical temperance movement – despite the Alliance's disdain towards the 1872 Act. Exploiting fears that the Liberal Party was in cahoots with temperance zealots helped the Tories snatch the political middle ground and contributed to their victory in the General Election of 1874. In a letter to his brother Robert following this defeat, Gladstone expressed no doubt about the 'operative causes [which] have determined the elections'. 'We have', he wrote, 'been borne down in a torrent of gin and beer'.[50]

The ethics of prohibitionism

Arguments over prohibition were about practical politics, but they were also about underlying philosophical principles. Prohibitionists believed that moral responsibility was always and everywhere strangled by alcohol. The anti-prohibitionist argument also appealed to moral agency, but it did so with the crucial proviso that 'absence of temptation cannot confer moral strength'. As far as anti-prohibitionist liberals were concerned, progress was measured by the capacity to choose virtue *despite* the temptations of vice, not simply because vice was made harder to access.

This, however, required a leap of faith. Prohibitionists simply felt that, all things remaining equal, unlimited individual freedom would simply encourage the mass of humanity to get drunk. Why, they asked, should unrestrained freedom encourage sobriety? In response, Millian liberals had to fall back on versions of Mill's notoriously problematic assertion that 'those who are equally acquainted with, and equally capable of appreciating and enjoying both, do give a most marked preference to the manner of existence which employs their higher faculties'.[51] In other words, the optimistic notion that, freed from the undue influence of the State, individuals will automatically choose to indulge their 'higher' faculties – something which, in the context of the debates over prohibition, presupposed a reasonable level of sobriety. However, what was left out of the equation on all sides was the possibility that drunkenness might sometimes be – to put it simply – a good thing. Not even the most vehement opponent of temperance fanaticism publicly ascribed a positive value to intoxication; at best it was acknowledged as the sometimes harmless side effect of a legitimate indulgence. The polite assumption that sobriety was always better than drunkenness, so novel a hundred years earlier, had by the mid-nineteenth century become an unquestioned orthodoxy among the British middle class.

What gave temperance campaigners confidence in the rightness of their cause was that this consensus seemed to be an example of the 'value convergence' which drove liberal conceptions of history. The widespread adoption of conspicuous sobriety by swathes of the middle class, and a significant portion of the respectable working class, seemed to confirm the liberal belief that given the right conditions (whether achieved through 'positive' or 'negative' means) the value systems of all rational, adult humans will eventually converge because the values encapsulated in liberalism are, fundamentally, universal. By the 1850s, this assumption was already under attack from the fringes of the artistic and literary avant-garde, but it also made many working-class activists suspicious that temperance was nothing more than a frontal assault on their class culture.

We have already seen the extent to which attacks on lower-class drinking cultures can be understood as a form of social control in the sphere of everyday cultural practices. However, one has to be careful when applying simplistic models of class conflict to the drink question in the nineteenth century. Working-class drinking was the prime target of paternalistic middle-class reformers: Neal Dow's insistence at a speech in London that prohibition was 'a thousand times more important' than franchise expansion exposes that depth of condescension plainly.[52] At the same time, however, much of the fire in the belly of temperance came from its radical working-class wing. Similarly, the deep divisions between those bourgeois Victorians (such as T. H. Green) who dreamed of imposing their private sobriety on society at large and those other bourgeois Victorians (like J. S. Mill) who were horrified at the thought of prohibition suggests little class unity on this crucial area of cultural and economic activity. Free traders, social conservatives, State interventionists, libertarians, religious reformers and rational recreationists – all, by and large, good middle-class liberals – fell about themselves where the drink question was concerned.

What makes it difficult to ascribe a clear ideological role to temperance is the fact that drink produced all sorts of ideological paradoxes. Wasteful expenditure on alcohol ran counter to the principles of thrift and accumulation which, on the surface at least, drove Victorian capitalism. On the other hand, the alcohol economy was a model of efficiency: cash laid out in wages was, through the alchemy of the bottle, re-circulated to the economic benefit of all – except the worker whose cash had been so easily teased from his wallet (and who, thereby, chained himself ever tighter to the wheel of his labour while experiencing that chaining as pleasure). It is not coincidental that the public house was so often the place where wages were paid in the early nineteenth century, nor that the abolition of this custom in 1883 was one of the temperance movement's most significant contributions to social welfare. The nineteenth-century drink question pitched eminently capitalist temperance reformers against eminently capitalist brewers and publicans, and it provides a concrete example of how cultural, economic and class interests are often wildly contradictory.

As John Greenaway points out, drink tends 'to generate its own ideological schools'.[53] However, in nineteenth-century England drink was more than just a political loose cannon promiscuously attaching itself to whichever reformist cause presented itself; rather, alcohol captured contradictions in Victorian capitalism and held them up for all to see. Economic growth required both production and consumption, and the brewers were certainly some of the most active producers at work. For many Victorian liberals, the economic necessity of consumption came up hard against the need for moral responsibility in one's private and public life.[54] While this was an issue for many forms of consumption, because alcohol represented intoxication *as* a commodity, it was especially problematic. Having no material presence once consumed, and no ethical value (according to temperance campaigners, at least), but stimulating huge amounts of economic activity, alcohol presented a moral and ideological conundrum that repeatedly escaped resolution.

By focusing on the trade, rather than on the drinker, prohibitionists sparked a debate about the morality of free trade which was made all the more tortuous because few of those involved were able to recognise that underpinning all this was a debate about markets at large, not just the specific issue of alcohol use. The drink question shook the foundations of the Liberal Party in particular because no one could resolve the problem of where State licensing stopped and free-market liberties started. Prohibitionists radicalised one portion of the Liberal Party's natural constituency by presenting a utopian vision linking prohibition to the liberal progressive dream of a rational and equitable society. By doing so, they exposed deep divisions within liberal thought more broadly. On the subject of alcohol legislation leading liberals like J. S. Mill and T. H. Green could find absolutely no common ground. For Mill, alcohol consumption was a natural and morally neutral activity which the State could only restrict when it clearly encouraged other, censurable activities. For Green, drinking was only natural inasmuch as other forms of human corruption were natural, and the State had a duty to create conditions in which corruption was curtailed. There was no way to bridge these two positions. In addition, the fundamental liberal belief in free trade was thrown into confusion by the alcohol market. Once the principle was allowed that the State could outlaw a commodity, which in some but by no means all cases produced social harms, then there was no saying where that principle ended. Liberals could agree on banning slavery because they agreed there was no acceptable or 'moderate' slave-owning. They couldn't agree the same for alcohol because, as even prohibitionists had to accept, most drinkers were moderate and well-behaved. Prohibition only made sense if alcohol was inherently evil. On this there was simply no scope for compromise in terms of either principle or policy. The debates over the 1872 Licensing Act certainly did not resolve any of these contradictions, nor did they dampen the enthusiasm of temperance campaigners. As a result, the political hostilities over the management of the drinks trade continued to intensify over the following decades – leading to a period of unprecedented activity during which the relationship between the drinks trade and the State would come to occupy the centre of the political stage.

Notes

1   House of Commons, Report from the Select Committee of Inquiry into Drunkenness (1834) 559, pp. vii–ix.
2   *Ibid.*, p. iv.
3   American Temperance Society, *Permanent Temperance Documents of the American Temperance Society* (Boston, MA: Seth Bliss and Perkins, Marvin, and Co, 1835), pp. 475–86.
4   L. Armstrong, *The Temperance Reformation* (New York: Fowlers and Wells, 1858), p. 31.
5   Dunlop, *The Philosophy of Drinking Usage*, p. 2.
6   Couling, *History of the Temperance Movement*, p. 112.
7   *Ibid.*, p. 117.
8   *Ibid.*, p. 118.
9   *Ibid.*, p. 217.
10 Wilson, *Alcohol and the Nation*, p. 332.
11 C. Dickens, 'Demoralisation and total abstinence', in M. Slater (ed.), *Dickens' Journalism, Vol. 2*, p. 161.
12 T. Wright, *Some Habits and Customs of the Working Classes* www.victorianlondon. org, accessed March 2006.
13 Dunlop, *The Philosophy of Drinking Usage*, p. 288.
14 J. Livesey, *True Temperance Teaching* (London: W. Tweedie, 1873), p. 13.
15 F. R. Lees, *An Argument for the Legislative Prohibition of the Liquor Traffic* (Manchester: United Kingdom Alliance, 1856), p. 114.
16 Harrison, *Drink and the Victorians*, p. 227.
17 Lees, *An Argument for the Legislative Prohibition of the Liquor Traffic*, p. 2.
18 *Ibid.*, p. 130.
19 *Ibid.*, p. 120.
20 *Ibid*, pp. 48, 15.
21 J. S. Mill, *On Liberty* (Harmondsworth: Penguin, 1980), p. 157.
22 E. H. Stanley and S. Pope, 'Lord Stanley, M. P., and the United Kingdom Alliance'

(*Times*, 2 October 1856), p. 8.

23 *Ibid.*

24 *Ibid.*

25 *Ibid.*

26 I. Berlin, *Liberty* (Oxford: Oxford University Press, 2002).

27 I. Kant, *Lectures on Ethics*, trans. Peter Heath, ed. Peter Heath and J. B. Schweewind (Cambridge: Cambridge University Press, 1997), p. 80–1.

28 *Ibid.*

29 Stanley and Pope, 'Lord Stanley, M. P., and the United Kingdom Alliance', p. 8.

30 Mill, *On Liberty*, p. 167.

31 *Ibid.*, p. 173; P. Nicholson, 'T. H. Green and state action: Liquor legislation', *History of Political Thought*, 6:3 (1985), 517–50, p. 536.

32 J. S. Mill and D. Burns, 'Mr Mill upon the Permissive Bill' (*Times*, 10 November 1868), p. 4.

33 *Ibid.*

34 *Ibid.*

35 *Ibid.*

36 R. Bellamy, *Liberalism and Modern Society* (Pennsylvania, PA: Penn State University Press, 1992), p. 41.

37 Cited in Nicholson, 'T.H. Green and state action', p. 517.

38 Bullock and Schock, *The Liberal Tradition*, p. 183.

39 Nicholson, 'T. H. Green and state action'.

40 Stanley and Pope, 'Lord Stanley, M. P., and the United Kingdom Alliance', p. 8.

41 House of Commons, *Report from the Select Committee on Public Houses* (1854) 367, p. xvi.

42 Livesey, *True Temperance Teaching*, p. 5.

43 House of Commons, *Report of the Select Committee of the House of Lords Appointed to Consider the Operation of the Acts for the Sale of Beer* (1850) 398, p. iv; House of Commons *Report from the Select Committee on Public Houses* (1854) 367, pp. ix, vii.

44 Harrison, *Drink and the Victorians*, p. 267; Greenaway, *Drink and British Politics*, p. 33.

45 J. Morely, *The Life of William Ewart Gladstone, Vol. III* (Edinburgh: Constable, 1903), p. 390.

46 Harrison, *Drink and the Victorians*, p. 275.

47 Cited in *ibid.*, p. 293.

48 Malcolm, *Ireland Sober, Ireland Free*, p. 271.

49 Harrison, *Drink and the Victorians*, p. 292.

50 Morely, *The Life of William Ewart Gladstone*, p. 495.

51 J. S. Mill, *Utilitarianism* (Oxford: Oxford University Press, 1998), p. 56.

52 Anon., 'The Maine Liquor Law' (*Times*, 21 May 1867), p. 7.

53 Greenaway, *Drink and British Politics*, p. 5.

54 M. Hilton, 'The legacy of luxury: Moralities of consumption since the eighteenth century', *Journal of Consumer Culture*, 4:1 (2004), 101–23, p. 106.

10

The State and the trade: the drink question at the turn of the century

It has come to be a struggle for mastery between the State and a trade, and the time has fully come for a decision of the question – Who is to be master? (Arthur Wellesley Peel)

Every government that has ever touched alcohol has burnt its fingers in its lurid flames. (David Lloyd George)

When, in 1903, Sidney and Beatrice Webb described the late eighteenth century as 'the most remarkable episode in the whole history of public-house licensing in England' they were wrong. What they had no way of realising was that they, in fact, were right in the middle of that most remarkable episode. The period between 1880 and 1918 saw the political furore over alcohol reach a level of intensity not seen before or since. It was a period that would see prohibitory legislation put on the statute books for the first time, the passing of legislation formalising arrangements for the reduction of licences, and the State itself taking direct control not only of licensing regulations, but the actual ownership of breweries and pubs. It would see the Liberal Party repeatedly stake its reputation on the drink question (and repeatedly suffer as a result), and a parade of leading politicians publicly identify the drink question as the single most important social problem facing the country.

The battleground on which the drink question was fought out in this period was the bigger political question of the relationship between the State and a trade which, to many, seemed to have run out of all control. It was a fear famously summarised by Lord Rosebery's assertion, made soon after becoming Prime Minister in 1894, that 'if the State does not soon control the liquor traffic, the liquor traffic will control the State'.[1] The collapse of the 1830 free trade experiment and the reassertion of licensing authority had shown, incontrovertibly, that the State was involved in the alcohol trade whether it liked it or not. The question that beset reformers around the turn of the century concerned the extent and nature of what that involvement should be. Prohibitionists, having put their eggs in the 'local option' basket, argued that control over the trade should be devolved to the local level: that licensing should be run by regional plebiscite. Others argued that the State should take direct control of the alcohol industry at either a national or municipal level by literally buying up brewers and retailers and running the trade as a non-profit making concern. Others still argued for State power to be vested in the local justices and their autonomous capacity to manage the number and nature of licences in their area. Whatever position people took, the idea that there was, or could be, such a thing as a free trade in alcohol became an absurdity. In this period the drink question once again acted as a test case for the concept of an unregulated market; once again, it showed that such a thing doesn't exist.

The sheer scale of activity in this period is daunting. Navigating the complexities of disinterested management schemes, municipalisation, local veto, monopoly value, compensation and State management projects is not an easy task. However, the debate on drink at this time was framed by a number of identifiable principles, which give shape to what can otherwise look like a bewildering array of plans and proposals carried on with no apparent political logic at all. These principles, framed as questions, are set out below.

Firstly: *does the State, while retaining free-trade principles, have a right to directly reduce the scale of the trade in alcohol?* State management up to this point operated through licensing alone. More direct intervention meant the State-sanctioned reduction (or 'suppression') of the number of licensed premises by licensing authorities. This raised the question of compensation: if the State, working through licensing authorities, was to directly intervene to close businesses, did it owe those businesses compensation?

The second question, put by prohibitionists, was: *should the trade in alcohol be placed under the direct control of local populations?* Although licensing magistrates acted on behalf of the State, they were unelected and, therefore, undemocratic. Many temperance groups argued for the creation of at least partially elected licensing boards to ameliorate this problem. The prohibitionist solution was far more radical because it implied a particular model of the relationship between the citizenry and business. Local option not only proposed a ban on alcohol, but the idea that an otherwise free retail trade should be put under direct democratic control.

The third principle put forward by those in favour of direct State control of the drinks trade was: *should the profit motive be removed from the alcohol trade?* In our contemporary world of global trade liberalisation this concept seems extraordinary. Nevertheless, it was a principle adhered to by numerous social reformers and leading politicians at the turn of the nineteenth century. That such a concept is, in both practical and ideological terms, more or less unthinkable today shows just how much the world has changed.

When placed under the microscope, many of the political decisions made at this time can be seen as driven partly by the vagaries of circumstance, short-term political manoeuvring, and the demands of self-protection. Compelling evidence for this is set out in studies by both John Greenaway and David Gutzke.[2] However, short-term decisions are made in the context of broader social and ideological contexts. It would have been of no tactical use for Liberal ministers to pander to prohibitionists if the idea of prohibition had not acquired real political currency, just as there would have been no political advantage to be gained by Wellington in promoting the 1830 Beer Act had free trade been off the political radar at the time. It is the way in which legal and political decisions act as a barometer for underlying social and political concerns which will provide the focus here.

Sharp v. Wakefield

Temperance groups loved to depict the 'trade' as a leviathan: immovable, venal and corrupt. The truth, however, is that while the trade was indeed economically and politically powerful, as a lobbying body it was both less well-organised and less well-financed than the temperance movement.[3] The Alliance in particular had substantial funds which it ploughed into the vigorous lobbying of sympathetic politicians and the equally vigorous harassment of opponents. They also had an extremely efficient publicity machine, and very able writers such as Frederic Lees and Dawson Burns, which meant that the Alliance position always got into the public domain. The trade, by comparison, was often its own worst enemy. It was disorganised, it had a terrible public image, and, apart from the County Brewers Society, founded in 1822, it had never bothered to put in place organisations which could respond to the economic, political and legal threats it faced.

Change began to occur in the early 1870s with the establishment of the Licensed Victuallers Defence League (LVDL). This was the first time the retail side of the trade began to organise itself, but it was hardly an effective body. Largely provincial and perennially underfunded, the LVDL was set up to defend publicans against threats posed by magistrates and politicians, but it also targeted the economic threat from off-licences.[4] Indeed, the one thing that publicans and temperance reformers could agree on was that they both hated off-licences. For temperance campaigners they represented a new threat to public sobriety, especially as they weakened social taboos on women purchasing alcohol in public houses. Similarly, publicans saw them as competition and were also aggrieved at the way that off-licences were immune to many of the licensing restrictions placed on pubs. A House of Lords Committee on Intemperance, reporting in 1879 confirmed that where full on-licence applications could be refused at the discretion of local justices, off-licence applications could only be denied in the case of bad character, disorderly conduct or legal disqualification. It was an injustice that publicans felt deeply and which exposed the myth that 'the trade' was a homogenous body with identical interests across the board.

The anomaly regarding magisterial control of off-licences was largely rectified by an Act of 1882 which gave justices the same powers of discretion regarding the grant of off-licences as they currently had regarding full on-licences. Many publicans saw the 1882 Act as opening up the possibility that the proliferation of off-licences could be stemmed, and their economic threat restricted. Soon after the law was changed the Licensed Victuallers Defence League, in collaboration with temperance campaigners, brought forward a legal case which tested whether this were true. It was the first action in a series of events which would end up backfiring badly on landlords.

In August 1882, publicans in the town of Lancashire town of Darwen appealed to the local justices for clarification as to whether annual applications for the renewal of off-licences should be treated as completely new applications, and therefore be made subject to the discretionary powers that magistrates now had over the granting of off-licences. The justices sitting at the Brewster Session decided that annual off-licence renewals should be treated as if they were new applications, and they agreed that – using the discretionary powers invested in them by the 1882 Act – they would refuse to renew 34 of the 72 off-licences put before them. Presiding over an appeal from a licensee, the senior judge William Ventris Field confirmed that 'every licence is a new licence, although granted to a man who has had one before, for it is only granted for one year'. Consequently, when both granting new licences *and* when approving the annual renewal of existing licences 'the legislature meant to vest the absolute discretion in the justices'.[5] It was, apparently, a decisive victory for the publicans. They had, in one stroke, effected the closure of almost half the off-licences in Darwen. According to the legal advisor to the Darwen justices at the time, the Licensed Victuallers Defence League quickly used the judgement to attack the Permissive Bill, claiming that the Darwen judgment showed that local justices already had the power to reduce licences and so no new legislation was needed.[6]

It was, however, a pyrrhic victory. The following year a petition of over half the registered voters in Darwen was presented to the Brewster Session requesting a similar reduction in on-licences. The petition was unsuccessful, but as Thomas Nash – legal adviser to the LVDL – commented a few weeks later in the *Morning Advertiser* the 'unfortunate result of the Darwen case was that it … divulged what had hitherto been, more or less, a professional secret – viz. that, subject to appeal, licensing magistrates can refuse to renew the licence of any and every holder of an on-licence'.[7] In other words, what the actions of the LVDA in Darwen revealed was that the right to run a public house of any kind was a gift from the State which lasted just one year at a time.

The implications of this were potentially enormous and four years later a test case was taken all the way to the House of Lords. In September 1887 the licensing justices at Kendal refused to renew a licence for an inn in Kentmere on the grounds that it was too remote to be supervised properly and that the local area did not require an inn in that location. The owner of the licence appealed to the Quarter Sessions, but they confirmed the decision. The case, now titled *Sharp v. Wakefield*, was taken to the Queen's Bench the following April, and was presided over by the same judge who heard the Darwen appeal, William Ventris Field. Field had not changed his opinion. Local justices, he insisted, 'are perfectly unfettered in the exercise of their discretion' regarding both new licences and the annual renewal of existing licences.[8] The case was taken to the Court of Appeal where William Brett, Master of the Rolls, concurred with Field and added that so far as licences were concerned 'not renewing is not taking away; it is not giving'.[9] The House of Lords upheld the judgment in March 1891, establishing its principles finally in law.

Legally, *Sharp v. Wakefield* was a turning point because it established once and for all that local magistrates did not just have the right to refuse new licence applications, they also had the right not to renew existing licences as well. In theory it meant that local justices could proactively *reduce* the number of licensed premises in their area simply by refusing to renew existing licences while refusing to grant new ones. Of course, licensing practice didn't suddenly become a tool for the blanket suppression of public houses. However, many authorities had taken a firmer line with licensees since the power of licensing justices had been bolstered in 1872. According to the 1879 Select Committee on Intemperance, magistrates had certainly 'become more alive to the importance of the licensing question', and in Birmingham the local authority, under its Liberal mayor Joseph Chamberlain, had been pro-active in encouraging a reduction in licences.[10] Across the country, pub numbers had already begun to stagnate despite an ongoing increase in population.[11] *Sharp v. Wakefield* contributed to this trend by further strengthening the arm of magistrates.

However, simply reducing the number of pubs never led directly to a reduction in consumption; often it simply meant that new and existing pubs were enlarged and made more efficient. Certainly, consumption levels of beer and spirits continued to spiral upwards throughout the period reaching a peak in the remarkably drink-sodden year of 1877, when collected beer, spirits and wine consumption reached levels unmatched before or since. Consumption dipped slightly in the 1880s, but revived the following decade. By the end of the nineteenth century the average per capita consumption of spirits was just over 1 gallon annually; per capita consumption of beer was 32½ gallons a year.[12]

The hard-line prohibitionists at the Alliance never had any respect for tinkering with licensing law, and the signal failure of the licensing authorities, however draconian their powers, to stem the consumption of alcohol only served to bolster their argument that the entire system had to be demolished and rebuilt from scratch. For prohibitionists *Sharp v. Wakefield* was a sideshow. What they wanted was local option – the right of local voters to decide directly and absolutely whether or not alcohol was to be sold in their area at all. Just a few months after the *Sharp v. Wakefield* judgment was passed down, the National Liberal Federation in Newcastle adopted local option as official policy. For many prohibitionists, it looked like their boat was about to come in.

Local option

There is an irony in the adoption of local option as a policy by the National Liberal Federation (NLF). The NLF was set up by Joseph Chamberlain as a way of bringing the grass-roots of the Party into the centre of decision-making, but Joseph Chamberlain was, as we shall see, one of the Alliance's most trenchant opponents. Nevertheless, the so-called Newcastle Programme drawn up by the NLF in 1891 contained, among its smorgasbord of policies, a commitment to local option which, when the Liberal Party won the 1892 Election on the Newcastle Programme platform, became official government policy.

While many senior Liberals were uncomfortable hitching their party to the principle of local prohibition others, such as the Chancellor William Harcourt, were enthusiastic. Harcourt told his constituents in Derby that the 'one subject above all which lies near to my heart and engages my most earnest attention' was nothing other than local option.[13] William Gladstone had voted alongside Harcourt in favour of Lawson's 'local veto' resolution in 1883 – although, like many other Liberal MPs, he may have backed Lawson as a sop to the Alliance knowing full well that nothing was going to come of it at that stage. Herbert Asquith, then Home

Secretary, joined Harcourt in drawing up a 'local option' Bill which was eventually put to Parliament in 1895, as did the more established pro-Alliance MPs George Trevelyan and Thomas Burt (who had presided over the Alliance's annual meeting in 1892). The distinction between 'local option' and 'local veto' was that 'local veto' meant a single vote on whether to allow or ban the sale of alcohol in the area, while local option included the option to limit the number of licences as an alternative to an outright ban. It was a fuzzy distinction, and one lost on many bemused observers (especially when terms such as 'direct veto' were thrown into the mix).[14] The Alliance were not keen on local option but it is that rare example of a principle on which they were prepared to compromise.

Whatever swung the public vote in favour of the Liberals in 1892 (land reform, Home Rule, education policy or licensing law), the Alliance saw the 1892 Liberal Election success as *their* victory. Addressing the annual meeting of the Alliance that year, Wilfrid Lawson claimed the new Parliament had given the Alliance 'a clear majority for the direct veto' and that the 'party in power knew it would not have been there but for the support of the prohibitionists'.[15] Indeed, Harcourt lost no time in drafting a local veto Bill, and he put one before Parliament in 1893. Temperance campaigners lobbied hard in support and gathered over 600,000 signatures in petitions backing the measure. The trade, however, was prepared this time. While the Alliance spent around £17,000 lobbying in support of local veto, the trade spent around £21,000 and gathered well over one million signatures against the Bill.[16] This was the first time a governing party had presented explicitly prohibitionary legislation to Parliament. The Bill was abandoned before its second reading.

The Liberal Party was not obligated to the Alliance (whatever Wilfrid Lawson said), nor was it dominated by fanatical teetotallers. However, the strategic decision on the part of the Alliance to promote prohibition at a local level, although taken initially as a purely expedient measure in the face of the impossibility of nationwide legislation, touched on a real nerve for the Liberal Party. George Trevelyan, as far back as 1872, had prophesied that the Liberal Party 'in spite of its antecedents, in spite of its fancied interests, in spite of itself, must ere long become a temperance party'.[17] One reason for this was that that Party owed an unimpeachable 'allegiance to the great principle which is the key-note of all Liberalism, the paramount and unlimited authority of popular control'.[18] As John Greenaway has pointed out, in 'advocating local veto, prohibitionists … helped reposition the Drink issue in terms of local government'.[19] Local veto and local option were experiments in devolved democracy which greatly attracted many Liberals and which held out the promise of a radical take on a seemingly intractable social problem.

The failure of the 1893 Bill only hardened the attitude of the Alliance. The Liberal MP, and acerbic Alliance advocate, W. S. Caine was in sabre-rattling mood when he told the annual Alliance conference in 1894 that 'they were in the position now, not to request, but to demand their measure from the Government, whom they helped to create'.[20] When Harcourt, Asquith, Trevelyan and Burt presented a redrafted Bill to Parliament in 1895, this time based on local option rather than local veto, they did so with the explicit backing of the Government. Anomalies, such as the suspiciously snobby exclusion of inns and eating-houses, had been expunged and the option of limiting, as opposed to prohibiting, alcohol retail had been added to the provisions of the Bill. Sponsored by men who had all, in one way or another, publicly declared the need to take on the trade, the Bill was never fully tested in Parliament because the administration collapsed before it reached a second reading. However, when the Liberals were trounced at the subsequent election, many saw it as a popular judgement on their decision to back local option.

In reality, the Liberals were defeated in 1895 for a variety of reasons, not least Home Rule. Nevertheless, many leading figures such as Herbert Gladstone saw local option as one of the 'heaviest burdens the Liberal Party had to bear' in 1895 and the defeat went a long way towards killing off prohibition as a plank of Liberal policy.[21] It also reopened old schisms between prohibitionists and their detractors within the temperance movement.[22] Whatever the machinations of the trade, local option proved politically unpopular and it became increasingly clear to temperance activists that it may well not be practical in Britain anyway. Joseph Rowntree and Arthur Sherwell's influential book *The Temperance Problem and Social Reform* (which went through nine editions between April 1899 and December 1900) looked in depth at local prohibition in America and decided that it was simply impractical in large urban areas.[23] While the Alliance stuck, as ever, to its guns the wider temperance movement began to look for more practicable alternatives to either the hopeful moral suasion of their earliest forebears or the militant prohibitionism of the Alliance.

The approach taken by the influential Church of England Temperance Society (CETS) was to campaign for licensing reform. The CETS backed enforced reductions in pub numbers, and further restrictions on opening hours, Sunday trading and the sale of alcohol to children. It also lobbied for establishment of locally elected licensing boards – an idea dismissed by the Alliance as 'peddling legislation'.[24] The CETS took the socially conservative line (hardly surprising for an organisation which had Queen Victoria as a patron) that while total abstention was a fine ideal, the role of the State was primarily to empower its devolved bodies to place rigorous controls on the excesses of the alcohol market. As far as the CETS was concerned, the pub was basically a bad place and its functions should be shackled as tightly as was possible by the local authorities.

This all went well with the middle- and upper-class membership of the CETS who never really had occasion to use pubs, and never truly understood their appeal. The problem was that, like all restrictive temperance groups, the CETS simply made no effort to grasp the fact that for vast numbers of people the pub was not just a necessary evil, it was a positive good. It failed to take seriously the idea that most people went to pubs not because they had to, but because they wanted to; and that the desire to go to pubs, while often driven by the paucity of alternatives and the squalor of home life, was not always driven by such things. People were not goaded into pubs: they went because they liked them, they liked the company, and they liked the drink. While just about everyone agreed on the need to provide counter-attractions for the working class so that the pub was not their *only* place of leisure, few temperance groups were willing to countenance the idea that there was some virtue in retaining the pub, albeit transformed, as a valid social institution. Nevertheless, from 1892 – just as the Alliance thought they had prohibition in their grasp – it was this very idea which began to establish itself as the most realistic way forward for the campaign to make England sober.

Disinterested management

There had never been consensus in the Liberal Party on local option, not even among those for whom the drink question was a pressing concern. In a pamphlet which outlined his proposals for the municipalisation of the drinks trade in Birmingham, Joseph Chamberlain described the Alliance as 'the worst friends of temperance which the cause has'.[25] Chamberlain had already overseen the municipal purchase of key utilities in Birmingham, and it was a project he wanted to extend to the alcohol business. 'You see,' he wrote:

> I want to treat the drink question as we have treated the gas question. I want to buy up existing interests, and carry on the trade for the benefit of the people; but with this distinction – that whereas our object is secured in the case of gas when we have tempted the largest possible number of persons to increase their consumption to the greatest possible extent, our object in the drink traffic is to reduce consumption to a minimum.[26]

This project was entirely in keeping with Chamberlain's unshakeable belief in the need for direct intervention in the management of key industries. However, he was also influenced by an experiment in Sweden that was beginning to gain attention among temperance campaigners in

England. It was a version of this experiment, which came to be known as the 'Gothenburg system', which Chamberlain hoped to carry out.

The Gothenburg system first came to public attention in the late 1870s, partly because of the interest expressed in it by the Select Committee on Intemperance. Put simply, the Gothenburg system arose out of legislation passed by the Swedish parliament in 1855 allowing for the establishment of private companies which were empowered to buy up the spirits trade in specific localities in order to run it on a not-for-profit basis. In 1865 the city of Gothenburg voted to support the creation of just such a company, known as the 'Bolag'. By 1868, the Bolag had acquired all sixty-one of Gothenburg's public-house licences. Eighteen of them were closed, twenty-seven were kept open and sixteen turned into hotels, clubs and restaurants.[27] The key point is that where bars remained open, the managers were no longer self-employed. Instead they became salaried employees of the Bolag, which meant that they no longer had any financial interest in pushing the sale of spirits. When the bar was their own business, owners had good reason to encourage customers to drink as much as possible since higher sales meant higher profits. Under the Bolag system, any profits made from the sale of spirits (though not from food or beer) went straight to the municipality to be absorbed into the local coffers. Managers' wages stayed the same whatever happened.

The actual effectiveness of the Gothenburg system in reducing consumption was never clear-cut. Reporting to Parliament in 1877, Henry Selwyn Ibbetson found that the consumption of spirits in Gothenburg had increased dramatically after 1866 and that many local papers condemned the scheme as a failure.[28] Local authorities blamed the increase on greater prosperity and asked sceptics, perhaps fairly, to consider what the figures would have looked like had the scheme not been introduced. Sales of spirits did fall significantly thereafter, but the sale of beer more than doubled in the last quarter of the century and arrests for drunkenness went up, although, as many commentators agree, arrests for drunkenness are a notoriously unreliable way of measuring actual consumption, reflecting as they do patterns of police practice as much as the activities of drinkers.[29] In Bergen, Norway, a more rigorous version of the Gothenburg system was applied in which licensed premises were stripped down to their most basic and unappealing and in which profits were not allowed to go towards the reduction of local rates, hence removing an anomaly in the original version which meant that while individual managers had no interest in pushing the spirit trade, tax-payers as a body certainly did.

When Joseph Chamberlain gave evidence to the Select Committee on Intemperance in 1877, he proposed a typically municipal version of Gothenburg. Rather than set up a private company to run the pubs of

Birmingham, Chamberlain suggested that the municipality itself buy up the drinks interest and run it as a municipal concern. Chamberlain had already put the proposal to Birmingham's local council and it had agreed the plan by a large majority. The Select Committee was equally impressed and while its final report rejected the other licensing schemes put before it (free licensing, local option and licensing boards), it recommended that legislation be put in place to allow Chamberlain to try his ideas out. When Chamberlain tentatively put his plans to Parliament, however, they failed to gain momentum and no legislation was forthcoming. For the rest of the 1880s interest in the Gothenburg system petered out, and Chamberlain turned his considerable energies in other directions.

The issue re-emerged in 1892 in the unlikely form of a letter to *The Times* from the then Bishop of Chester, Francis John Jayne. Jayne's letter, published on 2 August, argued that while those 'who take a darker view of alcohol may be justified in advocating its total prohibition ... the large majority of thoughtful men allow that its moderate use has much to say for itself, and that in any case the deep-rooted habits of the nation are to be modified rather than set at defiance'. Jayne's larger argument was that 'private enterprise cannot bear the weight of [the] vast national responsibility' of running the country's public houses. Instead, he insisted that the State should step in to provide pubs which contained 'comfortable, spacious, well-ventilated accommodation', where 'newspapers, indoor games and ... music' would be available, and where the financial interests of the managers would 'depend entirely on the sale of eatables and non-alcoholic beverages'.[30]

This was radical stuff: a leading churchman suggesting that not only might pubs have an intrinsic value, but that the State should become, in effect, the nation's publican. It is no surprise that Dawson Burns had penned a lengthy condemnation of the proposals on behalf of the Alliance within days. In response, Jayne reiterated his views in a second letter to *The Times* insisting that 'it would be worse than folly to shut our eyes to the achievements of the Gothenburg system, and to refuse it a fair trial in this country'.[31] The CETS was horrified to read that an Anglican Bishop was seriously advocating constructive support to improve public houses; 'in God's name,' appealed its Treasurer, 'do not induce the working men to use "the public" as a club house ... the real centre of a man's life should be, for his own sake, for his family's sake, and his country's sake, his home'.[32] In October 1892, Jayne was even called before a convention of the Church hierarchy in Shrewsbury to explain himself. He insisted that he 'did not represent a movement outside the Church of England Temperance Society', but there was no discernable way that his support for the Gothenburg system could be reconciled with the CETS's demanded for purely restrictive reform.[33]

Jayne's intervention, coupled no doubt with increasing concern over the parliamentary successes of the Alliance, led to a renewed interest in the Gothenburg system and the whole idea of disinterested management. Even Joseph Chamberlain – who by now had other political fish to fry, not least leading the Liberal Unionist opposition to Gladstone's plans for Home Rule – returned to his old theme, calling for the establishment of a 'Public-house Reform Association' and blaming his lengthy silence on the subject on the 'hostility of the temperance party'.[34] To the Alliance, Jayne's proposals may have been 'sheer quackery',[35] but they struck a chord with many who saw them as a way out of a destructive impasse between all-or-nothing prohibitionists on the one hand and increasingly determined trade interests on the other.

Joseph Rowntree and Arthur Sherwell came out in favour of disinterested management, although they objected to Jayne's notion that pubs should be made pleasant and attractive; they approved instead of the sparse and depressing type of pub developed by the authorities in Bergen, where 'not even seats are provided, nor are customers permitted to loiter on the premises'.[36] The Duke of Westminster, who had presided over the 1879 Select Committee and who had enforced the closure of all but eight of the forty-seven pubs on his Mayfair estate, joined up with Jayne and Chamberlain in supporting a Gothenburg-inspired scheme of reform.

In 1896 Jayne founded the People's Refreshment House Association (PRHA). His goal was to create a company which, while not incorporating the municipal principles of the Gothenburg system, did introduce a system of disinterested management. Funded by shareholders who would receive a maximum 5 per cent dividend on their investment, it bought up pubs and employed managers whose salaries were not dependent on sales. Additional profits were returned in the form of small donations to local communities surrounding PRHA pubs. Jayne's organisation was reasonably successful but extremely limited in scope, only ever buying up a handful of businesses. In 1901, the Central Public House Trust (CPHT) was founded along similar lines to the PRHA, but with greater ambition and a more robust organisational structure. The CPHT oversaw the activities of a series of regional Public House Trusts which, similarly to the PRHA, bought or opened pubs on the basis of shareholder investment and salaried management. The attraction of Public House Trusts to shareholders was that they got to invest in a company which promised reasonably high returns while ostensibly promoting the eminently respectable cause of temperance. This was a far cry from Chamberlain's municipalisation, and, as critics pointed out, the pubs involved still produced profits for investors, but it was an experiment in both disinterested management and the development of a retail model which did not rely absolutely on the unlimited sale of alcohol.[37]

Bricks and mortar

Nevertheless, the number of establishments opened by these Gothenburg-inspired companies was, in the grand scheme of things, miniscule. By 1914 there were a grand total of 250 trust houses in England and Wales: hardly enough to match the number of pubs in a couple of London boroughs at the same time.[38] In the 1890s, as disinterested management campaigners vied with their opponents in the prohibitionist camp, the brewers themselves were undercutting both by turning themselves from private into public companies. In 1886 Guinness had floated itself on the stock market. The shares were oversubscribed fifty times and the flotation raised £6 million for the company.[39] The Guinness flotation sent a shockwave through the British brewing industry, triggering off a spate of similar flotations by the other brewing giants as well as a raft of mergers between leading companies. The profits generated were enormous, and the impact was significant. By the mid-1890s all the brewing giants were publicly owned, and they all had money to invest in expanding their operations. Fortunately for the brewers, the market in the 1890s was buoyant and met their increased capacity for production. However, as we have seen previously, individual brewers relied on vertical integration to protect their markets: that is, they relied on controlling the supply as well as the production, the pubs as well as the breweries. With plenty of capital to spend, the large brewers became embroiled in a fierce competition to build, buy and develop licensed premises, which triggered a property boom of spectacular proportions.

Competition between brewers for ownership of licensed premises saw property prices spiral dramatically in the late 1890s and early 1900s, and it ensured that, whatever might be going on in the handful of Gothenburg-inspired pubs, the thousands of tenants and managers installed by breweries in their tied houses were most certainly interested in profits. A number of factors drove this price inflation and the competitive practices that ensued. One of these, ironically, was the success temperance organisations had achieved in gaining influence over the management of licences at a local level.

Sharp v. Wakefield had confirmed that licensing authorities had complete discretion in the grant of licences, and it had increased the confidence of many justices in using their powers more punitively. The influence of respectable temperance organisations like the CETS, however, also began to be felt at a local level. The CETS had always campaigned for reductions in licence numbers, and it was an organisation whose membership was dominated by precisely the kind of respectable, Anglican and socially conservative classes who packed the licensing benches of the country. The very fact that, towards the end of the nineteenth century, increasing numbers of local justices began to implement temperance principles and put restrictions on the number of licences they granted meant that those licences which were granted became increasingly valuable. As justices became more hawkish, and brewers more competitive, the market price for properties which possessed a licence shot up in value. Rowntree and Sherwell listed examples of astronomic price inflation for licensed properties: the price of one house, valued in 1897 at £3,500, increased to £24,500 as soon as a licence was granted.[40] While local option floundered at the polls, and disinterested management schemes sputtered into ineffectual life, the reticence of local justices to grant licences in large numbers coupled with the increasing range of counter-attractions for customers to choose from meant that brewers were more desperate than ever to shore up their economic base by attracting customers into their pubs.

Vested interests

Between 1900 and 1903, licensing magistrates across the country started taking on the trade to an unprecedented degree. As in previous periods of licensing restriction, justices attempted to suppress a popular institution (the pub or alehouse) backed by more or less powerful brewers eager to defend their markets. So far as the pub, as a social institution, was concerned little had changed. Once again a social class who had no cultural investment in the public house launched an attack on an institution they saw as both distasteful and socially damaging. This time, however, the brewers were a different animal. Since becoming public companies they were able to claim that their interests were the interests of their shareholders – good, middle-class shareholders at that.[41] Because they had invested so heavily in property, they were also able to claim that the well-being of their shareholders rested heavily on the value of the licensed properties the brewery owned. The shareholders' investments had gone into buying up properties which, because of the restrictions imposed by licensing justices, were inflated in value. Despite *Sharp v. Wakefield*, brewers argued that justices who refused to renew licences were not simply destroying the livelihood of the licensee, they were punishing brewers, landlords and investors (often depicted in the trade literature as frugal widows and housewives) by stripping licensed properties of thousands of pounds of value.

This additional value which accrued to licensed properties became known as 'monopoly value'. The 'monopoly value' of a licensed premises was the amount added to its market value by the fact that it possessed a licence. So, in the case of the example given by Rowntree and Sherwell cited above, the monopoly value was the difference between the £3,500 the house was worth on its own and the £24,500 it was worth with a licence. Brewers and publicans argued that because stripping a property of its licence effectively meant stripping it of a large part of its market value as well, anyone who had an application for licence renewal refused by justices for reasons other than misconduct or mismanagement, should be compensated accordingly. The argument ran that if licensing authorities wanted to reduce the number of pubs in their area, they should compensate the people whose livelihoods and investments they destroyed along the way. The fact that the investors were now 'the public' added considerable weight to the brewers' case.

Continued concern over the seemingly intractable drink question had led to the establishment of yet another committee of inquiry in 1897. The Royal Commission on Licensing was chaired by Arthur Wellesley Peel, a man chosen for his neutrality on the subject. By the time it concluded in 1899, it had heard from more than 250 witnesses over 134 sittings. Lord Peel had come down on the side of temperance, and the rest of the Commission had become so divided that it was unable to produce a single report acceptable to all members. In the end, the Commission produced two. A minority report was signed by Peel, the erstwhile temperance campaigners Thomas Whittaker and William Caine, and six others. The majority report was signed by the rest of the Commission, which included a number of leading brewers. Both reports agreed that the Government had to legislate to enforce a reduction in the number of licensed premises. However, Peel's minority report set out a clear limit for the number of pubs that should be allowed (1 per 750 inhabitants in towns and 1 per 400 elsewhere) whereas the majority report merely stated that 'the number of licensed houses should be largely reduced'.[42] More critically, the two reports differed on the issue of compensation. The majority report called for a tax on licences which would create a fund out of which compensation would be paid to anyone stripped of their licence as part of a general reduction in numbers. The minority report also called for a compensation fund financed by a tax on the trade, but it wanted a seven-year time limit on any compensation payments, after which justices should be able to close premises without compensation and after which 'the field would be clear for any legislation, experimental or otherwise, that Parliament might be disposed to enact'.[43]

At first sight the issue of whether there should be a time limit on compensation for people whose licences were not renewed seems a relatively minor issue. However, it would become the most contentious question in the debates over alcohol policy for the next ten years; a principle over which vast amounts of ink would be spilt, over which the trade would once again flex its considerable political muscle, and one to which the Liberals would once again hitch their political fortunes.

Why did the ostensibly obscure question of a time limit for compensation payments matter so much to so many people? The answer can be found in the wording of Peel's minority report. Peel insisted that compensation was not a right, but rather a 'matter of grace and expediency'.[44] The trade, by contrast, argued that compensation was a right: licensees invested or managed their finances in the expectation that their properties were worth a certain market value; if the State stepped in and reduced that market value by withdrawing the licence, then it owed the licensee compensation as a matter of natural justice.

It was this idea that compensation was a right which provoked fury among those calling for a time-limit. The point was that the grant of a licence to sell alcohol was a gift from the State: since 1552 it had been established that no one had the inalienable right to sell alcohol (a principle partially abrogated by the 1830 Beer Act, but reasserted in 1869). Because licences were a finite commodity, and because of the nature of both the retail and property markets, it so happened that granting a licence added significant value to the property attached to that licence. In effect, then, by granting a licence the State was not only allowing a retailer to sell alcohol, it was effectively adding thousands of pounds to the property value 'as an absolutely free gift'.[45] The irony, as Rowntree and Sherwell pointed out, was that monopoly values were 'State-created values, accidentally conferred upon private individuals in the effort of the State to safeguard a dangerous trade'.[46] By imposing a time limit on the payment of compensation, the State would be recognising the inconvenience to which individuals were being put in the process of restricting alcohol retail, but it would be maintaining the principle that those values never really belonged to the licensees in the first place. By not placing a time limit on compensation, the majority report attempted to establish the principle that the grant of a licence gave licensees a vested interest in their property which they had an absolute right to protect or be compensated for. In other words, for the authors of the majority report, the gift of added value handed to a licensee by the State through the grant of a licence should be held in perpetuity as the property of the recipient.

This principle, however, ran counter to the precedent laid down by *Sharp v. Wakefield*. Indeed, it was argued by temperance campaigners that the entire property boom of the late 1890s and early 1900s was based on the systematic pretence by the brewers that *Sharp v. Wakefield* had simply not happened.[47] A licence should only add value to a property if it is assumed that that licence is held in perpetuity; the property value of public houses, and the profits promised to investors during the flotations which were largely based on those property values, rested on a de facto convention that licence renewals were usually passed unchallenged, not on the letter of the law.

A monstrous betrayal

The issue of licence suppression came to a head in 1903. Throughout the country, licensing justices were asserting themselves to an unprecedented degree: more licences were denied renewal that year than in the previous six years put together.[48] Not only were the rights under *Sharp v. Wakefield* being applied vigorously, but justices were also aggressively applying a clause under a Licensing Act of 1902 which made the power to order structural renovations a condition of licence renewal. Properties which were deemed unsuitable could be ordered to carry out punitively expensive repairs or go under. In the absence of dramatic anti-drink legislation, the temperance movement had started to achieve some of its key goals by targeting, and often packing, the licensing benches themselves. The activities of licensing authorities in 1903 triggered a spate of public comments on the issue; the Webbs's historical study of licensing was largely supportive of active licence suppression, while the economist Arthur Shadwell dismissed the idea that more pubs meant more drinking as a 'temptation fallacy'.[49]

All this took place as a downturn in consumption, which had in fact started in 1900 and which was caused in part by the destabilising effects of the Boer War, began to have a devastating impact. Pub closures caused by a decrease in demand created a glut in the market which, along with the increasing awareness of the 'professional secret' that it was quite possible for a licence to add nothing to the value of a property, comprehensively burst the property bubble.[50] Brewery share values collapsed, leaving a swathe of investors out of pocket, brewery managers faced with debts which their properties were unable to cover, and publicans faced with an uncompensated loss of livelihood.

Consequently, when Arthur Balfour's Conservative administration passed a Licensing Act in 1904 based on the majority report of the Royal Commission, many Liberals saw it as a debt paid by the Tory party to the trade.[51] The 1904 Act sought to clarify the law regarding the organised suppression of licences, but in doing so it actually reduced the power of local magistrates. *Sharp v. Wakefield* had confirmed that local justices had the authority to refuse to renew any licence they liked; the 1904 Licensing Act required that anyone refused renewal in this way should receive financial compensation. The fund for compensation payments was to be raised by the trade itself, through a levy charged to publicans, so the State was not covering the loss of monopoly value directly. However, justices could only suppress licences *if* there was sufficient compensation available, which obviously put a limit on their powers. Furthermore, while licences granted after 1904 could be refused without compensation, there was to be no time limit on the period for which compensation would be given to existing businesses.

The National Liberal Foundation described the Act as 'a monstrous betrayal of the rights of the State'.[52] Speaking in the debates on the Bill, Lord Rosebery insisted that the failure to put a time limit on the period when refused renewals would trigger compensation undermined a key function of the state. The 'only way we would ever achieve a real temperance reform in this county,' Rosebery argued:

> was by fixing a date at the expiration of which all interest in the licence would be held to be exhausted, and the nation would resume its claim, its absolute dominion, over interests which had been created at the expense of the State, and of no other. [53]

Even for a free-trader such as Rosebery, the limits of market freedom did not extend to the business of alcohol.

The State and the trade

The 1904 Act was presented as a strategy to support licence reduction without punishing those retailers who were put out of business. It was a measure which acknowledged that, ultimately, the State had the right to intervene in the functioning of the alcohol market but which also recognised that selling alcohol was a private industry. However, the attempt to use licensing as a means of controlling the trade had created an important, and unintended, consequence: limiting the number of licences had made the ownership of a licence all the more valuable. At the same time, because licensing was devolved there was no central planning in terms of licensing policy, and the rigour with which restrictive powers were applied depended entirely on the whim of the local magistrates. As the social reformer Charles Booth put it, it 'is the restriction in the number of licenses that has given them their special value; and it is because unrestricted trade in alcohol is impolitic that we seem unable to handle these licenses to the public advantage'.[54] As a system of State management, magisterial licensing was mucky and murky and it left politicians in an almost impossible position: having to negotiate the conflicting demands of drinkers, retailers, brewers, temperance campaigners and constituents while unable to oversee directly the application of the laws that they introduced. If there was a battle going on between the State and the trade, then it was the un-elected and unpredictable magistrature that held the balance of power.

For many, this situation was unsupportable: brewers felt magistrates were too harsh, temperance campaigners felt they were too soft. The rolling system of compensation introduced under the 1904 Act did little to clarify things; if anything it made the legal status of the annual licence even less clear-cut. Over the next ten years many politicians and campaigners would turn to an option that seemed to cut through this mess of legislative confusion: the direct control of the trade by the state. However, such a radical move remained in the realms of optimistic speculation until the government's hand was forced by the outbreak of war.

Notes

1   Anon., 'Lord Rosebery in Birmingham' (*Times*, 24 May 1894), p. 6.
2   Greenaway, *Drink and British Politics*, D. Gutzke, *Protecting the Pub: Brewers and Publicans against Temperance* (Woodbridge: Royal Historical Society, 1989).
3   Gutzke, *Protecting the Pub*.
4   *Ibid.*, p. 65.
5   House of Commons, *Final Report of Her Majesty's Commissioners Appointed to Inquire into the Operation and Administration of the Laws Relating to the Sale of Intoxicating Liquors* (1899) C. 9379, p. 334.
6   F. C. Hindle, 'Licensing Bill: Compensation time limit' (London: Liberal Publications Department – leaflet no. 2168, 1908), p. 2.
7   T. Whittaker, 'The fall in brewery stocks: When and why it occurred' (London: Liberal Publications Department – leaflet no. 2166, 1908), p. 5.
8   House of Commons, *Final Report of Her Majesty's Commissioners Appointed to Inquire into the Operation and Administration of the Laws Relating to the Sale of Intoxicating Liquors*, p. 334.
9   *Ibid.*
10 J. Chamberlain, *Licensing reform and local option* (Birmingham: Journal Printing, 1876), p. 14.
11 House of Lords, *Report from the Select Committee of the House of Lords on Intemperance* (1879) 113, p. xxxi.
12 Wilson, *Alcohol and the Nation*, pp. 332–3.
13 Anon, 'Sir William Harcourt at Derby' (*Times*, 24 January 1895), p. 6.
14 Shiman, *Crusade Against Drink*, p. 222.
15 Anon, 'United Kingdom Alliance' (*Times*, 26 October 1892), p. 7.
16 Gutzke, *Protecting the Pub*, pp. 120–1.
17 G. O. Trevelyan, *Five Speeches on the Liquor Traffic* (London: Partridge & Co., 1872), p. 30.
18 *Ibid.*, p. 12.
19 Greenaway, *Drink and British Politics*, p. 29.
20 Anon, 'United Kingdom Alliance' (*Times*, 24 October 1894), p. 1.
21 P. Snowden, *Socialism and the Drink Question* (London: Independent Labour Party, 1908), p. 112.

22 Shiman, *Crusade Against Drink*, p. 229.
23 J. Rowntree and A. Sherwell, *The Temperance Problem and Social Reform* (London: Hodder and Stoughton, 1900).
24 H. J. Ellison, *Local option* (Edinburgh: John Menzies, 1882), p. 11.
25 Chamberlain, *Licensing Reform and Local Option*, p. 8.
26 *Ibid.*, p. 12.
27 Rowntree and Sherwell, *The Temperance Problem and Social Reform*, p. 451.
28 House of Commons, 'Report of the Municipality of Stockholm' (1877) 212, pp. 7–9.
29 Rowntree and Sherwell, *The Temperance Problem and Social Reform*, pp. 457–61.
30 F. J. Jayne, 'County councils and the public-house problem' (*Times*, 2 August 1892), p. 2.
31 F. J. Jayne, 'The Bishop of Chester and the drink question' (*Times*, 20 August 1892), p. 8.
32 W. Hicks, 'The Bishop of Chester on the drink question' (*Times*, 26 August 1892), p. 6.
33 J. Johnson, *The Gothenburg System of Public-House Licensing: What It Is and How It Works* (London: Church of England Temperance Society, 1883), p. 71.
34 Anon., 'Mr Chamberlain on Licensing Reform' (*Times*, 7 July 1894), p. 13.
35 Anon., 'United Kingdom Alliance' (*Times*, 26 October 1892), p. 7.
36 Rowntree and Sherwell, *The Temperance Problem and Social Reform*, p. 572.
37 Snowden, *Socialism and the Drink Question*, pp. 152–3.
38 D. Gutzke, *Pubs and Progressives: Reinventing the Public House in England, 1896–1960* (Dekalb, IL: Northern Illinois University Press, 2006), p. 43.
39 Haydon, *Beer and Britannia*, p. 240.
40 Rowntree and Sherwell, *The Temperance Problem and Social Reform*, p. 517.
41 Greenaway, *Drink and British Politics*, p. 74; Gutzke, *Protecting the Pub*, p. 25.
42 House of Commons, *Final Report of Her Majesty's Commissioners Appointed to Inquire into the Operation and Administration of the Laws Relating to the Sale of Intoxicating Liquors*, p. 57.
43 *Ibid.*, p. 289.
44 *Ibid.*
45 C. Booth, *Life and Labour of the People in London, Notes on Influences and Conclusion* (London: Macmillan, 1902), p. 102.
46 Rowntree and Sherwell, *The Temperance Problem and Social Reform*, p. 524.
47 H. Spender, *'The Trade' or the People* (London: Liberal Publications Department, pamphlet no. 4., 1908), p. 33.
48 Gutzke, *Protecting the Pub*, p. 154.
49 A. Shadwell, *Drink, Temperance and Legislation* (London: Longmans, Green and Co., 1903), p. 148.
50 Haydon, *Beer and Britannia*, p. 243.
51 Greenaway, *Drink and British Politics*, p. 78.
52 Liberal Party, *Proceedings at the annual meeting of the Council of the National Liberal Federation* (London: Liberal Publications Department, 1908), p. 35.
53 Liberal Party, *Ninth Year of the Tory Government* (London: Liberal Publications Department, 1904), p. 48.
54 Booth, *Life and Labour of the People in London*, p. 103.

11

Central control: war and nationalisation

Granted it be impossible literally to make men sober by Act of Parliament, it is not impossible to throw the force of the law and social arrangements upon the side of sobriety and, by a proper control of the traffic, to restrict the inducements to insobriety without unduly or improperly interfering with the legitimate liberty of the individual. (Joseph Rowntree and Arthur Sherwell)

A necessary element of any thoroughgoing scheme of reform is the removal of the barrier of private interests in the sale of drink. (Henry Carter)

In 1906, the Liberals won a landslide General Election victory. Once again they found themselves in a position to make their mark on the future direction of the drink question. This time, there was no ambivalence from the leadership about the importance which they attached to new drink legislation, and two years after coming to power they introduced a radical new Licensing Bill. Speaking to the Birmingham Liberal Association the new Prime Minister Herbert Asquith announced that he had staked his own political fortunes on the Licensing Bill, and that, furthermore, he had 'staked the fortunes of the Government and my party upon it'.[1] The Bill introduced by Asquith in 1908 represented, in his words:

The latest phase of the perpetual conflict which, generation after generation, the Liberal party has been waging to assert the paramount supremacy of public over private and of general over particular interests.[2]

What did this almighty struggle require? Among its provisions the Bill included a restriction of licences to 1 per 1,000 inhabitants in the cities, a fourteen-year time limit on compensation for licences suppressed in pursuit of this figure, local option for new licences, and – ill-advisedly, as it turned out – a ban on women working in pubs.

In the Commons, the Bill was secure but its popularity on the street, and in the pubs, was far less certain. In fact, opposition to the Bill was vocal from all sides: publicans feared the threat to their livelihoods, pub-goers objected to Government interference in their everyday activities, brewers feared financial distress, and industrialists objected to the confiscatory principles which the Bill enshrined. In July temperance campaigners organised a pro-Bill rally in Hyde Park which was attended by over 100,000 demonstrators: an anti-Bill demonstration held two months later attracted something nearer a quarter of a million.[3] The trade was able to harness popular mistrust at the Bill all the more effectively since it was seen by many as an attack on barmaids, which threatened not only the traditional character of the pub but the livelihood of thousands of 'poor, wage-earning, hard working women'.[4] In March the Liberals lost the seat of Peckham in a by-election which was seen by many as a political test of the entire Liberal programme, not least their stance on the drink question. Over the year they lost eight further by-elections. While no one of these losses can be singularly ascribed to the furore over the Licensing Bill, it all added to the impression that the Liberal administration – which, in its own words, had 'staked its existence' on the Bill – had, for the moment at least, lost the support of an electorate which had backed them resoundingly just two years earlier.[5]

In the end the Bill, which passed comfortably through a radically-minded Commons, was scuppered by the Lords. Conscious perhaps that it would play well with the public, but also acting in defence of their own previous legislation, the Tory-dominated Upper House refused to accept the legislation. It was another blow for temperance-minded Liberals and one which confirmed the deep distrust felt by the Liberal Party towards the Lords as a whole. The rejection of the 1908 Licensing Bill formed part of a larger constitutional crisis which culminated the following year when the Lords refused to confirm Lloyd George's 'People's Budget'. Rejecting the 1908 Bill was one of the last actions of a House whose power was to be severely curtailed by the 1911 Parliament Act. For Liberals it was another example of the unholy alliance between established business interests and a social elite whose power was rooted in the injustice of hereditary privilege. The State, whose role was to represent 'the people' as a whole, had once again had its purpose undermined by the collective power of big business and the landed gentry. It was, in some ways, a serendipitous get-out for the Liberals since it deflected attention from the genuine popular distaste for the Bill (albeit a distaste harnessed to its fullest extent by brewers and publicans), and presented its failure as an example of corrupt self-interest by a political institution whose unreconstructed powers belonged to a previous era.

Socialism and the drink question

In the same year that the Liberals saw their much-vaunted Licensing Bill collapse, one of the leading figures in the newly formed Independent

Labour Party, Phillip Snowden, published a book entitled *Socialism and the Drink Question*. Organised labour had not stood on the sidelines while liberals of various shades fought out how best to manage the drink trade. Perhaps surprisingly, given the extent to which the history of alcohol control had often been part of the wider control of lower-class culture, the trade union movement at the turn of the century was largely in favour of temperance reform (and many of the founding members of the Independent Labour Party, including Keir Hardy, had close links to the temperance movement). Since 1902, every Chairman of the Trades Union Congress had been a total abstainer and in 1906 the London conference of the TUC had voted overwhelmingly to pass a motion in favour of local veto.[6]

Like the radical teetotallers of the 1830s and 1840s, socialist temperance campaigners identified the drinks trade as an industry which conspired to disenfranchise and exploit working people. Unlike their teetotal forebears, however, they absolutely rejected the simplistic 'absurdity' that drink was the sole cause of poverty.[7] The drink problem was part of a wider problem of exploitation, lack of opportunity and cultural denigration. Nevertheless, it was a crucial part of the system of social and economic power that acted against the interest of workers. The pub may have been the social institution at the heart of most working-class communities, but for socialist temperance campaigners the brewers, all solid capitalists, had absolutely no interest in the welfare of the class of people who did most to line their ample pockets. In 1893, a manifesto published by two hundred labour leaders attacked those in the trade who opposed local veto on the grounds that it attacked the freedoms of the working class. It insisted that such unwelcome defenders of working-class interests:

> profess to be interested in the protection of the liberties of the working classes. It is a fraudulent profession. The liberty which most of them really desire is to maintain the liberty of the privileged monopolist to exploit the working classes, and to draw and suck from them their money by indirect means.[8]

For many of the leaders of organised labour, as for many the leaders of Irish nationalism, the supposed association between the social class they represented and a culture of drinking was a ruse which served only those who exploited them. As 'long as beer remains one of the main planks on the platform of the masses,' wrote one pamphleteer, 'so long will they be governed by the monopolist and the sweater'.[9]

For many socialists, the fact that time, money and energy were diverted into an activity which did nothing to ameliorate their conditions was bad enough. However, that situation was exacerbated by the fact that the drinks industry was such a prodigious work of capitalist machinery. Left-wing temperance campaigners were under no illusions that a thin line of blue-blooded magistrates were going to stem the power of the trade behemoth, even if some of them, for culturally conservative reasons, may have wanted to. Local option provided one opportunity for the democratisation of the trade, but it did little to address the systemic problem at hand because it would simply have led to the suppression of the industry in isolated regions while retaining the principle that drink should be the subject of the usual mechanisms of capitalist competition.

John Greenaway suggests that one reason political debate over licensing at the start of the twentieth century was so heated and partisan was because the drink question 'was now interpreted in the light of confiscatory "socialism" *versus* the rights of property, or of predatory vested interest *versus* the aspirations of the people'.[10] This had been the case for some time. Indeed, from the moment the Alliance turned the focus of temperance campaigning from moral suasion to legislative action, the problem of what the 'licensed liberty' to sell alcohol meant in terms of private property rights became key to the drink question. The rise of the Independent Labour Party, alongside the development of 'New Liberalism' in the 1890s, meant that many in the temperance movement now framed the drink question explicitly as part of the larger question of properly defining the relationship between the State and trade in general. Attempts to put strict statutory limits on the activities of the drinks industry had failed in 1871, 1895 and 1908; this, combined with the enormous financial power of an increasingly concentrated brewing industry, exacerbated the sense among temperance campaigners that the drink question was nothing less than, in Peel's words, 'a struggle for mastery'.[11] Although some socialist leaders would have no truck with the forces of 'rum and reaction',[12] many began to move towards the idea that some form of direct State control was the only practical answer to the drink question – even if it was only the least worst option.[13]

Germany, Austria and drink

Temperance did have some victories. In 1908, Lady Astor's Children's Act included a section banning under-fourteens from licensed premises – although, as Charles Booth argued, excluding children from pubs risked making things worse by simply reinforcing the already problematic distinction between the behavioural norms of home and public house, and by further establishing the pub as that mysterious place where adulthood began.[14] When Lloyd George's 1909 budget was finally passed in 1910 it contained some considerable tax increases on both brewer and pub licences. These certainly put the squeeze on the trade, but the impact was limited.

Things were different for Scotland, however. In 1913, prohibitionists finally achieved a victory with the passing of the Temperance (Scotland) Act which set a timetable for local option to be introduced across the country in 1920. Prohibitionists finally had the chance to give the people their say, though they would have to wait seven years to discover the true scale of their vindication. When the people finally spoke in 1920, just 3 per cent of eligible areas voted for the 'no-licence' option.

In England, the flagging fortunes of political temperance were revived by war. Within weeks of Britain entering hostilities with Germany, the Defence of the Realm Act (DORA) was passed, allowing for emergency legislation to be enacted affecting a swathe of domestic activities. The first of the regulations affecting alcohol supply gave naval and military authorities the power to set closing hours in and around defended harbours and imposed rules controlling the supply of drink to servicemen. Concerns over drunkenness among soldiers and sailors surfaced early in the First World War, especially after Lord Kitchener issued an appeal in October 1914 that citizens 'avoid treating [servicemen] to drink, and give them every assistance in resisting the temptations which are often placed before them'.[15] However, it was not so much worries over drunken soldiers as worries over the impact of drinking on the efficiency of domestic labour that triggered off one of the most extraordinary episodes in British licensing history.

In February 1915 the then Chancellor of the Exchequer, David Lloyd George, addressed a meeting in Bangor at which he outlined the state of the war so far. In the course of his address he turned to the 'lure of the drink' and its detrimental impact on the efficiency of a small but significant proportion of the workforce. His startling conclusion was that 'Drink is doing us more damage in the war than all the German submarines put together'.[16] Lloyd George had a history of fairly active temperance campaigning. He had introduced a Welsh local veto Bill into Parliament in 1894 and had addressed the annual meeting of the Alliance in 1907, during which he tried out an early version of his more famous rhetorical flourish, describing the liquor traffic as 'a greater handicap to our trade, commerce, and industry than all the tariffs of the world put together'.[17] According to one contemporary, the Bangor speech 'made history. It changed the perspective of the question ... From the morrow of the speech, for nearly three months, the drink question was the main subject of debate in the Press and in private circles'.[18]

The next three months certainly saw some furious activity. In March Lloyd George met with a deputation of shipyard owners who called, in all seriousness, for the total prohibition of alcohol for the duration of the war. In responding to the deputation Lloyd George trumped his previous statements on the subject by announcing that 'we are fighting Germany, Austria and Drink; and as far as I can see the greatest of these deadly foes is Drink' – a remark that prompted one *Times* leader writer to suggest the whole thing was 'getting a little out of perspective'.[19] A few days later a 'Memorandum on practical temperance reform' was sent to Herbert Asquith signed by almost one hundred of the nation's great and good, including Edward Elgar and Sir Arthur Conan-Doyle. The Memorandum acknowledged that prohibition was impractical, but called instead for severe restrictions to be placed on opening hours and the compulsory closure of pubs in the vicinity of military instillations.[20]

One factor driving calls for reform was the fact that Britain's two key allies, Russia and France, had both introduced radical temperance legislation in response to the war. Within months of each other Russia had banned vodka and France had banned absinthe. In both cases, especially absinthe-drinking in France, there was a long pre-history of campaigning for legislation which the war made viable. Clearly, the war opened up the possibility for legislation which would otherwise have been inopportune. But it also meant that complex devolved processes like local option were completely out of the question. The solution that the Government came up with – the creation of a Central Control Board to oversee the liquor trade – turned out to be the most original contribution to the drink question for a considerable time.

The Central Control Board

Originally, Lloyd George had supported the nationalisation of the entire drinks industry, but his radical plan failed to gain the backing of cabinet colleagues who baulked at embarking on such an ambitious project in the middle of a war. Instead, what Lloyd George put through Parliament was a Liquor Control Regulation establishing a Central Control Board (CCB) empowered to manage the sale and supply in specific areas of the country where war materials were 'made or loaded or unloaded or dealt with in transit'. The CCB was also to be given power of compulsory purchase, the power to set up refreshment rooms and to enforce tighter restrictions on opening hours.

Having been formally created by Royal Assent in May 1915, the CCB brought ten shipbuilding areas under its control the following July. In these areas opening hours were reduced by up to two-thirds, treating was banned, as was buying drinks on credit, spirits were to be sold diluted and clubs were placed under the same control as all other licensed premises. Soon, however, the regions under CCB control expanded so that by 1916, CCB orders were in force across virtually the entire country – an expansion of powers justified by the CCB on the grounds that the entire country had been effectively militarised and so could be legitimately considered as falling under the CCB remit.[21]

What was unusual about the CCB, however, was not the fact that it enabled emergency restrictions to be placed on alcohol retail across the country. That was hardly an original approach to managing the drink question in a time of crisis. Rather, the originality of the CCB lay in the fact that it took an overtly constructive approach to the control of the drinks trade; that is, it revisited some of the ideas that had been circulating among the promoters of the Gothenburg system and applied them to its own projects. One of the first CCB campaigns was to provide industrial workers with an alternative to the pub on their breaks. Conventionally, factory employees had had to take their lunch breaks in the local pubs, since there were not usually any facilities on site. Because there was no real tradition of food provision in most pubs, this meant that workers often ate insubstantially, relying instead on a 'liquid lunch' for sustenance. Between 1915 and 1918, the CCB built 840 industrial canteens in factories across the country. These were often huge facilities serving hot food and drinks – sometimes including beer in limited amounts – to hundreds of workers at a time. When Henry Carter, the CCB's semi-official historian, wrote that the 'industrial canteen is here to stay' he wasn't wrong.[22] It would be hard to overstate its impact on the culture of lunchtime drinking among factory workers, at least.

The creation of industrial canteens was nothing, however, compared to the experiments in State ownership which the CCB embarked upon in the first half of 1916. In Enfield Lock, north London, the Royal Small Arms Factory – one of the key rifle manufacturers in the country – did not have a proper canteen. Because there was no space to build one, the CCB came up with the novel idea of purchasing the four nearest pubs to the factory in order to transform them into places where workers could buy a decent meal. Consequently, as Henry Carter, himself a committed teetotaller, proudly observed, 'on January 4th, 1916, the State, for the first time in modern England, entered business as a retailer of liquor'.[23] The newly acquired pubs were not demolished or closed, but they were transformed into 'spacious, airy and comfortable' premises in which, alongside beer, workers could buy coffee, tea, soft drinks and hot food.[24]

What happened on a small scale in Enfield was repeated on a larger scale in April 1916 when the CCB bought up the licensed premises around the Cromarty Firth on the north-west coast of Scotland. The most dramatic of the CCB's actions, however, was the wholesale purchase of the entire drinks trade in and around Carlisle later that year. As in both Enfield and Cromarty, the CCB were responding to local conditions – this time an enormous influx of navvies and construction workers employed in the creation of a large munitions factory in Gretna which swelled the local population dramatically. In the first half of 1916, convictions for drunkenness in nearby Carlisle went up from 72 to 563 – an increase of around 800 per cent.[25] The normal control orders appeared inadequate to deal with the unusual conditions around the new factory, so the CCB repeated its experiment in Enfield and Cromarty, this time on a huge scale. In total, 207 pubs, 20 off-licences and 4 breweries came under the direct control of the CCB in an area covering 500 square miles. Once again, the CCB combined conventional licence suppression (104 licences were terminated in total) with the establishment of disinterested management and physical improvement to the pubs themselves.

The CCB encouraged pub managers to promote the sale of soft drinks and, more importantly, food. The Chairman of the CCB, Lord D'Abernon, had been a member of the Surrey Public House Trust Company, and he used their Gothenburg-inspired principle of salaried management in CCB pubs.[26] As in all disinterested management schemes, the licensee's income ceased to depend on maximising sales of alcohol while his job security came increasingly to depend on the maintenance of good order in his premises.

More surprisingly still, the CCB opened its own purpose-built pubs. A post office in Gretna was converted by the CCB and re-opened as the Gretna Tavern in July 1916. A second pub, the London Tavern, was opened soon after. To the east of Gretna, in Longtown, a pub called the Globe was rebuilt to incorporate a bowling-green, billiard-room and large dining rooms. To the west, in Annan, a new CCB pub called Gracie's Banking was built from scratch with a restaurant, bowling-greens, a billiard room and a cinema. Five CCB pubs were also opened in Carlisle.

The CCB board contained members sympathetic to temperance such as Henry Carter and Phillip Snowden, but it also contained two of the country's leading brewers: Sydney Nevile, head of Whitbread, and William Waters Butler, head of Mitchells and Butlers. It was this uniquely collaborative approach – and, frankly, the exclusion of anyone sympathetic to the Alliance – which allowed the CCB to combine restriction with development so successfully. The creation of the Gretna Tavern, the Globe and Gracie's Banking saw the CCB return to the model of pub improvement first mooted by the Bishop of Chester over twenty years earlier. Henry Carter was explicit in positioning the CCB's strategy within debates over the concept of pub improvement. 'These reconstruction schemes,' he wrote:

> have a significance beyond the mere fact that good property replaces bad. They should, in due time, furnish a measure of guidance for the answering of a much-

debated question which can be stated in these terms: How far would the general provision of a better type of public-house in which drink is sold in wholesome surroundings, under regulations devised to repress intemperance, and where the sale of food is encouraged ... promote public sobriety?[27]

As we shall see later, this question would dominate debates on alcohol throughout the 1920 and 1930s.

The nation's landlord

Leaving the promotion of sobriety through pub improvement aside for now, the key political opportunity presented by the establishment of the CCB was the nationalisation of the drinks trade as a whole. Joseph Chamberlain's municipalisation scheme may have looked like a mere idiosyncrasy to many temperance campaigners in 1876, but the political failure of local option in England, coupled with the patchiness of its successes in America, led many in the movement to look towards some form of State purchase as the only realistic way to bring the drinks industry under control. Phillip Snowden had long since come to see some form of State ownership as the only solution to the drink question which was not doomed to failure. The leading temperance figures Joseph Rowntree and Arthur Sherwell had come out in favour of municipalisation in 1900, but the example of the CCB led them to publish a trenchant essay backing complete State purchase in 1919. 'Parliament has demanded the impossible,' they wrote. 'Public sobriety and private profit cannot be combined. They are in the nature of things irreconcilable'.[28] Instead what Rowntree and Sherwell, two of the most influential temperance campaigners alive, called for was nationalisation: 'not a catalogue of restrictions, but *recovery of control* – the transfer of power from the Trade to the State'.[29]

By the end of the First World War, then, the focus of the drink question had shifted. In Scotland local option waited in the wings and in America, of course, the huge experiment of nationwide prohibition was about to embark on its doomed course. In England, by contrast, prohibition was effectively dead: it had failed repeatedly to carry the will of Parliament and it had failed to achieve widespread support outside of the committed temperance movement. In an era of social massification and the integration and expansion of business interests, not to mention global war, the regional direct democracy of local option began to look both fantastical and quaint. What did a 'dry' borough mean in the era of the motorised transport, industrial production and electronic communications? The federalisation of prohibition in America made sense from this perspective, but whereas the trade was often depicted in American temperance as an alien presence whose expulsion would return the nation to its purer condition, no such nativist propaganda was going to fly in England where beer and the pub were so deeply embedded in cultural life and history.

The idea of State purchase was a logical conclusion of all the debates over licensing that had taken place since the repeal of the 1830 Beer Act. The question of licensing *is* the question of State control: it is the question of how the State should manage a trade which is like no other. In an obvious sense licensing is a series of restrictions placed by the State on an otherwise free trade – and this is certainly how licensing has tended to be perceived not just by brewers and publicans but also by ordinary pub-goers. However, the temperance campaigners of the late nineteenth and early twentieth century were not wrong in pointing out that, strictly speaking, a licence to retail alcohol was a gift rather than a restriction. A complete free trade in alcohol is as far-fetched an idea as complete prohibition; the drink question, politically, is the question of what the balance of power should be between the State and the trade. Lord Rosebery was overstating things when he suggested that if the State did not control the trade, the trade would control the State – but, as Lloyd George illustrated repeatedly, the drink question had a knack of making Liberal politicians gild the rhetorical lily. Nevertheless, it was about government taking seriously the proposition that the drinks industry demanded to be in some way democratically accountable. Of course, as consumers, drinkers voted with their feet and continued to frequent pubs in spite of, and in addition to, other, newer, attractions. But while the 'temptation fallacy' was grossly overplayed by prohibitionists (pub-goers were not beseeching Parliament to strip them of opportunities to drink), as citizens those same drinkers did have the right to expect that an industry which, in some instances, could have detrimental social impacts would be properly managed by the legislature. The conventional approach to licensing – in which power was devolved to unelected local magistrates – was a way of asserting State control while protecting elected authorities from answerability. The debates over licensing between 1880 and 1918 went a long way towards exposing this as a fallacy, but, as we shall see, the political expediency of this principle for both government and the drink industry means that it remained firmly in place long afterwards.

Notes

1 Liberal Party, *Proceedings at the Annual Meeting of the Council of the National Liberal Federation*, pp. 87–8.
2 *Ibid.*
3 Anon, *The Licensing Bill. Demonstration in Hyde Park* (*Times*, 28 September 1908), p. 7.
4 E. Booth and E. Roper, 'Barmaid's political defence league' (*Times*, 1 May 1908), p. 2.

5   Spender, *'The Trade' or the People*, p. 3.
6   Snowden, *Socialism and the Drink Question*, pp. 28–30.
7   *Ibid.*, p. 86.
8   *Ibid.*, p. 27.
9   'Mile End Socialist', 'Socialism, atheism and temperance: A defence of socialism' (London: Arthur Warren, 1898), p. 10.
10 Greenaway, *Drink and British Politics*, p. 89.
11 A. W. Peel, 'The Royal Commission on Licensing: The struggle for mastery between the state and a trade' (London: Central Temperance Legislation Board, 1899), p. 4.
12 J. Burns, *Labour and Drink* (Bristol: Western Temperance Press, 1914), p. 29.
13 Snowden, *Socialism and the Drink Question*, pp. 189–90.
14 Booth, *Life and Labour of the People in London*, pp. 65–6.
15 Anon., 'The New Army. Appeal to the Public by Lord Kitchener' (*Times*, 25 October 1914), p. 4.
16 Anon., 'Mr Lloyd George on the Drink Peril' (*Times*, 1 March 1915), p. 8.
17 Anon., 'United Kingdom Alliance' (*Times*, 16 October 1907), p. 8.
18 H. Carter, *The Control of the Drink Trade* (London: Longmans, Green and Co., 1919), p. 48.
19 Anon., 'Conference on Drink' (*Times*, 30 March 1915), p. 11; Anon, 'The Ends and the Means' (*Times*, 3 April 1915), p. 9.
20 Anon., 'Practical Temperance Reform' (*Times*, 3 April 1915), p. 5.
21 Carter, *The Control of the Drink Trade*, p. 127.
22 *Ibid.*, p. 197.
23 *Ibid.*, p. 174.
24 *Ibid.*
25 *Ibid.*, p. 202.
26 Gutzke, *Pubs and Progressives*, p. 45.
27 Carter, *The Control of the Drink Trade*, p. 218.
28 Rowntree and Sherwell, *The Temperance Problem and Social Reform*, p. 583; J. Rowntree and A. Sherwell, *State Purchase of the Liquor Trade* (London: Allen and Unwin, 1919), p. 26.
29 Rowntree and Sherwell, *State Purchase of the Liquor Trade*, p. 5.

12

The study of inebriety: medicine and the law

For once grant that inebriety is a disease over which the victim has little or no control, and it follows that the inebriate, like the lunatic, needs to be protected, not only for his own, but for the public good. (Harry Campbell)

Prison is no cure for alcoholism. (Hugh Wingfield)

The period between 1870 and 1918 saw extensive debate on licensing, management of the drinks trade and the social effects of public drinking. However, it also witnessed intense intellectual and political activity around a parallel, but closely related, concern: the nature and treatment of what we might now call alcohol addiction. As we have seen, the drink question has always hinged on both the social effects of drunkenness and the habit-forming tendencies of alcohol. Puritans warned against the 'bewitching sin' and the political temperance movement demanded legislative action partly because alcohol produced 'habitual drunkards' whose condition amounted to a form of slavery. Prohibitionists and moral suasionists took a very different view of what to do with habitual drunkards, and there was certainly no consensus as to what either caused or cured the 'drink crave', but both wings of the temperance movement put the subject of habituation at the centre of their world-view.

Historians of addiction often suggest that the key historical transformation in ideas around what we now call alcoholism centred on a shift from seeing addiction as a vice (a sin for which the drinker was responsible) to seeing it as a disease (a compulsion which afflicted certain drinkers through no fault of their own). There is clearly some truth in this: the moral opprobrium directed towards habitual drinkers in some early modern texts is unthinkable today. However, there was no neat transition from one paradigm to the next, nor have the two viewpoints ever been entirely distinct. Even in the diatribes of fire-and-brimstone Puritans, the vice of drunkenness was recognised as peculiarly compulsive. Similarly, despite the dominance of 'disease' models of addiction today, the issue of moral responsibility has not gone away. As we shall see, many writers in the late nineteenth and early twentieth centuries saw the drink question as a straight conflict between defining habitual drunkenness as vice or disease. In truth, however, it could never be fully accounted for as either. Even the most ardent proponents of medical models of alcohol addiction could not escape the theme of individual responsibility, nor could the most high-handed moralists ever deny that there was something about the compulsive use of alcohol that went beyond ordinary demands that an individual 'pull themselves together'.

The late nineteenth century certainly witnessed a marked increase in the use, and influence, of disease-based models of alcohol addiction. But even among the numerous doctors and psychiatrists who struggled to redefine the problem in medical, rather than moral, terms significant differences of interpretation remained. It was one thing to call habitual drunkenness a disease, quite another to agree on precisely what kind of disease it might be, and what one thinks a disease *is* defines how one thinks it should be treated.[1] Because there were numerous competing disease models, there was also an array of conflicting prognoses and cures.

The other key fact to bear in mind when assessing the rise of disease models of addiction is that they did not emerge in a political vacuum. As Virginia Berridge has observed, what was new in this period was not the discovery of previously unimagined medical ideas, 'but rather a particular combination of social forces which made such concepts assume hegemony'.[2] This achievement of hegemony was stuttering and partial, but the overlap between medical developments and wider social, political and ideological developments is significant. Medical approaches to alcohol use had their roots as much in the ideological assumptions of late Victorian England as they did in any politically neutral process of scientific discovery. Similarly, the first treatment regimes which disease models gave rise to were inextricably linked to the institutional management of social order and of deviant populations. Indeed, the disease model of alcohol addiction first entered the public domain in Britain not through a change in the activities of doctors, but through the introduction of legislation which allowed for the creation of quasi-penal institutions to which 'habitual drunkards' could be committed for periods of restraint and rehabilitation. In Britain, the disease model was not beyond politics.

Habitual drunkards

The idea that the State should oversee the creation of institutions specifically designed to house habitual drunkards was first mooted around 1850 by the Edinburgh-based physician, Alexander Peddie. Peddie was frustrated with the lack of provision for what he saw as the victims of a disease which caused them to behave in antisocial and self-destructive ways. In 1858 he published a detailed outline of both the reasons why he felt legislative reform was needed and the kind of treatment he felt should be made available. Peddie proposed the creation of reformatories, managed under the auspices of the local authorities, which could accommodate individuals who entered voluntarily as well as people sent by the courts for compulsory treatment. Peddie was clear that his motive was one of protection for habitual drunkards. He believed that as the system stood, too many people who were suffering from a disease either ended up in prison or were left to fend for themselves against the terrible desire for drink. There was, he claimed 'a deliberate injustice and inhumanity in ... permitting a man to expose himself to the penalties of law, when it has long been apparent that he has not the power to govern his own will and reason'.[3]

Peddie's ideas were not taken up in Britain immediately. In fact, the first reformatory of this kind was opened in Binghampton, New York in 1864. Nine more were created in America over the following decade. In England, Peddie's idea finally found a political figurehead in the person of the Liberal MP for Bath, Donald Dalrymple. Dalrymple spent the last years of his life campaigning for the creation of asylums for the treatment of habitual drunkards, and although he died before seeing any such legislation enacted, his campaign would eventually bear fruit with the passing of the Habitual Drunkards Act in 1879. The Habitual Drunkards Act marked a new phase in the treatment of alcohol addiction, and although it would ultimately prove a failure it would dominate thinking about the treatment of habitual drunkenness in England for forty years.

Retreat and rehabilitation

Donald Dalrymple was no friend to prohibitionism, which he considered illiberal and unworkable.[4] Rather than back the Alliance's Permissive Bill, Dalrymple put his energies into promoting his own Habitual Drunkards Bill. The Bill failed to achieve a second reading when it was first introduced in 1870, and Henry Bruce persuaded Dalrymple to withdraw the Bill in 1871, perhaps concerned that it would further complicate the already tortuous process of his own doomed licensing legislation. Not deterred, Dalrymple organised a Select Committee on Habitual Drunkards which published its report in June 1872. The report stated that:

> occasional drunkenness may, and very frequently does, become confirmed and habitual, and soon passes into the condition of a disease uncontrollable by the individual, unless indeed some extraneous condition, either punitive or curative, is brought into play.[5]

The report went on to propose the establishment of asylums similar to those suggested by Peddie, although it supported separating voluntary retreats from compulsory reformatories. Although Dalrymple died the following year, the campaign was revived by the Glasgow MP Charles Cameron in 1877. Cameron's Habitual Drunkards Bill, based on the 1872 Committee report, passed through the House successfully in 1878 after Cameron agreed to remove the clause allowing for the compulsory committal of drunkards – a crucial shift, as we shall see. The Bill received Royal Assent in 1879 under the title the 'Habitual Drunkards Act'.

The 1879 Act allowed local authorities to grant licences to private or-ganisations to set up retreats for the care and rehabilitation of habitual drunkards. Entry to a retreat was voluntary and the cost of treatment was paid for by the patient. The peculiarity of the system was that once some-one signed up to enter a retreat, they were then not allowed to leave until the duration of their treatment was completed. In other words, entering a retreat literally meant signing away one's liberty. Anyone absconding before the completion of their treatment could, by law, be forcibly returned.

The Act also clarified the term 'habitual drunkard', establishing for the first time a legal definition of the concept. A habitual drunkard was defined as 'a person who by means of habitual intemperate drinking of intoxicating liquor is dangerous to himself, or herself, or to others, or incapable of managing himself or herself, and his or her affairs'. Anyone applying for committal to a retreat had to be signed off as a habitual drunkard, according to these terms, by a magistrate. Although 'habitual drunkenness' was defined by the 1879 Act as a condition requiring medi-cal treatment, the decision as to who was or was not a fit subject for this treatment was made by the courts, not doctors.

Perhaps unsurprisingly the retreat system was not a great success. Applicants had to be affluent (because they were liable for the cost of treatment), prepared to be legally designated as incapable of managing themselves, and willing to sign away their own liberty for up to a year. The number of wealthy, self-declared drunkards who saw enforced con-finement as the best solution to their condition was always going to be limited. Five years after the Act was passed there were just six retreats in operation, ministering to a grand total of forty-five patients.[6] By 1891 there were seven retreats and the total number of inmates had swelled to sixty-two.[7]

The Inebriates Act

In 1893, a Departmental Committee was set up to look into the work-ings of the 1879 Act. While it skirted the question of whether habitual drunkenness was, strictly speaking, a disease, the final report argued strongly that allowing only voluntary committal undermined the entire system.[8] To counter this, it called for new legislation allowing people defined as habitual drunkards by the courts to be *forcibly* entered into reformatories. In 1898, an Habitual Inebriates Act was passed based on these recommendations. It created two new classes of reformatory. The first, 'certified local reformatories', were funded and managed by local authorities; the second, 'state reformatories', were managed directly by the Home Secretary and housed more serious offenders. Under Section 1 of the Act, serious criminals who the court decided were also habitual drunkards could be committed to State reformatories in lieu of part of their prison sentence; under Section 2 anyone convicted of minor crimes directly involving drunkenness (being drunk and incapable, drunk in charge of a carriage, and so forth) four times in a single year could be committed to a local reformatory for up to three years.

Under the 1898 Act then, convicted criminals could be sent to institutions where their drunkenness, not their criminality, was the focus of the disciplinary regime. More radically, anyone arraigned for simple drunkenness four times in one year could be forcibly sent for treatment in a quasi-penal institution. Compulsory commitment to an inebriate asylum presupposed that habitual drunkenness was a kind of disease, but equally that it came under the jurisdiction of the courts.

By 1903, there were around twenty private, voluntary retreats, six local authority reformatories, and two State reformatories – one for women at Aylesbury prison and one for men at Warwick prison. The vast majority of inmates in the reformatories were women. Between 1898 and 1903, 876 women were committed under Section 2 of the Act as compared to just 136 men. In 1903, the female State reformatory at Aylesbury held 70 women – twice the number of men held at Warwick.[9] Around 80 per cent of the women sent to the State reformatory under Section 1 of the Act were mothers charged with child neglect by the NSPCC; the majority of women committed under Section 2 were prostitutes.[10]

Whatever the motives of those who introduced inebriate reformatories, the gender bias of the committals shows that in practice they acted as institutions for policing public order and morality rather than for treating the victims of a disease. As Mariana Valverde has argued:

> The skewed reformatory figures, in particular the near-complete absence from the compulsory committed population of the hard-drinking violence-prone working-class man one might have expected to find in such institutions, certainly suggests that the inebriate reformatories in Britain were involved in the policing of women's sexual and reproductive conduct as much or more than in the regulation of alcohol.[11]

When Dalrymple's committee had reported in 1872, *The Times* had warned that compulsory rendition 'would treat vice as disease, and punish it as crime'.[12] What it did not predict was that compulsory committal would provide a means by which 'deviant' women could be both punished and pathologised. Once again, institutional attitudes to drunkenness bore down far more heavily on women than on men. 'The drunken woman', wrote the coroner for North East London in 1903, 'is a reckless, depraved, dissolute being, with only half a mind and no conscience'.[13] His language was not unusual. The common use of the term 'criminal inebriate female' in the literature of the time reflected the extent to which the gendered politics of sexual morality, the enforcement of social control and the medicalisation of drinking were conflated in the inebriate reformatory movement as a whole.

The drinker's disease

The inebriate asylum movement fitted into the context of wider late-Victorian attempts to medicalise deviancy, but the 'disease-ing' of habitual drunkenness had been under way for some time.[14] However, while doctors had been writing about the 'disease' of drunkenness since the late seventeenth century, none had outlined a specific medical condition, afflicting only some of the population, which made certain people unable to drink in a controlled way. Habitual drunkenness, in writing prior to the nineteenth century, was always the effect of something else: a mental, physiological or spiritual problem which manifested itself through destructive drinking because of the habit-forming propensities of alcohol itself.

A turning point in the development of the disease concept occurred with the suggestion that there may be a *pre-existing* condition, an illness which could appear *before* the sufferer had even tasted their first drink, which made some people unable to drink alcohol moderately.[15] One of the first writers to clearly describe habitual drinking in these terms was the French psychiatrist Jean-Étienne Esquirol who, in 1838, suggested there was a mental disease – 'dipsomania' – which caused some people to drink to excess. For Esquirol this was one manifestation of a partial insanity which he called 'monomania': that is a condition in which the sufferer 'was unable to reason properly on one particular subject but was otherwise lucid'.[16] Someone suffering from a monomania of the will – that is, an inability to control one's behaviour where a particular activity was concerned – could become a dipsomaniac. This was not because of the addictive properties of alcohol, and not because of some associated physical or mental condition, but because that person suffered from a pre-existing condition which was triggered by exposure to drink.

In Britain, Alexander Peddie was insistent that dipsomania (his preferred term) should be understood as 'symptomatic of some abnormal cerebral condition which gives it the form of insanity', and that this condition was 'not so much produced by intoxicating drinks, as it [was] that which created the desire for them'.[17] The 'dipsomaniac, the chronic insane drinker,' Peddie insisted, 'should be suitably restrained *since he can no longer control himself*. This is the full and true limit to liberty of person. In this state he must forfeit his freedom for a while'.[18]

The nomenclature surrounding drunkenness becomes somewhat convoluted around this time. 'Dipsomania', coined by Brühl-Cramer in 1819 and literally meaning 'manic thirst', came to be used to describe a mental condition that led an individual to indulge in bouts of heavy and uncontrolled drinking. The term 'alcoholism', coined by Magnus Huss in 1849, was generally applied to prolonged heavy drinking over an extended period of time. Huss distinguished between chronic and acute alcoholism. Chronic alcoholism could involve constant drinking without the drinker necessarily ever getting blind drunk, while acute alcoholism was characterised by bouts of extreme intoxication. Dipsomania tended to be a term used by people who, like Peddie, defined habitual drunkenness as a specifically mental disease, while alcoholism tended to be used by those who, like Huss, regarded the problem as a disease of the nervous system or as having a primarily physiological basis: that is, something that arises out of the physical effects of alcohol on the body itself. However, the fluidity of thinking at the time meant that the terms were often used interchangeably.

An imperious impulse

The concept of 'inebriety', as distinct from alcoholism or dipsomania, was popularised in Britain by a Glaswegian doctor called Norman Kerr. Kerr had joined the United Kingdom Alliance when it was formed in 1853 but joined the more moderate CETS in 1874.[19] Kerr was, in many ways, the heir to Peddie, and although he had not been involved in the Select Committee of 1872, he became a dominant figure in the resurgent campaign for legislation after he founded the Society for the Promotion for the Control and Care of Habitual Drunkards in 1877. Most importantly, in 1884 he founded the British Society for the Study of Inebriety, an organisation modelled on the Society for the Study of Inebriety which had been established in America in 1870. Kerr's organisation was dedicated to the medical study of habitual drunkenness, and in particular to proving that it was a disease rather than a moral failing.

The word 'inebriety', as used by Kerr, referred to:

a diseased state of the brain and nervous centres, characterised by an irresistible impulse to indulge in intoxicating liquors or other narcotics, for the relief which these afford, at any peril.[20]

The main distinction between the words 'inebriety' and 'dipsomania' was that the former denoted the inability to resist drugs in general, not just alcohol. In this, the Society for the Study of Inebriety was unusual.[21] For Kerr, inebriety became dipsomania (or alcoholism – Kerr often used the terms interchangeably) when an inebriate was exposed to alcohol; just as it could become opium addiction were an inebriate exposed to opium.

Despite Kerr's best efforts to clarify the concept, inebriety remained a deeply contradictory idea. It was, as Kerr defined it to the inaugural meeting of the Society for the Study of Inebriety, a 'true disease, as unmistakably a disease as is gout, or epilepsy, or insanity'.[22] In comparing inebriety to three completely distinct types of diseases Kerr succeeded in illustrating the extent to which his disease model relied on analogy and fuzzy distinctions. This confusion was not ameliorated by his insistence that inebriety was sometimes hereditary (in about 30 per cent of cases), but equally could be triggered by nervous shock, overwork, 'lack of healthy stimuli', head injuries, indigestion, and, indeed, excessive drinking itself.[23] Indeed, Kerr went on to tell his audience that he was not actually able to decide finally if inebriety was a sin, a vice, a crime, or a disease. 'In my humble opinion,' he concluded, 'it is sometimes all four, but oftener a disease than anything else, and even when anything else, generally a disease as well'.[24] Kerr was moving towards a disease model, but with uncertain steps.

In fairness, Kerr's circumspection may well have reflected a desire to protect the fledgling society from accusations of quackery. Fifteen years later, shortly after the 1898 Act further established the principles of medical temperance in political practice, Kerr was more assertive, writing that:

a revolution has taken place in medical and public opinion till, at the present day, the overwhelming majority of professional and philanthropic persons, as well as social and political reformers [believe] most confirmed drunkards are drunken, not of choice, but of an imperious impulse arising from mental and sometimes bodily disease.'[25]

Without stripping habitual drunkenness of its moral aspect entirely, Kerr tried to move away from simplistic moral condemnation and towards some degree of medical understanding. As we have seen, however, this did not demand fewer interventions in the lives of habitual drinkers, but more. As a strictly medical condition, inebriety demanded not mere condemnation, but analysis, observation, cure and even incarceration. Social historians influenced by the ideas of Michel Foucault will see in this a classic example of the extension of the 'clinical gaze' and the control of populations through the pathologisation of deviancy. However, the wide-spread resistance to pure forms of medicalisation which was voiced from many groups outside of, and in some cases within, medicine undermines the Foucauldian tendency to see such processes as more or less coherent expressions of institutional power.[26]

Drink and criminal liability

The question of whether inebriety was a vice or a disease went right to the heart of liberal notions of selfhood and responsibility. The 'patholo-gisation' of deviant behaviours may have proved a relatively efficient way of managing problematic social groups, but it played havoc with some basic concepts of justice. Harry Campbell, who succeeded Norman Kerr as President of the Society for the Study of Inebriety in 1902, wrote 'once grant that inebriety is a disease over which the victim has little or no control, and it follows that the inebriate, like the lunatic, needs to be pro-tected'.[27] His views were reflected by William Sullivan – Deputy Medical Officer at Pentonville Prison, and a leading figure in medical temperance – who argued that 'if by reason of disease of mind [the inebriate] is to suffer an abatement of liberty, he will also benefit in restricted responsibil-ity'.[28] The psychiatrist Hugh Wingfield insisted that because 'the normal man is not, and cannot be subject' to the temptations faced by alcohol-ics, society tends to 'judge these unfortunates with harshness and injus-tice'.[29] At the same time, however, other people equally involved in the medicalisation of drunkenness remained deeply uncomfortable about the disease concept. One ex-chairman of the Inebriates Acts Committee on London County Council complained that inebriety may be a disease of sorts, but it was 'assuredly a disease in which the individual possessed has in many cases an essential co-operative influence in his own worsement or betterment'.[30]

The vice/disease debate was an issue for the law just as much as it was for medicine.[31] Under the so-called M'Naughten rules established in 1843, a defendant could plead diminished responsibility if, by reason of insanity, they were incapable of knowing if their actions were criminal or immoral. If habitual drunkenness was a disease of the mind, then it was surely a form of insanity – which undermined the idea that an inebriate was legally responsible for his or her actions. This came on top of the already confused legal position regarding the extent to which drunken-ness itself could act as a defence. In law it had never been established whether drunkenness should be recognised at all as a factor in criminal cases – and, if so, whether it should be taken as an aggravating or mitigat-ing circumstance.[32] Donald Dalrymple's Select Committee had stated that 'there is a difference between the paroxysm of intoxication and insanity proper, so distinct as to forbid the plea, in bar of punishment, that an offence was committed while drunk'.[33] Some judges insisted drunkenness was a 'madness for which the madman is to blame', thereby aggravating the crime, yet juries were often directed to consider whether the drunkenness of a defendant might diminish their responsibility.[34] Others said the law took no cognisance of drunkenness at all 'except where it forms part of the charge'.[35] One exasperated law professor wrote that the problem was insoluble:

> until we are ready with an answer to a previous enquiry: 'Is the habit of inebriation a vice or a disease?' If a vice, it might be proper to punish it. If a disease, it might be possible to cure it. In the first case the drunkard is a candidate for the prison; in the second for the hospital and the asylum.[36]

Throughout the period, the legal position on drunken culpability remained 'far from clear or logical'.[37] Indeed, it was only recently clarified when, in 2004, the Sentencing Guidelines Council identified the 'commission of an offence while under the influence of alcohol' as 'indicating higher culpability'.[38]

In 1908 a Departmental Committee set up to look at the inebriate reformatories acknowledged the lack of consensus on the question of vice and disease, and insisted that 'the two views are irreconcilable'. For its part, the Committee decided that the inability to control one's drinking was indeed a 'constitutional peculiarity', but that it was no more disease-like than 'the possession of a sixth finger [or] the absence of a taste for music'. There were, it claimed, 'cogent reasons why the term disease should not be used to characterise the inebriate habit', not least the question of legal responsibility.

Overall, then, the rise of more thoroughly medicalised models of habitual drunkenness and inebriety posed unsettling questions for the notion that rights and responsibilities were dependent on the proper functioning of reason. Criminals, being presumed rational, were liable to the full punitive force of the law; the insane, being presumed irrational, were not criminally liable but were subject to both incarceration and compulsory treatment. Inebriates did not just fall awkwardly between these two stools: they presented a legislative, juridical and philosophical problem which undermined any neat distinction between rationality and insanity. They were both rational *and* insane depending on which part of their evidently conflicted, possibly multiple, selves one chose to look at. The question of inebriety was, then, part of a wider set of questions about the nature of identity itself.

Inebriety and degeneration

Not all the proponents of the disease model saw inebriate asylums as places whose role was to cure habitual drunkards. For a significant number, the best inebriate asylums could achieve was to take otherwise helpless inebriates out of the community for as long as possible, with luck ameliorating some of their symptoms along the way. There was, obviously, a social order motive for supporting inebriate asylums even if you doubted that inebriety could be cured. If inebriates tend to commit crime, then three years in an asylum was three years struck off from their criminal career. However, there was another very different motive for incarcerating inebriates put forward by some within medical temperance: the belief 'that the treatment at least restrains for the time [the inebriate's] tendency to procreate offspring that are likely to be parasitic or dangerous to the community'.[39] In other words, incarceration might not make people better, but it could act as a form of eugenic control.

The disease concept of inebriety was tied to the late-Victorian obsession with the idea of racial degeneration. That is, the idea that criminality, immorality, certain forms of disease and even industrial inefficiency could be explained by a kind of reverse evolution in which 'degenerate' characteristics acquired by one generation (such as sexual perversity or alcoholism) could be passed on to their offspring, and furthermore that such degenerate traits would then snowball through those subsequent generations producing ever more deviant individuals until the genetic line died out altogether. The idea relied on a Lamarckian model of evolutionary change – the idea that traits *acquired* by parents were passed on to offspring – as opposed to the Darwinian principle that change in offspring is always the result of random mutations which either are or are not well-adapted to the specific environment. Degeneration theory came under increasing pressure as Lamarckianism began to lose credibility towards the end of the nineteenth century, and its influence on the eugenic policies of Nazi Germany finally put into the political wilderness an idea which had been consigned to the scientific dustbin some time previously.

The relationship between nineteenth-century ideas about alcoholism and contemporary degeneration theory is well-known. Benedict Morel, one of the fathers of degenerationist thought, believed excessive alcohol consumption was one of the driving factors behind degeneration. Famously, Émile Zola produced a literary study of alcoholic degeneration in his novel *L'Assommoir*. Conventionally, degeneration theory tends to be associated with continental medical writers such as Bénédict Morel, Cesare Lombroso and, in the cultural sphere, with the splenetic anti-modernist Max Nordau – who, in the course of his widely-read book *Degeneration*, called Paul Verlaine 'a repulsive degenerate', Walt Whitman 'a reprobate rake', Maeterlinck a 'pitiable mental cripple', Ibsen a 'malignant, anti-social simpleton', Nietzsche 'a madman' and Zola 'a sexual psychopath'.[40]

However, degeneration theory was alive and well in Britain as well. Articles in *The Lancet* debated not so much if, but by what specific means, physical degeneration was taking place in British towns and cities,[41] and an 1895 Departmental Committee on Prisons (which, incidentally, asserted that the 'physical craving for drink is a disease which requires medical treatment not provided by the present prison system') considered it 'not unreasonable to acquiesce in the theory that criminality is a disease, and the result of physical imperfection'.[42] It was the English evolutionary theorist Francis Galton who coined the term 'eugenics'.

Degenerationist ideas dovetailed into late-Victorian medical temperance, but then branched off in a number of conflicting directions. At the heart of the issue was the belief held by many in the movement that inebriety, like all forms of degeneration, was hereditary. An influential study carried out by T. D. Crothers – the leading figure in the American Society for the Study of Inebriety – claimed that out of 1,744 cases of alcoholism analysed, 1,080 had a 'distinct history of heredity'.[43] Crother's findings seemed to bear out both anecdotal evidence and common-sense inferences about the effect of parental drinking on children. Norman Kerr was convinced that inebriety was a hereditary condition, as was William Sullivan. Victor Horsley and Mary Sturge published a compendious study of the physiological effects of alcohol in 1907, in which they concluded that 'parental intoxication tends to produce impulsive degenerates and moral imbeciles'.[44]

Of course, all this smacks resoundingly of Daniel Defoe's 'fine spindle-shanked generation'. The Victorians certainly did not invent the idea that parental alcohol use led to defective offspring, although the anti-gin campaigners of Georgian England had no concept of evolution – progressive or regressive – on which to hitch this idea. However, late-Victorian concerns about alcoholic degeneration were no less fixed on the role of drunken mothers than those expressed in the gin craze. The exact means by which degenerative traits were inherited remained open to debate. Physiologists such as Horsley and Sturge tried to find empirical evidence for cellular damage which might be passed on to children, but did not go much beyond pointing to the fact that cress and geraniums tended to wither when raised in alcoholic solutions.[45] The influential Swiss psychiatrist Auguste Forel suggested that drunkenness at the time of conception might damage reproductive cells, leading to cases of the impressively titled 'blastophthoric degeneration'.[46] Whatever the specific means of transmission, though, while paternal alcoholism was not dismissed as a factor it seemed self-evident to many that maternal drinking was the more dangerous. Indeed, previously low levels of maternal drinking seemed to some to explain the otherwise baffling fact that European civilisation, having always been exposed to alcohol, had not died out long ago. An Inter-Departmental Committee on National Deterioration, reporting in 1904, stated that 'the abuse of alcoholic stimulants is a most potent and deadly agent of physical deterioration', but continued by observing that while historically many drunken nations had been unaffected by degeneration, that was because in those nations only the men drank; however, 'if the mother as well as the father is given to drink, the progeny will deteriorate in every way, and the future of the race is imperilled'.[47] This was not an unusual comment, and the literature of the time is filled with dire warnings that the future – or at least the imperial dominance – of European civilisation itself was under threat because women, as well as men, had taken to drink.

The usual version of this kind of degenerationist thinking was that there was something in the nature of modern civilisation which, if not managed properly, held within it the seeds of its own destruction. Overcrowding (and the promiscuity born of proximity), poor sanitation, easy access to alcohol and narcotics, and the enervating effects of over-stimulation appeared to give rise to degenerative diseases which required intervention to prevent them gnawing away at the very fibre of modern civilisation itself, rotting it from within. Arguments for medical intervention in the prevention of inebriety were part and parcel of this: the implication was that unless inebriety was dealt with where it occurred, then it would be passed on to the subsequent generations, intensifying and spreading in the process. This provided a strong argument for prohibition: not only did progress require sobriety, but sobriety was needed to protect against cultural regression. However, there was a counter-argument to this which suggested that far from being a 'curse of civilisation', a degree of hard drinking was both a measure and guarantee of civilisation.

An evolutionary protective

The architect of this idea was a British doctor called George Archdall Reid. Reid argued that the whole idea of hereditary inebriety, as conceived by the majority of writers on the subject, was simply preposterous. He followed Darwin in insisting that acquired characteristics were never passed on to offspring; consequently, there was no evolutionary mechanism whatsoever by which the drunkenness or otherwise of a parent could impact upon the predispositions of their children. He did accept that heavy drinking by pregnant women could damage children, but this was only because of the effect of alcohol on the foetus. Nevertheless, Reid remained a degenerationist of sorts. He did so because he argued that the 'drink crave' – the 'susceptibility to the charm of alcohol', as he described it – was 'inborn in primitive man, and lay latent and harmless in the early races until the discovery of alcohol made it harmful'.[48] The discovery of alcohol, Reid argued, damaged those in whom that natural 'drink crave' was strong, but at the same time gave an evolutionary advantage to anyone born with a mutation which weakened that susceptibility. This, he argued, was identical to the introduction of alien diseases into native populations: an event which invariably killed off the weak and the susceptible, but benefited those with inherent resistance, thereby making the community stronger overall. Alcohol 'like disease,' Reid claimed, 'is the cause of an evolutionary protective against itself. Drunkenness among the ancestry is the cause of temperance among the descendents'.[49]

Reid's novel, and deeply imperialist, suggestion was that 'civilised' western races consumed alcohol because a long process of evolution had weeded out the majority of those who had a 'primitive' intolerance. By the same token, this explained why colonised people seemed to suffer so much alcoholism: not because of any kind of colonial trauma, but because they had not evolved an alcohol tolerance in the way Europeans had. Consequently, Reid was vehemently opposed to prohibition and total abstinence. For Reid, the very worst thing a civilised society could do was prohibit alcohol since that would simply stop the genetically primitive from dying off. There were, he argued, 'two methods of temperance reform: the reformer's plan, the elimination of drink; and Nature's plan, the elimination of the drunkard'.[50] For Reid, there was no question which was the right course.

Reid's ideas, when they were first published in 1896, caused a storm among medical temperance commentators.[51] Nevertheless, his ideas found a degree of acceptance inside the Society for the Study of Inebriety, despite Norman Kerr's objections. Reid helped produce a report for the Society in 1899 which rejected the idea of hereditary alcoholism while asserting the hereditary nature of the basic desire for drink. It was too much for William Sullivan and Victor Horsley, both of whom refused to sign the report.[52] When Harry Campbell took over presidency of the Society in 1902, he backed Reid's position and distanced the Society from the principle of total abstention.[53] As a result, the Society began to move away from the conventional degenerationist position and towards the counter-intuitive idea that a level of alcohol consumption was essential as a means of protecting 'civilised' genetic stock.

This idea caught on quickly among anti-prohibitionists. The economist Arthur Shadwell used it to counter 'bigoted and self-righteous' temperance propaganda in 1903.[54] Some years later the eminent surgeon Ernest Starling used exactly the same argument, arguing that 'the total withdrawal of alcohol from a civilised community would help perpetuate the existence of an inherently unstable stock which would tend to degenerate still further in subsequent generations'.[55]

The conventional degenerationist strand in medical temperance was dealt a body blow in 1910 when two researchers at the Galton Laboratory for National Eugenics at University College London published the findings of research into health among the children of alcoholic parents.[56] Ethel Elderton and Karl Pearson's findings completely undermined the predictions of hereditary models. They found that there was no difference in the average family size of drinkers and non-drinkers, that there was no discernable evidence that parental drinking affected the intelligence of children, and that the higher death rate among the children of alcoholics was due to accidents rather than disease. Indeed, they concluded that the 'general health of the children of alcoholics appear[ed] on the whole slightly better than that of sober parents'. Furthermore, 'the physically strongest in the community have probably the greatest capacity and taste for alcohol'.[57] What Reid had proposed in theory, Pearson and Elderton appeared to prove empirically. The conventional degenerationist idea that alcohol consumption led to a reversing of evolutionary progress was trumped by the eugenicist belief that non-problematic alcohol use was a sign of genetic strength.

The decline of medical temperance

In early twentieth-century England, as conventional degeneration theory began to lose credibility, medical temperance came no closer to arriving at a clear position on either the nature or proper cure of the disease of inebriety. The 1898 Inebriates Act led to the creation of a handful of reformatories but, partly because of the lack of any clear guidance as to the proper treatment of inebriety, it remained unclear exactly what the purpose of compulsory committal was.[58] Furthermore, local authorities had to justify the expense of maintaining institutions whose methods and efficacy were unproven to a public who remained suspicious of the idea that they should be footing the bill for the reclamation of common drunks. Just before the outbreak of the First World War, London County Council stopped administering the 1898 Act – a move which fatally undermined the asylum movement as a whole. By 1921 there were no inebriate asylums left.

The debate on the physiological and psychological effects of alcohol continued throughout the First World War. The concept of inebriety, however, came under criticism from a number of directions. In keeping with its desire to address the drink question in all its aspects, the Central Control Board carried out a comprehensive review of the existing evidence.[59] Its report, published in 1917, sought to establish a clear distinction between the scientific analysis of alcohol and any calls for legislative action; it explicitly distanced the study of habitual drinking from 'ethics, administration, or national economy'.[60] The authors resisted making firm assertions about the effects of alcohol on offspring on the grounds that it was too important a question to be concluded without further research. Similarly, having decided that alcohol was a narcotic, not – as was widely assumed – a stimulant, the authors hedged their finding with the observation that there was 'nothing intrinsically good about a stimulant, and nothing intrinsically bad about a narcotic'.[61] Ultimately, the report lent its support to broadly physiological explanations for alcoholism: to the idea that 'the continued abuse of alcohol leads in many instances to changes in mental and bodily functions which create a need or craving for alcohol'.[62] It also, however, asserted the harmlessness of moderate drinking.[63] It was a typically pragmatic approach that mirrored CCB licensing policy: drink sensibly, it said, and you should be fine.

Towards the end of the First World War, studies into shellshock began to suggest that psychological trauma could trigger behaviours previously associated with degeneration in even the most robust and respectable individuals.[64] Some anti-temperance doctors even noted that there seemed to be a preponderance of total abstainers among the victims of shellshock, and they drew their own conclusions about the robustness or otherwise of such people.[65] Shellshock also reinforced the growing trend towards seeking psychological explanations for problematic behaviours. R. C. Brainthwaite, once an exponent of the organic disease model, changed his view after the war and began to 'consider whether habitual drunkenness could not more reasonably be regarded as a syndrome than a disease'.[66] That is, as the result of the kind of psychological traumas that both the study of shellshock and the popularisation of Freudian ideas had brought to light, inebriety began to be seen as rather more like neurotic compulsion than a disease 'like gout'.

Partly as a result of the political failure of the inebriate asylums, partly because of the decline of the socio-medical idea of degeneration that underpinned early disease models, and partly because of a turn towards psychological explanations the drink question began, towards the end of the First World War, to split in two. The twin issues of habitual drunkenness and social order had been inextricably linked throughout the nineteenth century. Prohibitionism had been as much about ending the enslavement to drink as it had been about preventing antisocial behaviour. Similarly, the Inebriates Act effectively turned the treatment of inebriety into a subset of police work. The failure of compulsory treatment, coupled with the theoretical failure of medical temperance to produce anything approaching a workable model of inebriety, dipsomania or alcoholism, led to an unhitching of the medical and legislative issues that was typified by the CCB's insistence that no political inferences be drawn from their scientific investigations. Slowly but surely, alcohol policy began to focus solely on those issues of social order which were quantifiable, actionable, and therefore an appropriate object of political practice. Habitual drunkenness, which remained a resolutely fuzzy and contradictory concept, lost its political dimension. However, a later shift in emphasis from disease models to public health would ensure that the medical profession ultimately retained its central role in defining the parameters of the drink question. Nevertheless, it would be some time before the influence of medical opinion would be felt to the degree it had been at the turn of the century.

Notes

1   R. Room, 'Governing images of alcohol and drug problems' (PhD: University of California, 1978) www.robinroom.net/dissert.pdf, accessed March 2007.
2   V. Berridge, 'The origins and early years of the Society 1884–1899', *British Journal of Addiction*, 85 (1990), 991–1003, p. 999.
3   A. Peddie, *The Necessity for Some Legislative Arrangements for the Treatment of Dipsomania, or the Drinking Insanity* (Edinburgh: Sutherland and Knox, 1858), p. 15.
4   Anon., 'Parliamentary Intelligence' (*Times*, 8 May 1873), p. 9.
5   House of Commons, *Report of the Select Committee on Habitual Drunkards* (1872) 242, p. iii.
6   House of Commons, Sixth Report of the Inspector of Inebriates under the Habitual Inebriates Act (1886) C. 4822, p. 5.
7   House of Commons, *Report from the Departmental Committee on the Treatment of Inebriates* (1893) C. 7008, p. 5.
8   *Ibid.*, p. 7.
9   T. N. Kelynack, (1904) 'Medico-legal aspects of inebriety', *The British Journal for the Study of Inebriety*, 2:1 (1904), 117–29, pp. 123–7.
10 M. Valverde, *Diseases of the Will: Alcohol and the Dilemmas of Freedom* (Cambridge: Cambridge University Press, 1998), p. 77; G. Johnstone, 'From vice to disease?: The concepts of dipsomania and inebriety, 1860–1900', *Social and Legal Studies*, 5:1 (1996), 37–56, p. 44.
11 Valverde, *Diseases of the Will*, pp. 265–6.
12 Anon., 'Habitual Drunkards' (*Times*, 14 August 1872), p. 10.
13 W. W. Westcott, 'Inebriety in women and the overlying of infants', *British Journal for the Study of Inebriety*, 1:2 (1903), 65–8, p. 68.
14 V. Berridge, 'Prevention and social hygiene 1900–1914', *British Journal of Addiction*, 85 (1990), 1005–16, p. 1009.

15 Valverde, *Diseases of the Will*, p. 47.
16 P. McCandless, '"Curses of civilization": Insanity and drunkenness in Victorian Britain', *British Journal of Addiction*, 79 (1984), 49–58, p. 53; Valverde, *Diseases of the Will*, pp. 45–6.
17 Peddie, *The Necessity for Some Legislative Arrangements*, p. 12.
18 *Ibid.*, p. 28.
19 T. D. Crothers, 'The Norman Kerr memorial lecture', *The British Journal for the Study of Inebriety*, 3:3 (1906), 105–15, p. 111.
20 N. Kerr, 'President's inaugural address', *Proceedings of the Society for the Study and Cure of Inebriety*, 1:1 (1884), 2–16, p. 3.
21 Valverde, *Diseases of the Will*, p. 50.
22 Kerr, 'President's inaugural address', p. 3.
23 *Ibid.*, pp. 3–8.
24 *Ibid.*, p. 14.
25 N. Kerr, 'Legislation for inebriates in Britain', *Medical Temperance Review*, 2:5 (1899), 100–1, p. 100.
26 Valverde, *Diseases of the Will*, p. 49.
27 H. Campbell, 'The study of inebriety: A retrospect and a forecast', *The British Journal for the Study of Inebriety*, 1:1 (1903), 5–14, p. 5.
28 W. C. Sullivan, 'The criminal responsibility of the alcoholic', *British Journal for the Study of Inebriety*, 2:1 (1904), 48–53, p. 53.
29 H. Wingfield, *The Forms of Alcoholism and their Treatment* (London: Hodder and Stoughton, 1918), p. 26.
30 J. W. Collins, 'An address on the institutional treatment of inebriety', *The British Journal for the Study of Inebriety*, 1:2 (1903), 97–115, p. 11.
31 Valverde, *Diseases of the Will*, p. 1.
32 D. Rabin, 'Drunkenness and responsibility for crime in the eighteenth century', *Journal of British Studies*, 44 (2005), 457–77.
33 House of Commons *Report of the Select Committee on Habitual Drunkards* (1872) 242, p. iv.
34 S. B. Atkinson, 'Some medico-legal relations of intemperance', *The British Journal for the Study of Inebriety*, 3:1 (1905), 4–15, pp. 5–6; N. Walker, *Crime and Insanity in England: Volume One* (Edinburgh: Edinburgh University Press, 1968), p. 178.
35 G. Slot, 'The medico-legal aspects of drunkenness', *British Journal for the Study of Inebriety*, 23:3 (1936), 113–24, p. 114.
36 R. W. Lee, 'Comparative legislation as to habitual drunkards', *Journal of the Society of Comparative Legislation*, 3:2 (1901), 241–51, p. 241.
37 Walker, *Crime and Insanity in England*, p. 180.
38 Sentencing Guidelines Council, 'Overarching Principles: Seriousness' (Sentencing Guidelines Secretariat, 2004), p. 6 www.sentencing-guidelines.gov.uk/docs/Seriousness_guideline.pdf, accessed April 2008.
39 W. C. Sullivan, 'The causes of inebriety in the female and the effects of alcoholism on racial degeneration', *British Journal for the Study of Inebriety*, 1: 2 (1903), 61–4, p. 64.
40 M. Nordau, *Degeneration* (London: University of Nebraska Press, 1993), pp. 119, 231, 239, 407, 416, 500.
41 D. Pick, *Faces of Degeneration: A European Disorder c. 1848–1918* (Cambridge: Cambridge University Press, 1989), p. 201.
42 House of Commons, *Report from the Departmental Committee on Prisons* (1895) C. 7702, p. 8.

43 V. Horsley and M. Sturge, *Alcohol and the Human Body: An introduction to the Study of the Subject* (London: Macmillan, 1907), p. 335.
44 *Ibid.*, p. 320.
45 *Ibid.*, pp. 53–5.
46 W. F. Bynum, 'Alcoholism and degeneracy in 19th century European medicine and psychiatry', *Addiction*, 79:1 (1984), 59–70, p. 64.
47 W. McAdam Eccles, 'Alcohol as a factor in the causation of deterioration in the individual and the race', *The British Journal for the Study of Inebriety*, 2:4 (1905), 146–55, p. 154.
48 G. A. Reid, 'Human evolution and alcohol', *British Journal for the Study of Inebriety*, 1:2 (1903), 186–201, p. 197.
49 *Ibid.*, p. 195.
50 *Ibid.*, p. 200.
51 F. C. Coley, 'Dr Reid's theories about alcoholism', *Medical Temperance Review*, 2:11 (1899), 245–48, p. 246.
52 Bynum, 'Alcoholism and degeneracy', p. 65.
53 H. Campbell, 'The study of inebriety', p. 13.
54 Shadwell, *Drink, Temperance and Legislation*, pp. 101, 126.
55 E. H. Starling, *The Action of Alcohol on Man* (London: Longmans, Green and Co., 1923), p. 166.
56 E. Elderton and K. Pearson, *A First Study of the Influence of Parental Alcoholism on the Physique and Ability of the Offspring* (London: Eugenics Laboratory Memoirs, 1910).
57 Bynum, 'Alcoholism and degeneracy', p. 68.
58 L. Zedner, *Women, Crime and Custody in Victorian England* (Oxford: Clarendon, 1991), p. 237.
59 Central Control Board, *Alcohol: Its Action on the Human Body* (London: HMSO, 1917).
60 *Ibid.*, p. 132.
61 *Ibid.*, p. 127.
62 *Ibid.*, p. 111.
63 *Ibid.*, p. 133.
64 C. May, 'Pathology, identity and the social construction of alcohol dependence', *Sociology*, 35:2 (2001), 385–401, p. 390.
65 Starling, *The Action of Alcohol on Man*, pp. 158, 206.
66 V. Berridge, 'The inter-war years: A period of decline', *British Journal of Addiction* 85 (1990), 1023–35, p. 1032.

13

The pub and the people: drinking places and popular culture

If anyone know of a pub that has draught stout, open fire, cheap meals, a garden, motherly barmaids and no radio, I should be glad to hear of it, even though its name were something as prosaic as 'The Red Lion' or 'The Railway Arms'. (George Orwell)

To drink beer is for your country's good as well as your own. (Brewers Society advert, 1938)

By 1918, the drink question in England had been transformed. The establishment of the CCB had shown that it was possible to impose central planning on the drinks trade. The restriction of opening hours had normalised the idea that special times should be set aside in which pubs were open, whereas previously the assumption had been that special times were set aside in which they were forced to close. The CCB had also encouraged leading brewers to work with the government in setting alcohol policy, rather than viewing legislation as a perennial threat.[1] Furthermore, the idea of improving the conditions in which people drank, rather than simply restricting access to alcohol, had become firmly established in the minds of both policy-makers and the wider public.

Equally importantly, however, levels of overall consumption had plummeted. At the start of the century, average annual consumption of beer stood at 214 pints per person; by the time the war finished it was just 80.[2] Beer was more expensive, it was weaker and pubs faced unprecedented levels of competition from new forms of entertainment such as the cinema and organised sports. The brewing industry had also shrunk: in 1900 there had been over 6,000 breweries in operation, by 1920 that figure had been halved.[3] The success of the CCB meant that nationalisation was a real possibility. The concept of State purchase had won over established temperance and had gained significant support within the Labour Party.[4] Although the CCB was formally wound-up with the passing of the 1921 Licensing Act, State management was retained in all the districts where it had been established during the war, leaving open the possibility that the experiment could be extended. Brewers were selling less beer, drinkers were abandoning the pub in unprecedented numbers, and the prospect of nationalisation was beginning to loom large.

Improving the pub

The most significant response to the post-war malaise within the brewing industry was driven by two brewing companies who had been closely involved with the work of the CCB: Whitbread, and Mitchells and Butlers. The chairmen of the two companies, Sydney Nevile and William Waters Butler, had advised the CCB and had been impressed by the success of the Carlisle experiment. In particular, they had seen that the public conception of the pub could be transformed by sloughing off its image as a mere drink shop and presenting it instead as a place where alcohol provided just one of a wide range of leisure choices. The great development projects of the CCB provided the blueprint for what became known as the 'improved pub', and throughout the inter-war years leading brewers would invest millions in building projects designed to replace the snug, but sometimes sordid, local with a new kind of pub: a genteel and airy establishment in which nutritious food and soft drinks would be as popular as beer, and dancing as popular as darts. Depending on your viewpoint, this represented either the civilising of an increasingly disreputable industry, or the imposition of middle-class values (and patterns of consumption) on the one social institution that the working class could truly call their own.

As we have seen, the idea of the improved pub had its roots in the adoption of the Gothenburg system by temperance campaigners in the late nineteenth century: in the belief that the worst excesses of drunkenness could be curbed by civilising, as it were, the public house itself. Where it had been tried, this approach had proved beneficial to the bigger brewers. In Birmingham, the systematic reduction of licences, which had been in place since 1897, was superseded from 1905 by a system of licence exchange which became famous as Birmingham's 'fewer and better' policy – designed to replace the plethora of low-grade pubs with a smaller number of more respectable establishments.[5] The 'fewer and better' system benefited those brewers who had the resources necessary to improve and expand their establishments. Mitchells and Butlers did especially well out of it; some years later their chairman commented to delegates at his organisation's annual general meeting that 'Birmingham can show types of houses which are unsurpassed for giving good service to the public, and the majority of them, I am proud to say, are the property of the shareholders of this Company'.[6]

As Birmingham magistrates attempted to oversee pub improvement through the management of licences, organisations like the People's Refreshment House Association and the Central Public House Trust Association strove to make the Gothenburg system a reality through buying up businesses and running them along disinterested lines. While the impact of such companies was numerically tiny, they played a significant role in influencing the activities of the CCB.[7] Furthermore, involvement with the CCB convinced Sydney Nevile and William Waters Butler that pub improvement was both socially responsible and economically viable. Consequently, by the 1920s pub improvement had been transformed from the experimental goal of eccentrically pragmatic temperance reformers to the business model of multi-million pound brewing interests.

In 1920, Whitbread established the Improved Public House Company to oversee investment into both the renovation of existing licensed properties and the pursuit of an ambitious project of new pub building. Whitbread were joined by Mitchells and Butlers, Watney, Combe & Reid, Barclay Perkins, Walker-Cain and many other breweries in the dash to polish up the pub's tarnished image. These new pubs did away with snugs and saloons, garish lighting and engraved glass panels and replaced them with spacious, open-plan seating areas, dining halls and even dance floors. Many improved pubs were built on an enormous scale; some incorporated bowling greens, tennis courts, even cinemas. Bar service was replaced by table service, purpose-built kitchens were installed to provide restaurant-standard food; mineral water, tea and coffee were made as easily available as beer and wine. Between 1922 and 1930 over 20,000 pubs were 'improved' to some degree, and over the whole of the inter-war period 79 new 'superpubs' were built at enormous cost to their developers.[8]

While brewers invested heavily in pub improvement, their supporters in Parliament sought legislative support for the movement. Between 1919 and 1928 three Bills were introduced proposing separate licence certificates for improved pubs. Although no legislation was forthcoming, a Select Committee was appointed to look at the issue, which reported in 1927. The Committee's findings acknowledged the good intentions of the pub improvers, and noted that some licensing Justices were not always as flexible as they could be in approving the extensions necessary to replace a traditional pub with an improved version. However, they also commented on the extent to which improved pubs alienated many traditional pubgoers, noting that 'where a public house is improved and enlarged there is a tendency for the old clientele which used to frequent it to remove to another unimproved house while another and better class of customer … comes to take their place'.[9]

The pub improvement movement opened a new frontline in the battle for control over the working-class drinking place. However, because it was driven by brewers themselves the goal was not the destruction of pub culture, but its incorporation into a new economy of leisure in which the biggest players were the ever-expanding middle class. George Orwell dismissed suburban superpubs as 'dismal sham Tudor' atrocities which represented a 'serious blow at [the] communal life' of the working class.[10] Orwell's own idea of a perfect pub (as set out in a 1946 article entitled 'The Moon Under Water') reflected his idiosyncratically lower-upper-middle-class vision of England as a sort of lower-upper-working-class idyll.[11] Nevertheless, Orwell understood the peculiarly fundamental role that the idea (whatever the reality) of 'the local' played in popular English culture and he was angered by the paternalistic social engineering which pub improvement attempted to achieve.

The motivation of the brewers involved in pub improvement was complicated. The fact that they were faced with collapsing beer sales, continuing temperance pressure and the real possibility of State purchase meant that brewers had to do something to reinvent their trade. As William Waters Butler put it, 'Carlisle has certainly roused in the trade the spirit of self-preservation if it has done nothing else'.[12] In addition to these pressures, brewers remained locked in conflict with licensing magistrates who were determined to pursue a 'fewer and better' policy, especially when granting licences for pubs on the new suburban estates. London County Council famously allowed for just one pub to be built on its Downham Estate, despite the fact that it contained homes for around 30,000 residents. The Downham Tavern, built by Barclay Perkins in 1929, would become one of the most enormous superpubs of the era. Brewers knew that they had a better chance of securing the potentially lucrative licence for such estates if they could convince the licensing authorities that their primary goal was the encouragement of sobriety rather than the sale of alcohol. Giant, improved pubs were expensive and their returns were by no means guaranteed, but they were seen by the brewers as providing a way of 'retaining trade which might otherwise be lost by the transference of population to a new district'.[13]

While it is tempting to dismiss pub improvement as a cynical attempt by the bigger brewers to secure their market position, it has more recently been suggested that their motivations were altogether more public-spirited. In a detailed study of the pub improvement movement, David Gutzke has argued that the improving brewers 'promoted pub reform as a tactic not to secure impressive profits, but to restore order, discipline, efficiency and fair competition to the marketplace'.[14] Indeed, Gutzke argues that the pub improvement movement was motivated primarily by the 'Progressive convictions' of the brewers.[15] While none of the key figures in the CCB or the pub improvement movement described themselves as 'Progressives' (and the London Progressive Party – who had dominated the London County Council at the turn of the century – supported a policy of simple licence reduction),[16] ideas associated with American Progressivism, such as a belief in the importance of the physical environment in developing social progress, were echoed in the thinking of the pub improvers. Pub improvement was certainly more closely akin to progressivism than it was to either the religious conservatism of the CETS or the political absolutism of the Alliance.

Pub improvement was an idea developed initially by temperance reformers who sought to 'civilise' the pub by turning it into a more respectable, more middle-class institution. The champions of pub improvement within the CCB – people like Henry Carter – were temperance men with a pragmatic approach to social engineering and a willingness to accept that the pub played a crucial role in the cultural lives of the working class. The adoption of pub improvement by leading figures within the drinks trade reflected the extent to which the idea provided a vision of the trade on which moderates from both sides could agree: a vision in which the business of selling alcohol was secured, but in a manner which stripped that business of its seemingly intractable associations with both drunkenness and the distasteful social habits of the lumpenproletariat. It also opened the trade up to the expanding, and increasingly affluent, middle class while presenting that expansion as an exercise in social responsibility.

The pub improvement movement was not confined to the work of brewers; numerous charitable and philanthropic organisations sprang up in the 1920s and 1930s which attempted to contribute to the transformation of the pub from 'an unclean place of furtive self-indulgence' to a 'centre of happy social life'.[17] One of these groups, the Committee for Verse and Prose Recitation (or 'Poetry in Pubs' as it soon became known), organised performances of Shakespeare and poetry readings in improved pubs, beginning with a performance of *Twelfth Night* in the Downham Tavern in June 1937. Their goal was to encourage 'a wider appreciation of our language and literature in its higher forms' and thereby pursue a self-declared ambition of bringing culture to the masses.[18] Like many of the brewers, Poetry in Pubs both looked forward to an age of mass cultural embourgeoisement and back to a mythic notion of the tavern as the centre of an authentic folk culture.

With the emergence of the pub improvement movement the drink question once again revealed itself to be a question about where and how people drank.[19] For the pub improvers, this question was to be addressed by training people to drink differently rather than through the coercion of draconian licensing policies. In the narrow sense this represented a conflict between two approaches to the drink question: between those who argued for restriction to access and those who argued for access to improved sources.[20] In a wider sense, however, it was a continuation of the attempt to establish social order through the civilisation of manners. From this perspective, many of the long-standing divisions between temperance reformers were tactical rather than fundamental. All temperance reformers saw excessive drinking as a brake on the establishment of social order, and most saw the establishment of more rational forms of recreation as key to the 'civilisation' of lower-class culture. The difference between those whose stated goal was 'fewer and better' and those who placed their faith in counter-attractions only, was simply that one group understood that the pub was not going to disappear, while the other believed it could be made to wither away. The coalition of interest groups who backed pub improvement represented a significant victory for the pragmatists – or, put differently, those who understood that the establishment of cultural hegemony always involved a degree of give and take.

That victory, however, turned out to be partial. Reporting in 1931, a Royal Commission on Licensing noted a marked change in manners, going so far as to assert that 'drunkenness has gone out of fashion'.[21] However, whether this was due to gentrification, counter-attractions, licensing restrictions or the price of beer was unclear. The brewers involved in pub improvement successfully sustained the meaningful channels of communication between themselves and policy-makers that had been established under the CCB, and they went a long way towards establishing the perception that some brewers at least had the interests of wider society at heart. Prominent sceptics such as Lord Astor may have insisted the whole enterprise was 'eyewash', but in the opinion of the chairman of Watney, Combe & Reid, the principle had been 'triumphantly vindicated' by the press, politicians and the clergy.[22] Of course, the brewers also obtained many potentially lucrative licences to service the new housing estates, even if that came at a significant short-term cost. However, despite investing up to £99 million in total on pub improvement over the inter-war period,[23] the improved public house proved to be a white elephant. By 1937 the *Brewer's Journal* was decrying the absurdity of 'freak public-houses', such as the Downham Tavern, which had been 'imposed at the behest of people who had never entered a public-house as customers in their lives'.[24] The same year saw the Downham Tavern's owners, Barclay Perkins, apply to the authorities for permission to reintroduce a stand-up bar – that symbol of old-style unreconstructed boozing – into their flagship superpub. Orwell's condemnation of improved pubs as inaccessible sham-Tudor eyesores reflected a widespread public feeling that the paternalism of the pub improvers, well-meaning or otherwise, was little more than class snobbery.

The pub and the people

As many commentators noted, the most significant flaw in the pub improvement movement was that it embodied a notion of what the pub could be which was conjured up in the minds of people who had very little idea of what the pub actually was. Of course, the brewers were intimately involved in the ownership, supply and, depending on the degree of autonomy allowed to tenant landlords, management of pubs. However, the boards and shareholder meetings of the big brewing companies, and the licensing benches who facilitated the improvement schemes, were simply not made up of the kind of people for whom the pub was the heart of their communal life.

Indeed, the alien nature of pub culture to sections of the middle class gave rise to a spate of quasi-anthropological investigations of pubs between the wars. In 1927, the social commentator Ernest Selley, who had written a pamphlet in support of nationalisation of the drink trade three years earlier, published a book-length investigation of pub life entitled *The English Public House As It Is*. Based on observations Selley made in pubs across the country, the book set out to counter the problem that most of what was written about pubs was produced by people who 'obviously never use them, and, therefore, fail to understand the point of view of those who do'.[25] However, while Selley clearly saw himself as contradicting the widespread 'rubbish written about what goes on inside public houses', his descriptions, though based on actual observation, were filtered by a sometimes narrowly judgemental perspective.[26] A drinker at one improved pub who objected to the 'continental system' of waiter service is dismissed by Selley as 'a member of what I once heard described as "The Flea and Sawdust School"; one of the type which prefers the stuffy "coziness" of the dirty, ill-ventilated taproom to any of the "new fangled" ideas'.[27] Like countless Select Committee reports, Commissions of Inquiry and journalistic accounts, Selley's drinkers were spoken on behalf of, described from the position of the 'neutral' observer, and defined by parameters not set by themselves. The one group, it seemed, who never got to state their view on the drink question was the actual people who did the drinking.

That default perspective was challenged when Mass-Observation published a study of pub life in 1943.[28] *The Pub and the People* was part of Mass-Observation's larger 'Worktown' study, which involved volunteers observing and documenting the minutiae of everyday life in Bolton. The difference between Mass-Observation's work and the work of people such as Ernest Selley was that while it remained primarily (though not exclusively) based on the observation of behaviour, subjective and largely condescending commentary was replaced by the presentation of detail which was, in theory at least, left to speak for itself. *The Pub and the People* sought less to demean the 'coziness' of the taproom than to mine its complexities (not least by setting out in minute detail the subtle, but critical, differences between taproom, vault, lounge and bar). Women, Mass-Observation noted, were excluded from taprooms – but nevertheless made up 31 per cent of the pub-goers in 'Worktown'. Under-25s represented the lowest proportion of pub-goers, but were the biggest frequenters of milk bars. Pushing attention to detail to entirely new levels, they recorded that standing drinkers finished a gill of beer in an average of five minutes and thirty-four seconds, while seated drinkers took over thirteen minutes (odd as such a calculation appears, it did serve the purpose of neatly illustrating the impact of the environment on drinking behaviours).[29]

The Pub and the People sought to overturn established myths about pub life. Having meticulously ascertained how long drinkers took to finish their beers at different times of the evening, the authors concluded that extended opening hours would not lead to more drunkenness since: 'First, people do not go to pubs to get drunk. Second, their drinking is limited by their spending capacity. Thirdly, as our timings show, they could easily get drunk in the available hours if they wanted to do so'.[30] The fact that significant numbers of women drank was not presented as a measure of social decay, but as a reflection of the complexity of the social rules which governed drinking – rules which, nevertheless, imposed all sorts of taboos on where and what women could drink. The fact that the pub-goers went to pubs to drink beer rather than eat food was presented not as a mark of their incivility, but as a measure of the importance they attached to beer as both a social lubricant and a source of nutrition.[31]

Throughout the study, the authors repeated their claim that the reasons for pub attendance were social, and that to understand the pub one had to strive to understand pub culture rather than obsess about levels of consumption, opening hours and public drunkenness. The 'basis of sound legislation,' they insisted 'must surely be the stabilization of what goes on *inside* the pub, not ... the minority that reel out from them blind-to-the-world and disorderly enough to attract a PC'; the reason so much legislation was unsound, however, was because it was usually drafted by 'persons who are automatically too high up the social scale to know much, if anything, about ordinary pubs'.[32]

Ultimately, however, Mass-Observation saw the greatest threat to the pub not in the cultural elitism of magistrates, but in the cultural narcosis of mass society: in the 'passive and individual' forms of leisure provided by the mass media. 'The pub,' the authors claimed:

stresses the fact that you are living among your fellow men, that the issues of life, whether faced or escaped, are not solitary but communal. The Church and the political party say the same thing, in a different way. The films and pools do not.[33]

The novel conclusion of Mass-Observation's study, then, was not that the pub needed improving, gentrifying or reinventing but that, if anything, in an age when popular culture was becoming increasingly commodified, individualised and passive, the traditional working-class pub needed to be saved.

Beer and Britishness

It was precisely this sense that the pub was losing out to the 'drug-like pleasures of the cinema and the radio', that attracted George Orwell to Mass-Observation's study.[34] Nevertheless, reviewing *The Pub and the People* in 1943, Orwell also noted that it was 'a pity that this large and careful survey could not have had a short appendix indicating what effect the war has had on our drinking habits'.[35] The fact that it had been unable to cover the impact of war on pub culture was *The Pub and the People's* greatest weakness. The Second World War may not have given rise to the dramatic changes in drinking culture that took place between 1914 and 1918, but its impact was significant nonetheless. In economic terms, the most important effect was an enormous increase in taxation: between September 1939 and April 1943, the basic duty on a barrel of beer went up from 48s to 138s, a rise of almost 300 per cent. Because the duties imposed on beer increase according to strength, beer also tended to become much weaker over this period.

Despite this, however, consumption actually rose. Significantly, the government made no attempt to suggest that beer-drinking was unpatriotic or detrimental to the war effort. In what was a far cry from Lloyd George's 'Germany, Austria and Drink' comments twenty-six years earlier, in 1940 the Minister for Food, Lord Woolton, declared that 'it is the business of the government not only to maintain the life but the morale of the country. If we are to keep up anything like approaching normal life, beer should continue to be in supply'.[36] In the context of a war in which distinctively 'British' values were being corralled by the government as part of their internal propaganda effort, beer was too rich a signifier of those values to be subjected to official condemnation. In the cultural imaginary of Churchill's Britain it was the hearty fellowship of honest ale (albeit weak and overpriced), not the prim decency of temperance, which provided the soundest bulwark against both the cultural and military threat of the German war machine.

Many underlying demographic shifts were also accelerated by the Second World War, the most significant of which was the popularisation of the pub among young women. Mass-Observation had already observed that a significant number of pub goers in the late 1930s were female, however the majority of these were women aged forty and above.[37] In the early 1940s, however, there was a measurable shift in the age profile of women drinkers so that by the end of the war up to two-thirds of female pub-goers were under forty.[38] There were a number of reasons for this: the real increase in wages which many women experienced when moving into traditionally male-dominated occupations, the liberation from familial controls which came from entering the workplace, the disruption of other forms of leisure activity such as cinema-going, and the fact that court-ship in pubs became increasingly acceptable as opportunities to engage in other leisure activities were curtailed.[39] Unlike the American saloon, the English pub had never been the site of an exclusive gender divide and the issue of women's rights had never overlapped with temperance to the de-gree that it did on the other side of the Atlantic. Nevertheless, many of the gender taboos surrounding public drinking, especially concerning young, single women, were undermined by the shake-up of gender roles enforced by wartime conditions.

Pub-going among young men also increased in the early 1940s, so much so that it led to something of a revival of temperance campaigning. In June 1943 the British Temperance League commissioned a report on juvenile drinking – ill-advisedly, perhaps – from Mass-Observation who concluded, much to the annoyance of their patrons, that such concerns were 'grossly exaggerated'.[40] Nevertheless, in December Henry Carter was moved to write to *The Times* reminding its readers of the success of the CCB in the previous war, and calling for the reintroduction of anti-treating orders to curb drunkenness among the young.[41]

The fact was, however, that while beer consumption had increased among men and women, the political sting had been drawn from the drink question by the experiences of the preceding quarter century. The drop in consumption during the course of the First World War had been enor-mous, and levels had never recovered since. The palpable threat posed by public drunkenness had, therefore, receded leaving temperance campaign-ers with little to point to but their own moral rectitude. The establishment of the CCB had led to a rapprochement between government and the brewing industry which was based, for the first time, on open coopera-tion rather than either mutual suspicion or surreptitious influence. The Licensing Act of 1921 had also provided a compromise in which many of the demands of the more moderate temperance campaigners had been met, especially regarding opening hours. The pub improvement movement had gone some way towards neutralising the cultural status of the pub by suggesting that its flaws were redeemable rather than fatal. Furthermore, the ungainly collapse of prohibition in America had dealt a mortal blow to the already weakened prohibitionist campaign in Britain.

The wartime mobilisation of 'Britishness' as an identity grounded in moderation, fellowship and good-humoured stoicism compounded the weakening of the traditional temperance movement by positioning beer and the pub as symbols of what was best, not worst, about British culture. In contrast to America, where the saloon and the brewing industry were successfully depicted as alien by a temperance campaign which came to rely increasingly on nativist rhetoric, in England beer's ambient associa- tion with national identity proved unshakable. It was this 'Beer Street' version of what beer-drinking meant – a version in which beer-drinking was presented as rational, social and civilised – which was shared by pub- improving brewers, social commentators like George Orwell, and, ulti- mately, the policy-makers of a wartime administration who needed to de- fend all the unifying national myths they could. Beer had always been 'the people's' drink, and how attitudes to beer changed said as much about the shifting role of the idea of 'the people' on the grand political scale as it did about anything else.

Market forces

For all that the Second World War helped see off the residual threat of the traditional temperance movement, it also put the brewers in a vulnerable position. High taxes and weak beers may have been accepted as a justifi- able imposition while the war continued, but once hostilities were over consumers were in a position to seek out alternatives. Mass-Observation had already noted that young people were more attracted to milk bars than old-fashioned pubs, and young people began to revert back to such establishments soon after war ended.[42] Add to this the increasing popular- ity of the cinema, the rise of television and the widespread availability of an array of soft drinks whose cultural connotations made them far more glamorous to young consumers than beer, and you had a recipe for real concern within the drinks industry.

Even before the war brewers had begun to respond to these cultur- al shifts by investing heavily in advertising. In the late 1920s, Guinness launched their 'Guinness for Strength' and 'Guinness is Good for You' adverts: a campaign which managed not only to convince one genera- tion of drinkers that beer made from overheated malt somehow acquired mysterious health-giving properties, it managed to establish that idea with such success that it remains a standard feature of drinking lore today. By

1931, the Royal Commission on Licensing estimated that at least £2 million was being spent annually on alcohol advertising.[43] This figure was further boosted by a controversial advertising campaign launched in 1933 after the chairman of the Brewer's Society, Sir Edgar Sanders, called for an advertising campaign to 'get the beer-drinking habit instilled into thousands, almost millions, of young men who do not at present know the taste of beer'.[44] Sanders had been vocal in his condemnation of increased beer duties, warning in the same year that increased costs were fostering 'sullen resentment' among working-class consumers.[45] However, his call for a nationwide advertising campaign raised the hackles of both temperance campaigners and newspaper editors who resented Sanders's suggestion that any advertising expenditure should be contingent upon editorial support from the papers in which adverts were placed. Samuel Story, president of the Newspaper Society, condemned Sanders's speech as an 'impudent threat' to the neutrality of the press, and emphatically denied that 'the editorial policy of the Press of this country can be dictated or influenced by the purchase of advertising space by any trade interest'.[46]

The subsequent 'Beer is Best' campaign followed Guinness in attempting to reinforce the notion that beer was a health drink.[47] Of course, this dovetailed neatly with the pub improvers' attempt to reposition the pub as a 'healthy' social space, and the campaign was strongly backed by Sydney Nevile. Whitbread also launched a campaign featuring endorsements from celebrities such as Douglas Fairbanks Jr. and images of Whitbread beer being drunk in an array of glamorous settings. Where 'Beer is Best' harked back to deeply held cultural beliefs around beer, Whitbread were innovative in trying to reposition their brand as unashamedly upper-class.

Post-war planning

Beer sales did increase in the years immediately following the 'Beer is best' campaign, but to nothing like the levels seen before the First World War. Despite the continued increase in consumption during the Second World War, the austere financial climate of the immediate post-war years only exacerbated the problems which had faced the drink industry in the 1930s. By the 1940s the combination of high taxation, low disposable incomes and proliferating counter-attractions was achieving outcomes that a century of temperance campaigning had signally failed to achieve. Beer was expensive, weak and often low-quality; the pub, by extension, was losing custom. The post-war Labour administration, meanwhile, sought piecemeal extensions to the State management of licensing which threatened to further undermine attempts by the brewers to re-establish the pub as the centre of social life. A Planning Act passed in 1945 empowered local planning committees in areas of extensive war damage to determine the licence requirements in their areas. Four years later, the Labour Government passed a Licensing Act which extended State management to all new towns under the auspices of locally-based licensing advisory committees. Had it been implemented, this would surely have represented the most significant extension of State control over the drinks trade since the establishment of the CCB, and it would have provided a platform from which supporters of complete State purchase could have forcefully argued their case. As it was, the legislation was repealed by the Conservatives before it could be acted upon. Nevertheless, the Licensed Premises in the New Towns Act, passed by Churchill's Tory administration in 1952, still brought in licensing committees for new towns which were empowered to identify what licensing needs were in their areas, and what types of licences would be most appropriate.

In 1953 a major Licensing Act further shored up the power of local authorities to put limits on the number of new licences in their jurisdiction by demanding that licences only be granted to buildings which were 'structurally adapted to the class of licence required'. Under these terms, only buildings with two rooms for public accommodation could be considered for an on-licence, and structural renovation could be imposed as a condition for licence renewal. In effect, this meant that licensing authorities could demand expensive renovation work to be carried out on pubs, with the threat of closure if the owner was unwilling, or unable, to stump up the necessary outlay.

By the mid-1950s, then, the drinks trade had seen off the organised temperance movement, and it had witnessed the fragmentation of the great Victorian drink question into a series of loosely connected debates over planning, mental health, economic efficiency, advertising and national morale.[48] Nevertheless, it remained mired in some familiar problems. On the one hand, the licensing system still placed significant control in the hands of local authorities, many of whom jealously protected their right to manage the number of drink outlets according to what they saw as the level of local need. On the other hand, the demand for drink remained sensitive to fluctuations in both production costs and levels of disposable income. Furthermore, every new leisure activity provided a counter-attraction which posed a threat to the traditional role of the pub as the centre of social life outside the workplace.

Consolidation

The response from the drinks industry came in the form of two related developments: the promotion of new drinks, especially lager; and the consolidation of the brewing and retail industry itself. The technological developments which transformed the retail end of the market were largely driven by the realisation that customers were being turned off by the unpredictable quality of traditional beers, a problem exacerbated by the fact those beers were now considerably more expensive than they had been. One response to this problem was the development of keg beers, which brewers began to produce in significant quantities from the mid-1950s onwards. However, while kegging had a significant impact (and would lead to the formation of the Campaign for Real Ale in 1971), the more seismic long-term change was the belated adoption of lager production by British brewers.

Imported lager had been available in bottles in Britain since the early years of the century, and the first lager brewery had been established in Wrexham, North Wales, in 1882. Throughout the early twentieth century, a small but significant number of British brewers attempted to produce lager on a profitable scale, despite the financial risks involved in buying the expensive refrigeration needed to successfully carry out the 'top' fermentation that distinguishes lager from other beers. While brewers saw the long-term market potential for a beer that was both attractive-looking and consistent, few had the will to take the economic gamble required to start up a large-scale lager concern.[49] In 1953, however, a deal between the Hope and Anchor brewery in Sheffield and the Canadian businessman Eddie Taylor saw the production of a new lager – Black Label – backed by the financial clout of the Canadian brewing giant Carling. Carling Black Label initially struggled to achieve a market share, not least because the tied-house system meant that it was hamstrung by Hope and Anchor's limited number of national outlets.[50] Taylor's solution to this problem would help set in motion a revolution not only in lager consumption, but in the shape of the drinks industry itself.

Taylor was a formidable operator.[51] Faced with the problem of tied houses, he responded by buying up a series of small brewers and, in 1959, established Northern Breweries. Within a year Northern Breweries had bought stakes in over twenty rival brewers, taken over six and, with the acquisition of Ulster Breweries, become United Breweries. Taylor's spectacular assault on the British brewing establishment coincided with an unexpectedly high valuation placed on Watney's during a takeover bid in 1959. It transpired that the bid was based on a valuation of the capital value of property that Watney's owned.[52] Although the bid fell through, potential buyers realised that many brewers were worth far more than their market listing suggested, because their properties had been consistently undervalued. Once again, the tied-house system blurred the line between brewers as commodity-producers and brewers as property-owners and provided the economic framework for a transformation of the industry.

Over the next three years the big brewers scrambled to both buy up smaller concerns, and to forge mergers which would protect them from their more voracious rivals (especially Taylor's ever-expanding empire). The mergers were also driven by a realisation that the brewing industry needed to modernise to survive. That meant pursuing the kind of efficiencies that could only arise out of conglomeration. Economies of scale in the production of beer, combined with the consolidation of distribution and retail networks required the merger of small and medium-sized breweries into enormous concerns, capable of competing on a national level.

The change was dramatic. In 1940, the ten leading brewers had produced 40 per cent of the beer consumed in Britain; by 1961 just eight brewers were producing 60 per cent of beer.[53] Part of this process involved a turn towards lager production on the part of many of the major brewers. By 1972, keg bitter and lager dominated beer sales, and the drinks trade as a whole was dominated by just six companies producing 82 per cent of beer for the domestic market.[54]

Easing restrictions

The consolidation of the brewing industry, and the development of new drinks, coincided with the decline of post-war austerity and the emergence of a new and affluent generation of consumers. It also coincided with a diminution of public concerns over drinking – something clearly reflected in the legislation. The Licensing Act of 1961 is notable for its focus on the relaxation of restrictions on access to drink: weekday opening was extended to 11p.m. in London and 10.30p.m. elsewhere, and Sunday closing put back from 10.00p.m. to 10.30p.m. At the same time, off-licence opening hours were extended so that, for the first time, off-licences could be opened throughout the day. In effect, this meant that the new supermarkets could sell alcohol as a standard commodity. Long opening hours for dancing clubs were extended from London to the rest of the country, new licences relaxing restrictions on the sale of alcohol in restaurants and hotels were introduced, and under-fourteens were permitted in bars where food was served. The 1961 Act also relaxed the rules so that pubs could play radio, television or recorded music without applying for a special licence, and for the first time billiards and music were allowed in pubs on a Sunday.

In 1961, for the first time in many years, licensing legislation was used to actively liberalise access to alcohol. This represented an important rejection of temperance ideology because it was legislation designed around the needs of the moderate drinker, rather than targeted towards the control of problem drinking. This is an important shift. Even when previous licensing legislation had veered towards liberalising the trade, it had always done so in terms which paid lip-service to temperance-led calls for greater control. The 1961 Act marked a clear change in tone, one further entrenched when a 1964 Licensing Act was passed, consolidating the Acts of 1953 and 1961. Under the 1964 Act (which provided the legislative framework for licensing until the system was overhauled in 2003) the new opening hours were retained, although Sunday closing was brought back to 10p.m. Exemption orders and special certificates were introduced, allowing for premises to apply for licence extensions for special occasions (something that would eventually contribute to the end of fixed opening hours altogether). The Carlisle system was retained, but its days were numbered. This last remnant of State control disappeared when the management of the drinks trade in Carlisle was returned to private hands by an Act of Parliament passed in 1971.

Under these conditions the alcohol industry fared well and sales began to increase considerably. One of the most significant developments was the expansion of the wine market. In 1950, around 14 million gallons of wine were being consumed in the United Kingdom annually. By 1960, this had doubled to 28 million gallons, and by 1970 it was over 51 million gallons.[55] In a sense, this increase represents the democratisation of a once exclusive market: it shows the fruition of Gladstone's vision of an expanded wine trade driven by the sale of wine in off-licences and grocery stores. Wine sales, as well as canned lager sales, were boosted enormously by the development of supermarkets – something which has driven up overall alcohol sales ever since. The popularisation of wine also represented the adoption of those 'continental' patterns of alcohol consumption so beloved of the moderate wing of the old temperance movement. Certainly, the increase in wine consumption was driven, in part, by the expansion of opportunities for foreign travel and the desire among British drinkers to adopt seemingly sophisticated modes of consumption. Wine continued to signify cultural capital, but in an age of expanding affluence and aspiration (as well as the expanding power of supermarkets and off-licence chains) those with the capacity and the desire to adopt wine-drinking increased massively.

The 1960s, of course, also saw the growth of other forms of drug consumption, and much of the energy of temperance was harnessed to the campaign to bring drugs other than alcohol under legislative control. Drugs legislation was passed in 1964, 1966 and 1967, all of which was consolidated in the 1971 Misuse of Drugs Act. Major reports into aspects of drug legislation were carried out by the Brain Committee in 1965 and the Wootton Committee in 1968. This flurry of activity reflected the development of a far more sophisticated market for intoxicants in which different states of mind became, for an increasing number of people, part of their smorgasbord of consumer choices. As we shall see later, it has been argued that the development of an advanced consumer market in intoxicants has had a profound impact on the alcohol market in recent years.[56] Drug use aside, the proliferation of lager, wine, exotic mixers and novel spirits reflected an increasingly diversified consumer culture – one which produced a demand to explore taste, identity and even consciousness in a market which was increasingly effective at providing just the array of commodities with which to service such desires.

By the mid-1970s, alcohol consumption had increased to levels unheard of since the outbreak of the First World War. Per capita consumption virtually doubled between 1950 and 1975 and the range of drinks being consumed had increased. Lager, which represented just 1 per cent of the beer market in 1961, represented 20 per cent of it by 1975.[57] In the same period spirit consumption had more than doubled and wine consumption more than trebled; the adult population, over the same period, had increased by less than 8 per cent.[58] Increased levels of disposable income, an upsurge in sales through supermarkets and off-licences, and a more efficient drinks industry selling more reliable and diverse products all contributed to a rise in consumption across the board. People were still drinking less than their Victorian forebears: the 1970s were more sober than the 1870s. Nevertheless, the marked rise in consumption over this period helped trigger a resurgence in debates on problematic drinking within the medical community and the reappearance of calls for government to use its power to actively reduce the amount people drank.

Notes

1 Greenaway, *Drink and British Politics*, p. 112.
2 Wilson, *Alcohol and the Nation*, p. 333.
3 Haydon, *Beer and Britannia*, p. 277.
4 S. G. Jones, 'Labour society and the drink question in Britain, 1918–1939, *Historical Journal*, 30:1 (1987), 105–22, p. 108.
5 Gutzke, *Protecting the Pub*, pp. 75–9.
6 Anon, 'Company meeting: Mitchells & Butlers, limited' (*Manchester Guardian*, 13 August 1927), p. 18.
7 Gutzke, *Protecting the Pub*, p. 45.
8 *Ibid.*, pp. 210, 249–51.
9 House of Commons, *Report of the Committee on the Disinterested Management of Public Houses* (1927) Cmd. 2862, p. 21.
10 G. Orwell, *The Road to Wigan Pier* (Harmondsworth: Penguin, 1989), pp. 66–7.
11 G. Orwell, *The Collected Essays, Journalism and Letters Vol. II: As I Please, 1943–5*, ed. S. Orwell and I. Angus (London: Secker and Warburg, 1968), p. 47.

12 Anon., 'Mitchells and Butlers, limited: Birmingham brewers' plans for licensed houses' (*Manchester Guardian*, 18 August 1928), p. 2.
13 *Ibid.*
14 Gutzke, *Protecting the Pub*, p. 222.
15 *Ibid.*, p. 5.
16 Progressive Election Committee, 'What the Progressive Party on the county council has done for temperance in London' (London: Alexander and Shepheard Ltd, 1904).
17 Anon., 'Poetry in Pubs' (*Times*, 7 June 1939), p. 17.
18 Anon., 'Art in the Inn' (*Times*, 8 June 1937), p. 17.
19 J. Gusfield, 'Benevolent repression: popular culture, social structure and the control of drinking', in Barrows and Room (eds), *Drinking: Behaviour and Belief*, p. 403.
20 Gutzke, *Protecting the Pub*, p. 138.
21 House of Commons, *Report of the Royal Commission on Licensing (England and Wales) 1920–31* (1931) Cmd. 3988, p. 9.
22 Anon., 'Lord Astor on the drink problem' (*Manchester Guardian*, 8 March 1926), p. 3; Anon., 'Company Meeting: Watney, Combe Reid and Co.' (*Times*, 12 August 1932), p. 17.
23 Gutzke, *Protecting the Pub*, p. 211.
24 A. Mutch, 'Shaping the public house, 1850–1950: Business strategies, state regulations and social history', *Cultural and Social History*, 1 (2004), 179–200, p. 97.
25 E. Selley, *The English Public House As It Is* (London: Longmans, Green & Co., 1927), p. 2.
26 *Ibid.*, pp. 19–20.
27 *Ibid.*, p. 115.
28 Mass-Observation, *The Pub and the People: A Worktown Study* (London: Victor Gollancz, 1943).
29 *Ibid.*, pp. 93, 105–10, 306, 314, 319.
30 *Ibid.*, p. 233.
31 *Ibid.*, p. 26.
32 *Ibid.*, pp. 230–1.
33 *Ibid.*, p. 218.
34 Orwell, *The Collected Essays*, p. 43.
35 *Ibid.*
36 Cornell, *Beer*, p. 197.
37 C. Langhammer, '"A public house is for all classes, men and women alike": Women, leisure and drink in Second World War England', *Women's History Review*, 12: 3 (2003), 423–43, pp. 426–7.
38 *Ibid.*, p. 436.
39 *Ibid.*, pp. 432–3.
40 *Ibid.*, p. 435.
41 H. Carter, 'Drink and Youth' (*Times*, 23 December 1943), p. 5.
42 Langhammer, 'A public house is for all classes', p. 436.
43 House of Commons, *Report of the Royal Commission on Licensing*, p. 156.
44 Burnett, *Liquid Pleasures*, p. 136.
45 Anon,, 'Burden of Duty on Beer' (*Times*, 31 October 1932), p. 20.
46 Anon,, 'Brewers and the Press' (*Times*, 16 November 1933), p. 14.
47 A. Barr, *Drink: An Informal Social History* (London: Bantam, 1995), p. 249; Burnett, *Liquid Pleasures*, p. 136.
48 Greenaway, *Drink and British Politics*, p. 150.

49 I. Hornsey, *A History of Beer and Brewing* (London: Royal Society of Chemistry, 2003), pp. 610–13.
50 *Ibid.*, p. 614.
51 P. Brown, *Man Walks into a Pub* (London: Macmillan, 2003), pp. 230–5.
52 Cornell, *Beer*, p. 210.
53 *Ibid.*, pp. 197, 211.
54 *Ibid.*, p. 217.
55 British Beer and Pub Association, *Statistical Handbook* (London: Brewing Publications Ltd, 2007), p. 27.
56 F. Measham, and K. Brain, 'Binge drinking, British alcohol policy and the new culture of intoxication', *Crime, Media and Society*, 1:3 (2005), 262–83.
57 British Beer and Pub Association, *Statistical Handbook* (London: Brewing Publications Ltd, 2007), p. 17.
58 *Ibid.*, pp. 34–5.

14

Prevention and health: alcohol and public health

The Government wishes to see progress made in tackling alcohol misuse, but the role the Government can play in encouraging sensible attitudes to drinking is ... still open to debate. (*Drinking Sensibly*, Department of Health and Social Security, 1981)

It is extremely difficult to answer the layman's question 'How much can I drink without damaging my health?' Indeed, it is impossible to provide an answer which is both simple and scientifically defensible. (R. E. Kendell)

The revival of the alcohol market in the 1960s was not attended by the re-emergence of political temperance. However, this is not to say that there was no action to control excessive drinking at government level. In 1962 fines for drunkenness, which were still set at the levels laid down by Acts of 1839, 1860, 1872 and 1902, were increased to reflect equivalent penalties in modern money. Under the 1964 Licensing Act a £10 fine was imposed for licensees who permitted drunkenness on their premises and the courts were given powers to imprison anyone procuring drinks for a drunken person for up to one month. All this, however, was in keeping with the notion that the management of drunkenness should be a matter for licensees and drinkers rather than the State. The exception to this principle was the law on drink-driving. The introduction of breath tests and statutory blood alcohol limits for drivers meant that, for the first time, the police had a quantifiable definition of drunkenness to work with and the powers to ascertain with precision, in legal terms at least, whether someone was guilty of posing a public risk through their insobriety. While this reawakened some of the most long-standing debates over the relationship between drink, the State and individual liberty it also strictly sectioned off one aspect of drunken behaviour, thereby contributing to the fragmentation of the drink question into a series of constituent concerns. Later, however, an approach to problem drinking began to emerge which would seek to re-establish drink as an issue of whole populations rather than narrowly defined groups (such as alcoholics and drink-drivers). Framing all of this were the concepts of harm prevention and harm reduction: the idea that the role of government intervention should not be to deal with grand moral questions over the rights and wrongs of intoxication, but to manage the risks posed by drink and drunkenness through both legislative action and the deployment of strategies which would encourage drinkers to internalise an awareness of risk and modify their own behaviour accordingly.

Drunk in charge

Drink-driving legislation was first introduced under the Road Traffic Act of 1930. Those framing the Act were faced with something of a conundrum, however. As one contemporary commentator observed, drunkenness 'used generally to imply an offence against social decorum or an incapacity to control oneself normally and safely in a street or public place ... but the Road Traffic Act of 1930 altered all that'.[1] The problem was that in order to be practicable, a definition of drunkenness had to be arrived at which was more precisely geared towards the specific problem of a driver's ability to perform a mechanical task effectively. In the end, the Act made it an offence to be in charge of a vehicle when 'under the influence of drink or a drug to such an extent as to be incapable of having control of a motor vehicle', which sounded fine until it came to be implemented by the police. Measuring, in concrete terms, whether this level of incapacity has been reached involved such impressionistic examinations as observing tremor and gait, analysing handwriting, and carrying out the 'finger-nose' and 'telephone directory' tests.[2] In one sense, these tests recognised that drunkenness is never quantifiable; however, they also made the law hard to enforce.

These problems were addressed partly by the 1962 Road Traffic Act, which made police tests for levels of blood alcohol permissible in court and which stated that levels of 150mg of alcohol per 100ml of blood could be taken as proof of impairment. For the first time, a quantifiable definition of drunkenness was introduced into English law. However, blood tests were only allowed following an accident and other proofs of impairment were still permissible in court if blood alcohol levels were lower than this limit. It was the Road Safety Act of 1967 which finally ironed out these anomalies, and thereby set the framework for the subsequent law on drink-driving. Under the 1967 Act, the maximum blood alcohol limit for anyone driving a motor vehicle was set at 80mg of alcohol per 100ml of blood. Police were also empowered to use the newly developed breathalyser to test anyone they suspected of driving under the influence, not just people who had been involved in an accident. As far as the law on drink-driving was concerned, then, drunkenness became a chemical measure which could be tested for prior to any visible crime being committed.

With the problem of drink-driving, a number of themes which had previously underpinned the drink question converged. One of the principal reasons why drunkenness became a social concern in the Victorian period was because alcohol and engines don't mix. The condemnation of workplace drunkenness in the nineteenth century was intensified by the threat posed to both efficiency and safety by the prospect of drunken workers operating industrial machinery. As we have seen, a second critical issue which framed the Victorian drink question was where the right to intoxication clashed with the responsibility not to harm others. The invention of the motor car brought the relationship between these two things into sharp focus. A drunken worker may threaten the efficiency of the company's earnings, and the safety of both himself and his colleagues; a drunk-driver threatens the safety of the public at large. Without further aggravating circumstances, a drunk and incapable pedestrian is a threat to no one but themselves; a drunk-driver, by contrast, presents a very real public threat. One can argue that a drinker has the right to be drunk in public so long as he or she does not actively seek to injure or abuse anyone else; the same is not so obviously true when that person is in charge of a vehicle. Internal combustion, in other words, adds a new dimension to the rights question regarding intoxication.

Dealing with this problem forced the Government to adopt a pragmatic and quantifiable measure of intoxication, even if that went against the experientially obvious fact that intoxication is not directly calculable according to units of consumption. The imposition of an 80mg blood alcohol limit under the 1967 Act, along with the attempt to introduce random breath tests, certainly triggered an angry response from some quarters. Indeed, the Government dropped the idea of fully random breath-testing under pressure that it represented an unjustifiable infringement on the liberty of sober drivers. The debate over the 1967 Act reignited many long-standing arguments over the relationship between the control of drunkenness and individual freedom, with one *Times* reporter claiming that 'three points about the introduction of breathalyser tests appeared to be uppermost in the minds of many motorists: the seeming unfairness of an inflexible law, the effect on individual liberty, and the feeling that when the novelty wears off things will be much as before'.[3]

The inflexibility of the law was, however, its strongest point. While studies had shown that blood alcohol levels could vary widely among drinkers who had consumed comparable amounts, the point was to instil as widely as possible the understanding that as long as one did not drink beyond a minimum level of two double spirits or two pints of beer, then there was no significant risk of exceeding the blood alcohol limit at all. What this meant in practice was that the object of moral censure shifted from driving badly while drunk to taking the risk of consuming an amount of alcohol that might contribute to drunk-driving. The goal of government policy in 1967, then, was to use a combination of coercion (breath tests and statutory blood alcohol limits) and persuasion (initially, a £350,000 advertising campaign launched by Barbara Castle in late September 1967) to shift the moral compass on drink-driving from act to intention. Where previously one was responsible for driving well, now one was responsible for avoiding the risk of driving badly. Success hinged on making the intention to drink and drive tantamount, in moral terms, to driving badly per se. This could only be practically achieved if debates over what precisely defined drunkenness were swept aside by the creation of a quantifiable measure.

Nonetheless, it was this inflexibility that exercised opponents even after the law was introduced. In December 1967, the Conservative MP Norman St John Stevas introduced a parliamentary motion condemning the 'tyrannical progress' of the government in its 'ever increasing destruction of the liberty of the subject'. St John Stevas cited breathalyser tests in particular as an instance of this, claiming that while drunk-driving 'was an anti-social menace … individuals did have rights'. The root of the problem, he insisted, was that the law 'was not flexible but absolute'.[4] Others complained that because the law allowed police officers to breathalyse when they simply *suspected* a driver was drunk, this was tantamount to the random testing which the Government had previously agreed not to introduce. While politicians condemned the attack on individual liberty, brewers warned of reduced profits (brewery share prices did dip briefly after the 1967 Act was passed), and publicans complained that responsible customers were being inconvenienced to a point whereby they were choosing not to drink in pubs at all.

However, for all that opponents attempted to frame the 1967 Act as an attack on the liberties of the pub-going people, it proved a successful piece of legislation. In the short term at least, it led to a decrease in road traffic casualties, while the number of people convicted of drink-driving more than doubled within two years of the Act coming into force.[5] The sharp increase in breath tests carried out by the police, which went up from 51,000 in 1968 to 142,000 ten years later, led to little public outcry despite the fact that less than one-third of breath tests actually led to a conviction.[6] Furthermore, a level of opprobrium towards drunk-driving was established which continues to have a significant impact on popular conceptions of the rights and wrongs of drunken behaviour today. When the Transport Act of 1981 allowed breathalyser results to be used in court as well as blood tests, the measure passed virtually unchallenged by a

public comfortable with the notion of roadside testing, and largely uncon-
cerned with the threat it posed to abstract notions of individual freedom.

Problem drinking

While the introduction of statutory blood alcohol limits for drivers represented a significant and unique development, it also fitted neatly with the
post-temperance view of the drink question. Drink-driving limits sectioned
off one specific aspect of drunken behaviour and subjected it to a discrete
set of regulations. Furthermore, the moral rhetoric of drink-driving never
overlapped with the logic of temperance rhetoric in that while someone
could be condemned as a repeat drunk-driver, there was no notion of a
habitual drunk-driver in the sense of someone who had lost control over
their ability to drive sober. In principle, the regulation of drunk-driving
had absolutely nothing to do with the regulation of drunkenness in other
walks of life.

However, the problem of the 'habitual drunkard' had certainly not
gone away. As Betsy Thom has shown, the disease model of alcoholism
re-emerged in the 1950s, driven by the adoption of the concept by the
World Health Organisation and by the spread of Alcoholics Anonymous
from America. The establishment of the first AA group in Croydon in
1952 provided a springboard for the extension of the AA approach to
alcoholism across the country.[7] The AA conception of alcoholism was by
no means the first or only model which posited alcoholism as a disease.
However, its unique 'twelve-step' treatment paradigm, with its emphasis
on continuing recovery based on the notion that one *is* an alcoholic ir-
respective of whether one still drinks or not, would go on to become
perhaps the single most influential version of the disease model. In Britain
the AA model never established quite the level of influence that it did in
America; however, its development contributed to a rise in the number of
treatment programmes being developed to tackle alcoholism in the late
1950s and early 1960s.

Initially, the resurgence of interest in alcoholism treatment was driven
by the work of a relatively small group of psychiatrists, many based at
the Maudsley Hospital in London, who were concerned with how to treat
what could be called 'skid row' alcoholics: that is, homeless drinkers who
would fit into the stereotype of what many people saw as the helpless,
drunken bum. Soon, however, they expanded their interest to consider
alcoholism in its less visible, and less stereotypical, aspects. The development of psychiatry-based treatment approaches for alcoholics developed
swiftly in the early 1960s at both national and local levels. In 1962, the
Ministry of Health recommended the establishment of specialist alcohol

treatment units in a number of psychiatric hospitals; in the same year Griffith Edwards – one of the psychiatrists based at the Maudsley – established the influential Camberwell Council on Alcoholism, and a National Council on Alcoholism was set up to oversee the establishment of further regional councils dedicated to promoting community and public health approaches to alcoholism.[8]

The widespread establishment of state-funded alcohol treatment programmes marked a continuation of the decoupling of alcohol policy noted in previous chapters. On the one hand, licensing legislation was geared towards the liberalisation of access to alcohol for moderate drinkers; on the other, the treatment of problem drinkers was seen largely as concerning the medical treatment of addiction. The conflation of penal and medical approaches which had characterised the late-Victorian asylum movement was a dim and distant memory, as was the degenerationist theory of the early twentieth-century study of inebriety. The discrediting of physiological models of addiction, in which repeated ingestion of alcohol was held to produce cellular changes which produced a craving for drink, meant there was little desire to look for the roots of addiction in the substance of alcohol itself. If the causes of addiction are psychological, then the amount of alcohol available in society at large should not have an impact on whether someone predisposed to alcoholism actually becomes an alcoholic. What remained were psychiatric treatment programmes and the new group-based therapy developed by AA. The development of the psychiatric models of alcoholism contributed to the fragmentation of the drink question in that they tended to isolate problem drinking from wider political questions around the relationship between sobriety, intoxication and social order.

This tendency was not absolute, however, and those promoting public health approaches to alcoholism were well aware that while treatment may be driven by psychiatry, local conditions – family, work, built environment – were key contributory factors. However, as consumption levels began to rise in the 1960s some people began to look once again at the wider social contexts which shaped the development of alcohol-related problems. The marked increase in per capita consumption in the 1960s and 1970s seemed to be accompanied by a rise in other social problems not necessarily linked to alcoholism and addiction. Convictions for drunkenness per head of population increased by 50 per cent between 1950 and 1970, while deaths from liver cirrhosis increased steadily throughout the 1960s, and then increased sharply from 1970 onwards.[9] The increased conviction rates for drunk-driving, although largely a consequence of increased roadside testing, also raised awareness of the fact that alcohol-related problems were not simply confined to addiction. The question all this raised was whether there was a causal connection between increased consumption generally and an increase in alcohol-related harms more usually associated with problem drinking.

Addressing this issue had important ramifications for government policy. The question it posed was as follows: when it comes to reducing alcohol-related problems, should government efforts be directed towards treating alcoholics (i.e. that small number of people who have an identifiable addiction) or should it be directed towards reducing the amount of alcohol drunk across the entire population? Historically, State policy had often been geared towards the reduction of overall consumption: the legislation passed during the 'gin craze' was designed to achieve just such a result, and the work of moderate Victorian temperance campaigners was also directed toward lowering consumption overall. However, the overall reduction argument tended to be obscured in the nineteenth century by the vociferous campaigning of those who insisted that the goal of legislation should be to effectively prohibit alcohol consumption altogether.

As we have seen, concern over the wider social impacts of alcohol, and the amount being drunk overall, remained muted in the 1950s and 1960s. The historically low levels of consumption, the collapse of organised temperance and the emergence of a raft of alternative targets for social anxiety – rock and roll, juvenile delinquency, drug use, etc. – created conditions in which individual problem drinkers remained an object of concern, while the broader drink question receded. However, this changed as the impact of increasing consumption began to be noticed in the early 1970s. Betsy Thom suggests that a turning point in government attitudes to alcohol came with the publication of a Home Office working party report in 1971 entitled *Habitual Drunken Offenders*. According to Thom, the conclusion of this report reflected a situation in which:

> Rising alcohol consumption, the perceived economic costs of alcohol misuse, and the interplay of competing interests … began to raise the policy salience of alcohol issues and alcohol policy gained increased attention on the policy agenda … It was during these years that the shift from 'treatment' to 'problem management' began to take place … policy concern focussed on per capita consumption of alcohol and alcohol-related harm rather than on 'alcoholism'.[10]

What this led to, Thom continues, was 'the adoption of an epidemiological rather than a medical definition of the alcohol problem'.[11]

Population approaches

Put briefly, medical lobbyists who formed part of the 'policy networks' around alcohol began, from the early 1970s, to take up the idea that alcohol needed to be thought about in terms of macro-level patterns of consumption and statistical analyses of alcohol-related harms. In terms of action, this meant turning the focus of government policy towards encouraging lower levels of consumption across the population and constructing a far broader definition of problem drinking. From a 'problem management' perspective, out-and-out alcoholics are not the sole concern; instead those 'moderate' drinkers who put themselves at risk of acquiring problematic drinking habits, or developing alcohol-related diseases, are the real issue. Rather than adopt a laissez-faire approach to 'ordinary' drinkers while treating addicts, this new approach set out to warn everyone that they might be at risk however much they felt they had their drinking under control.

In many ways, this represented a return to the old 'moderate drinker' problem posed by Victorian temperance campaigners. Old-fashioned temperance groups may have claimed the solution was total abstinence, but they (especially the prohibitionists) also argued strongly that the issue was not those people with an identifiable alcohol problem, but those who thought that drinking regularly could be a harm-free activity. The difference is that the modern epidemiological approach exchanged the moral argumentation of F. R. Lees, T. H. Green and others for an approach grounded in statistical analysis, risk-assessment and the language of harm reduction rather than total abstinence. This de-moralisation of the effort to make people drink less has been described as a strategy of 'normative neutralisation'; that is, a process in which the attempt to manage public behaviour becomes expressed in terms that are, on the surface at least, grounded in the morally neutral language of science, in which the 'value of drinking is not commented upon; only consequences matter'.[12] It is telling that one of the seminal studies in the development of epidemiological approaches to problem drinking was carried out by a demographer – Sully Ledermann – rather than a doctor or a moral reformer. Ledermann's analysis of the relationship between per capita consumption and levels of alcohol abuse in populations, published in 1956, provided a touchstone for the statistical analysis of alcohol problems. The 'Ledermann curve', as it became known, seemed to show that increased consumption across populations as a whole led to an increase in the number of heavy drinkers, and that the number of heavy drinkers increased in multiples: if overall consumption doubled, for example, the number of heavy drinkers would increase eightfold.[13] It also suggested that overall consumption was the only factor driving levels of alcohol abuse, and that cultural considerations played a limited role at best.

Ledermann's study had an impact on alcohol researchers in both Europe and North America. The Canadian Alcohol Research Foundation developed the approach, and the Finnish Foundation for Alcohol Studies, under the leadership of Kettil Bruun, worked hard to promote the idea that there was a quantifiable relationship between overall consumption levels and problem drinking.[14] In 1975, the publication of a study entitled *Alcohol Control Policies in Public Health Perspective* – authored by Kettil Bruun, Griffith Edwards and a number of other public health researchers – provided a coherent outline of the population approach.[15] In Britain, the idea was further promoted by many of those who had become powerful figures in the nexus between medical organisations, alcohol campaign groups and government policy-makers. In 1979, the Royal College of Psychiatrists published a report, under the chairmanship of Griffith Edwards, entitled *Alcohol and Alcoholism* which strongly argued for government intervention to ensure that '*per capita* alcohol consumption does not increase beyond the present level, and is by stages brought back to a lower level'.[16] This call for government action was based on the grounds that it 'can be asserted that if the average man or woman begins to drink more … then the number of people who damage themselves by their drinking will also increase'.[17]

But what was to be the mechanism for effecting this reduction in overall consumption? *Alcohol and Alcoholism* proposed two approaches: the use of taxation to increase the retail cost of alcohol and the development of agreed safe drinking limits. The safe drinking limits proposed by the Royal College of Psychiatrists were four pints of beer, four doubles of spirits, or one standard-sized bottle of wine per day.[18] This may come as a surprise to anyone familiar with the current guidance that no one should be drinking more than four units a day – which is roughly two pints of beer, two doubles of spirits or half a bottle of wine. As we shall see, however, the setting of safe drinking limits was understood by those involved as being strategic rather than analytical. In other words, safe drinking limits were initially designed to provide a guideline for attitudes to drinking rather than reflect a medically quantifiable reality.

State duties

Unit-based definitions of sensible drinking would, eventually, become established across the range of interest groups surrounding alcohol use. The drinks industry would agree to promote awareness of those guidelines through labelling, while health professionals, government departments, social researchers and alcohol lobbyists would all broadly accept the same framework.[19] The same cannot be said for the idea that tax rises should be used to reduce alcohol consumption by inflating the retail price. Far from it. In 1977 a cross-departmental White Paper on 'Prevention and Health' described the idea that the price of drink should not be allowed to fall in terms relative to price or incomes as 'the most controversial recommendation' in its section on alcohol misuse.[20] It would remain so as alcohol campaigners came to focus increasingly on the argument that the Government had a duty to intervene to reduce overall consumption; an argument that ran directly counter to the resurgent market liberalism which, in 1979, was about to reset the foundation on which British economic policy was made.

In typically forceful terms, *Alcohol and Alcoholism* asserted that there was an unquestionable relationship between the price of alcohol and the amount people drank: 'when price goes up,' it stated, 'consumption falls; when price goes down, consumption rises'.[21] The neat simplicity of this equation has subsequently been challenged; however, pricing – or rather the cost of alcohol relative to disposable income – does play an important role in shaping consumption.[22] This is politically critical because government has the capacity to directly influence the cost of alcohol through both taxation and licensing policy. The implication of an epidemiological approach to alcohol problems which insists on a direct link between pricing and consumption is that government has a duty to use its tax-raising powers to control the overall amount of alcohol being consumed.

As we have seen, drink has repeatedly revealed fault-lines in otherwise coherent ideological positions. The same was true for Thatcherism after the 1979 General Election. The moral conservatism of Thatcher's administration may have given hope to alcohol lobbyists campaigning for greater government controls over excessive drinking; however, that moral conservatism was trumped by the free-market liberalism which drove the Thatcherite revolution. In the case of alcohol, this meant that while Thatcher's moral ideologues may have spoken of a return to 'Victorian values', the economists engineered a return to laissez-faire – which, as many Victorian liberals had found, flatly contradicted the goals of temperance. When faced with the old problem of negotiating the relationship between the State and the trade, the new Conservative administration resisted the idea that economic leverage should form part of the equation.

In 1981, the Department of Health and Social Security published a booklet entitled *Drinking Sensibly* as part of the ongoing series of 'Prevention and Health' studies. The Forword, signed by the Secretaries of State for Social Services, Scotland, Wales and Northern Ireland, stated that the 'misuse of alcohol has implications beyond the field of public health', and that 'central to these is the question of the respective roles individuals and the Government must play in curbing a problem which stems primarily from the exercise by individuals of their freedom of choice.[23] In other words, here was a classic dilemma: alcohol had the potential to cause problems of public health and social disorder – both of which were properly the domain of government intervention; at the same time, drinking was a matter of individual choices made in a free market – and these, readers could assume, were not areas upon which this government was about to encroach.

Drinking Sensibly, as its title suggests, was not designed to promote some neo-temperance attack on drink; rather, it explicitly set out to 'encourage sensible attitudes towards the use of alcohol'.[24] In pursuit of this, it addressed in some detail the health effects and economic costs of alcohol misuse and made clear the need for proactive measures to be taken in order to counter excessive drinking. However, it rejected both of the key suggestions put forward in *Alcohol and Alcoholism*. The promotion of a precise safe drinking limit, it stated, 'might be counter-productive if it seemed to confer official approval on drinking levels which were in fact quite high'.[25] Instead it recommended more general advice, promoting moderation, the consumption of alcohol only in appropriate circumstances and the social disapproval of drunkenness. Such an approach 'would leave the onus of decision firmly on the individual drinker and would not enable him or her to shelter behind "authoritative" advice on how much it was safe or sensible to drink'.[26] To this extent, *Drinking Sensibly* was an expression of the classic liberal argument in which moral responsibility was inextricably tied to individual freedom. Tell people exactly how much they can drink and you simply take away their responsibility to work out for themselves what kind of behaviour is appropriate in the circumstances in which they find themselves. Safe limits, from this perspective, treat people like children. They subject everyone to arbitrary rules which take no account of circumstance, and they remove the responsibility of the individual to ascertain the parameters of reasonable behaviour for themselves.

Drinking Sensibly also rejected the 'systematic use of tax rates as a means of regulating consumption'.[27] The argument for this was also couched in liberal terms. On the one hand, the authors argued that increased taxation would have a very limited impact on highly dependent drinkers, who would simply switch to cheaper drinks or spend less money on other essential goods. Consequently, increased taxation would have a disproportionately detrimental impact on moderate drinkers who would be forced to pay more for something which they had every right to consume in order to effect a minimal change of behaviour among problem drinkers. This, the report claimed, 'raises the question of how far it is justified to take measures that would restrict – or increase the cost of the enjoyment of the great majority in order to check misuse or potential misuse by a minority'.[28] Finally, the report insisted that the influence of government on drinking behaviours was always going to be limited and that while taxation may have some impact on consumption the primary purpose of taxation was to raise revenue, not to manage behaviour. On the issues of both safe limits and taxation, then, the arguments set out by the Government were remarkably similar to those set out by Lord Stanley, in his rebuttal of prohibitionism, over a century earlier.

The rejection of increased taxation in *Drinking Sensibly*, however, proved to be deeply controversial. It turned out that a report had been prepared in advance of *Drinking Sensibly* by the Central Policy Review Staff (CPRS). This report had accepted both the epidemiological approach to drinking problems (in which increased overall consumption was seen as driving increases in problem drinking), and had strongly insisted on the central role taxation could play in reducing consumption. Alcohol duties, it stated, were 'the single most important instrument the Government had for influencing alcohol consumption'.[29] Furthermore, the CPRS report insisted that the Government 'cannot avoid taking a stance. Whatever it does to duties will in practice involve some change in the real cost of alcohol' and, by extension, overall levels of consumption.[30] Of course, the authors of *Drinking Sensibly* were not beholden to the findings of the CPRS report, and it was up to them to arrive at their own conclusions on the role of taxation. What caused the stir, among alcohol campaigners at least, was that the CPRS report was never made public. It only came to light when a leaked copy was published by the Finnish researcher Kettil Bruun three years later.

The suppression of the CPRS report was seen by many as evidence that the Conservative government was prepared to ignore, and even bury, its own advice on public health in order to protect its economic principles. *Drinking Sensibly* called for greater investment in health education and it encouraged advertisers to promote better awareness of the alcoholic strength of various drinks. It also called for more money to be put into alcohol research. As Thom has pointed out, the very fact that it addressed the subject of overall consumption levels did also show that the population approach had made inroads into government thinking.[31] However, for those who argued that the State had a duty to manage overall consumption in order to limit problem drinking the report refused to acknowledge the bottom line: tax increases would reduce consumption. This was doubly mysterious given that in all other areas of activity low taxation was seen by the Thatcher administration as a means of stimulating demand. Alcohol, so it seemed, was strangely resistant to the mechanics of a market in which making things more expensive tended to make them less attractive; suddenly a government which sought to use tax reforms to drive through economic change lost all faith in the capacity of taxation to have much effect on consumption at all.

In fairness, *Drinking Sensibly* never flatly denied that tax levels could have an impact on consumption; instead it combined an insistence that any impact would be limited with the argument that moderate drinkers should not be punished for problems caused by those who drank to excess. However, by blurring the lines between 'normal' and 'abnormal' drinking, in statistical terms at least, new epidemiological models were starting to construct a counter-argument to conventional reasoning on this point. According to the Ledermann Curve, when moderate drinkers became slightly less moderate, alcohol-related health problems increased disproportionately. In *Drinking Sensibly*, the Government had rejected tax rises on the grounds that there was a clear distinction between moderate and problematic consumption, and on the grounds that only problem drinkers needed to be subject to State interventions. However, for many medical campaigners the belief that most of the adverse effects of alcohol consumption were caused by heavy, rather than 'moderate', drinkers was a fallacy.[32] So long as this distinction between moderate and problematic drinking remained self-evident to policy-makers, the arguments forwarded in *Drinking Sensibly* could be successfully sustained. But if the definition of 'moderate' drinking was further scaled down – if the gap between safe and unsafe drinking could be narrowed – then pressure for government intervention could be increased. This is precisely what happened a few years later when medical experts dramatically expanded their definition of problem drinking by lowering their recommended daily limits.

Sensible drinking

We saw previously that in the nineteenth century, two liberal perspectives on alcohol clashed. One insisted that reasonable individuals should be free to make their own choices, since this both protected individual freedom and encouraged moral responsibility. The other argument called for apparently illiberal interventions on the grounds that alcohol was a substance which, by definition, blurred the ability of drinkers to make rational judgements. The debate over safe drinking limits revisited some of these issues, albeit in different terms.

When the Royal College of Psychiatrists proposed safe drinking limits in 1979, they were not adopting the moral high ground in the way that nineteenth-century temperance campaigners had. They were not, as had been the case with the likes of T. H. Green, suggesting that they understood the moral issues surrounding intoxication better than the average drinker, and that they, therefore, had the right to pronounce on what the best course of action for moderate drinkers might be. Nevertheless, by exchanging moral expertise for medical expertise, they arrived at a similar conclusion. That conclusion was that the average drinker is not in a position to make the kind of independent judgements regarding his or her own drinking that *Drinking Sensibly* called for. This, however, was not because they did not understand the moral framework but because they were unlikely to be aware of the underlying medical risks. Here again, we see the argument for controlling behaviours stripped of explicit moral judgement, but reinforced by the rhetorical weight of expert discourse. Everyone knows, roughly, what amount of alcohol is likely to lead to a thudding hangover: it is a knowledge gained through (painful) experience, and something that varies from person to person. Few of us, however, know how much alcohol is likely to cause us cirrhosis of the liver for the simple reason that the cause and the effect are set at such a distance from each other. Put absurdly, you do not wake up with liver cirrhosis and think 'I shouldn't have had that second bottle of wine last night.'

It is this inability to accurately judge the impact of drink on our long-term physical health which gave such weight to the pronouncements of medical authorities on the subject, and which provided the grounds on which campaigners in the medical community argued for the establishment of safe drinking limits. As one leading psychiatrist put it, the 'ordinary citizen certainly doesn't believe that he and millions of others moderate drinkers like him is drinking more than is good for him … Unfortunately, the facts do not support these convenient assumptions'.[33] In the mid-1980s, this idea that moderate drinkers were incapable of understanding for themselves what may or may not be a reasonable level of alcohol consumption began to gain ground among practitioners in a range of medical disciplines. The argument was that you did not need to be drunk, or an alcoholic, to be unable to know your own safe limits; identifying those limits was something that could only be done safely by those (i.e. medical professionals) who knew the physiology, the pharmacology and the figures.

In 1986 and 1987, the Royal Colleges of General Practitioners, Psychiatrists and Physicians all produced reports which called for safe drinking limits to be set at 21 units per week for men and 14 units per week for women. Suddenly, moderate drinking had a figure attached to it – and it was half as much as had been proposed less than a decade earlier by the Royal College of Psychiatrists. Much has been made subsequently of the fact that Richard Smith, a member of the Royal College of Surgeons, admitted in an interview that these figures were, in his words, 'plucked out of the air'.[34] Indeed, the 'rough and ready and arbitrary' nature of these figures was recognised at the time by the people who proposed them.[35] The argument was, however, that it was better to come up with a figure that everyone could understand, than to get embroiled in the complexities of trying to work out what might represent problematic drinking on a case-by-case basis. Safe drinking limits, then, were a pragmatic solution to the assumption that non-specialist individuals were not in a position to accurately measure long-term health risks by themselves.

The Royal Colleges strove to avoid giving the impression that they were simply telling otherwise reasonable people what to do with their lives. 'Doctors are not prohibitionists', insisted the Royal College of Physicians, although the title of their report – *A Great and Growing Evil* – would not have looked out of place on the cover of a United Kingdom Alliance broadside.[36] For the Royal College of Physicians, the fact remained, however, that no meaningful distinction between moderate and problem drinking existed. It was not that all drinkers were problem drinkers, but that 'social drinkers merge into heavy drinkers; some people who drink a little experience greater problems than some who drink more; and an individual who is drinking 'heavily' today may be 'dependent' tomorrow and vice versa'.[37] In the nineteenth century, temperance campaigners had struggled unsuccessfully to resolve the problem of how to reconcile the claims of 'moderate drinkers' with the problem of 'habitual drinkers'. Medical campaigners in the late twentieth century went some way to resolving this problem by both presenting a more complex typology of drinkers – social drinkers, heavy drinkers, problem drinkers, dependent drinkers (with 'binge drinkers' yet to be added to that list) – while insisting that the lines between these categories were fuzzy and permeable.

Alcoholism treatment programmes still continued, of course, and Alcoholics Anonymous continued to expand its role in shaping both treatment regimes and popular conceptions of alcoholism. However, at the high end of the alcohol policy network there was a perceptible shift away from a specific focus on alcoholism and towards the consideration of alcohol in both broader demographic terms (i.e. questions surrounding overall levels of consumption) and more precise behavioural and health-related terms (i.e. questions surrounding what exactly constituted safe drinking for the apparently moderate drinker). In 1984, the work of the National Council on Alcoholism was taken up by the newly-founded Alcohol Concern. A year earlier the United Kingdom Temperance Alliance – the same Alliance that had spent almost a century campaigning for prohibition – rebranded itself as the Institute of Alcohol Studies: a public health research organisation, rather than an old-style group of temperance radicals. A broad-based approach, which addressed potential problems facing all – rather than just some – drinkers, gained ground while safe drinking limits began to establish themselves as both recognisable and workable benchmarks for public health campaigns. In wider public and media discourse drink remained a relatively marginal issue compared to earlier periods, partly because alcohol consumption stagnated in the 1980s: per capita consumption among over-15s had increased by 23 per cent between 1971 and 1981, but fluctuated only slightly over the following decade and ended just 3 per cent higher in 1991 than it had been ten years previously.[38] Nevertheless, the framing of the issue had changed in ways that meant a far wider constituency of drinkers could now be identified as potentially problematic. Towards the end of the 1980s football hooligans and 'lager louts' turned public attention towards social problems associated with youth and alcohol, but as we shall see in Chapter 16, it would be a liberalising intervention in the alcohol market – an attempt by the Government to once again break the monopolising power of the drinks industry – that would kick start a process which, ultimately, would see the drink question return to the forefront of political debate.

Notes

1   A. Baldie, 'A definition of drunkenness', *Journal for the Study of Inebriety*, 23:3 (1936), 125–7, p. 125.
2   Slot, 'The medico-legal aspects of drunkenness', p. 124.
3   Anon., 'Bar trade cut by test' (*Times* 10 October 1967), p. 1.
4   Anon., 'MPs examine threat to individual liberty' (*Times*, 2 December 1967), p. 4.
5   H. L. Ross, 'British drink-driving policy', *British Journal of Addiction*, 83 (1998), pp. 863–5; British Beer and Pub Association, *Statistical Handbook*, p. 72.
6   *Ibid.*
7   B. Thom, *Dealing with Drink: Alcohol and Social Policy from Treatment to Management* (London: Free Association, 1999), p. 36.
8   *Ibid.*, pp. 41, 74.
9   Royal College of Psychiatrists, *Alcohol and Alcoholism* (London: Tavistock, 1979), p. 69; Department of Health and Social Security, *Drinking Sensibly* (London: HMSO, 1981), p. 18.
10   Thom, *Dealing with Drink*, p. 7.
11   *Ibid.*, p. 8.
12   P. Sulkunen, 'Ethics of alcohol policy in a saturated society', *Addiction*, 92:9 (1997), 1117–22, p. 1120.
13   D. Hanson, *Preventing Alcohol Abuse: Alcohol, Culture and Control* (Westport, CT: Greenwood, 1995), p. 85.
14   Thom, *Dealing with Drink*, pp. 110–13.
15   K. Bruun, G. Edwards, M. Lumio *et al.*, *Alcohol Control Policies in Public Health Perspective* (Helsinki: Finnish Foundation for Alcohol Studies, 1975).
16   Royal College of Psychiatrists, *Alcohol and Alcoholism*, p. 139.
17   *Ibid.*, p. 90.
18   *Ibid.*, p. 140.
19   See, for example, the Best Practice Guidelines (Annex 1) of the Portman Group *Code of Practice on the Naming, Packaging and Promotion of Alcoholic Drinks*, 4th edn (London: Portman Group, 2008), p. 15.
20   Department of Health and Social Security, *Prevention and Health* (London: HMSO, 1977) Cmnd. 7047.

21 Royal College of Psychiatrists, *Alcohol and Alcoholism*, p. 97.
22 The issue of 'price elasticity' (the extent to which commodity sales are affected by price changes) is the mediating factor here. See, for example, J. Fogarty, 'The own-price elasticity of alcohol: a meta-analysis' (University of Western Australia, Dept. of Economics Discussion Paper, No. 4:1), http://msc.uwa.edu.au/?f=150991, accessed November 2007; P. Meier, A. Booth, T. Stockwell, *et al.*, 'Alcohol pricing and promotion effects on consumption and harm' (ScHARR: University of Sheffield, 2008), www.dh.gov.uk/en/Publichealth/Healthimprovement/Alcoholmisuse/DH_4001740, accessed January 2008.
23 DHSS, *Drinking Sensibly*, p. 6.
24 *Ibid.*, p. 7.
25 *Ibid*, p. 32.
26 *Ibid.*
27 *Ibid.*, p. 59.
28 *Ibid.*, p. 53.
29 R. E. Kendell, 'Drinking sensibly', *British Journal of Addiction*, 82 (1987), 1279–88, p. 1285.
30 *Ibid.*
31 Thom, *Dealing with Drink*, p. 119.
32 Kendell, 'Drinking sensibly', p. 1285.
33 *Ibid.*, p. 1282.
34 R. Smith, 'A row plucked out of the air' (*Guardian* online: 22 October 2007), http://commentisfree.guardian.co.uk/richard_smith/2007/10/a_row_plucked_out_of_the_air.html.
35 Kendell, 'Drinking sensibly', p. 1281.
36 Royal College of Physicians, *A Great and Growing Evil* (London: Routledge, 1987), p. 7.
37 *Ibid.*, p. 5.
38 British Beer and Pub Association, *Statistical Handbook*, p. 36.

15

Beer orders: the changing landscape in the 1990s

We now need modern laws to deal with what is an old problem. They should allow people to enjoy their leisure as they wish, provided that they do not disturb others. (Jack Straw)

We may note at this point that the continental café has been held up as the type of establishment at which reform of the public house should aim. We think there is some tendency to idealize the conception of the average continental establishment. (Royal Commission on Licensing, 1931)

While the public health lobby became more influential in the 1970s and 1980s, it struggled to have an impact on policy. The political mood, which had swung towards the liberalisation of the drinks trade in the early 1960s, did not change under Margaret Thatcher's Conservative administration. If anything, it became more firmly established. This is not to say that there were no concerns over drink and drunkenness. Legislation designed to tackle the problem of drunken anti-social behaviour through the use of exclusion orders was introduced in 1980, as were special regulations to tackle football hooliganism by restricting the sale of alcohol on trains. In 1988 a wave of public concern over drunken violence – captured in the newly coined phrase 'lager lout' – emerged after the Association of Chief Police Officers (ACPO) published a report showing that drunken disorder usually associated with urban centres was starting to proliferate in more rural areas. The ACPO report not only led to a flurry of media activity, but also to two detailed studies into non-metropolitan violence – one funded by the Home Office, and a later report funded by the newly formed drinks industry organisation the Portman Group.[1] The 'lager lout' brought the issue of social disorder back to the centre of public discussions of alcohol just as the policy trend was moving towards increased liberalisation of the trade.

However, neither of the reports into this new phenomenon of small-town drunken violence suggested that it required a rethink of overall approaches to alcohol retail. The Home Office report focused on the need for more careful management of a new breed of 'youth pubs', as well as the need to avoid the creation of 'congestion sites' where there were high concentrations of youth pubs and takeaways in a small area.[2] The Portman Group study made similar observations, but also called for trials in the extension of opening hours. Both suggested that fixed closing exacerbated problems of drunken violence by chucking large numbers of drunken people onto the streets at the same time.[3] Indeed, rather than triggering more repressive controls on licensing, the findings of the studies into 'lager louts' had their most significant long-term impact in persuading the Government that a liberalisation of opening hours was needed in order to address problems of antisocial behaviour associated with town and city-centre drinking.

Public concerns over 'lager louts', then, signalled a return of social order issues to the centre of the debate on drink. However, they also reinforced the existing principle of government intervention, which was to regulate the activities of problematic minorities rather than target consumption among the general population. In 1985, the number of pubs per adult living in England and Wales was actually lower than it had been twenty years earlier.[4] These trends muted calls for tighter State controls of the alcohol market. At the same time, the neoliberal model of consumer choice which drove government policy militated strongly against restrictive market intervention of any kind.

Most changes to licensing law, therefore, were liberalising measures. The abolition of the of the 'afternoon gap' in 1988 meant that for the first time since 1915 pubs were able to open from 11a.m. to 11p.m. In 1995, all-day opening was expanded to cover Sunday trading, thereby rolling back the special restrictions on Sunday hours that had been in place since the middle of the nineteenth century. However, while these changes provided tangible evidence of the continuing liberalisation of licensing law, there were some more fundamental changes going on at the same time.

Cutting the tie

As has been noted above, while the drinks industry underwent a series of changes in the 1960s and 1970s (the introduction of keg beers and lager, the consolidation of national brewing, the expansion of domestic drinking, etc.) many long-standing features of the market remained effectively the same as they had been for centuries. The most important of these was the tied house. In the late 1980s three-quarters of all public houses were tied to brewers,[5] and this brought with it exactly the same concerns regarding consumer choice and quality that prompted the Beer

Act of 1830 and fuelled the mistrust of the 'trade' among liberals and socialists in the early twentieth century. The monopolisation of the drinks market by property-owning brewers seemed to be utterly intractable: it had accompanied the rise of mass production, it had shaped the physical development of the 'English pub', and it had survived at least 150 years of attacks from campaigners of every political stripe. All that, however, was about to change.

In 1989 the Monopolies and Mergers Commission (MMC) published a report on the supply of beer which looked specifically at the question of tied houses. The findings amounted to a scathing condemnation of the 'complex monopoly' that existed as a result of brewers controlling the production, distribution and retail of beer.[6] Not only were 75 per cent of pubs found to be tied to brewers, but of the remaining 'free houses' around half were controlled by brewers through loan ties.[7] Furthermore, the vast majority of tied houses were owned by one of the 'big six' brewers, who also produced 75 per cent of the beer consumed.[8] The MMC report specified the various characteristics of the existing monopoly and declared each of them to be against the public interest. In particular, it stated that tied houses allowed brewers to inflate artificially the price of beer by restricting competition and it allowed them to strangle the development of independent breweries by ensuring that the pubs which big brewers owned only stocked the beer that they produced.[9]

The report's authors stated that their goal was to 'free up the present system to the benefit of greater competition, while maintaining the British public house as it is widely admired'.[10] To that end, they set out a series of radical proposals. Most dramatically, they recommended that all brewers who owned over 2,000 pubs should be forced to sell their remaining stock or stop brewing altogether. Since the 'big six' brewers owned almost 35,000 pubs between them at the time, this would mean that 22,000 pubs would be put onto the open market.[11] The MMC also called for the abolishment of loan ties, thereby further shrinking the extent of control brewers would have over the beer supplied in ordinary pubs. Finally, the MMC called for brewers to allow all landlords in their remaining tied houses to stock at least one 'guest beer' not brewed by the parent company.

The MMC report was a bombshell. Rather than attempting to tackle the tied-house problem through licensing, it tackled it through the statutory regulation of the free market (and, in doing so provided a reminder that 'free' markets are also the creation of State intervention). The report was accepted by the Department of Trade and Industry and formed the basis of the Supply of Beer (Tied Estate) Order – otherwise known as the 'Beer Orders' – which was introduced in December of the same year.

The MMC proposals did not enter the statute books unscathed. The limit of 2,000 pubs was modified in the Beer Orders so that brewers only had to divest half of their stock over that number (e.g. Courage, who owned 5,000 pubs, were only required to sell half of the remaining 3,000). More crucially, the MMC had proposed that no brewer, after selling their excess pubs, should be allowed to enter into long-term supply agreements with the new owners. This made sense: if a brewer sold a pub cheaply to a property investor as part of a deal which effectively continued the old supply arrangements, then little would have changed in terms of consumer choice. Nevertheless, that requirement was removed from the Beer Orders in their final form. When the regulations were introduced, brewers were left free to draw up contracts of sale which included long-term supply agreements, and most of them did just that.[12] Furthermore, because the guest beer regulations only applied to pubs which continued to be *owned* by brewers, pubs which were sold off did not even have to comply with that requirement.

The impact of the Beer Orders has been described as 'by far the biggest shake-up the British brewing industry has ever seen in its history'.[13] Two things, principally, followed. Firstly, 11,000 pubs were put onto the market, many of which were bought up by retail companies who specialised in selling, but not producing, alcohol. These retail companies – which would become known as 'pubcos' – quickly began developing branded outlets (Slug and Lettuce, Pitcher and Piano, Scream, O'Neill's, All Bar One, Edwards, and so on) which soon became familiar features of high streets across the country. The pubcos were able to buy properties cheaply, draw up supply agreements with producers, and negotiate ever more substantial discounts as their retail interests expanded. Within a decade 30 per cent of all pubs would be owned by a retail chain of this kind, with the five biggest pubcos controlling 23 per cent of the overall market.[14] At the same time, the established brewers looked to separate their production and retail arms as swiftly as they could. In 1991 Grand Metropolitan sold its brewing interests to Courage, and four years later Courage sold its brewing interest to Scottish and Newcastle. Courage and Grand Metropolitan set up Inntrepreneur Estates to manage the pubs that they owned as a separate interest. In 1995 Allied Breweries, having already transferred its brewing to a joint venture company and rebranded itself as Allied Domecq, sold its last brewing shares to Carlsberg.[15] In 2000, Whitbread sold its brewing operations to Interbrew and concentrated instead on retail. Bass did the same, although the Competition Commission ruled that the sale breached competition rules and Interbrew had to sell most of their interest in Bass Brewers Ltd on to the American brewing giant Coors.

The details of mergers, restructures and takeovers since the Beer Orders are labyrinthine. What matters is that the seemingly immutable system of vertical integration between brewing and retail which had dominated the alcohol market in England for over two centuries suddenly ceased to exist. The power of the brewers, which had for so long been seen as unfairly influencing the development of alcohol policy, was now augmented by the power of vast retail organisations many of whom were subsidiaries of global investment companies (such as the Japanese investment bank Nomura) with an interest in both retail and property management. The number of tied pubs fell by just over 30 per cent in the decade after the Beer Orders (from 45 per cent to 11 per cent of the total), but that fall was matched almost precisely by the rise of pub chains who simply entered into supply agreements with an even more concentrated brewing industry.[16] Whatever the intentions of the Monopolies and Mergers Commission in 1989, they failed to predict that by severing the tie between production and retail they would usher in a new age of voracious commercial expansion based on brand-oriented monopolies which would prove at least as detrimental to their conception of consumer choice as what had existed previously.

The Beer Orders were revoked in 2003 following a report from the Office of Fair Trading which suggested that the problems the MMC had identified no longer existed. By then, however, the alcohol retail landscape had been transformed almost beyond recognition. Few people were concerned about the now quaint problem of tied houses; instead, what had emerged as the object of public concern was the proliferation of theme bars and superpubs on the high streets of towns and cities across the country. The Beer Orders had made the mass pub retail chain a reality, and it was these outlets which were starting to become the focus of increasingly vociferous complaints about the drinking habits of young people. However, the saturation of high streets with huge numbers of themed drinking outlets was not only the result of the Beer Orders. A number of other factors – political, economic and sociological – contributed to transformation of alcohol retail in this period. We will briefly outline these factors here.

The end of 'need'

Throughout this history, we have seen that the contours of everyday drinking culture have been carved out by the clash of two great forces: the economic power of property-owning brewers and the regulatory power of licensing magistrates. The question of how the discretionary power of magistrates was exercised, and how they defined the 'need' for new licences within their jurisdiction, triggered many of the most seminal events discussed in this book. The 1830 Beer Act, the Permissive Bill, *Sharp v.*

Wakefield, the battles over compensation, and the debates over municipal control all hinged on the problem of who should decide how many public houses were required in specific areas and how that power should be applied. Many of the fiercest political battles in the history of the drink question were fought out on the territory of 'need'.

It is extraordinary, then, that the principle of need should have ended up being derailed in the space of three years by a series of seemingly minor events: a licence hearing in Nottingham, an Inter-Departmental Working Group meeting, a report from the Better Regulation Task Force, and a Good Practice Guide distributed by the Licensing Clerks' Society. Nevertheless, between 1996 and 1999 these incidents – all largely unnoticed by non-specialists in the wider world – went a long way towards consigning 'need' to history.

The question of 'need' had faced its first significant post-war challenge with the publication of the Erroll Committee report on licensing in 1972. This Committee was established, under the leadership of Lord Erroll of Hale, following an MMC report on tied houses in 1969. The findings addressed issues including opening hours, licensing procedures and legal drinking ages. 'Need' was identified as 'one of the most important matters' that the Committee had looked at.[17] In a chapter dedicated to the subject, the Committee concluded that magisterial discretion was 'unnecessary and inappropriate' and that the principle of need was 'out of date' and should be abandoned.[18] So far as the granting of licences was concerned, the Committee insisted that the 'only relevant consideration [was] market demand', and it was landlords and brewers, not local magistrates, who were qualified to decide whether or not that demand existed.[19]

The Erroll Committee report failed to produce any legislative change, and was badly received by many who objected to its liberalising tone.[20] However, its discussion of 'need' illustrated the stark terms by which the logic of the free market countered the principle of magisterial discretion. The Erroll Committee's rejection of 'need' was not based on an abstract theory of rights but on a simple economic equation: if there is a licence application, then there must be need. In previous eras any such claim would have triggered impassioned debates over the responsibility of moral and legislative authorities to manage the desires of drinkers. And even in the early 1970s it remained a subject which demanded the kind of extensive exegesis afforded it by the Erroll Committee. In the neoliberal 1990s, by contrast, the notion that a licence application justified itself simply by proving *ipso facto* that a market demand existed came increasingly to be accepted as a kind of self-evident statement of the obvious. Under the pressure of a rampant free-market ideology, the idea that the market should *not* be left to decide such things began to look like a rather curious anachronism. In the 1990s, 'need' came to be seen by many as something which could simply be dismissed as a mere inconvenience.

The inconvenience of 'need' manifested itself in the problem of ensuring consistency and fairness in licensing decisions. It had always been the case that some licensing districts had applied their powers more firmly than others, and in the late 1980s and early 1990s many brewers complained that licence applications were unfairly harder to come by in certain regions.[21] In 1993 a Home Office consultation paper on licensing proposed the removal of justices' discretion on the grounds that the use of 'need' had led to both confusion and inconsistency.[22] Three years later, a Departmental Working Group on Licence Transfers was asked to consider the findings of this consultation paper and, in a meeting held on 7th March 1996, the members of this obscure committee decided that 'any system of codified ground for refusal [for licence applications] should *not* include a test of "need"'.[23] The surprising result of this brief finding was that, as far as the Home Office was concerned, it settled the issue: from then on official guidance proceeded on the principle that need was no longer to be considered by licensing magistrates.[24] According to one licensing lawyer, the Government quickly began to put pressure on magistrates to fall in line by suggesting that intransigence over 'need' could lead to licensing being taken out of their hands altogether.[25]

Two years later the influential Better Regulation Task Force (BRTF) produced a report on licensing legislation. Their report objected to the use of 'need' by local justices and insisted that market demand should not be massaged by the use of regulatory power.[26] The BRTF also went further than simply suggesting new guidance for the application of the law; it proposed that licensing should be managed by local authorities working to nationally set guidelines rather than by magistrates working to their own subjective principles.

The BRTF report was taken extremely seriously by local magistrates who saw in it a serious threat to their long-standing control over the licensing process. In response the Justices Clerks Society included in its *Good Practice Guide* for 1999 the recommendation that local magistrates abandon the use of 'need' as a criterion when making licensing decisions. Although, strictly speaking, *Sharp v. Wakefield* remained valid, and while the overall proportion of licence applications being refused did not fall dramatically,[27] in practice local magistrates were now being directed by their own official body to proceed as if 'need' was not a valid consideration. Having stoked the furnace of the drink question for a century after 1830, the principle of need was being quietly snuffed out by a handful of administrative paperwork.

A lost generation

The Beer Orders and the challenge to 'need' cleared the legislative ground for the transformation of the high street alcohol retail market. However, two other factors drove the economic investment required to put that infrastructure in place. One was the response of the alcohol industry to the threat presented to it by the emergence of rave culture in the late 1980s, and the other was the response of local planning authorities to the progressive dereliction of city centres following recession and the shift of capital towards the suburbs. A number of detailed and critically incisive studies of these processes have been published elsewhere.[28] What follows is intended primarily as an overview which will identify some key issues as regards the place of recent developments in the larger history of drink discourse.

Put at its simplest, the development of rave culture from 1987 onwards threatened the alcohol industry because the drug of choice for an ever increasing number of young ravers was Ecstasy, not alcohol. Indeed, in the early years of the rave scene alcohol was not simply bypassed in favour of Ecstasy, it was positively shunned. It may seem strange to an outsider looking at today's alcohol-centred youth culture, but there was a time in the late 1980s and early 1990s when for a significant number of young people alcohol was decidedly unhip. Furthermore, these were precisely the kind of new consumers the alcohol industry needed: young, pleasure-seeking and with access to high levels of disposable income. The response of the alcohol industry was to begin a process of rebranding – of both its drinks and the locations in which drinking could take place – in order to position alcohol as a party drug: to sell drunkenness as a psychoactive experience on a par with the illicit drug experiences that young people were increasingly comfortable experimenting with.[29] While celebrating drunkenness in advertising was illegal, the introduction of high-strength mixers, two-for-one and drink-all-you-can offers, the promotion of shooters, and the use of imagery culled from the rave scene in the branding of new alcopops represented a critical shift in the way drinks were marketed. Intoxication had always been part of the pleasure of drinking, but it was always the suppressed element in alcohol marketing: drink was never sold on the prospectus that it would get you drunk, even though that was always part of its appeal. As the drinks industry responded to the increased normalisation of drug use in youth cultures, and the 'development of new psychoactive consumption styles',[30] for the first time drunkenness itself started to be exploited by the drinks industry as the selling point for many of its products. Never before had the industry so explicitly sold drunkenness as the aim and point of drinking.

The desire of the alcohol industry to capture the psychoactive market was helped in no small way by the simultaneous suppression of rave culture by the Government. After the 1994 Criminal Justice Act specifically targeted the free, outdoor rave scene (by, notoriously, making special provision for the closure of events where the music was 'wholly or predominantly characterised by the emission of a succession of repetitive beats'), clubs and bars began competing to offer similar experiences.[31] The new breed of retail-centred bar chains were in an ideal position to blur the lines between pub and club: to invest in sound systems, lighting rigs, dance floors and DJs and thereby draw a generation of young people more attracted to repetitive beats than to real ale into their establishments.

Planning for the night

A further contributing factor to the rise of the new, youth-oriented, late-night bars in town and city centres was the desire among many planning authorities to use the promotion of a 'vibrant' urban nightlife as a means to achieve much-needed urban regeneration. Following the recessions of the 1980s and early 1990s, and the widespread development of out-of-town shopping malls, many town and city centres were increasingly run-down and economically unstable places: perceived as both depressing (by day) and dangerous (by night). At the same time, central government was encouraging increased housing development on 'brown field' (i.e. ex-industrial) sites in response to an impending housing shortage caused by increased demand for single-occupancy dwellings among both the unmarried and the divorced. The problem faced by local planning authorities was how to both re-stimulate local economies and encourage greater numbers of people and businesses to move into city-centre locations.

For many planners the solution to this conundrum lay in developing a more 'continental-style' city centre. Planners looked to cities such as Barcelona as the model for the successful regeneration of post-industrial urban environments. It was a model which suggested ex-industrial cities could be transformed by the development of new urbane cultures characterised by the promotion of arts, the culture industries and – most importantly – a 'vibrant' nightlife. Paris provided another, older, model for this – having been reinvented when Eugène Haussman pulled down the old streets following the uprisings of 1848 and replaced them with wide boulevards that housed grand cafés at every intersection. Parisian café society – in part the consequence of a monumental exercise in social engineering – also provided an ideal type to which the planners of late twentieth-century England aspired. The '24-hour city', modelled on continental café culture, was going to provide the royal road to a lasting urban renaissance.

Of course, this played well with the new breed of alcohol retailers – even if they were more interested in selling Kahlua than cappuccino. At the heart of the '24-hour city' was the idea of 'mixed use' development. In principle this meant encouraging developers to produce buildings which included work, accommodation and leisure facilities in the same space. In reality, it often meant expensive single-occupancy flats built above an enormous bar. Drink retail chains were in the ideal position to market themselves as key to the development of a vibrant urban culture: they were not traditional pubs, they appealed to both men and women and they looked sophisticated. No one wanted to plonk a Red Lion in the middle of a city-centre redevelopment, but an All Bar One or a Bar Havana was an altogether different proposition.

Of course, local planning authorities had no power to promote such developments through the grant of alcohol licences; that remained in the gift of local magistrates. However, they were responsible for granting the Public Entertainment Licences (PELs) required by premises which provided public music and entertainment. Phil Hadfield has documented the marked increase in PELs handed out by local authorities to licensed premises in the late 1990s. These allowed for live and recorded music to be played, but also made it easier for licensees to then apply to magistrates for Special Hours Certificates (SHCs), which allowed premises providing public entertainment to extend their opening hours to 2a.m. Put briefly, the liberal granting of PELs by local authorities keen to develop their night-time economies, and the subsequent granting of SHCs by local magistrates who were encouraged to support this model of urban regeneration, led to a de facto lifting of standard licensing restrictions in city centres across the country. By 2003, 61 per cent of high-street bars were trading beyond normal hours and the idea of 11p.m. closing was already becoming an anachronism to many young urban drinkers.[32]

Not all local magistrates fell in line with this new vision, however. Many, suspicious that increased competition between outlets might lead to more, rather than less, drunkenness, continued to apply their increasingly fragile discretionary powers to reject licence applications. The magistrates in Nottingham were especially notorious for their stringent application of 'need', and it was a challenge to their authority that further weakened local controls on retail development. In 1996, a new bar – appropriately named Liberty's – was refused a licence by Nottingham magistrates after police objections. Liberty's owners appealed and hired a local law firm, Poppleston Allen, to argue their side in court. As Phil Hadfield has shown in precise detail, the adversarial nature of licensing appeals gave a significant advantage to private law firms who had the experience and resources to manage the court environment effectively. Liberty's won their appeal in what was seen as a test of the right to apply 'need' to proposed city-centre developments.[33] Poppleston Allen would go on to become the solicitors of choice for affluent alcohol retail chains seeking to overturn licence refusals by local justices. As decisions were successfully challenged across the country, the last vestiges of 'need' were further demolished.

With hindsight it is tempting to dismiss the attempt to create a continental café society in English towns and cities as at best cackhanded and at worst deeply cynical. We should remember, however, that local planning authorities were faced with a very difficult problem to which the development of the night-time economy appeared to provide a tangible solution. Faced with the prospect of watching their cities go the way of Flint, Michigan or the way of Barcelona, it is hardly surprising that most planning authorities opted for the latter, especially when the architectural models never depicted the scene at a taxi-rank at 2a.m. The pubcos had the money and the will to invest in run-down city centres, and if an urban renaissance required the promotion of leisure industries whose prime market was alcohol then that was acceptable as long as individuals could be persuaded to drink sensibly. As Hobbs *et al.* put it, the consumption-based model of urban renaissance 'created a fog of city boosterism shrouding the heavy episodic alcoholic consumption that lay at the heart of the night-time economy'.[34] Nevertheless, it was a boosterism born out of a lack of viable alternatives, and many city centres were spared the worst effects of postindustrial recession by pushing the leisure economy.

In relation to the longer history of the drink question, this boosterism represents more than a novel anomaly. In fact, it marks a sea-change in the relationship between the alcohol economy and civic governance. For the first time, municipal authorities began to see their role as not simply managing the alcohol economy, but actively promoting it to the extent that it became critical to their long-term strategic visions. Alcohol consumption ceased to be simply an adjunct to regional economies, and became instead a key driver. When drinking was transformed from a regulated form of transgression to an activity on which whole urban economies depended, something very significant had taken place.[35]

The 1990s, then, saw seismic shifts in the alcohol market. The historic tie between brewers and retailers collapsed following the Beer Orders; the principle of 'need' collapsed under pressure from both central government and the magistrates' own advisory bodies; for the first time, the alcohol industry began to market drunkenness as a primary aim of drinking as they sought to compete with other psychoactive youth markets; and, again for the first time, local authorities began to see their role as promoting the alcohol market rather than simply managing it. While the basic principles of licensing law remained as they had since the war, the landscape within which they worked had been transformed.

Time for reform

Despite the de facto extension of licensing hours in many city centres, in the mid-1990s the majority of premises still turned their customers out at 11p.m. While the problems now associated with the night-time economy may blur our memories of just how run-down many city centres had become in the late 1980s, the problems associated with 24-hour licensing make it easy to forget just how anachronistic many people found the old system of 11p.m. closing. In the late 1990s, the feeling among many drinkers (and not just New Labour spin doctors) was that 'Cool Britannia' simply wasn't the kind of place where fully grown adults should be told they had to drink up and trundle home a whole hour before midnight. This was all the more true as increasing numbers of people took holidays abroad and experienced the strange thrill of being able to finish a drink late at night without being harassed by tired and irritable landlords. To many people, fixed closing times smacked of an unsophisticated paternalism better suited to the England of Ted Heath than Tony Blair.

Extended opening was not a new idea, and it had been strongly supported by the Erroll Committee back in 1972. The Erroll Committee proposed that pubs open from 10a.m. to midnight as standard, precisely on the grounds that there was 'an expressed demand for ... continental type cafes ... and for modern amenities more generally'.[36] It was suggestions such as this (and the reduction of the legal drinking age to 17) which saw the report fall foul of public health campaigners who condemned it as a manifesto for the development of a nationwide drink problem.

What fell on stony ground in the early 1970s, however, landed in fertile soil in the 'noughties'. By 2000, the licensing system was a tangled mess of complex and contradictory rules. Anyone entering the ever more economically important leisure services had to negotiate whole thickets of overlapping legislation: public entertainment licences, special hours certificates, restaurant licences, 'two in a bar' rules, temporary event notices and a mass of other regulations which made the system daunting and unwieldy. Few denied that the system needed clearing out and when the Home Office presented a White Paper on the reform of the licensing laws in 2000 it contained many of the proposals that had previously appeared in the Erroll Committee report.

The White Paper, entitled *Time for Reform*, called for the various existing licences covering everything from alcohol retail to food provision to film performances and public entertainment to be scrapped and replaced by just two licences: one for premises, and one for individuals. A premises licence would allow all the licensable activities previously covered by different legislation to be carried out on these premises (a single licence could, therefore, cover the sale of food, the provision of public entertainment, the showing of films and the sale of alcohol). The personal licence would allow the holder to sell alcohol in any premises that was licensed. In one clean stroke, then, the tangled complexity of existing licensing legislation would be swept away.

Time for Reform also accepted the recommendation contained in the BRTF report that licensing should be managed by local authorities acting according to national guidelines, not by magistrates acting according to their own discretion.[37] In other words, the principle of magisterial control which had been at the heart of licensing procedure since 1552 would be removed. Secondly, fixed closing hours would be lifted entirely. For the first time in almost two centuries, retailers would be free to sell alcohol at any time of day or night, seven days a week.

John Greenaway has suggested that the history of licensing provides ample evidence that the 'rational actor' theory of policy-making (the theory which assumes government policy is driven primarily by research and the rational analysis of evidence) is mistaken. Instead, Greenaway suggests that policy is more often driven by political expediency, which is then given the sheen of legitimacy through *post hoc* reference to a highly selective evidence base.[38] *Time for Reform* seems to bear this claim out. Its discussion of magisterial licensing extends no further than the BRTF report, its position on opening hours is based solely on the Portman Group study of lager louts and the proposals on young people and alcohol include one passing reference to another report carried out by the Portman Group in 1997. While the literature which informed the White Paper has sometimes been unfairly dismissed simply because it was funded by the drinks industry (the Portman Group study of lager louts was, in reality, a rigorous piece of social research), the lack of wider analysis which appeared to have gone into *Time for Reform* is startling, especially given the radical changes it proposed. No space was given to international studies looking at the effects of extended hours on consumption, and the history of licensing given in the appendix did not even mention the 1830 Beer Act, never mind the countless Select Committees and Royal Commissions which had thrashed out the questions of 'need', licensing procedure, access and policing over the centuries. *Time for Reform* was a document written as if history was a mere diversion.

Last orders

Nevertheless, *Time for Reform* underwent only minor modifications before providing the basis for a Licensing Bill that was introduced to Parliament in November 2002.[39] By this time responsibility for licensing had been moved from the Home Office to the Department for Culture, Media and Sport: signalling that it was now seen as an issue of leisure promotion, not the maintenance of law and order. From the start, New Labour focused on the extension of opening hours in their publicity for the Bill. Even though moving licensing to local authorities was the more historically radical proposal, the ending of fixed hours was the measure which most explicitly marked the Bill out as an attempt to modernise British social habits. Shortly before the 2001 Election, Labour sent a text message to thousands of young people which read 'cdnt give a xxxx 4 lst ordrs? thn vte Lbr on thrsday 4 xtra time'. That text has since become notorious as an illustration of the cavalier way in which Labour spin doctors attempted to bribe young voters with the promise of easier access to alcohol (one newspaper headline later ran 'Labour doesn't give a xxxx for the nation's livers').[40] However, the extension of opening hours was not simply presented as an issue of individual liberties; in its press releases, parliamentary statements and explanatory documents the Government also emphasised their claim that extended opening hours would 'reduce the problems of disorder and disturbance associated with fixed universal closing times'.[41] In terms of evaluating the success of the measures, this is a crucial point. The extension of opening was not presented as a rights issue which would have limited or negligible effects on crime and disorder, it was explicitly presented as a crime *reduction* measure which would have happy benefits for individual freedom. Both the research used in *Time for Reform* and the Erroll Committee had argued that the late-night violence was exacerbated by fixed closing times. Furthermore, it was an experiential truth to anyone who drank in pubs that people downed their drinks more quickly as closing time approached, and that the streets usually were more intimidating between 11p.m. and midnight than they were either before or after. While it turned a blind eye to research showing the negative effects of extended licensing in other countries (especially Ireland), the crime reduction element of 24-hour licensing was supported by research into English drinking patterns. Furthermore, it spoke to the common-sense perspective of drinkers and it was also supported by many within the police.[42]

The Bill initially had a good degree of public support, but its passage through Parliament was far from smooth. The Lords challenged the Government on a number of provisions, and they successfully removed a clause allowing unaccompanied children to enter licensed premises. While all-day licensing was the subject of an attempted amendment, the coverage of 24-hour licensing was muted in the press and was by no means the subject of widespread condemnation.[43] Indeed, insofar as the press covered the debates on the Licensing Bill, the majority of column inches were devoted to a row that erupted between the Musicians Union and the Government over the requirement for all premises which held live music performances to apply for a licence. The Conservatives and Liberal Democrats both backed the Musician's Union in its attempt to derail what it saw as a 'draconian' piece of legislation, and it was on this issue that the Bill came closest to parliamentary failure as the Lords repeatedly insisted on an amendment allowing small, unlicensed venues to provide unamplified music.[44] In the end, a compromise was reached protecting morris dancers, but the requirement for all other live music to be licensed remained in place. Once compromise on this issue was reached the Bill passed its final reading and the Licensing Act became law. A timetable for implementation was prepared which meant that, while the legislation received Royal Assent in 2003, it would become fully operational in November 2005.

Notes

1   M. Tuck, *Drinking and Disorder: A Study of Non-Metropolitan Violence*, Home Office Research Study 108 (London: HMSO, 1989); P. Marsh and K. Fox-Kibby, *Drinking and Public Disorder* (London: Portman Group, 1992).
2   Tuck, *Drinking and Disorder*, pp. 50, 66.
3   Marsh and Fox-Kibby, *Drinking and Public Disorder*, p. 156; Tuck, *Drinking and Disorder*, p. 68.
4   Department of Culture, Media and Sport (DCMS), 'Statistical bulletin: Liquor licensing' (2004) p. 8.
5   Monopolies and Mergers Commission, *The Supply of Beer* (London: HMSO, 1989), p. 2.
6   *Ibid.*, p. 4.
7   *Ibid.*, p. 2.
8   *Ibid.*, p. 3.
9   *Ibid.*, pp. 267–8.
10 *Ibid.*, p. 295.
11 *Ibid.*, p. 288.
12 J. Bridgeman, *The Supply of Beer* (London: Office of Fair Trading, 2000), p. 38.
13 Cornell, *Beer*, p. 228.
14 Bridgeman, *Supply of Beer*, p. 42.
15 *Ibid.*, p. 3.
16 *Ibid.*, p. 38.
17 House of Commons, *Report of the Departmental Committee on Liquor Licensing* (1972) Cmnd. 5154, p. 76.

18 *Ibid.*, pp. 87, 90.
19 *Ibid.*, p. 90.
20 R. Light and S. Heenan, *Controlling Supply: The Concept of 'Need' in Liquor Licensing* (Bristol: University of the West of England, 1999), p. 33.
21 MMC, *The Supply of Beer*, p. 2.
22 Light and Heenan, *Controlling Supply*, p. 37.
23 *Ibid.*, p. 42.
24 *Ibid.*, p. 40.
25 BBC, *Panorama: Cdnt give a xxxx 4 lst ordrs?* (6 June 2004) transcript, http://news. bbc.co.uk/nol/shared/spl/hi/programmes/panorama/transcripts/xxxx.txt.
26 Light and Heenan, *Controlling Supply*, pp. 43–4.
27 DCMS, 'Statistical bulletin: liquor licensing', p. 10.
28 See for example, K. Brain, 'Youth, alcohol and the emergence of the post-modern alcohol order' (London: Institute of Alcohol Studies, 2000); P. Chatterton, 'Governing nightlife: Profit, fun and (dis)order in the contemporary city', *Entertainment Law*, 1:2 (2002), pp. 23–49; P. Chatterton and R. Hollands, *Urban Nightscapes* (London: Routledge, 2003); D. Hobbs, P. Hadfield, S. Lister and S. Winlow, *Bouncers: Violence and Governance in the Night-time Economy* (Oxford: Oxford University Press, 2003); P. Hadfield, *Bar Wars: Contesting the Night in Contemporary British Cities* (Oxford: Oxford University Press, 2006); S. Winlow and S. Hall, *Violent Night: Urban Leisure and Contemporary Culture* (Oxford: Berg, 2006); M. Plant and M. Plant, *Binge Britain: Alcohol and the National Response* (Oxford: Oxford University Press, 2006).
29 Brain, 'Youth, Alcohol and the Emergence of the Post-modern Alcohol Order'; F. Measham and K. Brain, 'Binge drinking, British alcohol policy and the new culture of intoxication', *Crime, Media and Society*, 1:3 (2005), pp. 262–83.
30 Measham and Brain, 'Binge drinking', p. 266.
31 Hadfield, *Bar Wars*, p. 59.
32 *Ibid.*, p. 52.
33 BBC, 'Cdnt give a xxxx'.
34 D. Hobbs, S. Winlow, P. Hadfield and S. Lister, 'Violent hypocrisy: Governance and the night-time economy', *European Journal of Communications*, 2:2 (2005), 161–83, p. 163.
35 A. Lovatt, 'The ecstasy of urban regeneration: Regulation of the night-time economy in the transition of the post-Fordist city', in J. O'Connor and D. Wynne, *From the Margins to the Centre: Cultural Production and Consumption in the Post-industrial City* (Aldershot: Arena, 1996), pp. 141–68.
36 House of Commons, *Report of the Departmental Committee on Liquor Licensing*, pp, 147–9, 313.
37 Home Office, *Time for Reform* (2000), p. 48, www.culture.gov.uk/Reference_library/ Publications/archive_2001/time_for_reform.htm.
38 Greenaway, *Drink and British Politics*, p. 201.
39 G. Berman and G. Danby, *The Licensing Bill* (Home Office Research Paper 03/27, 2003), p. 12, www.parliament.uk/commons/lib/research/rp2003/rp03–027.pdf.
40 J. McCartney, 'Labour doesn't give a xxxx for the nation's livers' (*Sunday Telegraph*, 30 January 2005).
41 Department of Culture, Media and Sport, 'Licensing Countdown' (2004), p. 12 www. culture.gov.uk/NR/rdonlyres/3FEABCCF-D8F4–48D8-B8B5–35800D9EF91A/0/ LCNewsletterDec.pdf.
42 Winlow and Hall, *Violent Night*, p. 167.

43 Methodological note: a survey was carried out by the author using the newspaper database NewsBank, which contains full copies of all national newspaper articles published since 2000. Searches were carried out for all national newspaper reports containing the phrases 'licensing bill' and 'licensing act' for all years 2003–07 and the resulting articles analysed.

   A further search was carried out into coverage of binge drinking. For this the search terms 'binge drinker' and 'binge drinking' were used. Further qualifiers were added to remove articles which dealt specifically with Scotland or Ireland (in Ireland binge drinking became the subject of heated media debate about two years before the same thing happened in England). The results provide only an imperfect snapshot of the rise of 'binge drinking' in the mass media; however, they so give a rough sense of the trajectory of the subject. The findings, in purely numerical terms, were as follows:

Table 1 Binge drinking in the British press

Year	No. of reports containing the phrases 'binge drinkers' or 'binge drinking'
2000	0
2001	4
2002	6
2003	24
2004	101
2005	136
2006	141
2007	73

44 M. Woolf, 'Musicians petition Blair over new "draconian" Licensing Bill' (*Independent*, 17 June 2003).

16

Drinking responsibly: media, government and binge drinking

Rights and responsibilities are at the heart of the Government's approach to alcohol. (*Safe. Sensible. Social.*, Department of Health, 2007)

The consistent picture which emerges is of a central government which is determined to be toothless with respect to alcohol policy. (Robin Room)

During the passage of the Licensing Bill there was some concern over 24-hour licensing but the issue in no way dominated public debate. It was not until the start of the following year that the tone changed. Over the course of 2004, what had been ripples of concern over the liberalising elements of the Act began to swell into something approaching a tidal wave of public disquiet.

On 11 January 2004, the *Sunday Times* ran a story under the headline 'Street violence jumps in binge Britain'.[1] It was the first time this provocatively alliterative phrase had appeared in the press, but by the end of the year it – and the variation 'booze Britain' – would become part of the everyday language of the debate on alcohol. Over the next few months disturbing frontline accounts from the streets of 'Binge Britain' became a feature of both tabloid and broadsheet reporting, and the principle of all-day drinking became the object of increasingly feverish hostility on the part of journalists, police and politicians.[2]

Booze Britain

There are a number of reasons why this delayed reaction occurred. Firstly, research emerged which showed that levels of alcohol consumption were increasing significantly across the country. In particular, heavy episodic consumption among young people was shown to be among the highest in Europe and levels of consumption among women were shown to have increased substantially.[3] The statistics regarding alcohol consumption were given a rhetorical force by the increasingly widespread use of the term 'binge drinking', which had been virtually unheard of five years previously.[4]

'Binge drinking' was a fuzzy concept but it allowed for alarming figures to be presented in a language which conveyed the sense of an impending disaster. '18% of women aged between 20 and 60 are binge drinkers,' wrote the *Sunday Times* a week after its report on street violence, while '36% of twentysomething women qualify and 33% of men'.[5]

Few people would have known precisely what 'binge drinking' meant at the time. The Institute of Psychiatry study on which the *Sunday Times* report was based defined a 'binge' as consuming twice the daily recommended limit in one session: this equates to eight units for a man and six units for a woman, and it has become the standard model by which most studies define binge drinking. However, it is far from being the only definition.[6] In 2004, as the concept hit the headlines, different research bodies applied a number of different definitions. The European School Survey Project on Alcohol and Other Drugs (ESPAD), who had produced a report which showed England to be near the top of the European league table for binge drinking among young people, defined it as drinking five or more drinks in one session.[7] The Prime Minister's Strategy Unit defined binge drinkers more broadly as 'those who drink to get drunk and are likely to be under 25'.[8] The Office of National Statistics defined 'heavy drinking' using the same measure as the Institute of Psychiatry had used to define 'binge drinking'. Later the Institute of Alcohol Studies would attempt to overcome these definitional problems by defining binge drinking as 'drinking which results in the drinker feeling at least partially drunk'.[9] This certainly addresses these problems, but also risks turning most drinking occasions into a potential binge.

The Government's own attempts to dovetail its Licensing Act into a wider strategy to reduce alcohol-related harm also contributed to the wave of anxiety over consumption. The Licensing Act had been presented as a measure which would help reduce excessive drinking late at night; as such, the Government had hoped that it would fit neatly with their publication of a delayed Alcohol Harm Reduction Strategy for England in March 2004. However, the publication of this Strategy (whose unfortunate acronym greatly amused sceptical commentators) reinforced the impression that England was facing a deeply worrying increase in consumption, while seeming – to its critics, at least – to provide a 'recipe for ineffectiveness' in dealing with that problem.[10]

The Alcohol Harm Reduction Strategy estimated that alcohol-related harm cost the economy £20 billion annually and that alcohol was responsible for around half of all violent crimes, 360,000 incidents of domestic violence, increased antisocial behaviour and up to 1,000 suicides each year.[11] Even though it put the overall value of the drinks market at £30 billion annually and employment in the alcohol industry at one million jobs, the tax revenues still only amounted to £7 billion a year.[12] The overall picture presented was, therefore, one of a sizeable problem which was only partially offset by the economic contribution that the alcohol industry provided. Furthermore, while the Strategy was meant to show that the Government was taking alcohol problems seriously, public health campaigners were outraged by the proposals set out to tackle excessive drinking. The four approaches which the Strategy outlined were education, treatment for problem drinkers, a focus on crime and disorder and partnership with the drinks industry. These strategies were in accordance with the findings of an interdepartmental working group on sensible drinking which had been published in 2005.[13] However, as Robin Room pointed out in a scathing review, the proposals outlined in the Strategy were precisely those which had been identified by many of the world's leading alcohol researchers as the *least* effective when it came to reducing alcohol-related harm.[14]

Both the AHRSE and the inter-departmental report on sensible drinking had explicitly rejected population approaches, but, as we have seen, public health campaigners had been calling for per capita consumption to be reduced through increased taxation and reduced access to alcohol since the early 1970s. In 1994, a major report entitled *Alcohol and the Public Good* had argued that focusing on problem drinkers was less effective than tackling overall consumption across the population, and had insisted that targeting a small minority of problem drinkers was mistaken. It had also claimed that expenditure on education was excessive given that most research showed that education and media-based campaigns had little impact on drinking habits.[15] These conclusions had been reiterated in another major international report compiled by public health researchers in 2003.[16] The consensus among these researchers was that population-based approaches were the only sure way to tackle alcohol-related problems, and that the most effective way to reduce overall consumption was through raising prices via taxation and reducing access to alcohol via licensing restrictions.[17] The Government's determination to pursue an education-based approach, and to rely on the meaningful cooperation of the drinks industry, was anathema to public health campaigners and they became increasingly vocal in their calls for greater regulatory control.

In March 2004, coinciding with the publication of the Government's Harm Reduction Strategy, the Academy of Medical Sciences published a report which, while acknowledging that the more clumsy applications of the Ledermann curve had been abandoned by subsequent studies, insisted nevertheless that overall per capita consumption of alcohol remained a 'crucial determinant of harm'.[18] It demanded that consumption be brought back to 1970s levels, and that this be achieved through increased taxation, restrictions on access to alcohol, a reduction of the blood-alcohol limit for drivers from 80mg to 50mg and the establishment of a public debate on alcohol and health.[19]

In the mainstream media a public debate certainly ensued as both press and broadcast journalists began to report on the realities of 'binge Britain' with increasing vigour and alarm. Often consumption figures provided by public health campaigners provided the statistical background to press reporting. At the same time, a visual language began to emerge in mass-media depictions of 'binge Britain': photographs and CCTV footage seemed to reveal a nocturnal pandemonium of violent young men, sexually vulnerable (or promiscuous) young women, and harassed police in luminous jackets struggling to cope with the disorder that exploded on the streets as young binge drinkers staggered from one garish venue to the next. One cable TV channel produced an entire series of hour-long 'documentaries' – *Booze Britain 2: Binge Nation* – which followed groups of young drinkers in cities across Britain as they drank themselves into various stages of oblivion.[20] The number of national newspaper reports mentioning binge drinking in England quadrupled between 2003 and 2004, and continued to increase for the next two years.[21]

The details of this public debate have been discussed in detail elsewhere.[22] In brief, the key concerns expressed in the mass media were under-age drinking, crime and disorder, drinking among women and public health. Opposition to the 2003 Licensing Act came to a head in the months prior to its implementation in November 2005 with press campaigns against 24-hour licensing (such as the *Daily Mail's* 'Great Rebellion') and political attempts to scupper the implementation of the Act through a series of arcane parliamentary procedures. Public health campaigners insisted that 24-hour licensing would only exacerbate the already significant increase in alcohol-related deaths that been taking place over the previous decade. Ian Gilmore, a liver specialist who would become one of the most prominent medical campaigners on alcohol issues, wrote in the *Daily Mail* that 'far from ushering in a new age of maturity ... 24-hour pub opening will lead to more excess and binge-drinking especially among young people whose current levels of consumption are already at dangerous levels'.[23]

Women in particular were identified as being at risk from increased levels of alcohol consumption. Part of the reason that statistics for overall consumption had increased since the 1960s was precisely because increasing gender equality had lifted some of the long-standing taboos that had excluded women from public drinking. While we have seen that there was never an absolute prohibition on women drinking in public houses, the culture of the pub had always been deeply masculine and the physical make-up of the 'traditional' pub, with its dark corners, booths and snugs, had – as the old pub-improvers knew very well – tended to exclude women. The new generation of bars that appeared following the Beer Orders were designed specifically to appeal to both male and female drinkers. Well-lit, open spaces and a wider range of drinks made the modern pub a far less sexist institution than its traditional forebear. Breaking the cultural restrictions on women's drinking also went some way towards undermining the disproportionate moral condemnation that had attached to drunkenness among women over the centuries, though by no means entirely.

Comparisons have been drawn between the representation of binge drinking, especially among women, and the fevered debate on gender and alcohol that characterised the gin craze.[24] There are, undoubtedly, many parallels to be drawn. In both cases public drunkenness among young women has been represented as a new and altogether more worrisome threat to social order than that presented by drunken men. The other notable similarity is that in both instances, women's drinking has been associated with sexual promiscuity, vulnerability and irresponsibility. While the media semiotics of binge drinking revolve around images of violent men, they equally revolve around images of provocatively dressed women, or women who appear sexually vulnerable. Two photographs by the Bath-based photographer Matt Cardy, both showing young women in short black skirts and stockings sprawled next to discarded bottles of vodka, became standard images of the female binge-drinker, appearing in numerous press reports (and on the cover of one major book on the subject). Cardy's elegantly framed images of young drunk women represent, in many ways, a contemporary reworking of 'Gin Lane'. However, the difference between the images reveals the differences between the eras as well. In the eighteenth century, women's drinking was presented as a sign of moral decline, but one which was framed primarily in terms of the economic risks presented by the impact of alcohol on mothers and their children. Today, women's drinking is still presented as a sign of moral decline, but the predominant framework in which concerns have been expressed tends to be public safety (the risk of date-rape and other forms of predatory attack) and public health (the increased health risks run by women who drink at the same levels as men). The democratisation of access to drink has re-established the fact that gender equality has never been a feature of public discourse on alcohol,[25] and, indeed, that drink is a subject on which the assertion of intractable gender differences remains an unimpeachable norm.

Drinking responsibly

The pressure exerted on the Government over the issue of binge drinking forced a change of policy focus. In May 2004, the Prime Minister, Tony Blair, announced a campaign to combat what he described as a 'new British disease' of excessive drunkenness. In the short term, this involved financing a police drive to tackle under-age drinking and antisocial behaviour over the summer months. Meanwhile, civil servants from the DCMS, the Home Office and the Office of the Deputy Prime Minister were preparing a consultation document on how new measures, outside the provisions of the Licensing Act, could be introduced to discourage binge drinking.

This interdepartmental report was published in January 2005 under the title *Drinking Responsibly*. It outlined a series of new proposals including tightening existing police powers to impose drink-banning orders on people arrested for drunken antisocial behaviour. It also resurrected an idea for the creation of Alcohol Disorder Zones that had originally been rejected when put forward by the Home Secretary David Blunkett in 2003.[26] Alcohol Disorder Zones (ADZs) would be established as an act of last resort when retailers in specified areas persistently failed to implement measures to reduce disorder in and around their establishments. Once imposed, any retailer operating within an ADZ would be required to contribute financially towards crime-reduction measures for a set period of time. The Government had resisted the idea initially on the grounds that it faced stiff opposition from licensees; however, the mood had changed enough by early 2005 for the official position on the subject to have altered radically. Both the strengthened drink-banning orders and the establishment of ADZs were incorporated into the Violent Crime Reduction Act (2006), although the commencement order allowing councils to impose ADZs was not finalised until June 2008 after the regulations guiding implementation completed a very rocky journey through their committee stages.

While *Drinking Responsibly* was notable for the change of position regarding retailer responsibility, it still reiterated the position, stated in both the publicity surrounding the 2003 Act and throughout the Alcohol Harm Reduction Strategy, that 'responsibility for ending the binge drinking culture [lay] with the individual as much, if not more, than ... with the industry or licensed premises'.[27] 'Rights and responsibilities,' the document asserted, were 'at the heart of the Government's approach to alcohol',[28] but while the right to sell and the right to consume alcohol were both held to be shared equally, the responsibility for avoiding excess was slanted towards the consumer. Even where *Drinking Responsibly* directly addressed the need for an end to irresponsible drink promotions, not only was statutory regulation ruled out but it was stated in no uncertain terms that 'normal price competition in line with competition law should not be put in doubt'.[29]

This focus on individual responsibility was in line with the tenor of the Harm Reduction Strategy published a year earlier. There the authors insisted that 'individuals make choices about how much and how often they drink' and that it was individuals who were responsible for those choices even though 'they both influence and are driven by their peers and the wider culture of society'.[30] The implication of this moral framework was, of course, that in the alcohol transaction responsibility for the effects of intoxication lay fundamentally on the side of the consumer, not the seller or the licensing authorities. To paraphrase Daniel Defoe, writing three centuries earlier: if the people get plastered, it's the magistrates' problem, not the producers (or, to quote *The Sun* in 2008: 'Binge drinking is down to individuals. Clamping down on it is a matter for the police, not a reason for raising taxes').[31] Of course, the magistrates now had no power to control the retail side at all, and under the strict national guidelines released to local authorities in 2004, licensing committees were told in no uncertain terms that 'need' was 'not a matter for a licensing authority', that fixed closing times should not be imposed as a condition of a licence, and that any 'vexatious or frivolous' challenges to licence applications were to be dismissed (even though, extraordinarily, the decision as to whether such challenges were vexatious or not were to be taken by council administrators rather than the licensing committee proper).[32] Since the new licensing authorities were already required to accept all licensing applications that were not specifically challenged by residents, police or other interested parties, this further hand-tying caused consternation. Under pressure from the Lords, the DCMS eventually agreed that councils could identify 'cumulative impact' zones in areas already saturated with drinking outlets. Here councils would be allowed to presume against granting licence applications, but again only if a challenge to that application was lodged in the first place.

The inclusion of the right to create cumulative impact zones reintroduced the principle of discretion into the Licensing Act, albeit in the most limited way possible. However, taken together with the rest of the guidance, the overall presumption remained that the suppliers of alcohol should be given the freedom to ply their trade with as little interference as possible. Producers were asked to draw up voluntary agreements to curb irresponsible promotions, but the fundamental responsibility for not drinking to excess fell to the consumer. This free-market model of rights and responsibilities made sense if alcohol was like other commodities; however, we have already encountered the many arguments which pointed out the fact that it was not. Indeed, all the old arguments about the role of the State in managing the alcohol trade were resurrected in the vociferous debates that followed the enactment of the Licensing Act: was alcohol an 'ordinary commodity', to be regulated with the same light touch applied to groceries or durables? Did the rights of moderate drinkers outweigh the responsibility of the Government to prevent the harms produced by excessive consumption? Did the English suffer from a peculiar 'disease' of drunkenness which required special regulatory measures? Was the political influence of the drinks trade disproportionate? Did women drinkers have the same rights as men? Did particular patterns of social drinking produce particularly detrimental effects? The reappearance of these questions in the early twenty-first century suggests that no lasting solution to them was ever arrived at in the centuries-long debates that went before.

Mounting pressure

In the years that followed the implementation of the 2003 Licensing Act, the Government came under increasing pressure both from newspapers demanding greater intervention to deal with law and order and from public health groups calling for greater intervention to curb levels of overall consumption. In August 2006, the North West Public Health Observatory (NWPHO) published a report showing that in some areas of England 30 per cent of people reported drinking over twice the daily recommended limit on at least one occasion in the previous week. The *Daily Mail*, under the front-page banner headline 'Binge Britain', quoted Mark Bellis, Director of the NWPHO, as stating that Britain was 'no longer a nation enjoying a harmless tipple but increasingly one developing a dangerous alcohol addiction' – an interesting, and presumably rhetorical, conflation of old-fashioned addiction discourse with newer epidemiological language.[33] The Government's own safe drinking guidelines, initially adopted as a strategic way of encouraging sensible levels of consumption, increasingly came to be used as yardsticks by which the prospect of a nationwide drink problem was expressed in concrete terms. The NWPHO began publishing figures for 'hazardous' drinking alongside those for 'harmful' drinking – and producing statistics which combined the two.[34] 'Hazardous' drinking refers to anyone consuming over 21 units a week for men and 14 units a week for women; when combined with the results for 'harmful' drinking (which requires drinking over twice that amount per week), the figures suggested nearly one-third of the population had a drink problem. What it literally meant was that around one-quarter of men and one-sixth of women were regularly drinking more than the weekly sensible drinking guidelines adopted by the Royal Colleges in the mid-1980s. Therefore, it is not to question the importance of such statistics to note that they also represent the increasingly effective use of epidemiological discourse in the public framing of debates around drink. The appearance of broadsheet headlines such as 'Hazardous drinking, the middle class vice' represents, among other things, the successful creation of a new category of problem drinker, albeit one based on the contravention of what were initially conceived of as merely advisory guidelines for sensible consumption.[35]

The public health research carried out by the NWPO and others provided ever more detailed statistical investigations into patterns of consumption across England, patterns which showed, importantly, that while overall consumption was high among affluent drinkers, alcohol-related health problems were far higher in areas of multiple deprivation.[36] The detailed material produced by the likes of NWPHO made them one of the key sources for media information on alcohol, thereby establishing the public health position as central to media definitions. In 2007 an array of medical groups and alcohol-campaigning organisations formed the Alcohol Health Alliance, whose goal was to coordinate the political and media campaign for increased taxation, stiffer industry regulation and better funding for treatment programmes. At around the same time, a long-awaited policy report on 'social breakdown' produced for the Conservative Party by its ex-leader Iain Duncan Smith identified increased taxation as 'the most effective way of preventing and reducing alcohol harm'.[37] Although the report as a whole was later undermined by senior Conservatives keen to distance themselves from its alarmingly non-traditional policy proposals, the acceptance of a tax-based control principle by a Conservative research group represented a significant victory for public health campaigners. Equally notable is the fact that the research on which these recommendations were based was carried out by the Institute of Alcohol Studies. It had been a very long time since the Institute's forebears, the Alliance, had gained this level of influence among policy-makers.

In the same year the Government released the latest version of its National Alcohol Strategy under the title *Safe. Sensible. Social.* Fundamentally, the updated Strategy represented a continuation of the principles which had guided the original AHRSE. Once again, it insisted that 'rights and responsibilities [were] at the heart of the Government's approach to alcohol',[38] and once again it resisted calls for consumption to be targeted at a population level – focusing instead on the 'significant minority' of drinkers (under-age drinkers, binge drinkers aged between 18 and 24, and harmful drinkers) who caused serious problems.[39] The updated Strategy did, however, make some concessions to those who had been campaigning for a change of direction. The eight key goals which were set out retained the emphasis on education and industry partnership, but also included 'brief interventions' for potentially problematic drinkers entering the criminal justice system, the development of locally defined alcohol strategies, and a period of public consultation on the use of pricing to reduce excessive consumption. The Strategy also acknowledged that consumption was probably even higher than many reports suggested, since the amount of alcohol cleared for sale by Revenue and Customs was consistently far higher than the amount that the questionnaires used by the General Household Survey (which formed the basis for the figures released by the Office of National Statistics) suggested were being consumed.[40] Furthermore, rather than simply discounting the need for further statutory regulation of the drinks industry, the Strategy warned that the Government would ensure that 'sufficient measures are in place to eliminate irresponsible promotions' by retailers.[41] It was not much of a threat, but it is a measure of how enormously the political ground had shifted that sixty years after nationalisation of the drinks trade had been a serious consideration, this rather meek piece of fist-waving actually represented a Labour administration trying to publicly reassert its authority with regard to the alcohol industry.

The cost of drinking

In January 2008, three teenagers were convicted of beating Garry Newlove, a 47-year-old father of three, to death outside his home in Warrington, Cheshire. According to witnesses, the killers had been drinking prior to the assault, and in a statement following the trial Newlove's widow called for parents, the police and retailers to work harder to tackle under-age drinking and the violent and antisocial behaviour which often accompanied it. The story was covered widely in the print and broadcast media, and it seemed to confirm all the worst fears over binge drinking that had been expressed in the previous few years. Young people, it appeared, had easy access to alcohol which was being sold by unscrupulous retailers at knockdown prices. Drink was fuelling a yob culture which the police, parents and residents were all unable to control as long as supermarkets and off-licences were willing to sell alcohol to children at prices which made it cheaper than most soft drinks.

Shortly after the conclusion of the Newlove trial, the Home Secretary, Jacqui Smith, gave a speech in which she reiterated the Government's commitment to tackling binge drinking. The case of Gary Newlove, she said, had 'brought into sharp focus how serious the consequences of alcohol misuse can be'.[42] In general terms, Smith's speech followed closely the approach outlined in *Safe. Sensible. Social.* She insisted that the

Government's focus remained 'squarely on … that problematic minority who cause the violence, disorder and disruption'.[43] However, she also signalled a small but significant shift in direction by stating that the three groups which would be the focus of her work were under-age drinkers, binge drinkers and 'those who sell alcohol irresponsibly'.[44] By foregrounding the role of the alcohol industry in this way, Smith revealed the extent to which media pressure was forcing the Government to address the role of the alcohol industry in fostering a culture of heavy drinking, rather than repeating the standard insistence that ultimate responsibility lay with the individual. There was no major announcement regarding the introduction of new rules to govern alcohol retail, but while Smith acknowledged the effectiveness of voluntary regulation she also cited research from Alcohol Concern which suggested that many retailers still used irresponsible promotions to attract customers. An independent review of self-regulation by the auditors KPMG was announced and Smith left open the possibility that if the review found flaws in the system, then 'statutory regulation' of the industry remained an option.[45] Two weeks after Smith's speech, the supermarket giant Tesco announced that it would support Government intervention to ban the sale of cut-price alcohol by retailers.[46] Other supermarkets followed suit, but all insisted that they could not act alone, nor could they agree to fix prices between them as that would contravene competition law. Not that this statement of intent prevented Tesco or their rivals from pressing ahead with widely advertised cut-price alcohol promotions over the following weeks and months.

The trial of Garry Newlove's killers did not create a sea-change in thinking about alcohol, but it did represent a tipping point of sorts. Long-standing concerns over under-age drinking, which had always overlapped with even longer-standing worries over youth crime and violence, now began to centre not on licensing laws, but on the availability of cheap alcohol in shops and supermarkets. The affordability of alcohol had been raised periodically as an issue for some time, especially as it was one of the key drivers that the public health lobby identified as contributing to increases in consumption; however, because the Licensing Act had impacted most significantly on pubs and bars, media concern had tended to centre on the issue of licensing hours, and where it did address pricing it tended to do so by reference to the problem of 'happy hours', two-for-one promotions and the sale of cut-price shots. But while such promotions undoubtedly encouraged heavy sessional drinking in pubs and bars, the off-trade was always expanding far more quickly in terms of sales. Indeed, since 2001 the amount of alcohol consumed outside the home had actually fallen by over 18 per cent.[47] Pub attendance had not increased since the introduction of the Licensing Act, in fact it appeared to have fallen slightly.[48] Meanwhile supermarkets remained the place where consumers were most likely to buy their drink.[49] According to the Office of National Statistics, alcohol was 65 per cent more affordable (in terms of retail price relative to disposable income) than in had been in 1980;[50] over the same period per capita consumption had increased by 20 per cent – although it had dipped from a peak in 2003.[51] While, for years, the focus of media concern over binge drinking had been the threat of late-night pubs and clubs it turned out that many of the changes in levels and patterns of consumption had little to do with conventional licensed premises and much more to do with the sale of alcohol in shops.

The wave of concern over cheap sales of alcohol to young people further bolstered the campaign already under way on the part of public health campaigners for consumption to be managed through increases in taxation. A report published by the British Medical Association in February 2008 reiterated these calls in terms which echoed previous publications by medical groups (one of the senior advisors to the report was Griffith Edwards who, as we have seen, had been at the forefront of public health campaigning on alcohol since the 1960s). The BMA report, while insisting that it did not intend to 'assail those who enjoy consuming alcohol in moderation', outlined the same policy proposals as had been set out by the Academy of Medical Sciences four years earlier.[52] It insisted that the Government should move 'away from partnership with the alcohol industry' and concentrate instead on providing the 'strong leadership' necessary to drive consumption down to 1970s levels. Once again, spending on education was condemned as 'disproportionate' and taxation, restrictions on opening hours and lowered blood alcohol limits for drivers were called for instead.[53]

Shortly afterwards, in March 2008, the Government published an independent review of the 2003 Licensing Act. The review's finding were ambivalent; it concluded that it was 'too early to say with confidence whether the Act has succeeded or failed in its intention to tackle night time crime and disorder'; indeed, all that 'could be said with a degree of confidence was that [the Act] has not made matters worse in the first year or so of the changes'.[54] Other independent studies had arrived at very similar conclusions: 24-hour licensing had moved peak hours for alcohol-related violence forward from around midnight to around 3a.m., but it had not led to a massive rise in antisocial behaviour associated with drinking, nor had it caused a significant increase in consumption.[55] It hadn't, so it seemed, made things worse or better. Had Labour presented 24-hour licensing purely as a rights issue rather than a crime-reduction measure – had they, in other words, distanced later opening from the question of alcohol harm reduction – then they may have prevented it from becoming the object of such widespread controversy. The fact was that per capita consumption peaked *before* the introduction of the Licensing Act and had actually fallen by between 2–5 per cent since 2004.[56] The peak had followed the loss of control over licensing by magistrates, rigorous marketing and point-of-sale promotion by producers, and a significant increase in the affordability of alcohol. In England at least, opening hours started to look like less of a cataclysm in terms of harm reduction than opponents of the 2003 Act had insisted it would be: w*hen* people drank, so the research suggested, did not have a decisive impact on how much they drank or how they behaved after drinking. The Government announced it was not planning a reconsideration of 24-hour licensing, and few opposition politicians were minded to object.

By contrast in March 2008, three months after the Newlove trial and two months after the BMA report, the Chancellor of the Exchequer, Alistair Darling, presented a budget to Parliament in which a blanket alcohol tax rise of 6 per cent above inflation was announced, to be followed by 2 per cent above-inflation increases for the following four years. It was a headline-grabbing announcement in an otherwise sombre Budget. It was also the first time for a decade that spirit duties had been increased. Indeed, in his final budget as Chancellor just one year earlier Gordon Brown had proudly told the House that 'for the tenth budget in a row I will freeze duty on spirits'.[57] It had still been possible in 2007 to gain political mileage from announcing measures to keep down the price of alcohol; this was no longer true in 2008. The tax increases were welcomed by the Alcohol Health Alliance and the British Medical Association. Publicans and brewers pointed to the failure to distinguish between different types of drinks, and complained that it would impact disproportionately on draught beer sales, which had been falling, both in real terms and as a proportion of the alcohol market, for decades.[58] Pubs had already suffered a decrease in takings since the introduction of a ban on smoking in public places a year earlier, and the blanket increase was one that could be absorbed more easily by supermarkets than by pubs.[59] Confusingly, Darling also announced that the money raised by the tax increase would go towards increased Child Benefit payments and support for pensioner's heating bills – which left the Exchequer in the rather invidious position of claiming to tackle excessive drinking while needing high levels of alcohol consumption to fund improvements to the welfare of children and senior citizens. Much of the press – even those which had been most furiously opposed to 24-hour licensing – gave it the thumbs-down, accusing the Chancellor of 'penalising responsible, middle class drinkers' while 'doing nothing to tackle the problem of teenage binge-drinking'.[60]

While it may have alienated numerous journalists, most publicans, and no small number of drinkers, the fact that above-inflation taxation was applied at all, and the fact that neither opposition party challenged the idea, represented a victory for public health campaigners. Certainly, such a tax rise, taken alone, fell short of the broader demands set out by the Alcohol Health Alliance; the issue of 24-hour licences had been settled against their wishes, and there was no sign as yet of legislation to tackle supermarket discounts. Furthermore, the ring fencing of the expected receipts somewhat undermined the claim that the tax increase was a consumption-reducing measure. Nevertheless, by framing the announcement in terms of affordability, and by effectively targeting all drinkers, the Treasury had accepted a key tenet of the population model – something they had resisted forcefully for decades. It was an illustration of the success with which campaigners had harnessed concerns over social order, energised in the wake of the 2003 Act, and directed them towards framing the drink question as a public health issue.

Notes

1 W. Iredale, 'Street violence jumps in binge Britain' (*Sunday Times*, 11 January 2004).

2 See, for example, T. Rawstorne, 'Binge Britain' (*Daily Mail*, 12 July 2004); D. Boffey, 'Reclaim our streets: Unhappy hours' (*Daily Mirror*, 16 August 2004); J. Rayner, 'On the streets of Binge Britain' (*Observer*, 5 September 2004); J. Chapman, 'Blair's all-day drink plans are "reckless"' (*Daily Mail*, 12 August 2004); O. Blackman, 'Blitz on binge drinkers' (*Daily Mirror*, 17 September 2004); M. Hickley, 'All-day pubs will bring us 24 hours of hell say police' (*Daily Mail*, 18 September 2004); M. Bright, and G. Hinsliff, 'Britain: A nation "in grip of drinks chaos"' (*Observer*, 21 November 2004).

3 B. Hibbell, B. Andersson, T. Bjarnasson, *et al.*, *The ESPAD Report 2003* (Stockholm: Swedish Council for Information on Alcohol and Other Drugs, 2004).

4 See Table 1 above.

5 J. Elliott, 'Girls binge-drink lads under the table' (*Sunday Times*, 18 January 2004).

6 Plant and Plant, *Binge Britain*, pp. vii–xii.

7 Hibbell, Andersson, Bjarnasson, *et al.*, *The ESPAD Report 2003*, p. 21.

8 Prime Minister's Strategy Unit, *Alcohol Harm Reduction Strategy for England* (2004), p. 7.

9 Institute of Alcohol Studies, 'Binge drinking: Nature, prevalence and cause' (London: IAS, 2005), p. 1, www.ias.org.uk/resources/factsheets/binge_drinking.pdf.

10 Room, R., 'Disabling the public interest: alcohol strategies and policies for England', *Addiction*, 99 (2004), 1083–9.

11 PMSU, *Alcohol Harm Reduction Strategy for England*, pp. 5, 7.

12 *Ibid.*, p. 75.

13 Department of Health, *Sensible Drinking: The Report of an Inter-Departmental Working Group* (2005), pp. 27–8, www.dh.gov.uk/en/Publicationsandstatistics/ Publications/PublicationsPolicyAndGuidance/DH_4084701.

14 Room, 'Disabling the public interest', p. 1083.

15 G. Edwards, P. Anderson, T. Babor, *et al.*, *Alcohol Policy and the Public Good* (Oxford: Oxford University Press, 1994), pp. 202–8.
16 T. Babor, R. Caetano, S. Casswell, *et al.*, *Alcohol: No Ordinary Commodity* (Oxford: Oxford University Press, 2003).
17 For a full list of public health approaches see *ibid.*, p. 270.
18 Academy of Medical Sciences, *Calling Time: The Nation's Drinking as a Major Health Issue* (2004), pp. 19, 22, www.acmedsci.ac.uk/p48prid16.html.
19 *Ibid.*, p. 9.
20 For an insightful discussion of this programme, see K. Hayward and D. Hobbs, 'Beyond the binge in "booze Britain": Market-led liminalization and the spectacle of binge drinking', *British Journal of Sociology*, 58:3 (2007), 437–56.
21 See Table 1 above.
22 Plant and Plant, *Binge Britain*.
23 I. Gilmore, 'Terrible toll of this binge that never ends' (*Daily Mail*, 12 January 2004).
24 Borsay, 'Binge drinking and moral panics'.
25 M. Plant, *Women and Alcohol: Contemporary and Historical Perspectives* (London: Free Association, 1997), 230.
26 N. Watt and H. Carter, 'Pub policing splits Blunkett and No. 10' (*Guardian*, 1 March 2003).
27 Department of Culture, Media and Sport, 'Drinking Responsibly: The Government's Proposals' (2005), p. 12, www.homeoffice.gov.uk/documents/2005-cons-drinking/2205-cons-drinking-doc?view=Binary.
28 *Ibid.*, p. 3.
29 *Ibid.*, p. 14.
30 PMSU, *Alcohol Harm Reduction Strategy for England*, p. 22.
31 Anon, 'The *Sun* Says' (*Sun*, 13 March 2008), p. 8.
32 Department of Culture, Media and Sport 'Guidance issued under section 182 of the Licensing Act 2003' (London: DCMS, 2004), pp. 19, 72–3, 33.
33 J. Slack, 'Binge Britain' (*Daily Mail*, 4 August 2006).
34 Association of Public Health Observatories, *Alcohol* (2007), pp. 97–9, www.apho.org.uk/resource/item.aspx?RID=39376.
35 D. Brown, 'Hazardous drinking: The middle class vice' (*Times*, 16 October 2007).
36 APHO, *Alcohol*, p. 14.
37 K. Gyngell, *Breakthrough Britain, Volume 4: Addictions* (Social Policy Justice Group, 2007), p. 174, www.centreforsocialjustice.org.uk/client/downloads/addictions.pdf
38 Department of Health, *Safe. Sensible. Social.: The Next Steps in the National Alcohol Strategy* (online: 2007), p. 39, www.dh.gov.uk/en/Publicationsandstatistics/Publications/PublicationsPolicyAndGuidance/DH_075218.
39 *Ibid.*, p. 15.
40 *Ibid.*, p. 14.
41 *Ibid.*, p. 10.
42 J. Smith, 'Alcohol – meeting our responsibilities, making a difference' (2008), p. 3, http://press.homeoffice.gov.uk/Speeches/speeches-archive/home-secretary-alcohol-speech?view=Binary.
43 *Ibid.*
44 *Ibid.*, p. 4.
45 *Ibid.*, p. 12.
46 P. Wintour, 'Tesco wants ministers to ban cheap alcohol' (*Guardian*, 21 February 2008).

47 Information Centre, *Statistics on Alcohol: England, 2007* (2007), p. 92, www.ic.nhs. uk/statistics-and-data-collections/healthand-lifestyles/alcohol/statistics-on-alcohol:-england–2007-[ns].

48 APHO, *Alcohol*, p. 86.

49 E. Goddard, *Drinking: Adults' behaviour and knowledge in 2007* (Office of National Statistics online: 2008), p. 3, www.statistics.gov.uk/downloads/theme_health/ Drinking_2007.pdf.

50 Information Centre, *Statistics on Alcohol: England, 2007*, p. 78.

51 British Beer and Pub Association, *Statistical Handbook*, p. 36.

52 British Medical Association, *Alcohol Misuse: Tackling the UK Epidemic* (2008), p. 1, www.bma.org.uk/ap.nsf/AttachmentsByTitle/PDFtacklingalcoholmisuse/$FILE/ Alcoholmisuse.pdf.

53 *Ibid.*, pp. 47, 2, 3–4.

54 M. Hough, A. Hirschfield, A. Newton, *et al.*, 'The impact of the Licensing Act 2003 on levels of crime and disorder: An evaluation' (Home Office, 2008), p. 18, www. homeoffice.gov.uk/rds/pdfs08/horr04c.pdf.

55 J. Foster, R. Herring, S. Walter and B. Thom, 'Implementation of the Licensing Act 2003: A national survey' Alcohol Education Research Council, 2008), www.aerc.org.uk/documents/pdf/finalReports/054_LARG_Survey.pdf.

56 British Beer and Pub Association, *Statistical Handbook*, p. 36; Information Centre, *Statistics on Alcohol: England, 2007*, p. 90.

57 Hansard, 21 March 2007, col. 823.

58 British Beer and Pub Association, *Statistical Handbook*, pp. 15–20; J. Wilmore, 'Fury over booze blitz' (*The Publican*, 13 March 2008).

59 P. Charity, 'The smoking ban has reduced the profit of the average tenanted licensee by 10%' (*Morning Advertiser*, 22 February 2008).

60 S. Poulter, 'Drinks tax soaks the middle class' (*Daily Mail*, 13 March 2008).

Conclusion: the drink question today

No subject has suffered more from over-statement, and from excessive violence of opinion and of language, and on none, therefore is caution in drawing conclusions more necessary. (Edgar Vincent (Lord D'Abernon))

The aim of this book is not to suggest that the story of the drink question is simply a cyclical history of repeating themes and moments. It is clearly anything but that, and this conclusion will seek to outline what some of the key shifts within the public debate on drink have been. However, three constant issues have tended to underpin the drink question in all its various forms. These are: *social order*, *health*, and *economic responsibility*. Of course, these are inflected by broader social frameworks, not least changing ideas about class, gender and national identity. Questions about drink have never been isolated from those larger themes; hence the question regarding the relationship between the drink question and, say, gender or class has never been *if* there is a relationship, but rather what the nature of that relationship is.

Nevertheless, class, gender and national or ethnic identity are extrinsic to drink: they are social categories through which ideas about drink are framed. By contrast, issues of social order, health and economic responsibility are intrinsic to drink: alcohol always has the potential to impact upon social order, it always has a potential impact upon health, and it always impacts upon economic activity. In all cases this impact can be good or bad, though public debates on drink have almost invariably accentuated the negative. Because they are intrinsic to drink, these concerns have always been at the heart of the discourse on alcohol. However, because they are also issues that have wider social relevance, the way in which they have been discussed in relation to drink has tended to be a reflection of how they are socially constructed at the same time.

In this sense, the history of drink discourse has also been a history of how a small number of characteristically modern concerns have been articulated differently depending on the cultural context. So, for example, in the early seventeenth century, concerns about the threat to social order posed by alcohol were overlaid with concerns over political instability and new class formations; in the gin craze economic concerns over the reproduction of a labouring class were expressed through gendered health concerns focused on the figure of the drunken mother. The emancipatory rhetoric of the radical teetotallers focused on the economic threat alcohol posed and its role in inhibiting upward social mobility at an early stage of industrial capitalism. State purchasers hitched alcohol control to the economic responsibility of workers facing the threat of war. More recently, public health campaigns frame our responsibility to protect our own health in terms of the economic responsibilities of citizens in a welfare state: the 'costs' of alcohol use feature prominently in public health literature, often regarding costs to the NHS or days missed through absenteeism.

It is not so much, then, that the drink question has, depending on what period we look at, been about either social order, health or economic responsibility. Rather, it is that the discourse on drink has often reflected the way in which the relationship between these three things is imagined. Of course, hegemony regarding this framing process is only ever partially established, so it is usually a matter of very public contestation as well: the claims regarding the economic costs of alcohol made by public health campaigners conflict wildly with the claims regarding the economics of alcohol made by the drinks industry. To this extent, the history of alcohol policy and law provides a measure of whose version of events has established its position most effectively.

Campaigning in context

In the years immediately following the 2003 Licensing Act, public concerns over drinking tended to focus on issues of social order. The phrase 'binge drinker' conjured up an image of either a violent young man or a sexually vulnerable young woman behaving badly in a dystopian city centre. As Virginia Berridge observed, in the early 2000s, as in the latter years of the twentieth century, public health campaigners struggled to have a significant impact on either the framing of public debates on alcohol or on government policy.[1] However, the increasing effectiveness with which public health groups have set the media agenda on alcohol, the subsequent rise in discussions over the health impacts of 'hazardous' as well as 'harmful' drinking, and the (partial) adoption of population approaches at policy level represents an important change of focus. The establishment of the Alcohol Health Alliance in 2007 also marked an important moment in the development of a coordinated campaign, led by public health campaigners, for action to reduce per capita consumption through tax increases and stronger licensing restrictions. Furthermore, the AHA brought together public health groups with others more closely associated with policy research and addiction treatment; to which extent it marked a new consensus among alcohol campaigners.[2] As such, it can be seen as the most recent phase in the long-running story of the battle to control the consumption of alcohol in Britain. We have seen that the different phases of the campaign against excessive consumption have often overlapped and merged into one another. However, for the sake of simplicity, Table 2 sets out the different campaigns that have been discussed in this book in a schematic form.

The period from the mid-1970s to the establishment of the AHA is certainly not the first time that health has been at the forefront of a campaign to control consumption. However, it is the first time that a population approach has been established in which the definition of moderate drinking has been given quantifiable parameters, and in which exceeding those parameters has been defined primarily as an issue of medical risk. This is not to say that social order and economic responsibility do not figure in the population approach; social disorder is also a public health issue and the increased burden placed on hospital Accident and Emergency departments is one of the central themes of the public health argument. Similarly, as has been pointed out above, the reason that health is taken to matter at all is, to a large extent, because ill health creates a drain on public services and prevents people from providing their full economic contribution to society. Illness arising from the pursuit of risky behaviours is increasingly constructed as a species of freeloading: something which tells us a lot about the way that the relationship between health, economic responsibility and social order are constructed in contemporary culture.

The latest moral panic?

When looking critically at news coverage of binge drinking it is tempting to see it as a species of moral panic. The public discourse on drink has often been characterised by elements of moral panic: the over-identification of problematic behaviours with 'deviant' social groups, the use of media pressure to effect policy changes, and the tendency to articulate broader social anxieties through an attack on public drunkenness. Today it remains true that many media stories about binge drinking are driven by the demands of media spectacle, by the simplicity of the narrative and by the media campaigns of alcohol-lobbying groups. Many conventional 'folk devils' have taken centre-stage in the media versions of the binge-drinking story: the young, the socially excluded, women engaging in traditionally male pleasures. However, dismissing media discourse on

Table 2 Drink campaigns in England

Campaign	Core argument	Target group	Preferred solution
Early anti-drink tracts	Drunkenness is a 'bewitching sin'	Drunkards	Encouragement of religious piety and moral rectitude
Alehouse suppression (early seventeenth century)	Alehouses cause social disorder	Lower-class drinkers	Regulation of alehouses through magisterial licensing
Anti-gin campaign	Spirituous liquors cause economic collapse and social breakdown	Lower-class gin drinkers	Prohibition of gin (to 1743)
		Women drinkers	Control through taxation and licensing (after 1743)
Alehouse suppression (late eighteenth century)	Alehouse legislation is not effectively applied	Lower-class drinkers	More rigorous application of existing licensing law
Early temperance	Distilled spirits are qualitatively different to other drinks	Spirit drinkers	Voluntary abstention from spirits
Teetotalism	All drinking is socially regressive	All drinkers	Voluntary abstention from all alcohol
	All drinking can lead to addiction		Moral suasion
Prohibitionism	All drinking is socially regressive	All drinkers	Legislative prohibition of drinks trade

[table 2 cont.] Campaign	Core argument	Target group	Preferred solution
	All drinking can lead to addiction		
Inebriate asylum movement	Habitual drunk-ards suffer from a disease	Habitual drunkards	The establishment of inebriate asylums
	Habitual drinking increases crime and causes racial degeneration		
Gothenburg/pub improvement	The drinking environment shapes the behaviour of drinkers	Disreputable outlets	Legislative support for pub improvement
State management	A privatised industry encou-rages high levels of consumption	The drinks industry	Nationalisation of the drinks trade
	Excessive drinking undermines efficiency		
Public health	Per capita increases in consumption lead to increases in all alcohol-related problems	The drinks industry All drinkers	Tax increases Restrictions on access to alcohol through licensing controls
	Drink should be tackled at a population level		

drink as a moral panic is far too simplistic.[3] For instance, while 'binge-drinkers' have often been conventional folk devils (the young, the poor etc.), the term has also been applied to non-marginal social groups: professionals who 'work hard and play hard', or middle-class couples overdoing the Shiraz on a Friday night. Indeed, the £6 million advertising campaign launched by the government in May 2008 – designed to further entrench an awareness of the unit levels of various drinks – was clearly targeted primarily at middle-class consumers. Furthermore, while the tabloid images of 'binge Britain' often consist of those all too familiar figures (young, aggressive men; young, sexually vulnerable women) caught in the grainy footage of CCTV, the targets of press opprobrium on this issue have also regularly included captains of the alcohol industry, senior civil servants, supermarkets and government ministers. This is not unique to recent events and is one of the idiosyncrasies of the drink question. Alcohol has always been a subject which, while magnifying questions of private morality, has also forced debates on the role of the State and commerce in encouraging, or controlling, behaviours which are seen as problematic or antisocial at an individual level.

Importantly, moral panic theory also presupposes that the mass media are engaged in the *exaggeration* of a perceived threat; if a threat is genuine then even the most feverish media response cannot be accurately described as a moral panic.[4] The statistics on drinking show that whatever else recent public debates on drinking may be, they are not simply hype. In 2004 adult per capita consumption was more than 26 per cent higher than it had been thirty years earlier, and in the same period rates of alcohol-related mortality have more than doubled.[5] Between 2000 and 2007 cases of liver cirrhosis increased by around 95 per cent, while alcohol-attributable hospital admissions increased by nearly one-third between 2001 and 2006.[6] In 2003, when the most recent comprehensive study was carried out, levels of heavy sessional drinking in England among under-15-year-olds were consistently among the highest in Europe.[7] Although there had actually been a decline in the overall number of under-age drinkers since 2001, those who did drink, drank more in 2007 than previously.[8]

This is not to say that the threats posed by drunkenness have not often been whipped up by journalists and editors eager either to sell copy or occupy the moral high ground. Nor is it to say that recent coverage has not used binge drinking as a way of revisiting old anxieties over the 'dangerous poor', deviant youth groups, and the moral policing of women's public behaviour; it certainly has done all these things. The point is that when looking at the drink question, we are rarely looking at simple moral panics but we are almost invariably looking at ways in which concerns over drink also reveal other, less explicit, social values, assumptions and beliefs. Looking at alcohol provides a way of identifying how explicit social anxieties reveal implicit ones, but without requiring us to dismiss those explicit concerns as meaningless.

A newer kind of drunkenness?

A number of recent studies have argued that the questions posed by alcohol since the mid-1990s are entirely new; that the issues of binge drinking, a deregulated retail market and the wider culture of consumption are 'more than simply a reinvention of the long-standing "problem" of British drunkenness'.[9] The key argument tends to be twofold. Firstly, that the liberalisation of licensing, the promotion of night-time economies and the aggressive marketing of intoxication by the alcohol industry have led to historically unique conditions in which drunkenness is encouraged as a lifestyle choice by an industry which enjoys the support of government at both a local and national level. Secondly, that this 'marketized liminality'[10] reflects a wider ideological set of conditions in which hedonistic lifestyles and excessive consumption are not simply tolerated but have become crucial to the maintenance of an economic system which demands the constant stimulation of expenditure. This, it is argued, produces a culture that promotes hedonism as a core value while masking that reality by condemning consumers among whom the pursuit of hedonistic lifestyles becomes obviously problematic. Young binge drinkers, from this perspective, are simply consuming in a manner which reflects the ideological values of consumer capitalism (have fun and buy cheap), and yet are the very people who are identified as a moral threat. What is more, they are also consuming in precisely the way that was encouraged by the deregulation of the retail market and the development of the night-time economy; both, after all, were designed to expand the alcohol economy. Simply blaming consumers for the effects of this, a number of recent commentators have observed, is deeply hypocritical.[11]

The extent to which all this shows that 'binge drinking' is historically unique, something tied specifically to postindustrial capitalism, remains open to question, however. It is undoubtedly true that the encouragement of the alcohol industries at both a local and national level has gone beyond anything seen previously. It is also true that the development of a psychoactive economy has meant that the alcohol industry now pitches its products against the other illicit drugs which are widely used by their target market. Equally, it is true that 'binge drinking' provides an attractive analogy for the rampant consumerism of late capitalism. However, it is here that some caution is required. A unique relationship between contemporary patterns of consumption and postindustrial capitalism can only be proposed if the patterns of consumption which shaped previous eras are underplayed or ignored.

It is sometimes argued that patterns of working-class alcohol consumption have changed from a mutually supportive, disciplined form of drinking to a new anomic and hedonistic style of excessive consumption, and that this is due to the collapse of traditional structures of working-class sociality caused by the decline of industrial capitalism.[12] However, it is mistaken to assume that working-class drinking was historically a matter of mutual support and constructive socialisation. Mass-Observation certainly made this claim, but they were largely reacting to a century of temperance-driven literature which had distorted the realities of pub culture out of all recognition. The reality is more messy. The early teetotal movement, for example, was driven by working-class campaigners who saw drinking as excessive, destructive and as tending towards both public and domestic violence. John Dunlop's study of workplace drinking practices set out in detail the ways in which drinking was used in early industrial society as a means of enforcing both conformity and social hierarchies within the workplace – practices which were backed up by very real threats of violence. The payment of wages in pubs was roundly condemned by temperance campaigners because it encouraged drunkenness which was anything but disciplined or mutually supportive. The likes of Phillip Snowden, John Burns and, for that matter, Keir Hardie saw little solidarity in the rituals of drink. This is not to say that the likes of Mass-Observation or George Orwell were wrong, but that the relationships between drink, drunkenness and working-class culture have always been complex and conflicted.

Similarly, the simultaneous encouragement and condemnation of excessive alcohol consumption has always been a feature of modern society. Daniel Defoe's defence of the free trade in gin set out a very familiar argument: that in a market economy it was the job of the legal system (rather than commodity producers) to police the behaviour of problematic consumers. Furthermore, drunkenness is subject to as much condemnation today as it was at some of the high points of the anti-gin and temperance campaigns of the past. Drink has *always* been a deeply problematic form of consumption; there has *always* been a tension between those who support free trade and those who fear drunken excess; what is more these have often been, and continue to be, exactly the same people. The point here is not simply to say that things are always the same, but to suggest that the tensions that alcohol exposes are not simply those of postindustrial capitalism, but those of capitalism per se. The alcohol industry was one of the first industries to operate on a mass scale, and it was always at the forefront of developments in marketing, integration, conglomeration and all the other techniques and mechanisms by which capitalist enterprises develop and expand. It has also always dealt in a commodity which is both ideal (in that it is attractive and needs constant replenishment) and problematic (in that it contradicts principles of thrift and can have highly visible negative social impacts). The analysis of alcohol consumption, therefore, should not be abstracted from the analysis of consumption in market economies more broadly.

The drink question has been kept alive for centuries not least because the contradictions which it exposes speak to some of the most deeply-held values within western modernity. Pekka Sulkunen, for example, has argued that the drink question exposes contradictions between two of the dominant ethical paradigms within which moral arguments have been framed since the Enlightenment. In his analysis, contradictions between the 'ethic of the rule' (the rationalist idea that social order requires the identification and acceptance of the 'common good'), and the 'culture of authenticity' (the Romantic idea that life hinges on unique individual experience) are intensified where drink is concerned.[13] From this perspective, public debates on alcohol constantly run up against the deeply held belief that a degree of rational sobriety is essential for both the understanding and maintenance of social order, and the equally deeply-held belief that one has the right to explore one's inner world, or the range of possible life experiences, through – among other things – intoxication. Anyone wanting to understand the phenomenon of celebrity rehab would do well to think about the cultural status of intoxication in these terms.

Tensions such as those identified by Sulkunen do not simply emerge from questions about drink or drugs; they run through all aspects of modern, liberal society. The drink question is interesting mainly because it exposes these tensions with more clarity than many other cultural activities. Again, looking at the discourse of drink, for what it is worth, is interesting not just for what it tells us about attitudes to alcohol, but for what it tells us about the contradictions of modern culture itself.

Licensed liberty

Perhaps the most fundamental contradiction that the drink question has exposed is that between the competing conceptions of freedom. Throughout this book we have seen that the drink question has often provided a way of articulating far bigger questions about the nature of freedom, its limitations, and how it should be policed.[14] We have seen that as far back as the gin craze, drink posed the question of whether political freedom could be guaranteed by freedom of trade, or whether the deregulation of markets encouraged behaviours which, perversely, undermined freedom if the commodity in question had the capacity to do so through creating irrational (and therefore, from a rationalist perspective, unfree) states of mind.

We have also seen that the problems of social order associated with drunkenness have a tendency to expose thorny problems in otherwise coherent-sounding models of liberty. In particular, J. S. Mill's classic expression of negative freedom – that one should be free to do as one wishes so long as doing so does not restrict the freedom of others – hits all sorts of problems when applied to drinking. That these cannot be resolved neatly does not mean Mill was simply wrong – it is in the nature of liberalism that ethical questions exist as problems, not totalitarian solutions. Nevertheless, simple assertions about the rights or otherwise of drinkers should be recognised as articulations of these broader questions.

We have also seen that questions about drink are often questions about economic freedom: what level of intervention is politically acceptable (or possible) in an industry operating in an otherwise free market? The alcohol market poses key questions for otherwise uncritical assumptions about the necessity of deregulation in sustaining a healthy economy. Drink has always illustrated the impacts of deregulation with an untypical immediacy because the lag between cause and effect is often far shorter than is the case with other commodities (e.g. the causal relationship between car-ownership and global warming). In addition, the idea that consumers behave rationally (i.e. weigh up the long-term and short-term costs and benefits) when the alcohol market is deregulated has proved fanciful. Again, this is only a particularly obvious example of the more general fact that commodity consumption is often not about calculating, rational decisions but about desire, pleasure and excess. Even given that alcohol is unlike many other commodities, it is important to consider what the deregulation of drink tells us about the basic principles of free market economics.

The question of addiction is, of course, also a question of freedom. What kind of 'slavery' is addiction? Should addicts, to paraphrase Stephen Hales, be 'forced into their liberty'; and, if so, how is that enforcement to be achieved? Such questions remain unresolved, and the answers given to them have always been shaped by the social context in which they are posed. Whatever addiction actually is, it is also cultural.[15] The continuing lack of consensus on the nature and treatment of addiction, not to mention its proliferation as a category for describing an ever-expanding array of behaviours, illustrates the extent to which, as many addiction theorists have argued, the idea of addiction is always a function, and reflection, of the way the concept of freedom operates in a society.[16]

Public health debates are also framed by basic questions about freedom.

Health campaigners support tax increases and restrictions on access partly on the grounds that you cannot expect drinkers to behave responsibly on their own behalves.[17] At the same time, the official government position is that drinkers should exercise their own freedom as consumers in such a way as to 'drink responsibly'. Arguably, this misconstrues the whole point of intoxication – which is that it is pleasurable precisely because involves a degree of letting go.[18] Or perhaps, from a more critical perspective, it illustrates the way in which risk-management in contemporary society couches disciplinary messages ('control your indulgence') in the language of individual freedom ('choose to drink responsibly'). It also presents a refusal to curtail the freedom of the market as a defence of the freedom of the individual: i.e. drinking responsibly is an expression of individual rights – because the alternative is that the State paternalistically limits your freedom through licensing legislation.

The pleasure principle

Behind all this lies the difficult question of whether or not intoxication itself can be understood an expression of freedom. We have seen that one legacy of Romanticism is the idea that intoxication is a way of exploring certain forms of psychic freedom. Indeed, the idea that intoxication has a philosophically positive value predates the Romantics by a long way. It is clearly visible in the Classical Greek ideas of both the symposium and the bacchanalia. By making oneself 'other' than what one is in everyday life, drunkenness may be a form of self-abnegation or it may be a form of liberation. It is on this question that some of the thorniest problems posed by drink lie.

The problem here concerns the value placed by any given culture on intoxication itself: on whether the pleasure of intoxication is understood as having any inherent validity. It has been pointed out by a number of writers on this subject that one characteristic of public health literature on alcohol is that it pays almost no regard to the pleasures of intoxication.[19] Griffith Edwards has addressed this issue from a public health perspective in his discussion of the 'drinker's dilemma'.[20] Edwards's argument is that sensible drinking messages cannot hope to compete 'at the table level' with the desire to drink because, after a glass of wine, the desire for more outweighs the desire to embark on a tedious calculation of long-term health risks. He uses this to support his argument for coercive measures (tax increases and licensing restrictions) on the grounds that the 'drinker's dilemma' means that purely advisory strategies are doomed to failure.[21]

Recognising the pleasure of intoxication is crucial to a meaningful discussion of drink; however, for Edwards, the bottom line remains that intoxication itself has no actual value. He suggests that 'perhaps the best overall public message on alcohol we can hope to see reach the home is, enjoy the drink, but less is generally better, getting intoxicated is never wise, drink is two-edged'.[22] This is an eminently reasonable set of aims. However, while people choose different drinks for different reasons, they also often drink alcohol (as opposed to fruit juice or tea) precisely because they *do* see a value in some level of intoxication. This is not to say people drink to get blind drunk – most people don't – nor is it to legitimise drunken antisocial behaviour. However, it is to suggest that alcohol control messages may be more effective if they accept more explicitly that there is a legitimate pleasure to be had in a level of intoxication, and that that intoxication does not necessarily lead to negative social consequences. Furthermore, it may not be that people simply do not have the desire to think about the risks associated with alcohol, but rather that they think those risks are worth taking because they see a certain level of intoxication as a good thing. This is certainly a conclusion that can be drawn from a number of recent studies into attitudes to alcohol among young drinkers in particular.[23] An insurmountable problem Victorian temperance campaigners faced was that moderate drinkers simply did not recognise their version of what happened when drink was taken; the failure of generations of temperance campaigns to convert moderate drinkers is a testament to the fact that for many perfectly reasonable people intoxication may not be wise, but it does retain a legitimate and valuable place in their lives. It may be that part of the process of tackling antisocial behaviour and risky drinking will involve a more open discussion of the positive, as well as the negative, place of intoxication in cultural life – if only to prevent those who enjoy drinking switching off from advisory messages altogether.

Drink talking

The aim of this book is not to set out a plan for effective health promotion, nor is it to finally answer the question of why the English drink the way they do. Instead, it is to show the extent to which drink exists as much as a subject of discourse as it does as an object of consumption. Hopefully, it has shown that public debates on drink – which have been a feature of public life for over three hundred years – have always also been about other cultural issues. Because it sits at the heart of so much cultural activity, drinking provides us with a way of looking at social relationships and social values. To that extent, it is simply one among many routes through history. However, if there is a problem with the way the English drink, if there is something in English drinking culture which needs to be addressed, then a clear sight of the cultural history of drink needs to be part of any attempt to achieve a culture change. The English don't 'just love to drink'; such statements are attractive only because they are so simplistic. Cultures change, and English drinking culture has changed over time. Certainly, it is not a Mediterranean viticulture and never will be – but domestic wine drinking has been one of the most dramatic developments in consumption over the last fifty years. Undoubtedly, England has had a culture of heavy sessional drinking since at least the days of Nashe and Gascoigne, but the rituals of drink have undergone all sorts of transformations over that time and there is no reason why they couldn't change again in the future. This book does not purport to set out a model for changing cultural values. Hopefully, however, it does show that understanding the discourses of drink is valuable because it allows us to understand that ubiquitous social practice a little more clearly. The questions drink poses are about much more than just drink alone; because this is the case, the answers to many of those questions are political before they are anything else.

Notes

1 V. Berridge, 'Temperance: Its history and impact on current and future alcohol poli-cy' (York: Joseph Rowntree Foundation, 2005), pp. 23–5.
2 Members of the AHA include Action on Addiction, the Institute of Alcohol Studies, Alcohol Concern, the Alcohol Education and Research Council and the Royal Colleges of Surgeons, Physicians, General Practitioners and Psychiatrists.
3 Measham and Brain, 'Binge drinking', pp. 263–4; Borsay, 'Binge drinking and moral panics'.
4 C. Critcher (ed.), *Moral Panics and the Media* (Oxford: Oxford University Press, 2006), pp. 16–19.
5 British Beer and Pub Association, *Statistical Handbook*, p. 36; DoH, *Safe. Sensible. Social.*, p. 26.
6 APHO, *Alcohol*, p. 42.
7 Hibbell *et al.*, *The ESPAD Report*, pp. 133–60.
8 Information Centre, *Statistics on Alcohol: England, 2007*, p. 1; DoH, *Safe. Sensible. Social.*, p. 6.
9 Measham and Brain, 'Binge drinking', p. 265; Hayward and Hobbs, 'Beyond the binge', p. 444.
10 Hayward and Hobbs, 'Beyond the binge', p. 439.
11 See also Brain, 'Youth, Alcohol and the Emergence of the Post-modern Alcohol Order'; Hobbs *et al.*, *Bouncers*; Hadfield, *Bar Wars*; Winlow and Hall, *Violent Night*.
12 See, for example, Winlow and Hall, *Violent Night*, pp. 17–23.
13 Sulkunen, 'Ethics of alcohol policy in a saturated society', pp. 1119–20.
14 This theme, particularly with regard to addiction, is dealt with at length in Valverde, *Disease of the Will*.
15 R. Room, 'The cultural framing of addiction', *Janus Head*, 6:2 (2003), www.janus-head.org/6–2/Room.pdf.
16 Valverde, *Disease of the Will*; E. Sedgewick, 'Epidemics of the will', in *Tendencies* (London: Routledge, 1994); G. Reith, 'Consumption and its discontents: addic-

tion, identity and the politics of freedom', *British Journal of Sociology*, 55:2 (2004), 283–300.

17 G. Edwards, *Alcohol: The Ambiguous Molecule* (Harmondsworth: Penguin, 2000), pp. 181–90.

18 S. Walton, *Out of It: A Cultural History of Intoxication* (London: Hamish Hamilton, 2001), pp. 205–7.

19 P. O'Malley and M. Valverde, 'Pleasure, freedom and drugs: The uses of "pleasure" in liberal governance of drug and alcohol consumption', *Sociology*, 38:1 (2004), 25–42; Sulkunen, 'Images and realities of alcohol', p. 1311.

20 Edwards, *Alcohol: The Ambiguous Molecule*, pp. 180–1; G. Edwards, P. Anderson, T. Baber *et al.*, *Alcohol Policy and the Public Good*, pp. 41–2.

21 Edwards, *Alcohol: The Ambiguous Molecule*, p. 190.

22 *Ibid.*

23 For recent discussions of this, especially concerning young drinkers, see J. Cherrington, K. Chamberlain and J. Grixti, 'Relocating alcohol advertising research: Examining socially mediated relationships with alcohol', *Journal of health Psychology*, 11:2 (2006), 209–22; R. Harnett, B. Thom, R. Herring and M. Kelly, 'Alcohol in transition: Towards a model of young men's drinking styles', *Journal of Youth Studies*, 3:1 (2000), 61–77; I. Szmigin, B. Griffin, W. Mistral, *et al.*, 'Re-framing "binge drinking" as calculated hedonism – empirical evidence from the UK', *International Journal of Drug Policy*, 19:5, 359–66; M. Sheehan and D. Ridge, '"You become really close … you talk about the silly things you did, and we laugh": The role of binge drinking in female secondary students' lives', *Substance Use and Misuse*, 36:3 (2001), 347–72.

Bibliography

Academy of Medical Sciences, *Calling Time: The Nation's Drinking as a Major Health Issue* (online: 2004) www.acmedsci.ac.uk/p48prid16.html

Addison, J., *The Papers of Joseph Addison Esq. Vol. II* (Edinburgh: William Creech, 1790)

Allen, R. (ed.), *Addison and Steele, Selections from* The Tatler *and* The Spectator (London: Holt, Rhinehart & Winston, 1970)

American Temperance Society, *Permanent Temperance Documents of the American Temperance Society* (Boston, MA: Seth Bliss and Perkins, Marvin, and Co., 1835)

Anon., 'An appeal to the inhabitants of Northampton by the committee of the Temperance Society' (undated)

Anon., *The Juice of the Grape, or Wine Preferable to Water* (London: W. Lewis, 1724)

Anon., *Occasional Remarks upon The Act for laying a Duty upon the Retailers of Spirituous Liquors, &c. and for Licensing the Retailers thereof* (London: A. Dodd, 1736)

Anon., *The Trial of the Spirits, or Some Considerations Upon the Pernicious Consequences of the Gin-trade to Great-Britain* (London: T. Cooper, 1736)

Anon., *A Short History of the Gin Act* (London: H. Goreham, 1738)

Anon., *A Letter to a Friend in the Country In Relation to the New Law Concerning Spirituous Liquors* (London: M. Cooper, 1743)

Anon., *The Consequences Of Laying an Additional Duty on Spirituous Liquors, Candidly considered* (London: H. Whitridge, 1751)

Anon., *A Dissertation on Mr Hogarth's Six Prints Lately publish'd* (London: B. Dickinson, 1751)

Anon., *The Speech of a Creek-Indian against the Immoderate Use of Spirituous Liquors* (London: R Griffiths, 1754)

Anon., *An Essay on Tea, Sugar, White Bread and Butter, Country Alehouses, Strong Beer and Geneva and other Modern Luxuries* (Salisbury: J. Hodson, 1777)

Anon., *Brief Statement of the Origin and Nature of the Society for Carrying into Effect His Majesty's Proclamation for the Encouragement of Piety and Virtue* (London: George Stafford, 1789)

Anon., *A Treatise on the True Effects of Drinking Spirituous Liquors, Wine and Beer on Body and Mind* London: 1794)

Anon., 'Licensing system' (*Times*, 30 August 1827)

Anon., 'Editorial' (*Times*, 22 September 1829)

Anon., 'Editorial' (*Times*, 21 October 1830)

Anon., 'Parliamentary Intelligence' (*Times*, 7 September 1831)

Anon., 'A Temperance Society' (*Times*, 6 September 1833)

Anon., 'Editorial' (*Times*, 31 October 1834)

Anon. (Y., I. C.), 'Teetotalism: absurd in its object and censurable in its agency' (London:

E. Grattan, 1838)

Anon., 'The Maine Liquor Law' (*Times*, 21 May 1867)

Anon., 'Habitual Drunkards' (*Times*, 14 August 1872)

Anon., 'Parliamentary Intelligence' (*Times*, 8 May 1873)

Anon., 'United Kingdom Alliance' (*Times*, 26 October 1892)

Anon., 'Lord Rosebery in Birmingham' (*Times*, 24 May 1894)

Anon., 'Mr Chamberlain on Licensing Reform' (*Times*, 7 July 1894)

Anon., 'United Kingdom Alliance' (*Times*, 24 October 1894)

Anon., 'Sir William Harcourt at Derby' (*Times*, 24 January 1895)

Anon., 'United Kingdom Alliance' (*Times*, 16 October 1907)

Anon., *The Licensing Bill. Demonstration in Hyde Park* (*Times*, 28 September 1908)

Anon., 'The New Army. Appeal to the Public by Lord Kitchener' (*Times*, 25 October 1914)

Anon., 'Mr Lloyd George on the Drink Peril' (*Times*, 1 March 1915)

Anon., 'Conference on Drink' (*Times* 30 March 1915)

Anon., 'The Ends and the Means' (*Times*, 3 April 1915)

Anon., 'Practical Temperance Reform' (*Times*, 3 April 1915)

Anon., 'Lord Astor on the drink problem' (*Manchester Guardian*, 8 March 1926)

Anon., 'Company meeting: Mitchells & Butlers, limited' (*Manchester Guardian*, 13 August 1927)

Anon., 'Mitchells and Butlers, limited: Birmingham brewers' plans for licensed houses' (*Manchester Guardian*, 18 August 1928)

Anon 'Company Meeting: Watney, Combe Reid and Co.' (*Times*, 12 August 1932)

Anon., 'Burden of Duty on Beer' (*Times*, 31 October 1932)

Anon., 'Brewers and the Press' (*Times*, 16 November 1933)

Anon., 'Art in the Inn' (*Times*, 8 June 1937)

Anon., 'Poetry in Pubs' (*Times*, 7 June 1939)

Anon., 'Bar trade cut by test' (*Times*, 10 October 1967)

Anon., 'MPs examine threat to individual liberty' (*Times*, 2 December 1967)

Anon., 'The *Sun* Says' (*Sun*, 13 March 2008)

Antal, F., *Hogarth and his Place in European Art* (London: Routledge and Kegan Paul, 1962)

Armstrong, L., *The Temperance Reformation* (New York: Fowlers and Wells, 1858)

Association of Public Health Observatories, *Alcohol* (2007), www.apho.org.uk/resource/item.aspx?RID=39376

Atkinson, S. B., 'Some medico-legal relations of intemperance', *The British Journal for the Study of Inebriety* 3:1 (1905), 4–15

Austin, G., *Alcohol from Antiquity to 1800: A Chronological History* (Santa Barbara: ABC-Clio Information Services, 1985)

'A Physician', *Sermons to the Rich and Studious on Temperance and Exercise* (London: Edward and Charles Dilly, 1772)

Babor, T., *et al. Alcohol: No Ordinary Commodity* (Oxford: Oxford University Press, 2003)

Bacon, F., *The Virtues of Coffee* (London: W. G, 1663)

Bakhtin, M., *Rabelais and His World*, trans. Hélène Iswolsky (Bloomington: Indiana University Press, 1984)

Baldie, A., 'A definition of drunkenness', *Journal for the Study of Inebriety* 23: 3 (1936), 125–7

Barr, A., *Drink: An Informal Social History* (London: Bantam, 1995)

Barrows, S. and Room, R. (eds), *Drinking: Behaviour and Belief in Modern History*

(Berkeley, CA: University of California Press, 1992)

Baxter, R., *A Christian Directory* (London: Robert White, 1673)

BBC, *Panorama: Cdnt give a xxxx 4 lst ordrs?* (6 June 2004, transcript), http://news.bbc. co.uk/nol/shared/spl/hi/programmes/panorama/transcripts/xxxx.txt

Beecher, L., *Six Sermons on Intemperance* (Boston, MA: T. R. Marvin, 1828)

Bellamy, R., *Liberalism and Modern Society* (Pennsylvania, PA: Penn State University Press, 1992)

Benezet, A., *The mighty destroyer displayed* (Philadelphia, PA: Joseph Cruikshank, 1774)

Berlin, I., *Liberty* (Oxford: Oxford University Press, 2002)

Berman, G. and Danby, G., *The Licensing Bill* (Home Office Research Paper 03/27 2003), www.parliament.uk/commons/lib/research/rp2003/rp03-027.pdf

Berridge, V., 'The inter-war years: a period of decline', *British Journal of Addiction* 85 (1990), 1023–35

Berridge, V., 'The origins and early years of the Society 1884–1899', *British Journal of Addiction* 85 (1990), 991–1003

Berridge, V., 'Prevention and social hygiene 1900–1914', *British Journal of Addiction*, 85 (1990), 1005–16

Berridge, V. 'Temperance: Its history and impact on current and future alcohol policy' (York: Joseph Rowntree Foundation, 2005)

Bindman, D., *Hogarth and his Times* (London: British Museum Press, 1997)

Blackman, O., 'Blitz on binge drinkers' (*Daily Mirror*, 17 September 2004)

Blocker, J., Fahey, D., and Tyrell, I. (eds), *Alcohol and Temperance in Modern History: An International Encyclopedia* (Oxford: ABC-Clio, 2003)

Boffey, D., 'Reclaim our streets: Unhappy hours' (*Daily Mirror*, 16 August 2004)

Booth, C., *Life and Labour of the People in London, Notes on Influences and Conclusion* (London: Macmillan, 1902)

Booth, E. and Roper, E., 'Barmaid's political defence league' (*Times*, 1 May 1908)

Borsay, P., 'Binge drinking and moral panics: historical parallels?' *History and Policy Papers* (2007), www.historyandpolicy.org/papers/policy-paper–62.html#top

Bourdieu, P., *Distinction: A Social Critique of the Judgement of Taste* (London: Harvard University Press, 1987)

Boswell, J., *The Life of Samuel Johnson* (London: J. M. Dent, 1978)

Brain, K., 'Youth, alcohol and the emergence of the post-modern alcohol order' (London: Institute of Alcohol Studies, 2000)

Bretherton, R. F., 'Country inns and alehouses', in R. Lennard (ed.), *Englishmen at Rest and Play: Some Phases of English Leisure 1588–1714* (Oxford: Clarendon, 1931)

Bridgeman, J., *The Supply of Beer* (London: Office of Fair Trading, 2000)

Bright, M. and Hinsliff, G., 'Britain: A nation "in grip of drinks chaos"' (*Observer*, 21 November 2004)

British Beer and Pub Association, *Statistical Handbook* (London: Brewing Publications Ltd., 2007)

British and Foreign Temperance Society, *The Temperance Magazine and Review* (London: Benjamin Bagster, 1833)

British Medical Association, *Alcohol Misuse: Tackling the UK Epidemic* (2008), www.bma. org.uk/ap.nsf/AttachmentsByTitle/PDFtacklingalcoholmisuse/$FILE/Alcoholmisuse. pdf

Brown, D., 'Hazardous drinking: The middle class vice' (*Times*, 16 October 2007)

Brown, P., *Man Walks into a Pub* (London: Macmillan, 2003)

Bruun, K., Edwards, G., Lumio, M., *et al.*, *Alcohol Control Policies in Public Health*

Perspective (Helsinki: Finnish Foundation for Alcohol Studies, 1975)

Bullock, A. and Schock, M., *The Liberal Tradition: From Fox to Keynes* (Oxford: Clarendon Press, 1967)

Bunyan, J., *The Greatness of the Soul* (London: Joseph Marshall, 1730)

Burke, P., *Popular Culture in Early Modern Europe* (Aldershot: Wildwood Press, 1988)

Burne, P., *The Teetotaller's Companion* (London: Arthur Hall, 1847)

Burnett, J., *Liquid Pleasures: A Social History of Drinks in Modern Britain* (London: Routledge, 1999)

Burns, D., 'The Bishop of Chester on the drink question' (*Times*, 5 August 1892)

Burns, J., *Labour and Drink* (Bristol: Western Temperance Press, 1914)

Burrington, G., *An Answer to Dr William Brakenridge's Letter* (London: J. Scott, 1757)

Bynum, W. F., 'Alcoholism and degeneracy in 19th century European medicine and psychiatry', *Addiction* 79: 1 (1984), 59–70

Cadogan, W., *A Dissertation on the Gout* (London: J. Dodsley, 1771)

Campbell, H., 'The study of inebriety: a retrospect and a forecast', *The British Journal for the Study of Inebriety* 1:1 (1903), 5–14

Carter, H., *The Control of the Drink Trade* (London: Longmans, Green and Co., 1919)

Carter, H., 'Drink and Youth' (*Times*, 23 December 1943), p. 5

Cascardi, A., *The Subject of Modernity* (Cambridge: Cambridge University Press, 1992)

Central Control Board, *Alcohol: Its Action on the Human Body* (London: HMSO, 1917)

Chamberlain, J., *Licensing Reform and Local Option* (Birmingham: Journal Printing, 1876)

Chapman, J., 'Blair's all-day drink plans are "reckless"' (*Daily Mail*, 12 August 2004)

Charles I, *The King's Majesties Declaration to His Subjects Concerning Lawfull Sports to be Used* (London: Robert Barker, 1633)

Charles II, *A Proclamation Against Vicious, Debauch'd and Profane Persons* (London: Christopher Barker and John Bill, 1660)

Charles II, *A Proclamation for the Suppression of Coffee-Houses* (London: John Bill and Christopher Barker, 1675)

Charles II, *An Additional Proclamation Concerning Coffee-Houses* (London: John Bill and Christopher Barker, 1676)

Charity, P., 'The smoking ban has reduced the profit of the average tenanted licensee by 10%' (*Morning Advertiser*, 22 February 2008)

Cherrington, J., Chamberlain, K. and Grixti, J., 'Relocating alcohol advertising research: Examining socially mediated relationships with alcohol', *Journal of health Psychology* 11:2 (2006), 209–22

Cheyne, G., *The English Malady* (London: George Strahan, 1733)

Cheyne, G., *An Essay on the Regimen* (London: C. Rivington, 1740)

Cheyne, G., *The Natural Method of Cureing the Diseases of the Body and the Disorders of the Mind Depending on the Body* (London: George Strahan, 1742)

Church of England, Province of Canterbury, *Articles to be Inquired of, by the Churchwardens and Sworn Men: In the Visitation of the Lord Archbishop of Cantebury: Within the Diocese of Norwich* (1605)

Clark, P., *The English Alehouse: A Social History* (London: Longman, 1983)

Clark, P., 'The "mother gin" controversy in the early eighteenth century', *Transactions of the Royal Historical Society* 5th ser.: 5 (1987), 63–84

Clej, A., *A Genealogy of the Modern Self: Thomas De Quincey and the Intoxication of Writing* (Stanford, CA: Stanford University Press, 1995)

Coleridge, S. T., *The Notebooks of Samuel Taylor Coleridge, Volume 3: 1808–1819*, (ed.) K. Coburn (London: Routledge and Kegan Paul, 1973)

Coleridge, S. T., *The Collected Works of Samuel Taylor Coleridge: Essays on His Times in* The Morning Post *and* The Courier *II* (London: Routledge and Kegan Paul, 1978)

Coley, F. C., 'Dr Reid's theories about alcoholism', *Medical Temperance Review* 2:11 (1899), 245–8

Collins, J. W., 'An address on the institutional treatment of inebriety', *The British Journal for the Study of Inebriety* 1:2 (1903), 97–115

Colquhoun, P., *Observations and Facts Relative to Public Houses* (London: J. Downes, 1795)

Cooke, M., 'De Quincey, Coleridge, and the formal uses of intoxication', *Yale French Studies* 50 (1974), 26–40

Cornell, M., *Beer: The Story of the Pint* (London: Headline, 2003)

Coryate, T., *Coryate's Crambe* (London: William Stansby, 1611)

Couling, S., *History of the Temperance Movement in Great Britain and Ireland* (London: William Tweedie, 1862)

Cowan, B., 'Mr Spectator and the coffeehouse public sphere' *Eighteenth Century Studies* 37:3 (2004), 345–66

Cowan, B., 'The rise of the coffeehouse reconsidered', *Historical Journal* 47: 1 (2004), 21–46

Cowan, B. *The Social Life of Coffee* (London: Yale University Press, 2005)

Critcher, C. (ed.), *Moral Panics and the Media* (Oxford: Oxford University Press, 2006)

Crothers, T. D., 'The Norman Kerr memorial lecture', *The British Journal for the Study of Inebriety* 3:3 (1906), 105–15

Darwin, E., *Zoonomia* (London: J. Johnson, 1794)

Darwin, E., *The Botanic Garden* (London: J. Johnson, 1799)

Defoe, D., *A Brief Case of the Distillers and of the Distilling Trade in England* (London: T. Warner, 1726)

Defoe, D., *Augusta Triumphans* (London: J. Roberts, 1728)

Dent, A., *The Plain Man's Path-way to Heaven* (London: 1607)

Department of Culture, Media and Sport, 'Guidance issued under section 182 of the Licensing Act 2003' (London: DCMS, 2004)

Department of Culture, Media and Sport, 'Licensing Countdown' (2004), www.culture.gov.uk/NR/rdonlyres/3FEABCCF-D8F4–48D8-B8B5–35800D9EF91A/0/LCNewsletterDec.pdf

Department of Culture, Media and Sport (DCMS), 'Statistical bulletin: Liquor licensing' (2004)

Department of Culture, Media and Sport, *Drinking Responsibly: The Government's Proposals* (2005), www.homeoffice.gov.uk/documents/2005-cons-drinking/2205-cons-drinking-doc?view=Binary

Department of Health, *Sensible Drinking: The Report of an Inter-Departmental Working Group* (2005) www.dh.gov.uk/en/Publicationsandstatistics/Publications/PublicationsPolicyAndGuidance/DH_4084701

Department of Health, *Safe. Sensible. Social.: The Next Steps in the National Alcohol Strategy* (2007), www.dh.gov.uk/en/Publicationsandstatistics/Publications/PublicationsPolicyAndGuidance/DH_075218

Department of Health and Social Security 'Prevention and health' (1977) Cmnd. 7047

Department of Health and Social Security, *Drinking Sensibly* (London: HMSO, 1981)

Dickens, C., 'Whole Hogs' (*Household Words*, 23 August 1851)

Dickens, C., *Miscellaneous Papers* (London: Chapman Hall, 1908)

Dickens, C., *Dickens' Journalism, Vol. 2*, ed. M. Slater (London: J. M. Dent, 2003)

Dillon, P., *The Much-Lamented Death of Madam Geneva: The Eighteenth-Century Gin*

Craze (London: Review, 2002)

Disney, J., *Thoughts on the Great Circumspection Necessary in Licensing Public Alehouses* (London: J. Johnson, 1776)

Dodsworth, F., '"Civic" police and the conditions of liberty: The rationality of governance in eighteenth century England' *Social History* 29:2 (2004), 199–216

Douglass, F., *The Narrative of the Life of Frederick Douglass, An American Slave* (Harmondsworth: Penguin, 1986)

Downame, J. *Four Treatises, Tending to Dissuade all Christians from Four no Less Heinous than Common Sins Namely the abuses of Swearing, Drunkenness, Whoredom, and Bribery* (London: Michael Baker, 1613)

Dunlop, J., *The Philosophy of Drinking Usage in Great Britain* (London: Houlston and Stoneman, 1839)

Eagleton, T., *Walter Benjamin or Towards a Revolutionary Criticism* (London: Verso, 1981)

Earle, J., *Micro-cosmographie, or A Piece of the World Discovered* (London: William Stansby, 1628)

Earle, J., *The Character of a Tavern* (London: D. A., 1675)

Earnshaw, S., *The Pub in Literature: England's Altered State* (Manchester: Manchester University Press, 2000)

Edwards, G., *Alcohol: The Ambiguous Molecule* (Harmondsworth: Penguin, 2000)

Edwards, G. *et al.*, *Alcohol Policy and the Public Good* (Oxford: Oxford University Press, 1994)

Elderton, E. and Pearson, K. *A First Study of the Influence of Parental Alcoholism on the Physique and Ability of the Offspring* (London: Eugenics Laboratory Memoirs, 1910)

Elliott, J., 'Girls binge-drink lads under the table' (*Sunday Times*, 18 January 2004)

Ellison, H. J., *Local Option* (Edinburgh: John Menzies, 1882)

Engels, F., *The Condition of the Working Class in England* (Harmondsworth: Penguin, 1987)

England and Wales, Sovereign, *Injunctions Given by the Queen's Majesty* (1559)

Erkkila, B. and Grossman, J. (eds), *Breaking Bounds: Whitman and American Cultural Studies* (Oxford: Oxford University Press, 1994)

Ferentzy, P., 'From sin to disease: Differences and similarities between past and current conceptions of chronic drunkenness', *Contemporary Drug Problems* 28 (2001), 362–90

Fielding, H., *An Enquiry into the Causes of the Late Increase of Robbers and Related Writings* (Oxford: Clarendon Press, 1988)

Fielding, J., *Extracts from Such of the Penal Laws as Particularly Relate to the Peace and Good Order of this Metropolis* (London: H. Woodfall and W. Strahan, 1768)

Foster, J., Herring, R., Walter, S. and Thom, B., 'Implementation of the Licensing Act 2003: A national survey' (Alcohol Education Research Council, 2007), www.aerc.org.uk/documents/pdf/finalReports/054_LARG_Survey.pdf

Foucault, M., *The Order of Things: An Archaeology of the Human Sciences* (London: Tavistock, 1970)

Foucault, M., *The Birth of the Clinic: An Archaeology of Medical Perspectives* (London: Routledge, 1993)

Foucault, M., *Madness and Civilisation* (London: Routledge, 2001)

'Gallobeligicus', *Wine, Beer and Ale, Together by the Ears* (London: John Grove, 1629)

Gascoigne, G., *A Delicate Diet for Dainty-mouthed Drunkards* (London: Richard Jones, 1576)

George, D., *London Life in the Eighteenth Century* (Harmondsworth: Penguin, 1992)

Gibson, E., *An Earnest Dissuasive from Intemperance in Meats and Drinks* (London: M. Downing, 1740)

Gies, F. and J., *Life in a Medieval Village* (London: The Folio Society, 2002)

Gilbert, L., *Reasons for Temperance: A Discourse* (Boston, MA: Lincoln and Edmonds, 1829)

Gilmore, I., 'Terrible toll of this binge that never ends' (*Daily Mail*, 12 January 2004)

Goddard, E., *Drinking: adults' behaviour and knowledge in 2007* (Office of National Statistics, 2008), www.statistics.gov.uk/downloads/theme_health/Drinking_2007.pdf

Gray, J., *The Two Faces of Liberalism* (Cambridge: Polity, 2000)

Greenaway, J., *Drink and British Politics Since 1830: A Study in Policy-Making* (Basingstoke: Palgrave Macmillan, 2003)

Gutzke, D., *Protecting the Pub: Brewers and Publicans against Temperance* (Woodbridge: Royal Historical Society, 1989)

Gutzke, D., *Pubs and Progressives: Reinventing the Public House in England, 1896–1960* (Dekalb: Northern Illinois University Press, 2006)

Gyngell, K., *Breakthrough Britain, Volume 4: Addictions* (Social Policy Justice Group, 2007), www.centreforsocialjustice.org.uk/client/downloads/addictions.pdf

Habermas, J., *The Structural Transformation of the Public Sphere*, trans. Thomas Burger (London: Polity Press, 1989)

Hadfield, P., *Bar Wars: Contesting the Night in Contemporary British Cities* (Oxford: Oxford University Press, 2006)

Hales, S., *A Friendly Admonition to the Drinkers of Gin, Brandy and Other Distilled Spirituous Liquors* (London: SPCK, 1751)

Hanson, D., *Preventing Alcohol Abuse: Alcohol, Culture and Control* (Westport, CT: Greenwood, 1995)

Harnett, R., Thom, B., Herring, R. and Kelly, M., 'Alcohol in transition: Towards a model of young men's drinking styles', *Journal of Youth Studies* 3:1 (2000), 61–77

Harrison, B., *Drink and the Victorians: The Temperance Question in England 1815 – 1872* (London: Faber and Faber, 1971)

Hartley, D., *Observations on Man, his Frame, his Duty and his Expectations* (London: J. Johnson, 1791)

Harwood, E., *Temperance and Intemperance: Their Effects on the Body and Mind, and Their Influence in Prolonging or Abbreviating Human Life* (London: T. Becket, 1774)

Haydon, P., *Beer and Britannia: An Inebriated History of Britain* (Stroud: Sutton, 2003)

Hayward K. and Hobbs, D., 'Beyond the binge in "booze Britain"': market-led liminalization and the spectacle of binge drinking', *British Journal of Sociology* 58:3 (2007), 437–56

Hazlitt, W., *The Selected Writings of William Hazlitt*, (ed.) Duncan Wu (London: Pickering and Chatto, 1998)

Herrick, R., *Hesperides* (London: John Williams and Francis Eglesfield, 1648)

Heylyn, P., *Cyprianus Anglicus* (London: A. Seile, 1688)

Heywood, T., *Philocothonista, or the Drunkard, Opened, Dissected, and Anatomized* (London: Robert Raworth, 1635)

Hibbell, B., Andersson, B. and Bjarnasson, T., *The ESPAD Report 2003* (Stockholm: Swedish Council for Information on Alcohol and Other Drugs, 2004)

Hickley, M., 'All-day pubs will bring us 24 hours of hell say police' (*Daily Mail*, 18 September 2004)

Hicks, W., 'The Bishop of Chester on the drink question' (*Times*, 26 August 1892)

Hilton, M., 'The legacy of luxury: Moralities of consumption since the eighteenth century', *Journal of Consumer Culture* 4:1 (2004), 101–23

Hindle, F. C., 'Licensing Bill: compensation time limit' (London: Liberal Publications Department: leaflet no. 2168, 1908)

Hobbs, D., Hadfield, P., Lister, S. and Winlow, S., *Bouncers: Violence and Governance in the Night-time Economy* (Oxford: Oxford University Press, 2003)

Hobbs, D., Winlow, S., Hadfield, P., and Lister, S., 'Violent hypocrisy: Governance and the night-time economy', *European Journal of Communications*, 2:2 (2005), 161–83

Hogarth, W., *The Analysis of Beauty*, ed. Joseph Burke (Oxford: Clarendon, 1955)

Holinshed, R., *The First and Second Volumes of Chronicles* (London: Holinshed, 1587)

Holt, M. P. (ed.), *Alcohol: A Social and Cultural History* (Oxford: Berg, 2006)

Home Office, *Time for Reform* (2000), www.culture.gov.uk/Reference_library/Publications/archive_2001/time_for_reform.htm

Hornsey, I., *A History of Beer and Brewing* (London: Royal Society of Chemistry, 2003)

Horsley, V. and Sturge, M., *Alcohol and the Human Body: An Introduction to the Study of the Subject* (London: Macmillan, 1907)

Hough, M., Hirschfield, A. and Newton, A., 'The impact of the Licensing Act 2003 on levels of crime and disorder: an evaluation' (Home Office, 2008), www.homeoffice.gov.uk/rds/pdfs08/horr04c.pdf

House of Commons, *First Report from the Committee on the State of the Police of the Metropolis* (1817) 233

House of Commons, 'An account of the number of brewers, retail brewers, licensed victuallers and intermediate brewers , in England, Scotland and Wales (1830)

House of Commons, *Report from the Select Committee on the Sale of Beer* (1830) 253

House of Commons, 'Report from the Select Committee on the sale of beer' (1833) 416

House of Commons, *Report from the Select Committee of Inquiry into Drunkenness* (1834) 559

House of Commons, *Report of the Select Committee of the House of Lords Appointed to Consider the Operation of the Acts for the Sale of Beer* (1850) 398

House of Commons, *Report from the Select Committee on Public Houses* (1854) 367

House of Commons, *Report of the Select Committee on Habitual Drunkards* London: House of Commons, 1872) 242

House of Commons, 'Papers relating to the Gothenburg scheme' (1877) 212

House of Commons, 'Report of the Municipality of Stockholm' (1877) 212

House of Commons, *Sixth Report of the Inspector of Inebriates under the Habitual Inebriates Act* (London: HMSO, 1886) C. 4822

House of Commons, *Report from the Departmental Committee on the Treatment of Inebriates* (London: HMSO, 1893) C. 7008-I

House of Commons, *Report from the Departmental Committee on Prisons* (London: HMSO, 1895) C. 7702

House of Commons, *Final Report of Her Majesty's Commissioners Appointed to Inquire into the Operation and Administration of the Laws Relating to the Sale of Intoxicating Liquors* (London: HMSO, 1899) C. 9379

House of Commons, *Report of the Committee on the Disinterested Management of Public Houses* (London: HMSO, 1927) Cmd. 2862

House of Commons, *Report of the Royal Commission on Licensing (England and Wales) 1920–31* (London: HMSO, 1931) Cmd. 3988

House of Commons, *Report of the Departmental Committee on Liquor Licensing* (London: HMSO, 1972) Cmnd. 5154

House of Lords, *The Lord's Protest Against an Act for Repealing certain Duties upon Spirituous Liquors* (London: 1743)

House of Lords, *Report from the Select Committee of the House of Lords on Intemperance* (London: House of Commons, 1879) 113

Houston, A. and Pincus, C., *A Nation Transformed: England After the Restoration* (Cambridge: Cambridge University Press, 2001)

Humphrey, C., *The Politics of Carnival* (Manchester: Manchester University Press, 2001)

Hunt, A., *Governing Morals: A Social History of Moral Regulation* (Oxford: Oxford University Press, 1999)

Hutton, R., *The Rise and Fall of Merry England: The Ritual Year 1400–1700* (Oxford: Oxford University Press, 1994)

Hutton, R., *Stations of the Sun: A History of the Ritual Year in Britain* (Oxford: Oxford University Press, 1996)

Information Centre, *Statistics on Alcohol: England, 2007* (2007), www.ic.nhs.uk/statistics-and-data-collections/healthand-lifestyles/alcohol/statistics-on-alcohol:-england–2007-[ns]

Institute of Alcohol Studies, 'Binge Drinking: Nature, Prevalence and Causes' (2005), www.ias.org.uk/resources/factsheets/binge_drinking.pdf

Iredale, W., 'Street violence jumps in binge Britain' (*Sunday Times*, 11 January 2004)

James I, *The King's Majesties Declaration to His Subjects, Concerning Lawful Sports to be Used* (London: Bonham Norton and John Bill, 1618)

James I, *A Proclamation concerning Ale-houses* (London: Bonham Norton, 1618)

James I, *A Proclamation for Repeal of certain Letters, Patents, Commissions, and Proclamations, concerning Inns, Ale-houses, and the Manufacture of Gold and Silver Thread* (London: Bonham Norton and John Bill, 1621)

Jayne, F. J., 'County councils and the public-house problem', (*Times* 2 August 1892)

Jayne, F. J., 'The Bishop of Chester and the drink question', *Times* 20 August 1892)

Jellinek, E. M., *The Disease Model of Alcoholism* (Brunswick, NJ: Hillhouse Press, 1960)

John, G., *Flagellum, or a Dry Answer to Dr. Hancock's wonderfully Comical Liquid Book* (London: Thomas Warner, 1723)

Johnson, J., *The Gothenburg System of Public-House Licensing: What It Is and How It Works* (London: Church of England Temperance Society, 1883)

Johnson, S., *A Dictionary of the English Language* (London: J. Knapton, 1756)

Johnstone, G., 'From vice to disease?: The concepts of dipsomania and inebriety, 1860–1900', *Social and Legal Studies* 5:1 (1996), 37–56

Jones, A., *The Dreadful Character of a Drunkard* (London: Elizabeth Andrews, 1663)

Jones, S. G., 'Labour society and the drink question in Britain, 1918–1939', *Historical Journal* 30:1 (1987), 105–22

Kant, I., *Lectures on Ethics*, trans. Peter Heath, (ed.) Peter Heath and J. B. Schweewind (Cambridge: Cambridge University Press, 1997)

Kelynack, T. N., 'Medico-legal aspects of inebriety', *The British Journal for the Study of Inebriety* 2:1 (1904), 117–29

Kelynack, T. N., 'The control of the inebriate', *The British Journal for the Study of Inebriety* 3:1 (1905), 92–6

Kendell, R. E., 'Drinking sensibly', *British Journal of Addiction* 82 (1987), 1279–88

Kerr, N., 'President's inaugural address', *Proceedings of the Society for the Study and Cure of Inebriety* 1:1 (1884), 2–16

Kerr, N., 'Legislation for inebriates in Britain', *Medical Temperance Review* 2:5 (1899), 100–1

Kethe, W., *A sermon made at Blanford forum* (London: John Daye, 1571)

Klein, L., 'Liberty, manners, and politeness in early eighteenth-century England', *Historical Journal* 32:3 (1989), 583–605

Lamb, C., *The Prose Works Vol. 1* (London: Edward Moxon, 1838)

Langhammer, C., '"A public house is for all classes, men and women alike": Women, leisure and drink in Second World War England', *Women's History Review* 12:3 (2003), 423–43

Lee, N., *Caesar Borgia, son of Pope Alexander the sixth* (London: R. E., 1680)

Lee, R. W., 'Comparative legislation as to habitual drunkards', *Journal of the Society of Comparative Legislation* 3:2 (1901), 241–51

Lees, F. R., *An Argument for the Legislative Prohibition of the Liquor Traffic* (Manchester: United Kingdom Alliance, 1856)

Lettsom, J. C., *Hints Respecting the Effects of Hard Drinking* (London: C. Dilly, 1798)

Levine, H. G., 'The discovery of addiction: Changing conceptions of habitual drunkenness in America', *Journal of Studies on Alcohol* 39:1 (1978), 143–74

Liberal Party, *Ninth Year of the Tory Government* (London: Liberal Publications Department, 1904)

Liberal Party, *Proceedings at the Annual Meeting of the Council of the National Liberal Federation* (London: Liberal Publications Department, 1908)

Light, R. and Heenan, S., *Controlling Supply: The Concept of 'Need' in Liquor Licensing* (Bristol: University of the West of England, 1999)

Lillywhite, B. *London Coffee Houses* (London: Allen and Unwin, 1963)

Livesey, J., *The Preston Temperance Advocate* (1 January 1837)

Livesey, J., *The Malt Liquor Lecture* (Ipswich: J. M. Burton, 1850)

Livesey, J., *True Temperance Teaching* (London: W. Tweedie, 1873)

Longmate, N., *The Waterdrinkers* (London: Hamish Hamilton, 1968)

McAdam Eccles, W., 'Alcohol as a factor in the causation of deterioration in the individual and the race', *The British Journal for the Study of Inebriety* 2: 4 (1905), 146–55

McCandless, P. (1984) '"Curses of civilization": Insanity and drunkenness in Victorian Britain', *British Journal of Addiction* 79, 49–58

McCartney, J., 'Labour doesn't give a XXXX for the nation's livers', (*Sunday Telegraph*, 30 January 2005)

Macnish, R., *The Anatomy of Drunkenness* (Glasgow: W. R. McPhun, 1827)

Maddox, I., *An Epistle to the Right Honourable the Lord-Mayor, Aldermen and the Common-Council of the City of London, and Governors of the Several Hosptals* (London: H. Woodfall, 1751)

Mainwaring, E., *The Method and Means of Enjoying Health, Vigour, and Long Life* (London: Dorman Newman, 1683)

Malcolm, E., *Ireland Sober, Ireland Free* (Dublin: Gill and Macmillan, 1986)

Mandeville, B., *The Fable of the Bees: Or Private Vices, Publick Benefits* (London: J. Tonson, 1724)

Marsh, P. and Fox-Kibby, K. *Drinking and Public Disorder* (London: The Portman Group, 1992)

Mass Observation, *The Pub and the People: A Worktown Study* (London: Victor Gollancz, 1943)

May, C., 'Pathology, identity and the social construction of alcohol dependence', *Sociology* 35:2 (2001), 385–401

Measham, F. and. Brain, K., 'Binge drinking, British alcohol policy and the new culture of intoxication', *Crime, Media and Society* 1:3 (2005), 262–83

'Mile End Socialist', 'Socialism, atheism and temperance: a defence of socialism' (London:

Arthur Warren, 1898)

Mill, J. S., *On Liberty* (Harmondsworth: Penguin, 1980)

Mill, J. S., *Utilitarianism* (Oxford: Oxford University Press, 1998)

Mill, J. S. and Burns, D., 'Mr Mill upon the Permissive Bill' (*Times*, 10 November 1868)

Monopolies and Mergers Commission, *The Supply of Beer* (London: HMSO, 1989)

Montagu, B., *Some Enquiries into the Effects of Fermented Liquors* (London: J. Johnson, 1814)

Morely, J., *The Life of William Ewart Gladstone, Vol. III* (Edinburgh: Constable, 1903)

Mutch, A., 'Shaping the public house, 1850–1950: Business strategies, state regulations and social history', *Cultural and Social History* 1 (2004), 179–200

Nashe, T., *Pierce Penilesse, His Supplication to the Divell* (Edinburgh: Edinburgh University Press, 1966)

Nicholls, J., 'Vinum Britannicum: The "drink question" in early modern England', *Social History of Alcohol and Drugs* 22:2 (2008), 6–25

Nicholls, J. and Owen, S. (eds), *A Babel of Bottles: Drink, Drinkers and Drinking Places in Literature* (Sheffield: Sheffield Academic Press, 2000)

Nicholson, P., 'T.H. Green and state action: liquor legislation', *History of Political Thought* 6:3 (1985), 517–50

Nordau, M., *Degeneration* (London: University of Nebraska Press, 1993)

O'Connor, J. and Wynne, D., *From the Margins to the Centre: Cultural Production and Consumption in the Post-industrial City* (Aldershot: Arena, 1996

Ogborn, M., *Spaces of Modernity: London's Geographies 1680–1780* (London: Guilford Press, 1988)

Orwell, G., *The Collected Essays Journalism and Letters, Vol. II: As I Please 1943–5*, ed. S. Orwell and I. Angus (London: Secker and Warburg, 1968)

Orwell, G., *The Road to Wigan Pier* (Harmondsworth: Penguin, 1989)

Parfect, C., 'The number of alehouses shewn to be extremely pernicious to the public' (London: R. Baldwin, 1758)

Paulson, R., *Hogarth: His Life, Art, and Times, Volume III* (London: Yale University Press, 1971)

Paulson, R., *Hogarth Volume III: Art and Politics, 1750–1764* (Cambridge: Lutterworth, 1993)

Peddie, A., *The Necessity for Some Legislative Arrangements for the Treatment of Dipsomania, or the Drinking Insanity* (Edinburgh: Sutherland and Knox, 1858)

Peel, A. W., 'The Royal Commission on Licensing: The struggle for mastery between the state and a trade' (London: Central Temperance Legislation Board, 1899)

Pennington, D. and Thomas, K. (eds), *Puritans and Revolutionaries: Essays in Seventeenth-Century History* (Oxford: Clarendon, 1978)

Phillips, J., *Wit and Drollery Jovial Poems* (London: 1661)

Pick, D., *Faces of Degeneration: A European Disorder c. 1848–1918* (Cambridge: Cambridge University Press, 1989)

Plant, M., *Women and Alcohol: Contemporary and Historical Perspectives* (London: Free Association, 1997)

Plant, M. and M., *Binge Britain: Alcohol and the National Response* (Oxford: Oxford University Press, 2006)

Porter, R., 'The drinking man's disease: The "pre-history" of alcoholism in Georgian Britain', *British Journal of Addiction* 80 (1985), 385–96

Porter, R., *London: A Social History* (Harmondsworth: Penguin, 2000)

Porter, R., *Flesh in the Age of Reason* (Harmondsworth: Penguin, 2004)

Portman Group, *Code of Practice on the Naming, Packaging and Promotion of Alcoholic*

Drinks, 4th edn (London: Portman Group, 2008)

Poulter, S., 'Drinks tax soaks the middle class' (*Daily Mail*, 13 March 2008)

Prime Minister's Strategy Unit, *Alcohol Harm Reduction Strategy for England* (London: Strategy Unit, 2004)

Proclamation Society, 'Brief statement of the origin and nature of the Society' (London: George Stafford, 1789)

Progressive Election Committee, 'What the Progressive Party on the county council has done for temperance in London' (London: Alexander and Shepheard Ltd., 1904)

'Protector', *A Proclamation Commanding a Speedy and Due Execution of the Laws Made Against the Abominable Sins of Drunkenness, Profane Swearing and Cursing, Adultery, Fornication, and Other Acts of Uncleanness* (London: Henry Hills and John Field, 1655)

Prynne, W., *Healthes: Sicknesse* (London: 1628)

Rabin, D., 'Drunkenness and responsibility for crime in the eighteenth century', *Journal of British Studies* 44 (2005), 457–77

Raleigh, W., *Remains of Walter Raleigh* (London: William Sheares, 1657)

Rawlidge, R., *A Monster Late Found Out and Discovered* (Amsterdam: 1628)

Rawstorne, T., 'Binge Britain' (*Daily Mail* 12 July 2004)

Rayner, J., 'On the streets of Binge Britain' (*Observer*, 5 September 2004)

Reid, G. A., 'Human evolution and alcohol', *British Journal for the Study of Inebriety* 1:2 (1903), 186–201

Reith, G., 'Consumption and its discontents: Addiction, identity and the politics of freedom', *British Journal of Sociology* 55:2 (2004)

Reynolds, D. S. and Rosenthal, D. J. (eds), *The Serpent in the Cup: Temperance in American Literature* Amherst: University of Massachusetts Press, 1997)

Roberts, M. J. D., 'The Society for the Suppression of Vice and its early critics', *Historical Journal* 26:1 (1983), 159–76

Room, R., 'Governing images of alcohol and drug problems' (PhD dissertation: University of California, 1978) www.robinroom.net/dissert.pdf

Room, R., 'The cultural framing of addiction', *Janus Head* 6:2 (2003), www.janushead.org/6–2/Room.pdf.

Room, R., 'Disabling the public interest: alcohol strategies and policies for England', *Addiction* 99 (2004), 1083–9

Rorabaugh, W. J., *The Alcoholic Republic: An American Tradition* (Oxford: Oxford University Press, 1979)

Ross, H. L., 'British drink-driving policy', *British Journal of Addiction* 83 (1988), pp. 863–5

Roth, M., 'Carnival, creativity and the sublimation of drunkenness', *Mosaic*, 30:2 (1997), 1–18

Rowntree, J. and Sherwell, A., *The Temperance Problem and Social Reform* (London: Hodder and Stoughton, 1900)

Rowntree, J.and Sherwell, A., *State Purchase of the Liquor Trade* (London: Allen and Unwin, 1919)

Royal College of Physicians, *A Great and Growing Evil* (London: Routledge, 1987)

Royal College of Psychiatrists, *Alcohol and Alcoholism* (London: Tavistock, 1979)

Rush, B., 'An Inquiry into the Effects of Ardent Spirits upon the Human Body and Mind', reprinted in *Quarterly Journal of Studies on Alcohol*, 4 (1944), 324–41

Scodel, J., *Excess and the Mean in Early Modern English Literature* (Oxford: Princeton University Press, 2002)

Scott, J., *Observations on the Present State of the Parochial and Vagrant Poor* (London:

Edward and Charles Dilly, 1771)

Sedgewick, E., 'Epidemics of the will', in *Tendencies* (London: Routledge, 1994)

Selley, E., *The English Public House As It Is* (London: Longmans, Green & Co., 1927)

Seneca, *Letters from a Stoic* ed. R. Campbell (Harmondsworth: Penguin, 1969)

Sentencing Guidelines Council, 'Overarching Principles: Seriousness' (Sentencing Guidelines Secretariat, 2004) www.sentencing-guidelines.gov.uk/docs/Seriousness_guideline.pdf

Shadwell, A., *Drink, Temperance and Legislation* London: Longmans, Green and Co., 1903)

Sharpe, H. L., *Early Modern England: A Social History, 1550–1760* (London: Arnold, 1996)

Sheehan, M. and Ridge, D., '"You become really close … you talk about the silly things you did, and we laugh": The role of binge drinking in female secondary students' lives', *Substance Use and Misuse* 36:3 (2001), 347–72

Shiman, L. L., *Crusade Against Drink in Victorian England* (Basingstoke: Macmillan, 1988)

Short, T., *A Rational Discourse on the Inward Uses of Water* (London: Samuel Chandler, 1725)

Short, T., *Vinum Britannicum* (London: D. Midwinter, 1727)

Sitch, C. and Davison, J., *Found Wanting: A Labour Verdict on Prohibition* (London: Harrison, Jehring & Co., 1921?)

Slack, J. 'Binge Britain' (*Daily Mail*, 4 August 2006)

Slot, G. 'The medico-legal aspects of drunkenness', *British Journal for the Study of Inebriety* 23: 3 (1936), 113–24

Smith, A., *The Wealth of Nations Books I–III* (Harmondsworth: Penguin, 1986)

Smith, A., *The Wealth of Nations Books IV–V* (Harmondsworth: Penguin, 1999)

Smith, J., *The Curiosities of Common Water* (London: J. Billingsley, 1723)

Smith, J., 'Alcohol – meeting our responsibilities, making a difference' (2008), http://press.homeoffice.gov.uk/Speeches/speeches-archive/home-secretary-alcohol-speech?view=Binary

Smith, R., 'A row plucked out of the air' (*Guardian Online*, 22 October 2007) http://commentisfree.guardian.co.uk/richard_smith/2007/10/a_row_plucked_out_of_the_air.html

Smollett, T., *The History of England from the Revolution to the Death of George the Second, Vol IV* (London: T. Cadell, 1880)

Smythe, A. (ed.), *A Pleasing Sinne: Drink and Conviviality in Seventeenth-Century England* (Cambridge: D. S. Brewer, 2004)

Snowden, P., *Socialism and the Drink Question* (London: Independent Labour Party, 1908)

Spender, H., *'The Trade' or the People* (London: Liberal Publications Department: pamphlet no. 4, 1908)

Stallybrass, P. and White, A., *The Politics and Poetics of Transgression* (London: Methuen, 1986)

Stanley, E. H. and Pope, S., 'Lord Stanley, M. P., and the United Kingdom Alliance' (*Times*, 2 October 1856)

Starling, E. H., *The Action of Alcohol on Man* (London: Longmans, Green and Co., 1923)

Strype, J., *Memorial of the Most Reverend Father in God, Thomas Cranmer* (London: Richard Chiswell, 1694)

Stubbes, P., *The Anatomy of Abuses* (London: New Shakespeare Society, 1879)

Sulkunen, P., 'Ethics of alcohol policy in a saturated society', *Addiction* 92:9 (1997), 1117–22

Sulkunen, P., 'Images and realities of alcohol', *Addiction* 93:9 (1998), 1305–12

Sullivan, W. C., 'The causes of inebriety in the female and the effects of alcoholism on racial degeneration', *British Journal for the Study of Inebriety* 1: 2 (1903), 61–4

Sullivan, W. C., 'The criminal responsibility of the alcoholic', *British Journal for the Study of Inebriety* 2:1 (1904), 48–53

Szmigin, I, Griffin, B., Mistral, W., *et al.*, 'Re-framing "binge drinking" as calculated hedonism – empirical evidence from the UK', *International Journal of Drug Policy* 19:5, 359–66

Taylor, A., *Bacchus in Romantic England: Writers and Drink, 1780–1830* (London: Macmillan, 1999)

Taylor, J., *Drink and Welcome* (London: Anne Griffin, 1637)

Thom, B., *Dealing with Drink: Alcohol and Social Policy from Treatment to Management* (London: Free Association, 1999)

Thompson, T., *A Diet for A Drunkard* (London: Richard Bankworth, 1612)

Trevelyan, G. O., *Five Speeches on the Liquor Traffic* (London: Partridge & Co., 1872)

Trotter, T., *An Essay Medical, Philosophical, and Chemical on Drunkenness and its Effects on the Human Body* (London: Routledge, 1988)

'T. S.', *A Proper Reply to a Scandalous Libel Intituled The Trial of the Spirits In a Letter to the Author* (London: J. Roberts, 1736)

Tuck, M., *Drinking and Disorder: A Srudy of Non-Metropolitan Violence* Home Office Research Study 108 (London: HMSO, 1989)

Tucker, J., *An Impartial Inquiry into the Benefits and Damages Arising to the Nation from the Present Very Great Use of Low-priced Spirituous Liquors* (London: T. Trye, 1751)

Uglow, J., *Hogarth* (London: Faber & Faber, 1997)

Valverde, M., '"Slavery from within": The invention of alcoholism and the question of free will', *Social History* 22:3 (1997), 251–68

Valverde, M., *Disease of the Will: Alcohol and the Dilemmas of Freedom* (Cambridge: Cambridge University Press, 1998)

Walker, N., *Crime and Insanity in England: Volume One* (Edinburgh: Edinburgh University Press, 1968)

Walton, S., *Out of It: A Cultural History of Intoxication* (London: Hamish Hamilton, 2001)

Ward, N., *A Complete and Humorous Account Of all the Remarkable Clubs and Societies in the Cities of London and Westminster* (London: J. Wren, 1756)

Ward, N., *The London Spy* (London: Colleagues Press, 1993)

Ward, S., *A Warning Piece to all Drunkards and Health-Givers* (London: 1682)

Warner, J., 'Resolv'd to drink no more': addiction as a preindustrial concept', *Journal of Studies on Alcohol* 55:6 (1994), 685–91

Warner, J., 'Good help is hard to find: a few comments about alcohol and work in preindustrial England', *Addiction Research* 2:3 (1995), 259–69

Warner, J., 'Historical perspectives on the shifting boundaries around youth and alcohol. The example of pre-industrial England, 1350–1750' *Addiction* 93:5 (1998), 641–57

Warner, J., *Craze: Gin and Debauchery in the Age of Reason* (London: Profile, 2003)

Warner, N., *Spirits of America: Intoxication in Nineteenth-Century American Literature* (London: University of Oklahoma Press, 1997)

Watt, N. and Carter, H., ''Pub policing splits Blunkett and No. 10' (*Guardian*, 1 March 2003)

Webb, S. and B., *The History of Liquor Licensing in England Principally from 1700–1830* (London: Longmans, Green & Co., 1903)

Westcott, W. W., 'Inebriety in women and the overlying of infants', *British Journal for the Study of Inebriety* 1:2 (1903), 65–8

Whitman, W., *Franklin Evans, or The Inebriate: A Tale of the Times*, in T. Bresher, (ed.), *Walt Whitman: The Early Poems and Fiction* (New York: New York University Press, 1963)

Whittaker, T., 'The fall in brewery stocks: When and why it occurred' (London: Liberal Publications Department: leaflet no. 2166, 1908)

Wilmore, J., 'Fury over booze blitz' (*The Publican*, 13 March 2008)

Wilson, G., *Alcohol and the Nation* (London: Nicholson and Watson, 1940)

Wilson, T., *Distilled Spirituous Liquors the Bane of the Nation* (London: J. Roberts, 1736)

Wilson, T. M. (ed.), *Drinking Cultures* (Oxford: Berg, 2005)

Wingfield, H., *The Forms of Alcoholism and their Treatment* (London: Hodder and Stoughton, 1918)

Winlow, S. and Hall, S., *Violent Night: Urban Leisure and Contemporary Culture* (Oxford: Berg, 2006)

Wintour, P., 'Tesco wants ministers to ban cheap alcohol' (*Guardian*, 21 February 2008)

Woolf, M., 'Musicians petition Blair over new "draconian" Licensing Bill' (*Independent*, 17 June 2003)

Wright, T., *Some Habits and Customs of the Working Classes* (2007), www.victorianlondon.org

Yeo, E. and S. (eds), *Popular Culture and Class Conflict 1590–1914* (Sussex: Harvester, 1981)

Young, T., *England's Bane, or the Description of Drunkenness* (London: William Jones, 1617)

Zedner, L., *Women, Crime and Custody in Victorian England* (Oxford: Clarendon, 1991)

Index

Lightning Source UK Ltd.
Milton Keynes UK
UKOW06f0424150616